What is Mental Disorder?

International Perspectives in Philosophy and Psychiatry

Series editors: Bill (K.W.M.) Fulford, Katherine Morris, John Z Sadler and Giovanni Stanghellini

Volumes in the series:

Forthcoming volumes in the series:

What is Mental Disorder?

An essay in philosophy, science, and values

Derek Bolton

Professor of Philosophy and Psychopathology,
Institute of Psychiatry, King's College London,
and Honorary Consultant Clinical Psychologist,
South London and Maudsley NHS Foundation Trust

OXFORD
UNIVERSITY PRESS

OXFORD
UNIVERSITY PRESS

Great Clarendon Street, Oxford OX2 6DP

Oxford University Press is a department of the University of Oxford.
It furthers the University's objective of excellence in research, scholarship,
and education by publishing worldwide in

Oxford New York

Auckland Cape Town Dar es Salaam Hong Kong Karachi
Kuala Lumpur Madrid Melbourne Mexico City Nairobi
New Delhi Shanghai Taipei Toronto

With offices in

Argentina Austria Brazil Chile Czech Republic France Greece
Guatemala Hungary Italy Japan Poland Portugal Singapore
South Korea Switzerland Thailand Turkey Ukraine Vietnam

Oxford is a registered trade mark of Oxford University Press
in the UK and in certain other countries

Published in the United States
by Oxford University Press Inc., New York

British Library Cataloguing in Publication Data

Data available

Library of Congress Cataloging in Publication Data

Bolton, Derek.
  What is mental disorder?: an essay in philosophy, science, and values / Derek Bolton.
    p.; cm.—(International perspectives in philosophy and psychiatry)
  Includes bibliographical references and index.
  ISBN-13: 978-0-19-856592-5
1. Mental illness—philosophy.
  [DNLM: 1. Mental Disoders. 2. Philosophy, Medical. 3. Psychological Theory. 4. Social
values. WM 140 B694w 2008] I. Title. II. Series.
  RC437.5.B653 2008
  616.99'449—dc22   2007041184

Typeset by Cepha Imaging Private Ltd., Bangalore, India
Printed on acid-free paper by the
MPG Books Group, Bodmin and King's Lynn

ISBN 978–0–19–856592–5

10 9 8 7 6 5 4 3

What health and illness mean in general are matters which concern the physician least of all. He deals scientifically with life processes and with particular illnesses. What is 'ill' in general depends less on the judgement of the doctor than on the judgment of the patient and on the dominant views in any given cultural circle.

Karl Jaspers

The fact is that any definition of disease which boils down to 'what people complain of', or 'what doctors treat', or some combination of the two, is almost worse than no definition at all. It is free to expand or contract with changes in social attitudes and therapeutic optimism and is at the mercy of idiosyncratic decisions by doctors or patients. If one wished to compare the incidence of disease in two different cultures, or in a single population at two different times, whose criteria of suffering or therapeutic concern would one use? And if the incidence of disease turned out to be different in the two, would this be because one was healthier than the other, or simply because their attitudes to illness were different?

Robert Kendell

Preface

The question of mental disorder is a curious one. On the one hand, the main groups involved have other problems to solve. Psychiatrists focus on their main task – the diagnosis and treatment of the problems people bring to the clinic – and they can get on with this without worrying too much about what 'mental disorder' really is; it is just assumed or known that the problems are mental disorders, and there is no need to be held up. Researchers in the sciences basic to psychiatry are clear about their main task of constructing causal models of the conditions of interest, but they do not need to assume that what they are studying are mental disorders in one sense or another, or that they are mental disorders at all. A particular kind of condition may turn out to involve, for example, brain disease, or expressions of normal traits in problematic environments, or perhaps normal at a particular age – but these options are a matter for the science and not assumption from the start. The other potential stake-holders in this problem are the people who at some time or another use mental health services and therefore receive a diagnosis of some mental disorder, and their parents, brothers, sisters, partners and children, who all together make up probably half the population, but their immediate concerns are managing and getting help, and this is not what this essay is about.

In this way to spend time with the question of mental disorder is idling, off main task. – On the other hand, the question matters much. Psychiatrists and other mental health professionals in some social and clinical contexts have to be clear about why some conditions are considered to be mental disorders and others not, about what the distinction is meant to be, and about related questions such as why psychiatric treatments are appropriate for some conditions and not for others. These same questions involve the users or potential users of mental health services. In constructing causal models of the conditions of interest, the basic sciences become involved with constructs that are essentially involved in the notion of mental disorder, such as what is normal or abnormal in the population, typical or atypical, the effects of lesions and disease processes and adverse environments, and the meaningfulness or otherwise of people's responses to them. The public interest is in the way psychiatry carries out the task of demarcating mental disorder from mental order, and in the fact that society assigns it this task, even though psychiatry for its main purposes hardly needs to worry about its meaning. Some way along in the development of the manuals for diagnosis of mental disorders – the American Psychiatric Association's DSM and the World Health Organisation's ICD – there was a need for a definition of what mental disorder is, for the purpose, among other things, of being clear why certain conditions should be included in them and others should excluded. Much hung on this, questions of whether difference or disadvantage or life-style choice was being pathologised and disqualified, questions of provision of services and funding for treatment – large scale social and economic questions, matters of public policy.

So the topic of this essay has a curious status, barely visible yet of widespread importance, many-sided and immensely complex. This I say partly by way of apology that my attempt to address it in this essay and the conclusions reached are not as clear as I would have liked. The place the essay has ended up can be described as sceptical – a scepticism of the gentle variety. Having considered the ways in which mental disorder is understood in psychiatric practice, the explicit definitions in the diagnostic manuals, and bearing in mind the clinical problems that they characterise, and having examined the more elaborate, rigorous definitions in the surrounding literature, the most influential of which is due to Jerry Wakefield, and the sociological approaches, and the paradigms and general findings of the current science – there ends up being, so far as I can see, no stable reality or concept of mental disorder; it breaks up into many, quite different kinds, some reminiscent of an old idea of madness or mental illness, others nothing like this at all. This instability and fragmentation corresponds to diversity in the phenomena, in current clinical services, and in current terminology. I would have settled for one clear proposal as to what mental disorder really is, but couldn't find one.

That said, the scepticism is just about whether there is something stable, fixed and distinctive here, for which 'mental disorder' is a suitable name. It does not include doubts about the reality of the phenomena: the distress and disabilities that people bring to the clinic, and the need for psychiatric, or more generally mental health professional care. The domain of healthcare as a response to personal distress and disability seems to me permanent, only mistakenly seen as something to be deconstructed away. There may be no clear basis for distinguishing between mental health problems and social problems, or between mental health problems and 'normal – more or less normal – problems of living', but what distinguishes healthcare is the response to the person involved. The response is care for the individual, based on professional training, science and expertise, distinct from social or political action, or religious judgement, or demands for self-reliance. By all means there is then a debate to be had as to the pros and cons of one kind of response as opposed to another, a debate involving many stakeholders, with some clear cases, and many controversial boundary issues, but healthcare has a permanent seat in the debating chamber.

I have brought to this essay various parts of my life. I read philosophy at Cambridge and went on to doctoral and post-doctoral work on Wittgenstein, following which I read psychology and trained in clinical psychology at the Institute of Psychiatry and Maudsley Hospital in London. Subsequently I have worked there as a clinician for many years in various settings, mostly in child and adolescent services, mainly in-patient and more recently out-patient. My research interests have been mainly in obsessive compulsive disorder and other anxiety disorders, including recently behavioural genetic modelling and treatment studies. The Institute of Psychiatry and Maudsley Hospital have been great places to work and to learn, full of people with enquiring minds with a wide variety of clinical and research ideas and expertise – without this educational environment I never could have attempted such an essay, and I hope the result does it some justice. The same applies for my experience in the clinic over many years working with the children, adolescents, parents and families with many kinds of problems – my gratitude is to them for teaching me about the reality and the details of these conditions and how they can be managed. At a personal level I have suffered from a stammer life-long, speech-long, one of the conditions in the psychiatric manuals of mental disorders, which figure large in this essay. A stammer produces characteristic communication difficulties and associated emotional problems which I have had to live with and for which I had many kinds of speech- and psycho-therapy at various periods, all of which helped, until finally several decades ago for some reason at that stage in my life I stopped minding and have been better since. I learnt much from all this, about a fraction of the great variety of mental health problems from the inside, and the complications of internalised social exclusion, and the subtleties of change, in and out of therapy.

Some years ago I began to teach a course the concept of mental disorder, part of a Masters degree in the Philosophy of Mental Disorder run jointly by the Institute of Psychiatry and the Philosophy Department of King's College London. This essay is an outcome of teaching that course, and I have to thank the postgraduates for many lively and instructive sessions on the topic. It became ever more apparent to me during these recent years of teaching that the problem of mental disorder criss-crosses many fields of enquiry: clinical, scientific, philosophical, literary and socio-political. Sometimes I have made sense of this by thinking that the subject of mental disorder covers all aspects of being human, from a certain point of view, as one of the boundary conditions.

My debt to Foucault's broad, penetrating analysis of the modern western idea of madness and mental illness is evident in the essay. My biggest intellectual debt is to Jerry Wakefield's work on the concept of mental disorder. His work has rightly dominated the field for nearly two decades; it draws together many crucial themes in the medical model of psychiatry, the roles of social norms and values, and the post-1960s idea that a proper understanding of mind and mental disorder has to have an evolutionary theoretic basis. This essay ends up in a quite different place, but it never would have got started without the stimulation of Wakefield's work, and it never would have got hold of key problems without having to wrestle with his well-argued, cogent proposals.

While writing the book I have benefited from many conversations on some of its key problems and from comments on drafts of parts or the whole. I want to thank particularly Jeremy Adler, Gwen Adshead, Matthew Bolton, Mary Douglas, Jonathan Hill, Jeff Poland, Jennifer Radden, Nik Rose, and Jerry Wakefield. The errors of all sorts are mine.

Derek Bolton, London, June 2007

Contents

Introduction

The effects of mental disorder are apparent and pervasive, in suffering, loss of freedom and life opportunities, negative impacts on use of education, work satisfaction and productivity, complications in law, institutions of healthcare, intensive scientific research into causes and cures and so on. Suffering, loss of functioning, and perceived threat are among the personal and social experiences that can lead to mental health services. Once the problems are brought to the attention of mental health services and mental disorder is diagnosed, a range of possible outcomes is licensed, including offer of treatment, funding and perhaps, depending on severity and other circumstances, paid leave from work due to illness, possible shame and stigma, and in extreme cases compulsory admission to hospital, or acceptance of no or diminished responsibility in the Courts. Mental health professionals engage with the problems inside institutional structures using manuals for diagnosis and providing treatments that are increasingly required to be backed by scientific evidence of effectiveness. The social and institutional outcomes of assigning a diagnosis are important topics for social scientific theory and research. However, earlier in the chain of events and consequences are the social manifestations of mental disorder, open for all to see, and most importantly the personal and interpersonal effects, experienced by the people with the problems, their families and friends.

Typically the experiences of the people with the problems are of anguish, confusion, of being in some respects and in some degree unable to carry on with their normal life. In other kinds of case, the problem is less for the person themselves and more for others, in the form of threats to safety from behaviour that deviates from fundamental standards of conduct. These are the kinds of phenomena that trigger involvement of mental health services and diagnosis of mental disorder. Labelling by a diagnosis, but behind that the phenomena themselves, belong with some positive responses, provision of care and treatment, but they equally belong with some negative responses, associated with perception of falling below the level of normal expectations. Add to this the fact that it is the person's mind that is in question, and the risks of denigration and shame are evident. If the person's behaviour is seen to present threat to others, then fear is also an obvious consequence. The negative connotations of mental disorder probably outweigh the positive, though the positive, the provision of care and treatment, are the point of mental health services. The same issues arise considering that 'normal' carries the implication *like us,* and 'abnormal' *not like us.* To this extent attribution of mental disorder is essentially socially excluding: it positions the speaker in the in-group and the recipient of the label in the out-group. 'Normal' mental functioning signifies belonging to a community of shared practices, emotions and beliefs, in which one person makes sense to another and is included in 'we'. By contrast 'abnormal' mental functioning signifies a break in perceived sense, a form of practice, emotion or belief which does not make sense, and which so far excludes the person from his position as an agent among us. Now in some cases of mental disorder, such as advanced dementia, or an acute psychotic episode, isolation from the group occurs regardless of any labelling process. However, the term 'mental disorder' in current usage does not discriminate between these kinds of case and others, between those and depression, say, or a debilitating social anxiety, or between the person who was in an acute psychotic state, but is now out-of-episode. The same term 'mental disorder' applies, and profoundly disqualifying significance clings to it.

There are two main sets of questions to be addressed in this essay, and the first set is alluded to above. What is the basis of the standards or norms by which we judge that a person has a mental disorder – that the person's mind is not working as it should, that their mental functioning is abnormal? Controversies about these questions since the 1960s have been dominated by the contrast between norms that are *medical* or *scientific* or *natural,* on the one hand, and *social* norms on the other. The norms that define mental disorder seem to belong to psychiatry, to be medical and scientific, but are they really social norms, hijacked and disguised by the medical profession?

There are social norms aplenty, familiar to us, and they can be applied to personal functioning. In many religious frameworks the fundamental issue is conformity or otherwise to divine law: piety and sin will be the fundamental division, and other important distinctions including normal as opposed to abnormal functioning may be interpreted in those terms, mental disorder then appearing as sin or devilish influence. In systems of morality generally, being good as opposed to bad is the main issue, and again other important distinctions are liable to be regarded in this light. A specific moral value, especially high in capitalist systems, is productive activity as opposed to uselessness and dependency, and this again may get muddled up with the concept of mental disorder. A further characterization of mental disorder is in terms of rationality, closely linked to the idea of the civilized man (the person tends to be male in this idea). From this perspective mental disorder will appear as fundamentally a deficit of reason, including such as acting on irrational beliefs or excessive emotions, implying absence of full humanity. Given that all societies function with systems of moral values, religious or secular, the negative linkage between mental disorder and immorality is a permanent risk, often enough experienced by the people involved.

A crucial and saving counterpoint to the moral interpretations of the phenomena is always the medical model, the recognition in all or most cultures that people may fail to do the right or the expected thing not because they have chosen to, or have been corrupted, or have weakness of will, but because they are ill, because the body is not in the right natural condition, that it has been damaged by diseases or lesions, or has imbalances in the materials involved in mental states, such as humours or neurotransmitters, these being matters for medicine and clinical science to determine.

These kinds of standards – the religious, the moral, the work ethic, the rational, and the medical – have for a long time provided the terms for discourse on mental disorder. The medical model stands out as the one that offers care and help to the individual, but generally it is not a good thing to be on the wrong end of any of the other distinctions: there lies sin, corruption, immorality, inadequacy and irrationality, these signifying in each case the opposite of what is regarded as the highest good. And the medical model can hardly avoid these implications either, because whatever may be the reason for the person's fallen state, fallen it is. Profoundly negative judgements, stigma and social exclusion are close partners with the judgement that someone has a mental disorder. A further aspect of the negative values associated with the medical model specifically has to do with the ambiguous nature of the mental illness attribution: on the one hand it excuses by reason of illness, but on the other it does so by apparently disqualifying the person's mental life and agency. This complication is highlighted by another kind of approach to be considered next.

There have been and there continues to be various large-scale social views of the norms of personal functioning corresponding to views as to what the person or the mind is for: realizing the divine will, economic productivity, rationality. They have existed alongside the medical model of dysfunction. A third kind of approach may be called the *psychological*, appearing distinctively over the past hundred years or so, with the birth of the new sciences of psychology and psychiatry. The primary focus of the psychological approach, like medicine and in contrast with the social sciences, is the individual rather than social organization, and it is as much or more concerned with normal as with abnormal functioning, unlike medicine. Psychological theories focus on the faculties of mental life – perception, belief, emotion, will – and on the intelligent activity that they bring about. These become the terms for describing psychological dysfunction, for construing the phenomena *as* 'psychological dysfunction' – as opposed to for example sin, or expression of a disease. Thus, perception of reality can be veridical or mistaken, or in an extreme kind of case, it can be hallucinatory. Memory likewise, and it can fail altogether. Beliefs may be true or false, reasonable or unreasonable, based on good evidence or authority, or lacking any evidence at all. Emotions may be understandable reactions to events, for example anger is an understandable response to being hurt, or not understandable, being angry for no reason; and so on. Desires are reasonable or otherwise depending of their relation to the person's needs. The will may fail to control action. Action may be reasonable or otherwise, depending on whether it follows from beliefs and desires, or on whether those beliefs and desires are themselves reasonable. Behaviour may be random, without any relation to the achievement of goals, without method, and in this sense may fail to be real action. A further issue is that we expect people to be able to give an account of their actions, at least of their important actions, to be able to explain why they are doing what they are doing, by citing beliefs and desires, reasons for action, and this capacity is intimately linked to the attribution of agency and responsibility.

These relatively uncontroversial observations indicate the range of psychological functioning and dysfunction. There may be problems in the relation between perception and reality, in memory, in the rationality of belief, in the appropriateness of emotions and desires, and in the role of reasons and method in the regulation of action. As well as having roots in medicine, modern psychiatry has developed within this broadly psychological thought-space and the manuals for psychiatric diagnosis of 'mental disorders' explicitly and inevitably operate with normative terms of the above kinds, such as 'rational', 'reasonable', 'meaningful', 'appropriate', 'proportionate', and their opposites.

There is probably no single word which ideally fits all these various kinds of standards for the variety of kinds of mental functioning, but some may be used as a cover for them all. One possible candidate is the word 'normal', so that we might say that in general psychiatry focuses on abnormal mental and behavioural functioning. Another option is the expression 'meaningful connection' which entered psychiatric theory mainly under the influence of Karl Jaspers in his *General Psychopathology*, published in the original German in 1913 and in English translation in 1963. Using this terminology we may say that psychological dysfunction is marked by breakdown of meaningful connections in psychic life: between perception and reality, between beliefs and evidence, between an emotion and its object (its cause), between reasons and action; and so forth.

This way of putting the matter, however, immediately raises the question that has dogged psychiatry since the beginning: is the break of meaning that characterizes mental disorder an absolute one, just fixed deficit – or, is there less obvious meaning underneath? That there is much method or meaning in madness was obvious in other places and times, for example to the Elizabethan audience in the tragic predicaments of Hamlet and Lear, and the comic of Malvolio. In Foucault's account this possibility was lost to the rational mind of the Enlightenment, to be reconstructed much later by Freud, at the start of the psychological paradigm. In the psychological paradigm – in Freudian theory, but also in conditioning theory and all their subsequent derivatives – the abnormal is treated in terms of the normal, typically construed as a meaningful response, more or less successful or adaptive, to abnormal circumstances. In this way the psychological approach to clinical problems constantly defines itself in opposition to what is usually called the 'medical model', charged – with some validity only – with supposing that 'symptoms' of mental illness or mental disorder have no sense or function whatever.

Another way of formulating the fundamental problem here is that the psychological approach tends to undermine the concept of mental disorder itself. 'Mental disorder' implies failure of psychological functioning, and psychological functioning is a matter of meaning and method, but then insofar as apparent mental disorder includes these things, it seems not to be a disorder after all. Or perhaps the condition is a disorder in some respects but not in others, perhaps the best solution to adversity which inevitably causes some functional loss, signifying order beneath disorder. Thoughts along these lines destabilize the notion of mental disorder, and the psychological models of psychopathology typically have negative or at least mixed feelings about the term.

The question whether the apparent disruption of meaning and reason is a pure deficit, or is rather on the surface, beneath which there is – after all – order, is connected to the second main question to be considered in this essay. Namely this: what is the nature and validity of the distinction between mental disorder and mental order? Broadly speaking there are two main approaches to this question, both already alluded to above. According to one, mental disorder essentially involves a breakdown of meaning at some point in the relations among mental states and between mental states and experience or behaviour. According to the other, mental disorder is a matter of functioning below the level of an appropriate 'normal' group. Of these two ways of approaching the question of mental disorder, the first is probably the most critical, but the second is inevitably always in the background.

The two main sets of questions central to the problem of mental disorder that will be considered in this essay are thus these:

- First, are the norms invoked in psychiatry really medical, or are they really social? Attempts to define medical disorder typically invoke diseases and lesions, or functioning below the level of the normal group, or failing to function as designed. Sociological critiques, by contrast, emphasize the role of psychiatry in regulating deviance from social norms. How can psychiatry define its proper domain as medical as opposed to social?

- Second, what is the validity of the distinction between mental disorder and order, between abnormal and normal mental functioning? To what extent, notwithstanding appearances, does mental disorder involve meaningful reactions and problem-solving? These responses may be to normal problems of living, or to not so normal problems – to severe psychosocial challenges. Is there after all order in mental disorder? And to the extent that there is, what implications does this have for the viability of the concept? Or again, taking a different approach to the distinction between mental order and disorder, what is the 'normal' group that provides a standard by which to judge what is normal as opposed to abnormal mental functioning?

These two sets of issues are connected and have often been merged by the main players in the debates. The medical model under a strong interpretation has mental disorder as the result of brain lesion or disease, determinable by natural science, obviously a medical matter, and by the same considerations, as devoid of meaning. Critiques of the medical model in the 1960s charged mainstream psychiatry with medicalizing and pathologizing what were essentially socially defined problems, and with becoming blind to sense and meaning in what had become 'mental illness', specifically meaning in relation to more or less normal problems of living. In their more nuanced forms the sociological critiques have social processes as not only defining the problems but also creating the domain of the meaningless for mental disorder, conscripting the medical model of brain lesions and diseases to elaborate, justify and cement the deed.

Nevertheless, while these several sets of problems have often been run together, they are distinguishable and are best now distinguished, mainly because the considerations relevant to the one are quite distinct from those relevant to the other. Whether and to what extent meaning is involved in mental disorders has largely become a matter for the science, especially now in the relatively recent paradigm in the behavioural sciences that can envisage meaningful processes as well as lesions and diseases as implicated in the aetiology and maintenance of the conditions of interest. Similarly the question whether there is a simple dichotomy between majority average functioning and minority below average functioning has likewise become a matter for the science. On the other hand, the question whether the norms involved in distinguishing mental disorder from order are a matter for natural science and medicine or are rather social, is a broader one, involving not primarily questions of causation and average functioning, but conceptual problems as to what these norms are meant to be and how they are to be defined.

The many issues surrounding the concept of mental disorder and associated practices have usually been framed and debated in terms of the validity of the so-called medical model in psychiatry. The medical model has been vigorously defended by some psychiatrists and philosophers, and vigorously criticized, in sociological critiques on the one hand, according to which the medical model mistakes social norms for medical norms, and in psychological critiques on the other, according to which the medical model pathologizes the meaningful and the normal. The debate has been historically conducted in terms of the medical model and it is inevitable to follow this to some extent, but the underlying issues have to do with the nature of the phenomena and their representation within the sciences and in society at large.

In some ways this essay seeks to update the position in the light of developments in the half century since the 1960s critiques of psychiatry, developments in diagnostic practices, in the sciences, in philosophical and conceptual approaches to the problem of defining 'mental disorder', and in the broader social context. It will be suggested that the dichotomy between what is medical, natural, and scientific and on the one hand, and what is social on the other, has not survived well. The various ways of making the dichotomy have all become doubtful: it turns out now that what is natural includes much that is social, this being clear in contemporary biobehavioural science, and this in addition to the fact that medicine including psychiatry is itself clearly a social institution. This shift since the 1960s – the blurring of the distinction between the medical and the social – has various implications for the ways in which psychiatry and mental health services generally engage with society at large. On the question of meaning in mental disorder, it is clear in the current state of the science that there is much meaning in what are called mental disorders, that meaningful processes are involved in their etiology, maintenance and treatment. Current behavioural science has also broken down the assumption of a simple dichotomy between what is psychologically normal and what is psychologically abnormal in the population, replacing it with the view that psychological traits are typically 'normally' distributed, with low, average and high levels distributed in a bell-shaped curve, with high degrees of variation among individuals. These changes are reflected in unhappiness about 'mental disorder' as a general term for the conditions of interest, and the current state of terminological flux.

The changes in the science have happened over the same period as large-scale social changes: the closure of the asylums, replacement by care in the community, and the increasing identification of common mental health problems such as anxiety or depression and increasing use of treatments, talking therapies of various kinds, and medications like Prozac. These social changes have affected the way we think about mental disorder, including questioning the term and finding others more fit for the present purposes.

Changes of these kinds in the science and in the social context over the past 50 years or so have all signified in one way or another flux in our understanding of mental disorder and its boundaries, and they are the subject matter of this essay.

Synopsis

The start place, in the first chapter, is the current psychiatric diagnostic manuals – the ICD-10 and the DSM-IV. These manuals are of enormous importance, summarizing and driving diagnostic practice and research in psychiatry throughout the world. They have been increasingly developed to maximize reliability of diagnosis, that is to say, to maximize the extent to which clinicians and researchers will agree about what constitutes a particular diagnosable condition, and in particular cases about whether it is present or absent. This has been achieved by characterizing symptoms in terms that are as descriptive as possible, limited to what is observable and accessible from informants in the clinic, and deliberately excluding speculation as to causes of the condition. Secondly, and notwithstanding the first point, the descriptions of symptoms and syndromes often though not invariably invoke norms of psychological functioning, specifying one or another kind of breakdown of normal linkages. These psychological norms are as indicated in the Introduction, in terms of 'meaningful', 'appropriate' linkages between beliefs and reason, between emotion and its objects, between reasons and actions; and so forth. Typically, though not invariably, diagnosis requires not only the presence of a clinical syndrome, but also associated significant distress or disruption of social functioning. In this way the notion of mental disorder at work in the diagnostic manuals can be captured (for many conditions, though not all) by the idea that *mental disorder is harmful disruption of normal psychological functioning*. The manuals also contain explicit definitions of mental disorder along something like these lines.

There are however many issues about mental disorder left unaddressed, including the basis of the norms of psychological functioning, and whether the associated harm is sometimes more for others than for the person with the dysfunction. It is acknowledged in the manuals that the matter of definition of mental disorder is problematic in various ways, though not fatally so.

Notwithstanding the problems, the diagnostic manuals go from strength to strength, being used increasingly in communication between various stakeholders, and as the basis for most research into causes and treatments. These two points about the current diagnostic manuals – lack of clarity about the concept of mental disorder on the one hand, and increasing influence on the other – appear somewhat paradoxical when put together, but they can be reconciled by the recognition that the manuals comprise at least two projects that are distinguishable and to a large extent separable. The manuals are primarily systems for describing and classifying the conditions of interest in as useful a way as possible for clinical and scientific purposes. A fundamental precondition of serving any useful purpose is clarity over what conditions we are talking about, and hence the drive for reliability in the description of symptoms and syndromes. The further aspect, at once headlined and axiomatic, but also problematic and implicit, is the characterization of these conditions of interest as being *mental disorders*. This distinction among the aims of the diagnostic manuals is barely attended to in the literature but is of major importance in understanding the criticisms of the manuals and diagnostic practice generally. The project of description and classification of the conditions of interest involves mainly issues of clinical and scientific reliability and utility, and its successes and limitations are generally discussed in these – fairly technical – terms. The second aspect, on the other hand, the axiomatic but barely explained characterization of these conditions as mental disorders, raises a host of criticisms that are primarily social, moral and conceptual. Here we find the complaints that diagnosis pathologizes and disqualifies the normal and the meaningful, that in so doing it contributes to stigma, that it medicalizes personal and social values, criticisms that the notion of mental disorder is unclear or even incoherent; and so on. These kinds of complaints and criticisms are frequently levelled at diagnostic practice as a whole, but this target is too broad. The familiar criticisms of diagnosis – the social, moral and conceptual – are rather best targeted specifically at the characterization of the conditions of interest as mental disorders.

Mental disorder and related concepts such as normality, function and meaning are the subject matter of sciences ranging from biology though to sociology, and the next broad topic, for Chapter 2, is what they have to say about them. Three points are noted about the sciences 'basic to psychiatry', including psychology, neuroscience and genetics. First, they search for causes of the conditions of interest, typically as defined by the psychiatric manuals; second, for this purpose it is immaterial whether these conditions are considered as disorders or not, and third, at least two of them – psychology and genetics – tend to be antithetical to the notion of disorder as discontinuous with the normal, or as meaningless/non-functional. Another basic science considered, neuroscience, has no notion of order/disorder independent of what derives from the distinction drawn at the psychological/behavioural level. In current models of psychopathology constructed in these basic sciences it is notable that meaningful/functional strategies typically play crucial roles, sometimes alongside other causal factors, including brain disease or lesion, or genetically based temperamental characteristics. These two characteristic features of the current science – that meaning has a causal role, and explanatory pluralism – are both signs of a paradigm shift that has been in progress roughly since the middle of the last century and which is crucial for the line of thought about mental disorder being pursued in this essay.

The next main theme in Chapter 2 is that increasingly the biobehavioural sciences are embedded in evolutionary theory. From an evolutionary point of view, what stands out is the essential linkage between behaviour and specific environments and task demands, and the process of more or less successful adaptation to more or less benign or adverse environments. In this context, what sense can be made of mental disorder? While behaviour may be more or less adaptive relative to specific environments and task demands, and this for a variety of reasons, the idea that some behaviour is just 'disordered' has no clear rationale.

Beyond the behavioural and brain sciences, the social sciences abound with theories of social functions and order, providing further scope for understanding what mental disorder may be. Sociological theories of mental disorder are relatively rare but they were prominent in the 1960s critiques of psychiatry and their influence continues. The sociological theories naturally tended to construe mental disorder as a kind of social deviance. This has much to be said for it, but it passes over distinctions among kinds of social deviance, some attributed to issues such as criminal intent and others to mental disorder, and it also passes over distinctions within mental disorders, in particular between the 'behavioural' disorders associated with antisocial activity, and emotional and other disorders that are characterized more by high levels of personal misery and help-seeking. A related problem is that problems at the individual level are not the focus of – are invisible to – social science and for this reason its grasp of what psychological dysfunction means is limited.

Having reviewed some main approaches of the sciences to concepts involved in mental disorder, Chapter 2 concludes with considering the norms which demarcate order from disorder, and specifically the validity of the old natural/social distinction. On this topic the basic sciences have not much to say: they are interested in causes, not norms. Norms of function can be defined in an evolutionary theoretic framework, but here the 'naturally evolved' and the 'social' are blurred, and both of these factors also involve individual differences. There are three kinds of factor involved in the design of human action – the evolutionary biological, the cultural, and individual agency – and each of them corresponds to a way of interpreting function and dysfunction, and hence order and disorder.

Chapter 3 considers definitions of mental disorder that attempt to clarify the medical, non-social basis for diagnosis in terms of a *natural fact* – the so-called 'naturalist' definitions. Two main naturalist definitions of mental disorder have been proposed, both important and highly influential, one by Christopher Boorse and the other by Jerome Wakefield. Both proposals have mental disorder (and related concepts such as mental or physical illness) as meaning a *harmful disruption of natural function*. The judgement of harm is taken to be primarily a matter of social norms and values, while the disruption of natural function is claimed to be matter of hard objective, scientific fact. Thus the definitions aim to resolve the 1960s debates by having both social norms and medical norms as components of the concept of mental disorder. Not much is said about the social norms and values involved, because the bulk of the arguments for and against the proposals have been taken up with the second part of the proposed definitions, the vexed issue of what natural function and dysfunction means. This problem goes to the heart of the matter of the justification of the standards by which we distinguish normal from abnormal functioning. Broadly speaking, Boorse and Wakefield between them explore the two available options for distinguishing normal from abnormal functioning in an objective, scientific way.

Boorse seeks to define natural or normal functioning in statistical terms, as average for the species, so that abnormal functioning is a matter of functioning below this species-typical level. There are many problems with this approach. The main one is that deviance from statistical normality in itself – independent of any problems that may result – does not warrant attribution of pathology, physical or mental. Another problem is that statistical abnormality is also relative to specific reference groups, and these can be selected in various ways, delivering different classifications of what is 'normal' or 'abnormal'. Boorse relies on human species-typical functioning to define an absolute gold standard group, which would avoid this relativity, but it is unclear whether there is such a thing.

The other approach to defining normal or natural function is to tie it to *design*, not just to a statistically normal level, and this is the one pursued rigorously by Wakefield. Wakefield links *function* explicitly to *functioning as designed,* and thus *natural function* to *functioning as designed in evolution.* According to Wakefield's analysis, then, mental disorder is a harmful failure of a natural mental or behavioural mechanism to function as designed in evolution. Wakefield's analysis has much to be said for it, and it may well be the best or the only way of providing an objective, scientific basis for the notion of mental disorder. It has, however, many problems associated with it. One is that diagnosis of mental disorder, according to the analysis, involves a risky hypothesis about causes. There are apparently pathways to conditions of the kind described in the psychiatric manuals that do not involve dysfunction in the sense defined in the analysis, and moreover, it is not generally clear which conditions or presentations do and which do not. The consequence is that it would be impossible to make a definite diagnosis of mental disorder in the clinic, because diagnosis would be conditional on a hypothesis that the presenting problem is or involves failure of an evolutionary designed mechanism to function as designed, a hypothesis that would typically be, for most psychiatric conditions, uncertain, speculative, provisional, for some quite likely false – and in probably all cases controversial. The resulting spectre of unreliability of diagnosis, however, is just the problem – writ large – that the diagnostic manuals have evolved to avoid. In practice, of course, diagnosis in clinical and research settings does not involve evolutionary theoretic speculations, but rather just the diagnostic criteria, which typically appeal to more accessible matters to do with, broadly, breakdown of perceived meaningful connections associated with harm as previously discussed.

The implication of this line of thought is that definition of mental disorder in evolutionary theoretic terms, whatever other virtues it may have, does not capture the usage of the term mental disorder in the diagnostic manuals. This requires further consideration of the way the manuals define the conditions of interest, and it opens up terminological problems – both topics deferred to later chapters. It is noted, finally, that the main rationale of the naturalistic definitions of mental disorder, resolution of the 1960s debates about medical vs social norms, is no longer valid, insofar as – as argued in the second chapter – the contrast natural vs social does not survive in the current science.

Chapter 4 pursues options for conceptualizing mental disorder without reliance on naturalist definitions. An implication from the third chapter is that if mental disorder is to be diagnosed reliably then it has to be defined within the clinical phenomena, not in terms of some hypothetical fact of nature. Other implications are that mental disorder so defined will probably not be readily distinguished from deviation from social and personal norms, and that it will commonly if not invariably involve some degrees of meaning, strategy, and so forth, typically in response to challenges in the internal and external environments. With these and other points in mind from previous chapters the definitions of mental disorder in the psychiatric manuals are reconsidered, particularly the one given in the DSM. It is noted that the DSM definition was prompted by the campaign of the gay lobby in the 1970s to have homosexuality removed from the manual of mental disorders, and is primarily focused on the *harm* that accrues from the conditions listed in the manual, this being understood in terms of distress and disability. It was remarked at the time that the conditions in the manual are there, as a matter of history, because they are the problems people have presented for attention at the clinic, and which the physicians have agreed warrant treatment. Mental disorder understood as arising in these ways does not have much to do with abstract speculations or technical hypotheses about evolutionary development – it is much more here and now, involving values in judgements of harm and the need to treat, and in which the personal, the social and the biological are hardly clearly distinguished, at least not up front. The DSM definition gestures towards demarcating mental disorder from social deviance, but without much detail. It requires that mental disorder is *not an expectable response*, this again being a gesture towards abnormality relative to some unspecified group, or towards lack of understandable connection, or both, but either way no detail is given. There are gestures towards these large-scale background assumptions and debates: that mental disorder is fundamentally a medical or scientific matter not involving social norms and values, that it excludes meaning, that it can be understood as normal as opposed to abnormal functioning – but that is apparently not the main point of the psychiatric manuals, which is to describe and classify as clearly as possible the conditions that are of interest to the folk and the clinicians.

The fourth chapter also contains my attempt to say something about the large-scale background assumptions still evident, though changing, in the psychiatric manuals and in psychiatric practice generally. Here I suppose that Foucault was right to identify medical psychiatry as growing up in Western European modernity, with its assumptions of absolute order in nature, in experience and reason, and in which disorder – madness – appeared as mere deficit, in the paradigm case as hallucination and delusion. These features shift in post- or late-modernity, and psychiatry is part of this change as it was in what went before. The general direction is towards flexible and negotiable boundaries, of many kinds in many contexts; for example, in meaning in disorder, in communication between 'patient' (whatever the name should now be) and clinician, and between cultures in diverse communities. A major boundary problem is between order and disorder itself, and this is taken up, in various forms, along with terminological problems, in the final chapter.

Chapter 5 explores the implications of giving up the idea that there is an objective, factual basis for the diagnosis of mental disorder – implications for a range of familiar problem areas. First on the list is the one that originally provided much of the rationale for naturalist definitions of mental disorder, the charge that unless some such definition is valid, there is apparently no defence against the charge that psychiatry is a form of social control. One important form this problem has taken is the perceived necessity of being able to give a principled reason why frank political abuse of psychiatry – for example several decades ago in the then Soviet Union – is wrong and illegitimate. So far as I can see the response consistent with conclusions so far in the essay has to be that the principled reason, the nature of the error and the illegitimacy, is not going to be made out in the philosophy or in the science of medicine and psychiatry, but has to be interpreted in terms of human rights legislation and the other principles and institutions of democracy. Democracies aim to protect freedom of expression of belief and of action, provided they pose no demonstrable risk to others. This leads to another form of the problem of psychiatry and social control, closer to home, the question whether mental disorders defined by antisocial behaviour are any different from profound and pervasive social deviance. The general implication of this essay is not to object to this coincidence, not to expect that the medical/psychiatric and the social can be kept apart, but it does require some shift of emphasis. It requires recognition that the 'harm' associated with mental disorder may be harm for others, not only harm for the person with the disorder. Risk to public safety raises problems and require solutions that are quite unlike those associated with medical care and healthcare generally: the control of individuals for the safety of others is fundamentally an activity of the state, not of the medical profession or any other healthcare profession.

Another topic for Chapter 5 is the consequence of tying diagnosis not to some natural fact that would define disorder, but to distress and disability, which in turn is closely linked to the perceived need to treat. Looked at in this way, decisions as to what conditions do and do not count as mental disorders are subject to influences from a variety of stakeholders, including the people with the problems, carers, purchasers and providers, and the manufacturers of treatment technologies. The question of what is included in and what is excluded from the diagnostic manuals can no longer be answered – if naturalist definitions are abandoned – by invoking a scientific, objective fact of the matter. The various well-known social, political and economic pressures for including or excluding conditions from the diagnostic manuals, or for allowing harm severity thresholds to lower or to rise, now appear as primary drivers, not simply practical complications. The same considerations apply to the vexed question whether the scope of diagnosable mental disorders is being extended illegitimately, beyond 'true disorders'. According to the line of thought being pursued here, there is no legitimacy or illegitimacy of the kind supposed by naturalist definitions, but only opinions to be reconciled about extent of harm and appropriateness and costs of treatment options. In short, there is a major boundary problem here, inevitably arising, I suggest, once the asylum walls come down and mental disorder is back in the community.

The boundary problem, uncertainty about the extent of mental disorder, recognition of its diversity and of the familiarity of some kinds, is connected to uncertainty and diversity in terminology – what name to use for the conditions of interest and the people who have them. Another way of putting this point is that the 'medicalization' of the conditions of interest, characterized historically by Foucault and criticized in the 1960s critiques, is back in the melting pot, though the outcomes now tend not to be ideological – all or none – but rather to involve recognition of diversity in the conditions, and in ways of responding.

It is evident enough that these implications of giving up on naturalism in this context, on the idea that mental disorder is fundamentally a matter of fact, leads to a characteristic post- or late-modern – the word 'mess' comes to mind. In place of absolute fixed facts and boundaries we find flux, appearing different from different points of view, and requiring negotiation between them. This outcome is not surprising: the social interplay of opinions and values is always apparent, the question is only whether there is some fixed order underneath or above it, and naturalism about mental disorder as elsewhere is just an expression of the opinion that there is. Give it up – because it is unviable – and we have to accept what is left. Science has a critical role in this problematic, because its methodology seems to track objective facts, to get beyond mere opinion and values. This is why through the essay I have assessed the two main naturalist definitions of mental disorder against paradigms and theories of current biobehavioural science, the outcome being that, far from supporting them, they undermine them.

I have kept references to articles, books and websites to a minimum in the text, wanting to avoid it being overwhelmed by them and thus harder to follow. Each chapter has an annotated bibliography which gives key references not already cited in the text, and some entry points into large literatures.

Chapter 1

The current diagnostic manuals
Aims, methods, and questions

1.1 Introduction and diagnostic criteria

As outlined in the Introduction the two main questions to be addressed in this essay are first, are the norms of psychological function medical, or really social?; and second, what is the validity of the distinction between mental disorder and normality, and in particular is there meaning, after all, in mental disorder? We start with how these issues play out in the psychiatric diagnostic manuals.

The *International Classification of Mental and Behavioural Disorders*, part of the *International Classification of Diseases and Related Health Problems* (ICD), produced by the World Health Organization, and the *Diagnostic and Statistical Manual of Mental Disorders* (DSM), produced by the American Psychiatric Association, are the two manuals in standard use for the description, classification and diagnosis of mental, or of mental and behavioural, disorders. Both have been through many revisions and editions, the current ones being the ICD-10 (World Health Organization 1992) and the DSM-1V (American Psychiatric Association 1994), and new editions, ICD-11 and DSM-V, are currently in the planning stage. The ICD-10 and DSM-IV differ in some ways, some minor and some major, partly reflecting their historical and cultural contexts, the ICD being international with roots in European psychiatry, the DSM originating in the United States though with increasing global reach. For the purposes of the present essay the two do not differ significantly, and main points made here about one or the other will generally apply to both unless otherwise stated.

The range of conditions in the manuals is wide and diverse, including mood and anxiety disorders, each of many kinds – schizophrenia, other psychotic disorders, adjustment disorders, somatoform disorders, dementias; childhood disorders such as enuresis, separation anxiety disorder, attention deficit hyperactive disorder, conduct disorder, autism – and the so-called personality disorders, adult lifelong conditions typically involving various sorts of difficulties in interpersonal and social relationships and so on, adding up to some hundreds of conditions when various kinds of subtyping are taken into account.

The psychiatric manuals describe well – albeit in cool, clinical language – the problems that people bring to the psychiatric clinic. The diagnostic criteria for a particular condition typically include description of particular symptoms, and specification that some number or range of these symptoms must be present, as a syndrome, for diagnosis to be warranted. The whole of this essay requires some familiarity with the psychiatric conditions, since they define its topic. Familiarity can come in many ways – personal experience of oneself, family or friends – though these sources alone are usually and thankfully restricted in scope. Clinicians have experience of a larger range of the problems, though probably not all of them; the diagnostic manuals represent an accumulation of clinical experience over generations and across a wide range of service settings. This essay has to do with all the conditions because psychiatry and its diagnostic manuals bring them all under the heading of 'mental disorder', and will focus especially on how this concept is defined in the manuals, explicitly and operationally for specific conditions. For those readers unfamiliar with the diagnostic manuals it may be helpful to give some examples of diagnostic criteria for specific disorders, to show how the diagnostic criteria work, but also to illustrate just some of the wide range. Diagnostic criteria for a few conditions are given as an Appendix to this chapter; some of the conditions are relatively common or familiar, and some controversial in various ways as follows:

◆ Major depressive episode
◆ Post-traumatic stress disorder (PTSD)
◆ Schizophrenia
◆ Autistic disorder
◆ Attention deficit hyperactive disorder (ADHD)
◆ Antisocial personality disorder.

Giving these illustrations should be accompanied with the caution that no illustrations are typical, just because of the great range and diversity of the conditions in the manuals. The illustrations are all taken from the DSM-IV (American Psychiatric Association 1994) and all page references are to this volume. The criteria in the ICD-10 are similar, though usually less algorithmic. The reader familiar with the manuals can of course skip this Appendix.

1.2 The projects of description, classification, and diagnosis of disorder

Several linked projects can be seen at work in the sets of diagnostic criteria: description of mental states and behaviours, regarded as symptoms, classification of symptoms into syndromes, and the diagnosis of a mental disorder.

Physicians have described psychological and behavioural symptoms and classified them into syndromes for centuries, with seminal work in the west being done in Europe and later in the United States. Modern western psychiatry, involving concepts and categories familiar now, is usually dated from about the end of the nineteenth to the beginning of the twentieth century. Research around the middle of the twentieth century in the UK and US brought to light major differences in diagnostic practices, however, and the search began for diagnostic criteria that could be agreed and applied more reliably by clinicians. 'Reliability' in this context is a matter of the extent to which clinicians will agree whether particular symptoms and disorders are present or absent in particular cases. This aim gave rise to the first editions of the formal diagnostic manuals, and these have been steadily refined through the subsequent editions. Broadly speaking the aim of increased reliability has been achieved, at least in research settings, by removing from descriptions of symptoms and disorders assumptions about hidden processes or causes, such as possible minor brain damage, or unconscious psychodynamics. This has involved making descriptions of symptoms more 'observational', so that presence or absence can be determined relatively straightforwardly by observation, including history-taking, without involving uncertain theoretical assumptions. In some conditions there remain explicit causal assumptions, such as in the criteria for PTSD, cited in the Appendix, or in the syndrome of 'psychosis due to substance misuse', but these are the exceptions and the causal assumptions are explicit.

A formative influence in steering the psychiatric diagnostic manuals to more observational descriptions of symptoms, without implicit causal or other theoretical implications, was a paper by the philosopher of science Carl Hempel, delivered in a psychiatric conference in New York in 1959. Drawing on familiar principles in the philosophy of the natural sciences, Hempel argued that the early descriptive phase in a science should use terms that are as observational, as theory-neutral, as possible:

> The vocabulary required in the early stages . . . will be largely observational: it will be chosen so as to permit the description of those aspects of the subject matter which are ascertainable fairly directly by observation.
>
> Hempel (1965, p.140)

This method optimizes the objectivity and reliability of descriptions. Thus:

> The concern of many psychologists and social scientists with the reliability of their terms reflects the importance attributed to objectivity of use: the reliability of a concept (or of the corresponding term) is usually understood as an indicator of two things: the consistency shown in its use by one observer, and the agreement in the use made of it by different observers.
>
> Hempel (op.cit. p.142)

The first task of the manuals is thus description of abnormal psychological phenomena, in terms that are as objective, as observational, as possible. Once symptoms are described, the next task is classification of symptoms into syndromes. This step is also made as well-defined and reliable as possible, for example by providing – especially in the DSM rather than the ICD – an algorithm leading from symptoms to syndromes, such as that either this or that symptom is necessary for diagnosis, or that some number, say five out of a possible ten, are sufficient. Using terms for the description of symptoms that are as observational as possible, and specifying symptoms or combinations of symptoms that are necessary or sufficient for diagnosis, helps to increase reliability of diagnosis. The need for reliability, for agreement between clinicians or researchers on whether the symptoms and conditions are present or absent, is clear enough. We cannot sensibly communicate about the conditions of interest, in the clinic or elsewhere, or research on their causes and treatments, unless there is a reasonable measure of agreement on what those conditions are. This requirement of reliability in description of the basic data and the methodology used to achieve it are evident in science generally. The application of this methodology in the diagnostic manuals has been straightforward and works reasonably well, though with room for continual improvements.

It may be noted here that while the description of symptoms may be made increasingly observational, they often contain reference to norms of psychological and behavioural functioning. This feature of symptoms has already been noted in the Introduction, and is inevitable given that they are indeed meant to be symptoms of abnormal psychological phenomena, whether in isolation or as part of a syndrome. However, normative concepts are not typically observational, and would not be so regarded in the empiricist tradition to which Hempel's work belonged. The importance of this point for the present purpose is that it is exactly the status of the norms invoked in demarcating mental disorders that has been controversial, specifically: are they a matter of objective, medical fact – or they really social? Issues here will be discussed in more detail in the next section.

The third aspect of the DSM and ICD projects is the diagnosis of disorder, the characterization of the mental and behavioural states that have been described and classified as *disorders*. In physical medicine, where the notion of diagnosis originated along with the related concepts of symptom and syndrome, diagnosis typically involves description of symptoms, classification of clinically observable symptoms into a syndrome, and further, if known, implication of a particular cause, such as a bacterium, virus, lesion, tumour, etc. As indicated above, diagnosis in psychiatry has increasingly emphasized the first two aspects of diagnosis, description and classification of symptoms, but the third aspect, implication of a particular cause, has been more problematic and has been correctly identified as complex and a matter for ongoing research. It has become clear and acknowledged that while some general medical conditions may have a single specific cause, no (practically no) psychiatric conditions have a single, specific cause. The causal stories will be complex, involving such broad factors as genetics, developmental neurobiology, early experience, social context, the person's attitude, current life circumstances and events, and so on. Since we know so far only fractions of the causal story for some conditions, and there is no way that causation in any particular person's case can be settled at the time of presentation in the clinic, diagnosis has come to be based on the limited criteria accessible at clinical interview, as specified in the manuals using one or more informants, with no commitment to what the causes may be.

The DSM-IV imposes a further requirement for the diagnosis of many disorders, over and above presence of the symptom syndrome, to the effect that the symptom syndrome is associated with significant distress or impairment. Typical is the wording for PTSD, (American Psychiatric Association 1994, p. 429): 'The disturbance causes clinically significant distress or impairment in social, occupational, or other important areas of functioning.'

The specification in the case of schizophrenia is slightly more elaborate:

> For a significant portion of the time since the onset of the disturbance, one or more major areas of functioning such as work, interpersonal relations, or self-care are markedly below the level achieved prior to the onset (or when the onset is in childhood or adolescence, failure to achieve expected level of interpersonal, academic, or occupational achievements).
>
> American Psychiatric Association (op. cit., p. 285)

The point of including a criterion of disorder of this kind is apparently to exclude cases where the person has a clinical syndrome, as defined in the diagnostic criteria, (such as avoidance of situations that are reminiscent of traumatic experience, hearing voices in the absence of speakers, or persistent cleaning compulsions, say), but does not mind, and is able to get on with their life.

In summary then, the psychiatric manuals require for diagnosis that the person has a mental/behavioural syndrome of the kind and range described in the diagnostic criteria, and also, in the DSM-IV for some conditions though not all, that the clinical syndrome be associated with distress or impairment. These are, in brief, the criteria for mental disorder in the manuals – but is it possible to construct a definition of the term?

Faced with the challenge of defining mental disorder the DSM and ICD have understandably been somewhat hesitant. Psychiatry was after all hounded away from the term 'mental illness' under the pressure of the 1960s anti-psychiatry critiques; mental disorder is a substitute, whether or not it is an improvement, and perhaps other terms will do better. ICD-10 introduces its definition of mental disorder unpromisingly under the heading 'problems of terminology':

> The term 'disorder' is used throughout the classification, so as to avoid even greater problems inherent in the use of terms such as 'disease' and 'illness'. 'Disorder' is not an exact term, but it is used here to imply the existence of a clinically recognizable set of symptoms or behaviour associated in most cases with distress and with interference with personal functions. Social deviance or conflict alone, without personal dysfunction, should not be included in mental disorder as defined here.
>
> World Health Organization (1992, p. 5)

Following caveats and qualifications, DSM-IV gives the following definition:

> In DSM-IV, each of the mental disorders is conceptualized as a clinically significant behavioral or psychological syndrome or pattern that occurs in an individual and that is associated with present distress (e.g., a painful symptom) or disability (i.e., impairment in one or more important areas of functioning) or with a significantly increased risk of suffering death, pain, disability or an important loss of freedom. In addition, this syndrome or pattern must not be merely an expectable and culturally sanctioned response to a particular event, for example, the death of a loved one. Whatever its original cause, it must currently be considered a manifestation of a behavioral, psychological or biological dysfunction in the individual. Neither deviant behavior (e.g., political, religious, or sexual) nor conflicts that are primarily between the individual and society are mental disorders unless the deviance or conflict is a symptom of a dysfunction in the individual, as described above.
>
> American Psychiatric Association (1994, pp. xxi–xxii)

Several points may be noted here about these definitions. First, the primary conceptualization of the mental disorders compiled in the manual is association with distress or disability, or risk of adverse outcomes. In brief, mental disorders are understood to be conditions associated with harm. This is so in both definitions, the ICD-10 as well as the DSM-IV. Second, qualifications are added so as to narrow down this class of conditions; that is to say, not all conditions associated with harm are to be understood to be mental disorders. One qualification is that to count as a mental disorder, a condition associated with harm has to involve a personal dysfunction, not to be just a matter of deviation from social norms. Another qualification, in the DSM-IV definition only, is that the condition must not be merely an expectable and culturally sanctioned response to a particular event, such as a major loss.

The above characterizations of mental disorder as used in the psychiatric manuals are helpful, and hard to improve on. They reflect well the way in which many of the sets of diagnostic criteria are laid out, and the use of the distress/impairment criterion. They add qualifications that are apparently essential, serving to distinguish mental disorders as personal/individual dysfunctions, distinct from normal reactions to life's adversities, on the one hand, and from social deviance on the other. Most attention in this essay will be to the DSM definition of mental disorder, largely the work of the editor of the DSM-III and DSM-III-R, Robert Spitzer, and his colleagues. Spitzer supplied background and commentary in a number of papers (e.g. Spitzer and Endicott 1978, Spitzer and Williams 1982), which will be considered at relevant points in the essay.

In summary, then, there are three main projects in the psychiatric diagnostic manuals: description of symptoms, classification into syndromes, and diagnosis of disorder. Arguably it all works reasonably well for many purposes in clinical practice and research, though with ample scope for ongoing improvements which can be worked on scientifically and clinically.

There are outstanding issues, however, and two of them that are relevant to topics of the present essay will be considered in the following two sections, one on norms of psychological functioning, and the second on the tension between diagnostic reliability and validity.

1.3 The problem of psychological normality/abnormality

There is a principled and not much discussed limitation inherent in the descriptive project, namely, that many though not all of the diagnostic criteria sets invoke norms of psychological/behavioural functioning. Some of these norms invoke what is being called here rupture of meaningful connections; others invoke below average functioning. Examples of the first kind can be seen in the criteria for schizophrenia and autism, quoted in full in the Appendix to this chapter. Positive symptoms of schizophrenia include 'distortions or exaggerations of inferential thinking (delusions) and perception (hallucinations)'. As other examples, the criteria for generalized anxiety disorder include reference to 'excessive' anxiety and worrying (American Psychiatric Association 1994, p. 435). The criteria for compulsions in obsessive compulsive disorder refer to lack of 'realistic' connection between compulsive behaviours and the negative event they are intended to prevent (op. cit., p. 423). Examples of norms that invoke below average functioning are found particularly in the criteria for disorders of childhood such as autistic disorder and ADHD, both quoted in full in the Appendix to this chapter; for autism, failure to develop peer relationships or lack of varied, spontaneous make-believe play or social imitative play appropriate to developmental level.

In other cases the norms seem to be implicit rather than explicit. For example most or all of the symptoms of *major depressive episode* (given in the Appendix to this Chapter), apparently contain no explicit reference to abnormal as opposed to normal functioning, as for example in persistent depressed mood, loss of interest, and recurrent morbid thoughts. That said, there is the well-known qualifier in the criteria, that 'the symptoms are not better accounted for by bereavement, i.e. after the loss of a loved one' (American Psychiatric Association 1994, p. 327). The background point is that some of the symptoms of *major depressive disorder* (though not all) may be indistinguishable from signs of bereavement, but no one wants to call bereavement a disorder – so the qualifier is there in effect to exclude at least one obvious case of normal depressed mood, where 'normal' can be understood as both meaningful and typical.

The pervasive but not much discussed use of norms in the diagnostic criteria raises various issues. First, it seems to be a principled qualification to the idea that the terms employed are just descriptive, or observational. Second, and this is a question obscured by assuming that all the terms are simply descriptive or observational, rather than normative, it is unclear what exactly is the nature of these normative distinctions. Behind that, there is the old problem of whether they are really medical and scientific norms, or rather social.

There is nothing wrong with normative concepts, but there is a problem with thinking of their application as involving just observation, the idea introduced into diagnosis by Hempel. Normative concepts are not generally regarded as observational, and were not so regarded in the empiricist tradition, of which Hempel's philosophy of science was a late expression. In empiricist thinking, observational data were regarded as objective facts, to be contrasted with values, which involved subjectivity. Norms would be regarded as falling on the value side of this dichotomy rather than the factual. Hempel in fact did consider the problem of norms in these terms, using as examples the (now defunct) diagnostic criteria for 'inadequate personality':

> It may be worth considering whether, or to what extent, criteria with valuational overtones are used in the specification of psychiatric concepts. . . Such notions as inadequacy of response, inadaptability, ineptness, and poor judgment clearly have valuational aspects, and it is to be expected that their use in concrete cases will be influenced by the idiosyncrasies of the investigator; this will reduce the reliability of these concepts.

> Hempel (op. cit., p. 145)

Two points may be noted about this. First, the empiricist fact/value distinction has trouble with norms of biological functioning. Biology – which came to maturity after the heyday of empiricism – is pervaded by concepts relating to norms of functioning, to systems (such as the cardiovascular or the auto-nomic nervous system) functioning more or less well or breaking down altogether. There is a pull to regarding these concepts and judgements as relat-ing to matters of fact, certainly if the option is that they are matters of subjective values. On the other hand, normative statements are hardly just observational, because they draw on a non-trivial theory about the normal functioning of the system in question. What about psychological norms? Are they like biological norms, basically factual, though not matters of observation, since they draw on a theory of psychological functioning? Or perhaps they are valuational, so that their use is influenced, as Hempel says, by the idiosyncrasies of the investigator, and behind that, we may suppose, by cultural or subcultural influences. Using biology as a model for psychology, norms of functioning assume the appearance of being a scientific, factual matter: on the other hand, if we focus on the links between the psychological and the social, then standards of functioning may instead involve social values.

While the diagnostic criteria are conceived in an empiricist way, as matters of observation and description, the use of norms of psychological functioning is unattended to. As indicated, it is obvious enough that there is a pervasive use of norms, and that many come under two main headings: rupture of meaningful connections, and deviance from the level of functioning of some reference group. Invoking norms of these kinds in the diagnostic criteria in fact seems to involve implicit assumptions of just the kind that mainstream psychiatry and its medical model have often been criticized for, and which have been sketched in the Introduction. It seems to be assumed that apparent ruptures of meaningful connections in mental life, such as in hallucination or delusion, or in performance of 'rituals' to avert harms with which the behav-iour has no realistic connection, are signs of the mental dysfunction, lack of order, but it may be, if we took a broader cultural or deeper psychological view, that these states and behaviours do have or may have meaning after all. The criteria for major depressive episode discussed above raise a similar prob-lem. Normal bereavement reactions are explicitly excluded, but normal, understandable intense and prolonged losses to other major losses are not, implying that they will count as warranting diagnosis of disorder.

Concerning the judgement of abnormality in terms of comparison with an average reference group, it is unclear exactly what normal reference group is being invoked, and why deviance from it should be considered a dysfunction rather than just difference. Relevant here is the point, to be considered in more detail in the next chapter, that the behavioural sciences typically do not envis-age a categorical cut-off between mental disorders and mental normality. So strong is the accumulating scientific evidence from psychological and behavioural genetic research that many psychiatric conditions are expressions of traits found in some degree in the general population that the authors have wisely allowed for this. Under the heading 'limitations of the categorical approach' the DSM-IV, for example, has

> In DSM-IV, there is no assumption that each category of mental disorder is a completely discrete entity with absolute boundaries dividing it from other mental disorders or from no mental disorder . . . It was suggested that the DSM-IV classification be organized following a dimensional model rather than the categorical model used in DSM-III-R. A dimensional system classifies clinical presentations based on quantification of attributes rather than the assignment to categories and works best in describing phenomena that are distributed continuously and that do not have clear boundaries. Although dimensional systems increase reliability and communicate more clinical information . . . they also have serious limitations and thus far have been less useful in clinical practice and in stimulating research . . . There is as yet no agreement on the choice of the optimal dimensions to be used for classification purposes.

American Psychiatric Association (1994, p. xxii)

To recap, the project of achieving reliability of diagnosis by characterizing symptoms and syndromes in descriptive, observational terms is essentially qualified by the pervasive use of norms of psychological/behavioural functioning, invoking either what is being called here rupture of meaningful connections, or below average functioning. A sign of the same issue reappears in the explicit definitions of mental disorder in the psychiatric manuals. As noted in the previous section, the definitions have mental disorders understood primarily as conditions associated with distress, disability and risk – in brief, harm – but qualifications are added so as to narrow down the broad class of harmful conditions, distinguishing mental disorders as a subset. It is stipulated that to count as a mental disorder a harmful condition must involve a personal or individual dysfunction, not to be just a matter of deviation from social norms, and, in the DSM-IV definition, it is stated that to count as a mental disorder a distressing or disabling condition must not be merely an expectable and culturally sanctioned response to a particular event, such as a major loss. These stipulations and statements in the definitions of mental disorder are not trivial, and straight away there is the possibility of tension between the aim of making sure that they are applied correctly in diagnosis, and the aim of making diagnosis reliable. This is another version of the problem in the diagnostic criteria sets for particular conditions: on the one hand they are meant to pick out abnormal psychological phenomena, while on the other they are meant to be purely descriptive or observational.

So the question of norms of psychological and behavioural functioning in the manuals is problematic: are they assumed or presumed or not? And if they are, what is their origin? As to this question of origin, standards that define what is meaningful as opposed to senseless, and expectations that people should function the same as some normal reference group, may rest on hard medical or scientific facts, or they may reflect features of social organization and values.

The operation of social norms in the psychiatric manuals is most obvious in the criteria for the antisocial conditions. The primary criterion (A) in the DSM-IV diagnostic criteria for antisocial personality disorder, (American Psychiatric Association 1994, pp. 649–50; quoted in the Appendix to this chapter), opens with: 'There is a pervasive pattern of disregard for and violation of the rights of others', followed by examples including 'failure to conform to social norms with respect to lawful behaviors'. This criterion seems to involve social norms – if anything does. Connected with this, the requirement that for diagnosis there has to be distress or disruption of social role functioning is not present in the diagnostic criteria for antisocial personality disorder. The absence of this kind of criterion allows for the fact that a person with this condition may not be distressed by it, nor need their social functioning be impaired by it, at least not in their own terms. There is also no explicit reference to disruption of psychological functioning, lending support to the interpretation that it is social norms not psychological norms that are being violated. In brief, it is unclear in the characterization of antisocial personality disorder that psychological norms are being invoked, or, if they are, that they are any different from social norms. By all means other people may be distressed by the person's behaviour, or may have their social functioning disrupted by it, but this introduces a whole other set of considerations – about effects on others – that again have more to do with social values. This of course is the kind of case that lends weight to the view that psychiatry is fundamentally in the business of defining social deviance under the guise of medical disorder. On the other hand it may be plausible to suppose that if a person persistently disregards and violates the rights of others, then they must have or may well have a psychological dysfunction, this supposition apparently drawing on the idea that some psychological functioning is bound up with concern for the rights, or the well-being, of others. This line of thought is plausible, but for the present purpose the point is that it effectively blurs the distinction between psychological and social functioning and their norms, rather than offering us a forced choice between the two; hence it opens up the possibility that the psychiatric manuals do rely at least in part on social norms after all. However, these issues, which echo the debates of the 1960s, are not explicitly discussed or explained in the manuals.

On the other hand one related point is clearly stated in the explicit definitions of mental disorder in the prefatory material of the diagnostic manuals. As quoted in the preceding section, both the ICD-10 and the DSM-IV have explicit statements to the effect that social deviance alone is not sufficient for the diagnosis of mental disorder: what is required is 'personal dysfunction', as opposed to just social deviance. What should this be taken to mean? The distinction here is made especially with reference to the pervasiveness of dysfunctional behaviour across contexts, using the principle familiar in personality theory, that constancy in behaviours across situations is attributed to the person, while variation is attributed to the situational context. Thus, an individual who only gets into trouble while in conflict with a particular social group, but who manages their affairs without problem otherwise, will be regarded as in conflict with that group, not as having an individual dysfunction. Conversely, a person who begins to have problems in one situation, perhaps in work or marriage, but who then, or in any case, develops problems of functioning generally, will be regarded as having an individual dysfunction.

Here for example are Spitzer and Williams elucidating this theme in the DSM-III definition of mental disorder:

> The next statement, that 'the disturbance is not only in the relationship between the individual and society', attempts to clarify the relationship between mental disorder and social deviance. An individual whose behaviour brings him or her into conflict with society should not be regarded as having a mental disorder unless there is strong evidence supporting the inference of a behavioural, psychological, or biological dysfunction. For example, anti-social behaviour that is sanctioned by sub-cultural norms, as in group delinquency, does not by itself warrant a diagnosis of a mental disorder. However, when it is part of a pervasive pattern that included inability to function at work or at school, the mental disorder Conduct Disorder or Antisocial Personality Disorder is diagnosed because a psychological dysfunction can then reasonably be inferred.
>
> Spitzer and Williams (1982, p. 21)

Understood in this way, the distinction between social deviance alone, as limited to a specific conflict, and mental disorder in the individual is relatively straightforward. It is different, however, from the question whether the norms of functioning implicit or explicit in the diagnostic criteria are social norms, or, by way of contrast, objective, medical, and scientific. It remains an open question, for example, whether pervasive disregard for the rights of others, pervasive across contexts and attributable therefore to the individual, is – what it seems to be – a pervasive violation of social norms. This raises the question whether the same may be true of other kinds of conditions. It may be the case, for example, that judgements as to whether worrying is excessive, or unrealistic, or as to whether hearing voices in the absence of speakers is dysfunctional, as to whether particular styles of interpersonal relating are dysfunctional and so on, are likewise fundamentally matters of social norms and values, rather than matters of medical or scientific fact.

What then is this contrast being made between social norms and norms that are objective, medical, and scientific? What does this mean? In part the answer lies in the complex debates of the 1960s, in the criticism of the so-called medical model of mainstream psychiatry by the various anti-psychiatry critiques – some of which, of course, were made by psychiatrists. Some details will be considered in the next chapter (in section 2.6), but I suggest the following here: that one fundamental question in those debates was over the origin and maintenance of the distinctions between mental health and illness, mental order and disorder, normality and abnormality. The question of medical and social norms would then be: are these distinctions, these boundary issues, made on the basis of special knowledge, medical and scientific, or they made by society? Or again: are they a matter for professional knowledge and expertise – or of what might be called 'folk psychiatry'?

These issues apparently do not surface in the psychiatric manuals, though by all means they embody and claim professional expertise. What they do have are the intriguing expressions that open the explicit definitions of mental disorder: 'clinically recognizable', or 'clinically significant' behavioural or psychological patterns. What do these expressions mean? They are left undefined and unjustified in the manuals, but they evidently carry a lot of weight. A superficial implication may be that these are matters of medical expertise, or the expertise of trained mental health professionals generally, not matters for the lay person. Beneath the surface however, discussed in the surrounding literature, is the background information that the idea behind these expressions is the recognition that the conditions listed in the manuals, and characterized there with accumulated professional expertise, are the kinds of problems people bring to the clinic – they are the presenting problems, the presenting complaints.

On this theme Spitzer and Williams remarked:

> The phrase 'clinically significant' acknowledges that there are many behavioural or psychological conditions that can be considered 'pathological' but the clinical manifestations of which are so mild that clinical attention is not indicated. For this reason, such conditions are not included in a classification of mental disorders ... [The] syndrome of caffeine withdrawal never leads to seeking professional help. Therefore it is not included in DSM-III as a mental disorder.

> (1982, pp. 19–20)

Another contemporary commentator, Donald Klein, wrote as follows on the need to have a definition of mental disorder:

> Strikingly there is no explicit statement within the *Diagnostic and Statistical Manual of Mental Disorders* [second edition] that defines the sort of condition categorizable within this document. Such a logical lapse is not restricted to psychiatry, however,

since the *International Classification of Diseases* also lacks such a statement. It seems plain that these compendia are actually compilations of the sorts of things that physicians treat; a circular classificatory principle but a useful historical clue. Our definitions of illness are derived from medical practice.

(1978, p. 41)

The insight that fundamental to the conditions in the diagnostic manuals is that they are the kinds of problems that people bring to the psychiatric clinic raises important issues about the relation between psychiatric expertise and folk psychiatry, and about the social organization that results in these kinds of problems being brought to the psychiatric clinic as opposed to elsewhere. These issues, I suggest, are critical in the debate as to whether psychiatric norms are social, as opposed to medical/scientific. These various issues will be considered in more detail in subsequent chapters: for the present the main point to be made is just that they are outstanding, unresolved and hardly addressed in the manuals.

The methodology recommended by Hempel to the American Psychiatric Association – to describe symptoms and syndromes in as observational terms as possible – worked reasonably well to achieve the desired result: more reliable diagnoses, more agreement between clinicians and especially between clinical researchers. However, as remarked above, one limitation inherent in the descriptive project is that most or all of the diagnostic criteria sets invoke norms of psychological/behavioural functioning, and this matters, because the status of these norms are the subject matter of critical debates within and around psychiatry. Yet the status of these norms is not discussed. Why should that be? Well, since we have observational descriptions we are only describing what is open to view, unproblematic. Or on the other hand, it may be that there are many underlying problems, so best leave them alone and get on with it – with classifying and diagnosing. Both of these contradictory attitudes are pragmatic and effective, the more so in combination. The unproblematic nature of observation is particularly interesting in the issues that it raises, as follows.

When 'observational' is tied to interrater agreement, as it is in Hempel's twentieth-century usage, it actually fails to force a principled distinction between facts on the one hand, and norms or values on the other. There is no reason why normative or valuational concepts should not be applied as reliably between raters as factual concepts, provided the group shares the relevant norms or values. It is a working assumption of the descriptive project in the diagnostic manuals that abnormal mental states and behaviour can be reasonably reliably recognized by psychiatrists and mental health professionals generally. However, this agreement is so far neutral to the question whether what is being recognized is just a matter of fact, or whether it is the implicit shared code – shared norms and values – of the group. Interrater reliability simply does not settle the issue one way or another. It is settled, rather, by inspecting the content of the descriptions, and what we find in the case of psychiatric symptoms and syndromes is pervasive use of norms and, perhaps, values. This implies that what we are all agreeing about, what we can recognize as if by eye alone, turns on a more or less implicit theory as to what is and is not normal mental and behavioural functioning. But what is this implicit theory, and what is its basis? Is the theory, or judgements in specific instances, based on medicine, on psychological science, on cultural tradition, or what?

This is, as it were, an academic question, but it comes to life in cross-cultural/subcultural contact. It was remarked above that normative judgements can be as reliable as factual judgements providing the group shares the relevant norms and know how to operate them. Normative judgements in these circumstances are then observational, a matter of perception: the members of the group can just see what is normal or abnormal. Or again, it will be seem to be just like a matter of objective fact. So the issue that arises in relation to the psychiatric manuals is this. Since psychiatrists and some other mental health professionals are all trained in using the kinds of normative judgements codified in the manuals, they will appear to be just like matters of fact – medical, clinical or scientific – and to the extent that the norms used in the clinic reflect those in society at large, so also society at large will have a similar view of the matter. It is only by exposure to other groups who may have other norms that the underlying position becomes clearer. It may be that other groups, different socio-economic classes or cultural communities, use the same norms, but it may be that they don't, and in this case what appeared to be a matter of fact shows up more as a subcultural or cultural option. In other words there is typically a within-group blindness to its own norms and a social anthropological perspective is necessary to see them. These problems have been attended to in cross-cultural psychiatry and anthropological critiques of psychiatry.

Various issues above will be taken up later, but the main point here is that the descriptive project in the psychiatric manuals makes little of or nothing of the fact that characterizations of symptoms are permeated by norms of functioning, and it remains unclear whether the norms of functioning are matters of medical or scientific fact, or whether they originate in and are maintained by broader society.

1.4 Tension between reliability and validity of diagnosis

There is a tension that arises between the several projects in the psychiatric manuals. On the one hand, they aim for perfectly good reasons to make diagnosis as reliable as possible, by basing it on data that can be reliably observed or otherwise ascertained during clinical interview, while on the other hand they want diagnosis to be valid as diagnosis of disorder. The tension that arises can be simply stated – that 'disorder' may not be a simple matter of observation or clinical ascertainment.

A way of stating the problem here is that the mental states and behaviours described in the various diagnostic criteria sets are supposed to be symptoms of disorder, and the syndromes comprising them are supposed to be mental disorders. It may be that these are after all theoretical matters, not something that can just be observed. In fact, from this point of view, it always was extraordinary to suppose that diagnosis of disorders, involving demarcation of disorders from normal functioning, could be run in simple descriptive terms, without using any normative distinctions. How can criteria for this purpose avoid normative distinctions, and how can those in turn not draw on a non-trivial theory about the normal functioning of the system in question (the mind)?

One answer to this is that we may already know (think we know) that the psychiatric conditions, the conditions that people bring to the clinic, are mental disorders, and the classification task just has to attend to features of the presentation, observed by the expert eye. Obviously all this means is that the background theory of order and disorder is implicit, somewhere in the process of people bringing the problems to the clinic, having clinics there for the purpose, and in the clinical science. Where and what the background theory is in all this entangled growth is hard to say – a formidable task to sort out. For many purposes, on the other hand, especially within the clinic itself, the issues can be fairly stable; problems arise more at the interfaces between psychiatric services and society at large, where the absence of an explicit understanding of the boundaries between disorder and order is keenly felt.

What might the theory of mental disorder be? There will be more detailed consideration of the many aspects of this question through the essay, but here is a very rough characterization of four key players, not incompatible with one another, listed here for the purposes of orientation:

1. Mental disorder is a matter of breakdown of meaningful connections in mental life. That is to say: it is a matter of an emotion having no appropriate object, or being excessive in relation to its object; or of beliefs having no basis in experience and/or education; or of behaviours that are not under the control of the person's will, or are inconsistent with the person's expressed aims and beliefs; and so forth.

2. Mental disorder results from a structural or functional lesion in the underlying neural processes.

3. Mental disorder is a matter of functioning below what is statistically normal for human beings.

4. In mental disorder the mind is not functioning as it has been naturally designed to do in the evolutionary process.

The first option has already been considered in various contexts so far: it is the most obvious marker of mental disorder, used frequently in the psychiatric manuals, and also familiar to the folk. The second approach to mental disorder is usually credited to the medical model, at least in a strong form, and can be seen as a or as the medical explanation of the surface features highlighted in option 1, breakdown of meaningful connections. The third option is a strong version of a marker that has also been considered above, defining abnormal function by reference to some reference group, also to be found in the manuals, and used by the lay person. It has been remarked already that some unclarity attaches to the question of what reference group is being invoked, and why, but the point about the strong version 3 is that it seeks to give a single, factual answer to this question in terms of the human species. It is elaborated in one of the two so-called naturalist definitions of mental disorder, due to Boorse, to be considered in detail in Chapter 3. The other naturalist definition, due to Wakefield, is along the lines of option 4, and will also be considered in Chapter 3.

These four approaches are probably the main options for making a distinction between normal and abnormal mental functioning, between mental disorder and mental order. The main point for here is that they all apparently go beyond what can be readily observed in the clinic, and what be described in reliable terms, in one way or another. That is to say, in brief: surface rupture of meaningful connections can be spotted readily enough, but judgement as to whether there is meaning after all, when life history and circumstances are taken into account, requires both more assessment and interpretation; deviation from the normal functioning of some readily available comparison group may be easy to see, but whether comparison with other groups would deliver the same result is unclear, as is the issue of which group is the critical one for comparison; finally, neither neural lesions nor failure of a mental mechanism to function as designed in evolution, are matters that can resolved reliably in the clinic. The implication then is that the drive to reliable descriptions of symptoms and syndromes in the psychiatric manuals runs the risk of losing validity in relation to diagnosis of disorder. In brief, we might be reliably diagnosing non-disorders as disorders.

To some extent the problem is mitigated by the fact that, while Hempel's recommendation was, and the official line is, that characterization of symptoms and syndromes should only be observational and descriptive, in practice normative distinctions are pervasively invoked. There is extensive reference to rupture of meaningful connections in mental life, and some more or less explicit reference to below normal functioning. On the other hand, as remarked above, neither of these criteria decisively demarcates disorder from normality. In any case, as indicated in the previous section, not all of the diagnostic criteria sets explicitly stipulate that the symptoms or syndromes as described constitute abnormal mental functioning. In these cases – true to the official line that symptoms are characterized in purely descriptive language – it seems possible for meaningful and typical psychological reactions to be brought in as disordered. The criteria for major depressive episode and for post-traumatic stress disorder, quoted in the appendix to this chapter, are examples.

The position is further complicated, though in the end not resolved, by the explicit definitions of 'mental disorder' given in the diagnostic manuals, considered above in section 1.2. The primary conceptualization of the mental disorders is association with harm, and there are stipulations that narrow down the general category of harmful conditions. One is that to count as a mental disorder a condition must involve a personal dysfunction and not be just a deviation from social norms. The other, in the DSM definition, is that to count as a mental disorder a harmful condition must not be merely an expectable and culturally sanctioned response to a particular event, such as a major loss. In brief, mental disorders are to be distinguished on the one hand from social deviance, and from normal reactions to life's adversities on the other. Problems with the dichotomy between personal dysfunction and social deviance (raised by the prospect of pervasive social deviance) were considered in the previous section. There are also problems with the second demarcation – between mental disorder and normal reactions to life's adversities. To the extent that the diagnostic criteria really are just descriptive – true to Hempel's recommendation but contrary to the spirit of the explicit DSM definition – then they cannot capture this difference, because distressing and impairing mental functioning might just be a normal reaction. In brief, validity of disorder diagnosis is lost. On the other hand, it seems that in some cases to some extent the diagnostic criteria really are not just descriptive but rather invoke abnormal psychological functioning – deviating from Hempel's recommendation but conforming to the spirit of the explicit definition. Here the risk is that in the attempt to achieve validity of disorder diagnosis, reliability is lost.

On the other hand, again, it would be possible to have both reliability and validity of diagnosis of disorder if the abnormality involved in disorder – the violation of the requisite norms – could be just observed in the clinic, maybe not in descriptive terms, but as good as, because it was obvious, open to view. So if we could just see the truth of points of the kind listed as options for theories of disorder, points 1 to 4 above, it would work. That is to say, if we could just see breakdown of meaningful connections, the effects of neurological lesions in the mental state, deviation from human statistical norms, failure of the mind to work as it – considering its natural design – should, then we could reliably pick out mental disorder – just by observing, or observing with an expert eye.

The problem here of course it that all we pick out like this are so far just matters of expert consensus, more or less reflecting wider social representations, not necessarily corresponding to the facts. What we can detect in the clinic might fall short of genuine disorder as defined in one or more of the four ways listed above. There are possible non-disorder variants of the main four options, which are or which might be indistinguishable in the clinic. Roughly as follows:

1. There is only apparent breakdown of meaningful connections. As one understands more about the context, e.g. the person's view of the world, life events, subcultural norms – meaning is evident after all.

2. There may be a primary lesion causing disturbance of mental state, but psychological processes can also cause disturbance, sometimes mimicking lesions – as in psychological models from Freud on.

3. The problematic functioning may deviate from the statistical norm of some reference group, but not another more similar in the relevant respects (e.g. exposed to the same life adversities). Or: the functioning may be just an extreme, or not so extreme, shift along from the broad average range of a normally distributed trait, whether temperamental or acquired or both.

4. No mental mechanism is working other than as designed, but problematic functioning arises from, for example, a mismatch between evolutionary design and current environment.

While we are diagnosing disorder in the clinic, either using purely descriptive criteria, or invoking abnormality in terms of either deviance from average group functioning, or apparent breakdown of meaning – either way, the possibility remains that we might be reliably diagnosing non-disorders as disorders – at least in terms of the theories of disorder listed in points 1 to 4 above.

The psychiatric manuals are clear in their explicit definitions of mental disorder that a primary feature of the conditions they describe and classify is that they are distressing and impairing, and this feature is reiterated in many of the diagnostic criteria for particular conditions. The DSM definitions also specify that to count as disorders conditions have not to be just expectable responses, though it is not clear how this qualification shows up in or is meant to apply in the diagnostic criteria. So some of the conditions in the manuals, or some types of them, or some individual presentations of them, while distressing and impairing, perhaps also unexpectable in some sense, may not be disorders after all, but problems associated with psychological functioning in the normal range. The position can be represented diagrammatically in Figure 1.1.

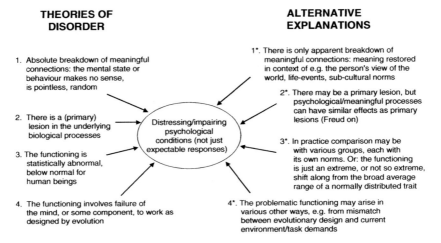

Fig. 1.1 This figure represents possible ways of explaining distressing psychological conditions, especially those that are not just expectable responses to life adversities. On the left-hand side are four theories involving attribution of mental disorder, on the right are related explanations that do not involve disorder of the specified types.

The conclusion is that what can be reliably ascertained in the clinic may not be mental disorder in one or more of the senses specified on the left side of Figure 1.1, but may be a non-disorder variant, of one of the kinds specified on the right side of Figure 1.1. This tension between reliability and validity of diagnosis of disorder is not one that is easily resolved – the problem is fundamental. Consider the two main responses.

One response is to say: OK then, Hempel was wrong – it was a wrong move to try to free up the psychiatric diagnostic manuals from theoretical commitments, especially wrong to free them up from those essentially involved in the attribution of disorder; these should rather be kept in. Following this option would lead to a lot of debate and controversy at a theoretical level as to which of theories 1 to 4 correctly captured the critical features of disorder, in general or for particular kinds of condition, and uncertainty within the science as to which applied to which conditions, and in the clinic as to which applied to particular presentations. However, let us suppose for the sake of argument that consensus could be reached on all this, so that it became clear which kinds of condition, or which subtypes, or which individual presentations, come in as disorders under the required theoretical assumptions, and which of them by contrast turn out to be normal, or at least not abnormal enough to be mental disorder, even though distressing and impairing. Suppose that by going down this route we would eventually secure validity of diagnosis of mental disorder (as opposed to mental normality), but even so, until agreement had been reached over the requisite theoretical and scientific issues and their application in the clinic, reliability of diagnosis would apparently be lost.

That is to say, apart from the substantial problems that would have to be solved to reach consensus over diagnosis of disorder, there is the more pressing problem of what to do in the meantime. How would we know what we are talking about when we are considering whether such-and-such a condition is or is not a disorder? Presumably it would be necessary to reintroduce or reaffirm the need for reliability in characterization of the conditions of interest, so that we could communicate in the clinic, and investigate the conditions in the science. We would need to follow Hempel's advice to get the project off the ground.

This takes us on the second response, sticking with Hempel's advice but acknowledging then that what we are characterizing is descriptive, reliable terms may or may not be mental disorder. An obvious implication then would be that we need another name for the conditions of interest until order/disorder status of each is sorted out. So the response is: Hempel was right – for scientific and clinical communication purposes we need as close to a reliable system of nomenclature and classification as possible, even if, as it turns out, we thereby lose or fail to gain purchase on whether what we are describing really are disorders or not. We would want to focus on conditions that were at least putative disorders, the most available criteria for which may be apparent breakdown of meaningful connections – in the broad sense in which this expression is being used here. These criteria will be shared at least in a culture or subculture, by clinicians and the people, or at least the majority thereof. We would want to stress also, as the psychiatric manuals do, and as the people do when they attend the clinic, that the conditions we are concerned with cause much trouble: distress and impairment. The question whether they are really disorders would be shelved until we had done the requisite theoretical work on the notion of disorder and on aetiological models in the science. In brief, the manuals would be collations of 'putative disorders', other words for which might be mental health problems, more or less severe and enduring, psychiatric conditions, distress, etc.

This second response – which prioritizes reliability of description and classification of syndromes over the validity of diagnosing them as disorders – is, I suggest, actually close to the current position and methodology of the psychiatric manuals. We start off with distressing/impairing states of mind or behaviour that folk bring to the clinic. If the clinician is following standard diagnostic practice as now codified in the psychiatric manuals, the distressing/impairing states of mind or behaviour can be characterized in relatively descriptive, reliable terms, though involving more or less explicit commonly agreed norms of psychological functioning. If the states of mind or behaviour are patterned into a recognized syndrome, and assuming there is associated distress or impairment (which there usually is in the clinic), then the clinician can make a diagnosis according to the criteria in the manuals. The tension arises to the extent that attribution of disorder might involve a further step, some theoretical hypothesis of the sort listed on the left hand side of Figure 1.1 above, over and above establishing the presence of a clinically significant syndrome together with the associated distress/impairment. For in this case, some of the problems listed in the manuals may not be mental disorders, and we need another name for them.

This is, at one level, a terminological problem, and as such the manuals acknowledge it. The manuals hang on to the term mental disorder, though apparently with little confidence in it and with plenty of reservations. As already noted, ICD-10 introduces its definition of mental under the heading 'problems with terminology' and says:

> The term 'disorder' is used throughout the classification, so as to avoid even greater problems inherent in the use of terms such as 'disease' and 'illness'. 'Disorder' is not an exact term.

> World Health Organization (1992, p. 5)

The DSM-IV definition is preceded by extensive caveats and qualifications:

> Although this manual provides a classification of mental disorders, it must be admitted that no definition adequately specifies precise boundaries for the concept of 'mental disorder' . . . Mental disorders have . . . been defined by a variety of concepts (e.g. distress, dyscontrol, disadvantage, disability, inflexibility, irrationality, syndromal pattern, etiology, and statistical deviation). Each is a useful indicator for a mental disorder, but none is equivalent to the concept, and different situations call for different definitions.

> American Psychiatric Association (1994, p.xxi)

So is this just a terminological problem? Well obviously yes and no. No – for reasons to be considered next.

1.5 Criticisms of the mental disorder concept

Problems surrounding the diagnosis of mental disorder are more or less the same now as they were in the heated debates within and around psychiatry in the 1960s and 1970s: problems of the validity of medical model, charges that it confuses social norms with medical norms, that it medicalizes and pathologizes problems of living, that it strips meaning from the problems and people's attempts to deal with them, that it is socially excluding; and so forth. There are certainly non-terminological issues here, symbolized by although muddled up with the terminological ones. To the extent that problems that are called mental disorders in psychiatry are meaningful responses to life's adversities, to ordinary or not so ordinary problems of living, then the name is problematic. Mental functioning, mental order, is defined by meaningful connections between experience and mental states, among mental states, and between mental states and behaviour. If conditions being called mental disorders in psychiatry are in fact meaningful responses, albeit associated with much trouble, then they are in order after all – and the name is problematic, or at least is destabilized. To the extent that the norms invoked to distinguish between mental disorder from order are social, then apparently they are not medical, and the medical model is inappropriate for psychiatry – or at least it is so if we make the assumption that medicine has to work with norms that are not socially defined. This line of thought too would question the use of the term mental disorder, with its history and possible allegiances to the medical model.

Psychological and social critiques of the medical model in psychiatry typically emphasize the 'non-disorder' options to the right side of Figure 1.1, stressing the importance and role of meaningful responses to and coping with adversities, relativity to social groups and environments, individual variations in temperament and personality – as opposed to illness or disorder. Related controversies are about appropriate responses to the problems, concern about medical treatments in particular medication for problems of this kind, emphasizing instead the need for talking therapies, empowerment of individuals and disadvantaged groups, corresponding changes in social organization, and acceptance and accommodation of diversity. All these problems are familiar and still pressing, and they are the non-terminological aspects of the question whether to continue to call the conditions in the psychiatric manuals disorders.

Importantly these were the kinds of social issues which prompted the American Psychiatric Association to attempt for the first time to construct a definition of mental disorder, for the third edition of the DSM. In an historical account of the development of the definition of mental disorder, Spitzer writes:

> Physicians rarely concern themselves with defining what a medical disorder is and instead spend their time, as best they can, diagnosing and treating individual patients. Psychiatrists as well, until fairly recently, ignored the issue of what a mental disorder is and left the problem to sociologists, psychologists, philosophers of science and members of the legal profession . . . In the early 1970s, however, gay activists forced American psychiatry to reassess its attitude toward the nosologic status of homosexuality . . . Arguing that homosexuality by itself was not evidence of illness, gay activists insisted that homosexuality be removed from the original classification (then DSM-II).
>
> Spitzer and Williams (1982, p. 16)

How this shaped the definition will be reviewed later (in Chapter 4) but for now the main point is that the term used – whether mental illness or disorder – has major implications which matter in broader society, and they arise specifically in boundary issues, over what is or is not included under in the category and consequent attitudes. As is well-known homosexuality was excluded from the DSM-III, so that issue was settled, but the same general problem reappears for other conditions, for example now over the question whether temperamentally high active children are being pathologized with the label ADHD and inappropriately medicated, and whether normal sadness in response to major losses is being pathologized and – perhaps – inappropriately medicated.

The relatively recent tension between reliability and validity of diagnosis was considered in the previous section, ending up with terminological problems, whether to keep or discard 'mental disorder'. Beneath the terminological problem there are of course the more interesting problems attaching to the concept. The 'problem of validity' of diagnosis of disorder – in effect the problem whether it is right to call the conditions in question disorders – already existed before the aspiration to achieve reliability and the subsequent tension between reliability and validity arose. The 1960s critiques of psychiatry mainly from sociological though also from psychological perspectives already identified problems for 'mental illness', and most of them transfer to the replacement term 'mental disorder'. Specifically: is there meaning in it – order after all? And are the norms social rather than medical?

The project of making the diagnostic criteria in the manuals more reliable, couched in descriptive terms, complicates the problems but does not cause them. To the extent that the diagnostic criteria are just descriptive, with no references to the phenomena being abnormal, then by all means the difference between normal and abnormal function is lost, and what we are left with is the fact that the conditions called mental disorders are associated with much trouble. Yet of course the diagnostic criteria are not like this; they are – some of them at least – characterized by reference to breakdown of meaningful connections, and lowered functioning compared with the normal. The explicit definitions too, especially the fuller one in the DSM, reinforce the idea that mental disorders are not just expectable responses. The problem of validity in the demarcation of mental disorder from normal functioning exists anyway, and it is the one addressed by the explicit definitions given in the manuals.

In the DSM definition, the expression 'unexpectable' is probably intended to do a lot of work, sorting out mental disorder from mental order – a major and problematic task indeed – which probably explains its admirable brevity. Both possible senses of 'unexpectable' – statistical deviance and absence of meaningful connections – are difficult to define: neither can bear much weight. The problems involved will be the subject of much of the essay, but they can be signalled briefly as follows.

While deviance in this statistical sense may be a typical marker of psychological dysfunction, it is questionable whether it captures what is meant by dysfunction. An obvious point is that some rare conditions do not involve any kind of dysfunction, such as high intelligence, or low aggression. There is also the problem that some of the conditions described in the manuals are not that uncommon; for example some estimates of lifetime population prevalence of major depressive disorder are as high as 25 per cent and possibly rising. In brief, statistical deviance seems to be neither sufficient nor necessary for a condition to count as a mental disorder. A further complication of the simple idea that mental disorder can be understood in terms of statistical abnormality is the current state of the science. As will be considered in more detail later (especially in section 2.2), in the behavioural sciences statistical normality and deviance are closely tied to the concept of a normal distribution – roughly bell-shaped – in the population. Most psychological traits are distributed in this way, and psychiatric conditions may represent the extreme or not so extreme ends of psychological traits. The critical point is that for traits that are normally distributed in the population, it is normal – natural, inevitable – for there to be extremes of the traits. This reinforces the point that statistical abnormality in the population does not in itself make a psychological condition dysfunctional, or – so far – anything to do with disorder. For these kinds of reasons, among others, it is not a happy interpretation of unexpectable (and hence disorder) that it just means: difference from what people usually are like.

Consider now the interpretation that unexpectable means: absence of meaningful connections among experience, mental states and behaviour. This raises a major issue lying dormant in the psychiatric manuals, as to whether mental disorder is supposed to exclude meaningfulness in this broad sense. This is a major problem with long historical roots, linked to the charge against a strong version of the medical model that in equating psychiatric problems with illness, and illness in turn with disease or lesion, it reduced the problems to mere deficit of mental functioning, mere absence of meaning or reason. So to what extant is the DSM definition of mental disorder, or its characterization of symptoms and syndromes, committed to this? Arguably the term unexpectable has the significance that to count as a mental disorder, a condition has not to be meaningful. Consider for example previously discussed of the criteria for major depressive episode. These exclude one kind of normal/meaningful case, namely bereavement, but this invites the question: why exclude just bereavement? Might depression also be a normal/meaningful response to other major losses, such as of limbs, or career? In general, what we are to say in cases of a depressive episode that seems proportionate to – with an appropriate meaningful connection to – the loss? Are we to say that in such cases that the depression is a disorder or not? The same issue arises in many other kinds of condition. Are phobic reactions after adverse conditioning events, or posttraumatic stress after trauma, excessive, or unreasonable, or disproportionate? And how does this issue affect the question whether they are mental disorders or not? Or take a more speculative possibility, that in some cases psychotic delusions may function to reduce unmanageable uncertainty in a chaotic sensory experience. If this were so, would we want to say that the delusions constituted mental disorder? After all, they are functional – we are supposing for the sake of argument – in relation to preserving order. The tension here arises because although depression, phobias, and delusions may be associated with all kinds of troubles, all kinds of harm, if they signify that the mind is responding appropriately/understandably to circumstances, or functioning in a strategic way towards a comprehensible goal, then so far they signify mental order, not absence of order – not mental disorder. In brief, if mental disorder is taken to exclude meaning, then there will be much reason to be dissatisfied with the inclusion of many of the conditions in the manuals. Alternatively, if mental disorder is primarily characterized by distress and disability, and the exclusion of meaning is not the main point, so that mental disorder may have meaning, then the very concept threatens to unravel.

This is a line of thought familiar in psychological critiques of the practice of diagnosing disorders and will be reconsidered in that context in Chapter 2 (in section 2.2). The contrast is with the medical model, in one of its old interpretations. Insofar as the medical model supposes that mental disorders are medical disorders caused by a disease or lesion, the implication will be that they do not make much sense, as for example an epileptic fit expresses no meaning. On the other hand, it is well-recognized now that psychological factors involving meaning and strategy play a prominent role in the production or maintenance of many symptoms or conditions. This is obvious now, so there is likely to be a tension in the psychiatric manuals, between having mental disorders as meaningless, consistent with this apparent implication of the word, and with the medical model, while recognizing or at least allowing for meaning in the conditions in mental disorder.

It is a moot point to what extent the current psychiatric manuals, the DSM-IV and the ICD-10, use or presuppose something like a strong medical model which would exclude significant roles for psychological factors. It may be that the explicit definitions of mental disorder, specifically the exclusion of expectable conditions, suggest the strong medical model, while the actual diagnostic criteria are ambiguous on this point. A recent debate in the literature between Follette and Houts on the one side, and Wakefield on the other (referenced at the end of this chapter), addresses the question whether the DSM-IV does or does not presuppose the medical model as opposed to a psychological model of the conditions of interest, and seems to come to similar conclusions: that the diagnostic criteria themselves apparently do not presuppose the medical model, but the surrounding texts, within and outside the manuals, in the context of the grounding of mental health services in psychiatry and that in medicine, do seem to show more commitment to the medical model.

It is not my intention or wish to attempt hermeneutic analyses of the manuals or the surrounding texts, and the main point for the present purpose is that there is an ambiguity in the manuals between understanding mental disorder in a way that excludes meaning, consistent with their roots in medical psychiatry, and acknowledging that meaning may well be involved, compatible with psychological models of the conditions. Connected with this point, there is no explicit statement in the psychiatric manuals that the conditions in them invariably result from lesions or disease processes. This may be believed by some, but generally speaking the science has left this general idea behind, as will be considered in the next chapter.

Four options for a theory of disorder previous are listed on the left side of Figure 1.1 (in the previous section), and so far we have considered the first three of them: absence of meaningful connections, statistical deviance, and lesions/diseases. All of them are problematic or wrong or both. The first two are alluded to in the explicit DSM definition of disorder, though with wise brevity, using the term expectable. The third, understanding mental disorder in terms of lesions and diseases, may remain as an affirmation of the medical model in psychiatry and the banner of some among many kinds of research programme, but it is generally hard to formulate and justify in the light of the current science. This leaves the fourth on the list: that the mind is disordered when it is not functioning as it has been naturally designed to do in the evolutionary process. This, as mentioned, is the option pursued by Wakefield and it is the most influential current theory of disorder. This is partly because of its strengths, but also partly because it is probably the only player left on the pitch. It will be considered in detail in Chapter 3 and the conclusion will be that it raises a number of problems. One is that it magnifies the tension between reliability and validity in the diagnostic manuals. Attractive though it may be to conceive physical or mental disorder in terms of evolutionary design, in terms of mechanisms not functioning in the way designed/selected for, such a concept is hard to pin down and to confirm in particular kinds of case, especially for mental functioning, the outcome being that mental disorder attribution becomes a somewhat speculative and uncertain hypothesis. This is a very poor fit with the requirement for the reliability of diagnosis in clinical and research settings. Therefore if Wakefield's proposal for a theory of disorder is taken to be correct, reliability of disorder attribution collapses, and we are faced with the prospect outlined earlier, needing another name for the conditions of interest until the evolutionary psychological theoretical dust has settled, and we are confident what types or subtypes or particular presentations are disorders in these terms and which are not. Or else we give up on the proposed analysis, because of this problem in combination with others, such as the questionable dichotomy between natural evolved functions as opposed to functions deriving from socialization processes and social norms.

This takes us on to the final point for this section, that over and above the already major problem of reliability and validity of diagnosis of mental disorder there is the radical possibility that there is no coherent, stable theory of mental disorder that would distinguish between when the mind is working properly, in order, and when it is failing to function properly, in disorder. This conclusion would amount to a kind of deconstruction of the concept, removing by critical evaluation the idea that it is fixed in some absolute matter of fact, in the nature of things. The consequence is both radical and puzzling, hard to follow through – or at least so I have found. Broadly speaking, the implications are along the lines that what is left is the reality of harmful, distressing and impairing conditions of mental life, with no clear theory that would enable us to demarcate what among this is mental disorder and what is normal, or at least not disorder, with indeed no clear meaning attaching to that distinction, with a range of different kinds of explanation (of the sort listed on the right side of Figure 1.1 in the previous section): hidden meanings, possible lesions and diseases, meaningful responses to adversities, cultural and subcultural variation, individual variation. Amidst the deconstruction of the idea of a general theory of mental disorder would be diversity rather than unity, problems of nomenclature, and questions as to what are appropriate responses to particular problems, whether medical, psychological, self-help/empowerment, questions that involve social organization and values. These complex issues exist for us anyway, but they become more open to view, unsettled in principle, if we were to give up the idea that there is a valid general theory of mental disorder, of one or other of the kinds listed on the left hand side of Figure 1.1: in terms of lack of meaningful connections, lesions/diseases, statistical deviance, and dysfunction of evolutionarily designed mental mechanisms.

All the problems of the validity of the concept of mental disorder sketched in this and the previous section and to be taken up through this essay, have not much to do, however, with the immediate aims of the psychiatric manuals. They have to be distinguished from the other problems that the psychiatric manuals have been designed specifically to solve, which are more to do with describing and classifying the conditions of interest in a clear and reliable way.

1.6 Functions, strengths, and limitations of the manuals

The various problems of psychiatric classification have a particular relevance at the current time because preparations are being made for the next editions of the DSM and the ICD, DSM-V and ICD-11, with much thought and an accelerating number of papers and books on how the manuals can and should be improved – some references are given at the end of the chapter. The kinds of question addressed in the original construction of the manuals and in their ongoing reconstruction are as follows:

1. Diagnosis should be reliable, with adequate agreement between clinicians, or between raters in research studies, as to what the conditions of interest are and when they are present or absent.

2. Classification should be valid, both classification of symptoms into syndromes, and syndromes into higher-level categories along with other syndromes. Examples of symptom-level questions are whether 'survivor guilt' should be included as a possible criterion for diagnosis of post-traumatic stress disorder, or whether being 'ego-dystonic' is necessary in obsessive compulsive disorder (OCD) (whether it is necessary that the person has recognized that the obsessions or compulsions they have are excessive or unreasonable). Syndrome level questions are more common, examples including whether bipolar disorder should be classified under psychoses along with schizophrenia, as opposed to being classified as an affective disorder alongside major depressive disorder, or whether OCD should be classified with the anxiety disorders or should be in a class of its own, or in a class with other, possibly OCD-related disorders.

3. The manuals should capture all and only mental disorders, excluding current false positives (non-disorders currently in the manuals), and bringing in current false negatives (disorders not yet included). This can be expressed as the aim of making the manuals more valid as manuals of mental disorders.

This last challenge of validity is the one considered in the previous section, where the tension between validity in this sense and reliability was highlighted and considered. This sense of validity in relation to the concept of mental disorder has to be distinguished from the problem of validity of classification of symptoms into syndromes and syndromes into higher-level classes of syndromes, as in point 2 above.

Broadly speaking, the issues that most preoccupy the psychiatric literature are those in 1 and 2, while the issues in 3 have mostly been assigned to the surrounding literature on the concept of mental disorder. The different issues are attended to in different literatures because they involve quite different rationales, problems and methodologies. In brief, with more detail to follow, 1 and 2 are ongoing problems for clinical science, while 3 broadens out beyond clinical science to include conceptual, social and ethical issues.

The issue of reliability – 1 above – is mainly a technical problem to be resolved by clinicians involved in the classification system and research. Its rationale is that without reliability we will not know what we are talking about, let alone whether what we are saying is true. In quantitative statistical terms, validity cannot exceed reliability. The challenge of making psychiatric diagnoses more reliable was explicitly taken up early on in the development of the psychiatric manuals, as reviewed earlier in the chapter. For research purposes, where much attention has to be paid to achieving and maintaining reliability (or else generalizability is lost straight away), structured and semi-structured diagnostic interviews have been developed with reasonable to good reliability for many common conditions, and to the extent that particular diagnostic categories have poor reliability, even under research conditions, there is a healthy scepticism about their utility.

The issue of validity of classification of symptoms and of syndromes – 2 above – is a further and complex topic. One major issue concerns the role of aetiology in classification. It was noted earlier in section 1.2 that the general medical model of linking symptoms into syndromes is in some cases underpinned by discovery of a single cause, such as a disease process or lesion. In psychiatry, however, causes have been difficult to pin down, with wide variation in candidate theories, so attention has focused on the prior task of reliable description and classification at the symptom and syndrome levels. However the aim remains to have a proper classification system based on aetiology. For example, to the extent that depression and anxiety share a common genetic influence, there is reason to classify them together. To the extent that different conditions share important neurological bases, again there is reason to classify them together. Critical in this enterprise would be determination of biological markers that would validate classification into a syndrome or subtype of syndrome by a laboratory test. Generally speaking these kinds of methodologies aiming to classify by aetiological principles tend to broaden or narrow the phenotypes, leading perhaps to (return to) a broad 'neurosis' phenotype, for example, or division of OCD into several subtypes.

The aspiration for psychiatry that its classification should be based on aetiology seems to me to be much complicated, however, by what is now known of the complex, multifactorial nature of the aetiology of psychiatric conditions. As noted in section 1.2 it is now recognized that influences typically involve, in some degree, many or all of such broad factors as genetics, developmental neurobiology, early experience, social context, the person's attitude, current life events and difficulties, and so on. All these various types of cause will pull an aetiologically based classification in various ways, choice between which would be probably based on a doubtful notion that some kinds of cause are more 'fundamental' than others, or else on the interests of particular research groups. A further point is that while aetiology based classification may be appropriate for the scientific community – theories and suggestions belonging for example in the scientific journals – the clinicians have other interests in the syndromes, such as course over time, specifically the change from one presentation to another, or response to specific treatments. Classification that is clinically useful may or may not coincide – given the complex nature of psychiatric conditions – with classification by aetiology, especially if this latter could be done in various ways.

Classification by aetiology can be subsumed under the more general principle that we expect predictive power from a classification system. Classification of A with B should enable predictions that A and B behave in some relevant similar ways. Here is Spitzer in a recent paper on principles of reliability and validity in the development of the DSM-III:

> A diagnostic concept is assumed to have validity to the extent that the defining features of the disorder provide useful information not contained in the definition of the disorder. This information may be about aetiology, risk factors, usual course of the illness, whether it is more common among family members, and most important, whether it helps in decisions about management and treatment.
>
> Spitzer (2001, p. 353)

In a simpler world, for conditions with a single main cause, the various associations of interest would all hang together, but with complexity of causal factors and pathways, they become diffuse, the end result being that there are various ways in which classification can be done – there is no single right classification. With this variety comes the need for a choice as to which kind of factors to base classification on, and which one is chosen depends partly on the purpose for which it is intended.

In summary, then, the rationale and challenges of the problems of reliability and validity of the psychiatric classification manuals – points 1 and

2 above – have to do with the clinic and clinical science. The contrast is with the problem of validity of manuals as manuals of mental disorders – point 3 – which involves not only the science but also conceptual and social issues of the kind reviewed in the previous section.

An instructive somewhat provocative way of making the same point is to say that the projects of making psychiatric classification reliable and valid (in the sense of having predictive utility) run practically free of whether the classified conditions are mental disorders or not. The conditions of interest as characterized in the manuals may be disorders in that they, for example, lack sense, are caused by lesions, are statistically deviant, or involve failure of a mental mechanism to function as designed in evolution. That is to say, they may be disorders in the sense of one or more of the theories of disorder sketched in the previous section and listed on the left side of Figure 1.1 (in section 1.4). Or, some or all may not be disorders in any of those senses, being attributable rather to processes listed on the right side of Figure 1.1, such as meaningful processes not apparent at first sight, reactions that are or would be typical for human beings in the same circumstances, or unfortunate fit between temperament and task-demands. None of this makes any or much difference to the way the psychiatric manuals are constructed, or to the way particular conditions are diagnosed.

This can also be made as a terminological point. The descriptive reliability project and the symptom/syndrome classification project are not dependent up any particular characterization of the conditions being described and classified. Those problems would stay the same if the conditions were characterized not as mental disorders but in other ways, for instance as psychiatric conditions, mental health problems, maladaptive behaviours, mental distress, treatable conditions, antisocial behaviour, plain social deviance, etc. The characterization of the conditions of interest as mental disorders is an additional step, a further claim or commitment, and of course a much criticized one at that.

It is, I suggest, those functions of the diagnostic manuals that are more or less independent of the term, concept and theory of mental disorder which are their main strengths and which underpin their success and increasing use. The strengths are as descriptions and classification of the conditions of interest, using terms and methodology that are transparent, open to view – unlike, it should be said, the psychiatric diagnostic practices that were current before the development of the manuals. The manuals enable us all to know what is being talked about. The main limitations are the ongoing problems of utility described above which can continue to be worked on, and, most important in the present context, the problematic notion of mental disorder.

Notwithstanding substantial and persistent criticisms of the medical model and its notions of mental illness and mental disorder the diagnostic categories of the DSM and the ICD have increasingly become the language of communication between various relevant stakeholders in clinical practice, including not only clinicians themselves, but also managers, service users, and the courts. The diagnostic categories have also become the basis of most clinical research, including basic science on causation and treatment outcome research. So, while one purpose of the psychiatric manuals is diagnosis of disorder, they have been increasingly designed to be mainly classification systems that are a prerequisite for communication generally and research specifically. The manuals describe and classify with reasonable precision the many and various 'conditions of interest', and this is the reason that they are increasingly used. However, these uses of the diagnostic manuals so far do not require that the conditions classified are disorders. This characterization is an additional description, and it is this that is problematic from many points of view, not only from some sociopolitical perspectives, but also, as will be seen in the second chapter, from within the sciences basic to psychiatry.

The point that current diagnostic systems have a crucial role in the description and classification of the conditions of interest which is distinguishable from their characterization of these conditions as disorders is a simple one, and important at the present time, but one that has generally not been entertained and explored in the literature. Many criticisms of the DSM and ICD from broadly anti-psychiatry points of view, for example by social scientists and psychologists, make much of the fact that their classification systems are inadequately supported or are always changing, but these kinds of criticism do not really count against the need for the classification project, which is necessary for communication and research, and which generally in the sciences and elsewhere is bound to involve provisionality, ongoing modification, and always some degree of arbitrariness. The intended target from anti-psychiatry perspectives is more likely to be the practice of diagnosing disorder, regarded as pathologizing and disqualifying, but the descriptive and classificatory projects run practically free of this issue. It simply does not matter. This is presumably one reason why the diagnostic manuals at first managed with no definition of mental disorder at all, and now acquiesce in what are recognized to be problematic terminology and definitions.

1.7 **Summary and outstanding questions**

As outlined in the Introduction, the two main questions to be addressed in this essay are first, are the norms of psychological function medical, or really social? and second, what is the validity of the distinction between mental disorder and normality, and in particular is there meaning, after all, in mental disorder? This first chapter takes a preliminary look at how these issues play out in the psychiatric diagnostic manuals, the ICD and the DSM.

The first section of this chapter briefly introduces the psychiatric diagnostic manuals to the reader unfamiliar with them, and illustrations of DSM-IV diagnostic criteria for several disorders are quoted in an Appendix to the chapter.

The second section of this chapter distinguishes three projects in the psychiatric diagnostic manuals: description of mental states and behaviours, regarded as symptoms, classification of symptoms into syndromes, and the diagnosis of a mental disorder. To increase the reliability of diagnosis, agreement between clinicians and researchers on what a particular condition is, and what counts as it being present or absent, the description of symptoms has been made as observational as possible. This methodology was recommended in the 1950s by the philosopher of science Carl Hempel, who worked in the empiricist tradition. It is remarked that while the description of symptoms may be made increasingly observational, they often still contain reference to abnormal psychological and behavioural functioning. Regarding diagnosis, it was noted that in general medicine diagnosis often specifies a cause of the symptoms or syndrome, but this has generally been dropped as a requirement for diagnosis of the mental disorders, partly because usually the cause is unknown, and partly because what is increasingly known is that causes of psychiatric conditions are likely to be complex: diverse and multifactorial. Apart from presence of a symptom syndrome, diagnosis of mental disorder is often taken to require significant distress or impairment. The diagnostic manuals also give explicit definitions of mental disorder, according to which its primary feature is association with distress, disability, or risk of adverse outcomes. It is further stated in the definitions that to count as a mental disorder a harmful condition has to involve a personal dysfunction, not to be just a matter of deviation from social norms. Further, in the lengthier DSM definition, it is stated that to count as a mental disorder a harmful condition must not be merely an expectable and culturally sanctioned response to a particular event, such as a major loss. In these ways mental disorder is distinguished from social deviance, on the one hand, and from normal reactions to life's adversities, on the other.

A major outstanding issue is the topic of section 1.3. While the description of symptoms may be made increasingly observational, they often still contain reference to abnormal psychological and behavioural functioning. Given that the phenomena being described are meant to be symptoms of disorders, this limitation to the aim of using purely descriptive, observational language is not surprising. Reference to abnormal functioning is of two main types: rupture of meaningful connections, and deviance from the level of functioning of some reference group. Both of these are problematic in various ways. Another kind of problem arises in those diagnostic criteria where there is no or no explicit reference to abnormal functioning; in these cases it may be that normal functioning is being included, e.g. normal reactions to life's adversities. In the lack of explicit attention to the norms being invoked in diagnosis, there remains the problem whether they might after all be social. Some of the diagnostic criteria sets do seem to invoke social norms – even if they are also medical norms. An important sign of the role of social factors is in the technical expression 'clinically significant' as applied to the conditions of interest, which turns out to refer to the fact that these are the kinds of conditions people have brought to the clinic, and thought by patient and physician to be in need of treatment. It is noted, finally, that the application of social norms and values within a group in which they are shared will typically exhibit agreement and reliability, thus mimicking simple observation of facts.

The fourth section considers another, related problem, the tension between reliability and validity of diagnosis. To the extent that diagnostic criteria are theory-free, can they really capture the difference between disorder and normality? Taking for granted that there is a difference, it seems plausible to suppose that diagnosis specifically of a disorder may have to involve theoretical assumptions. Some possible theories as to what mental disorder is are roughly characterized in this section, pending detailed consideration through the essay. They run in terms of deficit of meaning, lesions, subnormal functioning, and not functioning as designed in evolution. None of these are easy to detect by clinical observation, and non-disorder variants may be incorrectly diagnosed. In this way the project of achieving reliability of diagnosis of disorder seems to have been at the expense of validity. This tension is not easily resolved; options involve either temporary or permanent abandonment of the concept mental disorder for characterizing conditions currently in the psychiatric manuals.

In any case, moving on to the fifth section, problems with validity of the diagnosis of mental disorder were already identified in the 1960s critiques of psychiatry; they predate the drive for reliability, which only serves to exacerbate the problems, or to make them more transparent. Over and above the already major problem of reliability and validity of diagnosis of mental disorder there is the radical possibility that there may be no fully coherent, stable theory of mental disorder that would distinguish between when the mind is working properly, in order, and when it is failing to function properly, in disorder.

In the sixth section of the chapter the strengths of the psychiatric manuals are disentangled from their problems. The strengths have to do with construction of a clear language for communication about the conditions of interest and specifically for research into causes and treatments. Room for improvement there no doubt is, but no one has yet come up with a better kind of classification system for these purposes. However, clear description and classification of the conditions of interest is a project separable from the diagnosis of these conditions as mental disorders, this being the real target of the critiques of psychiatry – because social norms are being medicalized, because meaningful mental life in adverse circumstances is being pathologized. Distinguishing the various projects, purposes and problems of the psychiatric manuals in this way opens up the prospect of being able to have the advantages of the manuals without the disadvantages.

1.8 **Annotated bibliography**

The main topics of this chapter, introduced in the first section, are the psychiatric manuals, DSM and the ICD, and their current editions, the DSM-IV (American Psychiatric Association 1994), and the ICD-10 (World Health Organization 1992). Readers who wish to learn more of their general assumptions and methodology and their detailed criteria for specific conditions are referred to them. There are substantial primary and secondary literatures on the origins and development of the diagnostic manuals, the working out of their fundamental and working assumptions, and methodological problems, for each of them separately and in relation to one another. Norman Sartorius has been instrumental in the evolution of the ICD, an early paper being his (1976), and a more recent one with colleagues (1995). Robert Spitzer has been instrumental in the evolution of the DSM, papers including Spitzer and Endicott (1978) and Spitzer and Williams (1982, 1988). A significant influence in the move to make the diagnostic manuals more reliable by operationalizing definitions in descriptive, observational terms was work by the philosopher of science Carl Hempel, in the logical empiricist school (Hempel 1965; Stengel 1959; Zubin 1961). An excellent recent major work on diagnosis that includes review of many points in the development of the current manuals, and which highlights the role of values, is by John Sadler in the current series (Sadler 2004a).

The clinical and scientific interest in the manuals has to do with the reliability and utility of the classification system – topics addressed from various points of view in sections 1.2 to 1.6. Progressive editions have sought to improve reliability and utility in various ways. New editions of the manuals, the DSM-V and the ICD-11, are in preparatory stages, and recent books and papers examine the underlying challenges and possible improvements, for example Maj, Gaebel, Lopez-Ibor and Sartorius (2002); Helzer and Hudziak (2002); Phillips, First and Pincus (2003); Kupfer, First and

Regier (2002), Widiger and Clark (2000). The task of classifying by aetiology is recommended from a point of view in the philosophy of science by Dominic Murphy (2006). Much recent literature on the definition of mental disorder including the tension between reliability and validity of disorder attribution has focused on the work of Jerome Wakefield. Wakefield's approach to the concept of disorder is mentioned only briefly in this chapter and will be considered in more detail in Chapter 3, where references are given.

Section 1.5 refers to sociological and psychological critiques of psychiatric diagnosis. These will be considered in Chapter 2 (especially in 2.2 and 2.6) and references will be given there. There is also reference to a debate in the literature as to whether the DSM does or does not presuppose a medical model, between Follette and Houts on the one side, and Wakefield on the other. Key papers on this topic include Follette and Houts (1996) and Wakefield (1999b). The status of the medical model in the DSM was set within the broader context of a wider debate about whether the manual is or should aim to be theory-neutral, the proposal taken from Hempel's philosophy of science. The debate began in a special section in the *Journal of Consulting and Clinical Psychology* 1996, edited by W. Follette, on the development of alternatives to the DSM system, specifically from a behavioural perspective. Key papers included Follette (1996) and Follette and Houts (1996), and these prompted a response from Wakefield (1998) and further debate (Houts and Follette 1998; Wakefield 1999a, b; Houts 2001a, b; Wakefield 2003). In exploring the question of the theory neutrality of the diagnostic manuals Wakefield becomes explicitly committed to the claim that diagnosis of disorder itself involves a hypothesis – this problematic consequence of Wakefield's approach is anticipated in section 1.4 and taken up in Chapter 3 (section 3.5).

1.9 Appendix: some illustrations of DSM-IV diagnostic criteria

The following diagnostic criteria sets are in the DSM-IV (American Psychiatric Association 1994) and all page references are to this volume.

1. Major depressive episode (p. 327) (NB major depressive episode is not itself a diagnosis, but is the basis for various diagnoses including most straightforwardly major depressive disorder.)

2. Post-traumatic stress disorder (pp. 427–9)

3. Schizophrenia (pp. 285–6), prefaced by a preamble (pp. 247–5)

4. Autistic disorder (pp. 71–71)

5. Attention-deficit/hyperactivity disorder (pp. 83–5)

6. Antisocial personality disorder (pp. 649–50).

DSM-IV criteria for major depressive episode (p. 327)

A. Five (or more) of the following symptoms have been present during the same 2-week period and represent a change from previous functioning; at least one of the symptoms is either (1) depressed mood or (2) loss of interest or pleasure.

Note: Do not include symptoms that are clearly due to a general medical condition, or mood-incongruent delusions or hallucinations.

1. Depressed mood most of the day, nearly every day, as indicated by either subjective report (e. g., feels sad or empty) or observation made by others (e.g., appears tearful). **Note:** In children and adolescents, can be irritable mood.

2. Markedly diminished interest or pleasure in all, or almost all, activities most of the day, nearly every day (as indicated by either subjective account or observation made by others).

3. Significant weight loss when not dieting or weight gain (e.g., a change of more than 5 per cent of body weight in a month), or decrease or increase in appetite nearly every day. **Note:** In children, consider failure to make expected weight gains.

4. Insomnia or hypersomnia nearly every day.

5. Psychomotor agitation or retardation nearly every day (observable by others, not merely subjective feelings of restlessness or being slowed down).

6. Fatigue or loss of energy nearly every day.

7. Feelings of worthlessness or excessive or inappropriate guilt (which may be delusional) nearly every day (not merely self-reproach or guilt about being sick).

8. Diminished ability to think or concentrate, or indecisiveness, nearly every day (either by subjective account or as observed by others).

9. Recurrent thoughts of death (not just fear of dying), recurrent suicidal ideation without a specific plan, or a suicide attempt or a specific plan for committing suicide.

B. The symptoms do not meet criteria for a mixed episode (see p. 335).

C. The symptoms cause clinically significant distress or impairment in social, occupational, or other important areas of functioning.

D. The symptoms are not due to the direct physiological effects of a substance (e.g. a drug of abuse, a medication) or a general medical condition (e.g. hypothyroidism).

E. The symptoms are not better accounted for by bereavement, i.e., after the loss of a loved one, the symptoms persist for longer than 2 months or are characterized by marked functional impairment, morbid preoccupation with worthlessness, suicidal ideation, psychotic symptoms, or psychomotor retardation.

DSM-IV diagnostic criteria for post-traumatic stress disorder

A. The person has been exposed to a traumatic event in which both of the following were present:

1. The person experienced, witnessed, or was confronted with an event or events that involved actual or threatened death or serious injury, or a threat to the physical integrity of self or others

2. the person's response involved intense fear, helplessness, or horror.

Note: In children this may be expressed instead by disorganized or agitated behaviour.

B. The traumatic event is persistently re-experienced in one (or more) of the following ways:

1. Recurrent and intrusive distressing recollections of the event including images, thoughts, or perceptions. Note: In young children, repetitive play may occur in which themes or aspects of the trauma are expressed.

2. Recurrent distressing dreams of the event. Note: in children there may be frightening dreams without recognizable content.

3. Acting or feeling as if the traumatic event were recurring (includes a sense of reliving the experience, illusions, hallucinations, and dissociative flashback episodes, including those that occur on wakening or when intoxicated). Note: In young children trauma-specific re-enactment may occur.

DSM-IV diagnostic criteria for post-traumatic stress disorder *(continued)*

    4. Intense psychological distress at exposure to internal or external cues that symbolize or resemble an aspect of the traumatic event.

    5. Physiological reactivity upon exposure to internal or external cues that symbolize or resemble an aspect of the traumatic event.

C. Persistent avoidance of stimuli associated with the trauma and numbing of general responsiveness (not present before the trauma), as indicated by three (or more) of the following:

    1. Efforts to avoid thoughts, feelings, or conversations associated with the trauma

    2. Efforts to avoid activities, places, or people that arouse recollections of the trauma

    3. Inability to recall an important aspect of the trauma

    4. Markedly diminished interest or participation in significant activities

    5. Feeling of detachment or estrangement from others

    6. Restricted range of affect (e.g., unable to have loving feelings)

    7. Sense of a foreshortened future (e.g., does not expect to have a career, marriage, or children, or a normal lifespan).

D. Persistent symptoms of increased arousal (not present before the trauma), as indicated by two (or more) of the following:

    1. Difficulty falling or staying asleep

    2. Irritability or outbursts of anger

    3. Difficulty concentrating

    4. Hypervigilance.

DSM-IV Schizophrenia: part of preamble and diagnostic criteria

Part of preamble, pp. 274–5.

Characteristic symptoms may be conceptualized as falling into two broad categories – positive and negative. The positive symptoms appear to reflect an excess or distortion of normal functions, whereas the negative symptoms appear to reflect a diminution or loss of normal functions. The positive

symptoms (Criteria AI–A4) include distortions or exaggerations of inferential thinking (delusions), perception (hallucinations), language and
communication (disorganized speech) and behavioral monitoring (grossly
disorganized or catatonic behaviour).

Diagnostic criteria, pp. 285–6

A. *Characteristic symptoms:* Two (or more) of the following, each present
for a significant portion of time during a 1-month period (or less if
successfully treated):

1. delusions

2. hallucinations

3. disorganized speech (e.g., frequent derailment or incoherence)

4. grossly disorganized or catatonic behaviour

5. negative symptoms, i.e., affective flattening, logia, or avolition.

Note: Only one Criterion A symptom is required if delusions are bizarre or
hallucinations consist of a voice keeping up a running commentary on the
person's behaviour or thoughts, or two or more voices conversing with each
other.

B. *Social/occupational dysfunction:* For a significant portion of the time
since the onset of the disturbance, one or more major areas of functioning such as work, interpersonal relations, or self-care are markedly
below the level achieved prior to the onset (or when the onset is in
childhood or adolescence, failure to achieve expected level of interpersonal, academic, or occupational achievement).

C. *Duration:* Continuous signs of the disturbance persist for at least
6 months. This 6-month period must include at least 1 month of symptoms (or less if successfully treated) that meet Criterion A (i.e.,
active-phase symptoms) and may include periods of prodromal or
residual symptoms. During these prodromal or residual periods, the
signs of the disturbance may be manifested by only negative symptoms
or two or more symptoms listed in Criterion A present in an attenuated
form (e.g., odd beliefs, unusual perceptual experiences).

D. *Schizoaffective and mood disorder exclusion:* Schizoaffective disorder and
mood disorder with psychotic features have been ruled out because
either (1) no major depressive, manic or mixed episodes have occurred
concurrently with the active-phase symptoms;. or (2) if mood episodes
have occurred during active-phase symptoms, their total duration has
been brief relative to the duration of the active and residual periods.

DSM-IV Schizophrenia: part of preamble and diagnostic criteria *(continued)*

E. *Substance/general medical condition exclusion:* The disturbance is not due to the direct physiological effects of a substance (e.g., a drug of abuse, a medication) or a general medical condition.

F. *Relationship to a pervasive developmental disorder:* If there is a history of autistic disorder or another pervasive developmental disorder, the additional diagnosis of schizophrenia is made only if prominent delusions or hallucinations are also present for at least a month (or less if successfully treated).

DSM-IV diagnostic criteria for autistic disorder

A. A total of six (or more) items from 1, 2 and 3 with at least two from 1, and one each from 2 and 3:

1. Qualitative impairment in social interaction, as manifested by at least two of the following:

    (a) marked impairment in the use of multiple nonverbal behaviors such as eye-to-eye gaze, facial expression, body postures, and gestures to regulate social interaction

    (b) failure to develop peer relationships appropriate to developmental level

    (c) a lack of spontaneous seeking to share enjoyment, interests or achievements with other people (e.g., by a lack of showing, bringing, or pointing out objects of interest)

    (d) lack of social or emotional reciprocity.

2. Qualitative impairments in communication as manifested by at least one of the following:

    (a) delay in, or total lack of, the development of spoken language (not accompanied by an attempt to compensate through alternative modes of communication such as gesture or mime)

    (b) in individuals with adequate speech, marked impairment in the ability to initiate or sustain a conversation with others

    (c) stereotyped and repetitive use of language or idiosyncratic language

    (d) lack of varied, spontaneous make-believe play or social imitative play appropriate to developmental level.

3. Restricted repetitive and stereotyped patterns of behaviour, interests and activities, as manifested by at least one of the following:

   (a) encompassing preoccupation with one or more stereotyped and restricted patterns of interest that is abnormal either in intensity or focus

   (b) apparently inflexible adherence to specific, non-functional routines or rituals

   (c) stereotyped and repetitive motor mannerisms (e.g., hand or finger flapping or twisting, or complex whole-body movements)

   (d) persistent preoccupation with parts of objects.

B. Delays or abnormal functioning in at least one of the following areas, with onset prior to age 3 years:
   1. social interaction,
   2. language as used in social communication, or
   3. symbolic or imaginative play.

C. The disturbance is not better accounted for by Rett's disorder or Childhood Disintegrative Disorder.

DSM-IV diagnostic criteria for attention-deficit/ hyperactivity disorder

A. Either 1 or 2:

   1. Six (or more) of the following symptoms of inattention have persisted for at least 6 months to a degree that is maladaptive and inconsistent with developmental level:

      (a) Often fails to give close attention to details or makes careless mistakes in schoolwork, work, or other activities

      (b) Often has difficulty sustaining attention in tasks or play activities

      (c) Often does not seem to listen when spoken to directly

      (d) Often does not follow through on instructions and fails to finish schoolwork, chores, or duties in the workplace (not due to oppositional behavior or failure to understand instructions)

      (e) Often has difficulty organizing tasks and activities

      (f) Often avoids, dislikes, or is reluctant to engage in tasks that require sustained mental effort (such as schoolwork or homework)

DSM-IV diagnostic criteria for attention-deficit/hyperactivity disorder (*continued*)

    (g) Often loses things necessary for tasks or activities (e.g., toys, school assignments, pencils, books, or tools)

    (h) Is often easily distracted by extraneous stimuli

    (i) Is often forgetful in daily activities.

2. Six (or more) of the following symptoms of hyperactivity-impulsivity have persisted for at least 6 months to a degree that is maladaptive and inconsistent with developmental level:

Hyperactivity

    (a) Often fidgets with hands or feet or squirms in seat

    (b) Often leaves seat in classroom or in other situations in which remaining seated is expected

    (c) Often runs about or climbs excessively in situations in which it is inappropriate (in adolescents or adults, may be limited to subjective feelings of restlessness)

    (d) Often has difficulty playing or engaging in leisure activities quietly

    (e) Is often 'on the go' or often acts as if 'driven by a motor'

    (f) Often talks excessively

Impulsivity

    (a) Often blurts out answers before questions have been completed

    (b) Often has difficulty awaiting turn

    (c) Often interrupts or intrudes on others (e.g., butts into conversations or games).

B. Some hyperactive-impulsive or inattentive symptoms that caused impairment were present before age 7 years.

C. Some impairment from the symptoms is present in two or more settings (e.g., at school [or work] and at home.

D. There must be clear evidence of clinically significant impairment in social, academic, or occupational functioning.

E. The symptoms do not occur exclusively during the course of a Pervasive Developmental Disorder, Schizophrenia, or other Psychotic Disorder and are not better accounted for by another mental disorder (e.g., Mood disorder, Anxiety Disorder, Dissociative Disorder, or a Personality Disorder).

DSM-IV diagnostic criteria for antisocial personality disorder

A. There is a pervasive pattern of disregard for and violation of the rights of others occurring since age 15 years, as indicated by three (or more) of the following:

1. Failure to conform to social norms with respect to lawful behaviours as indicated by repeatedly performing acts that are grounds for arrest.

2. Deceitfulness, as indicated by repeated lying, use of aliases, or conning others for personal profit or pleasure.

3. Impulsivity or failure to plan ahead.

4. Irritability and aggressiveness, as indicated by repeated physical fights or assaults

5. Reckless disregard for safety of self or others.

6. Consistent irresponsibility, as indicated by repeated failure to sustain consistent work behaviour or honour financial obligations.

7. Lack of remorse, as indicated by being indifferent to or rationalizing having hurt, mistreated, or stolen from another.

B. The individual is at least age 18 years.

C. There is evidence of Conduct Disorder with onset before age 15 years.

D. The occurrence of antisocial behaviour is not exclusively during the course of Schizophrenia or a Manic Episode.

Reprinted with permission from the Diagnostic and Statistical Manual of Mental Disorders, Fourth Edition, Text Revision, (copyright 2000). American Psychiatric Association.

Chapter 2

The sciences on mental order/disorder and related concepts
Normality, meaning, natural and social norms

2.1 Introduction and overview of chapter

The purpose of this chapter is to review what the sciences have to say about the various issues relevant to mental disorder that have been identified in the Introduction and first chapter:

+ The distinction between medical, scientific, objective standards of mental functioning, and social standards – this is relevant to the question whether the norms involved in diagnosis of mental disorder are of the one kind or the other.

+ Whether mental disorders are caused by brain lesions and diseases – consistent with a strong interpretation of the medical model of mental disorder.

+ Whether there may be meaning in mental disorder (understandable responses, method), notwithstanding apparent absence – this is relevant because to the extent that there is, mental disorder involves order after all, and the concept destabilizes.

+ Is mental disorder a matter of functioning below the statistically normal level?

Because the chapter covers many complex areas, this opening section provides an overview to aid orientation. It gives a summary of main points by section (2.1 to 2.7), but all the points are considered in greater length and detail in the sections themselves.

The chapter starts (in 2.2) by considering the sciences basic to psychiatry – psychology, genetics, neuroscience, particularly neuroimaging, and medicine. Psychology tends to deflate the difference between order and disorder, looking for order – normality, function, strategy, meaning – even in disorder. According to this methodological tendency, 'disorder' turns out to be primarily mental states and behaviour that are relatively problematic and maladaptive – as opposed to being just random, chaotic outomes of lesions or disease processes. Psychiatric genetics points in the same general direction as psychology, deflating the difference between normality and abnormality, emphasizing adaptation including in adverse circumstances, and having the additional startling fact at the foundations that 'error' underpins the evolutionary process. The neuroimaging sciences provide many kinds of important data about structural and functional features of the brain, about lesions and diseases causing some mental disorders, and about the neural structures involved in both normal and abnormal mental processing. However, they do not and cannot define the difference between mental/behavioural normality and abnormality, order and disorder, which is drawn rather at the mental/behavioural level itself, by psychology for example, as above.

The medical model of mental disorder that has often been contrasted with the psychological approach would have symptoms as random, chaotic outcomes of lesions or disease processes. However, this medical model is too crude, and especially so compared with general medicine itself, which has elaborate theories of biological protection mechanisms, restoration, compensation, etc., analogous to the psychological approach to mental disorder. The underlying problem was an historical one, namely, that the understandable, protective, functional aspects of mental disorder had been split off from medical psychiatry, into psychoanalysis and its many offspring. The following two sections examine the historical problem and its resolution in a new paradigm, leading to more holistic understanding of the variety of factors implicated in mental disorder.

The historical problem is sketched at the start of section 2.3. When psychiatry emerged as scientific discipline at the turn of the nineteenth century the thought-space was defined by two great philosophical, cultural assumptions both of which converged on the view that mind and what was essential to it, meaning, had no place in the domain of science and scientific explanation. One of the background assumptions was several centuries old – mind/body dualism – and it affected mostly the early development of psychological science, defining behaviourism as the study of mind-free mechanical behaviour. The other background assumption was new at the time – the distinction between causality and meaning, or explanation and understanding: it was constructed by the new social sciences in the recognition that the methodology of the natural sciences did not apply well to their subject matter. This contemporary distinction impacted directly on the then new psychiatry, with tensions growing between hard-headed science searching for material causes, and soft-headed hermeneutics finding meanings. The outcome of these various developments and splits was that scientific psychology as behaviourism and scientific psychiatry eventually rounded on psychoanalysis, accusing it of being pseudo-science, while on the other hand the so-called anti-psychiatry critiques rounded on mainstream psychiatry for stripping the meaning out of madness, and pathologizing ordinary problems of living. Since the 1960s these splits have been resolved in the new biobehavioural science paradigm, the information processing, cognitive paradigm. In this new kind of general model, information carrying or meaningful states are involved in the regulation of behaviour, and (then inevitably) they are encoded in and processed by the brain. The appearance of what is fundamentally a semantic, information-regulated form of causation links biology to psychology, and psychology to social science, in a way not possible in the previous paradigms with splits and dichotomies as above. In relation to psychopathology, models can now be more holistic, and in particular mental causation can now join other kinds of causal factor in models of the aetiology and maintenance of psychiatric conditions.

In the following section, 2.4, it is noted that models of psychopathology in the paradigm are typically complex, multifactorial, and multilevel, able to comprise lesions and disease processes, but also genetics/design features, and psychological and cultural factors involving meaning. Conceptual points are illustrated using Daniel Dennett's work on three kinds of explanatory stances: the physical, the design, and the intentional. Explanation of systemic functional breakdown may seem to require dropping to the physical stance, and in its more or less real strongest form the medical model always wants to do just this. But there are also explanations of dysfunction from the design stance, in terms of genetic design or learning. Further and crucially, there are for systems beyond minimal complexity also explanations of loss of function from the intentional stance, implicating such as one function being sacrificed to preserve another of higher value. These kinds of explanation are typical in the psychological models underpinning psychological therapies. The point is partly that these three kinds of explanation exist, but the main point is that they can now coexist in the same space, and also – being within the same space – they can interact. Current models of psychopathology are accordingly complex and multifactorial, and specifically they include some role for mental causation. The old ideologies that assumed one kind of explanation a priori – lesion, genes, or meaning – are no longer viable.

Section 2.5 shifts the focus to the evolutionary theoretic framework. This offers some grip on the concepts of function and dysfunction, and most attempts to define mental disorder since the 1970s have invoked evolutionary theoretic considerations in one way or another, the best worked out and most influential version being Wakefield's. The concepts of function and dysfunction appear in the sciences for the first time in biology, then also in psychology, where they underpin diagnosis of mental disorder. The concepts in biology are tied into the notion of design: normal, correct functioning is functioning as designed – selected for – in evolution; dysfunction is otherwise. The evolutionary approach in psychology can envisage dysfunction arising from failure of an evolutionary designed mental mechanism, but the approach is much broader than this, creating space for other pathways to dysfunctional behaviour, including strategies that involve sacrifice of functions, design/environment mismatch, and maladaptive generalization of learnt behaviours. This turns out to have major consequences for Wakefield's analysis of disorder because it turns out to involve a theory, and one quite possibly not true of many conditions and presentations described in the psychiatric manuals – details and implications are deferred to the third chapter. Implications of the evolutionary psychological approach for psychiatry have been developed in the new subject of evolutionary psychiatry. It is recognized in this evolutionary theoretic approach, as in the psychological, that some psychiatric conditions may be extremes of normal variation, or otherwise not sharply separated from the normal, and some may have adaptive functions.

The following section, 2.6, continues on the theme of order and disorder in the sciences, beyond psychology into social science. This topic is important for the present purpose for completeness – the notion of order figures large in social science, not only in biology and psychology – but also of course because it is the perspective of social science that provides the main counterpoint to the medical model of mental disorder, having it as not medical disorder but rather social disorder, so-called social deviance. Some key themes in the sociological critiques of psychiatry are reviewed. Foucault's critique of the modern western idea of madness brings out that in the mechanized world of modern science, dominated by principles of reason, madness becomes defined as mere deficit, absence, and is thereby silenced, excluded from civilized society; psychiatry itself – according to this story – was constructed for the purpose of managing madness, out of mind and sight. Other critiques of mainstream psychiatry in the 1960s charged it with stripping the meaning from madness, from mental illness generally, disqualifying and dehumanizing those so labelled. The sociological critiques recognized that these processes were social, not originally psychiatric. These kinds of criticism remain, and they have often been counter-charged with failing to recognize the reality with which psychiatry deals, individual suffering and need for treatment.

A dominant theme in the 1960s debates was whether social norms were being disguised as medical facts, and much of the work on the concept of mental disorder since has continued in these terms. The assumption on both sides has been that there is a valid distinction between what is natural and what is social, and the closing sections of the chapter revisit this assumption in the light of the current science. The proposal in section 2.7 is that evolutionary psychology, combined with genetics, serves to break down the underlying contrast between what in the domain of the psychological is natural (evolved) and what is determined by social processes. This happens in two main ways. First, because some evolved functions are social – human evolution having been in social groups. Second, evolved factors may contribute a degree of specific content, but social factors elaborate this in diverse ways, with the evolved content typically identifiable at a more abstract level than the concrete social expression. The implication of this is that natural norms of psychological functioning are typically instantiated by social norms, in which case breaking one kind involves breaking the other. In current genetics the emphasis on gene–environment interactions brings out that psychological phenotypes – including some psychiatric conditions – are not simply evolved functions, nor are they produced by environmental conditions alone, including by social processes, but are rather the product of interaction between the two. Insofar as natural and social are not well distinguished in mental and behavioural functioning, the terms of the 1960s debates as to whether mental disorder is medical as opposed to socially defined break down, and so also the rationale for the naturalist approaches to defining mental disorder to be considered in detail in Chapter 3.

We turn now to consider these topics in detail.

2.2 Sciences 'basic to psychiatry': psychology, genetics, neuroscience, medicine

Psychiatry inherited from medicine its fundamental character as a clinical activity, concerned with the management and treatment of illness, based in the best current science. Medicine draws on the sciences of physiology, biology, genetics and mechanics, for example, and the sciences 'basic to psychiatry' include, as well as medical sciences, psychology and the neurosciences. This chapter begins by considering what these sciences basic to psychiatry have to say about the concepts relevant to mental or behavioural order and disorder.

Psychology is the science of mental and behavioural functioning. It comprises principles for understanding and explaining normal, everyday functioning, and applies these principles to the problems that are presented at the clinic, in clinical psychology. It is characteristic of psychology that it typically understands the 'abnormal' in terms of principles of normal functioning, and hence tends to be antagonistic to the assumption attached to medical psychiatry, that there is a radical difference between mental order and disorder. In brief, psychology tends to 'normalize' apparently abnormal mental conditions, as opposed to pathologizing them.

There are various ways in which psychology understands the abnormal in terms of the normal, including the following four. First, it may regard the abnormal as within the normal range of functioning, in a statistical sense, and in this sense as not abnormal. Second, it supposes that abnormal emotions may appear as more appropriate, more understandable, more like the normal case, when the person's experience of the situation is better understood and taken into account. Third, it emphasizes that much of what presents as symptoms of abnormal functioning are in fact strategies for solving problems, strategies that are reasonable within their own terms, and which signify order rather than disorder. Fourth, psychology typically emphasizes that patterns of behaviour are learnt, and that dysfunction may arise when behaviours that are reasonable in the context in which they were originally acquired are applied in different contexts, but again the psychological processes involved are not qualitatively different from those operating in the normal case. Let us consider these four points, which may all interact, in turn.

Mental and behavioural traits are typically distributed normally, in the statistical sense, in the general population, with the majority of the population falling within a broad average range, and smaller proportions falling at either extreme. The normal distribution, in the statistical sense, is shown in Figure 2.1 (copied from Wikipedia, 2006).

Figure 2.1 shows the percentage of the population falling within 1, 2 and 3 standard deviations above or below the population mean. About 68 per cent of the values are within 1 standard deviation away from the mean, about 95 per cent of the values are within two standard deviations and about 99.7 per cent lie within 3 standard deviations.

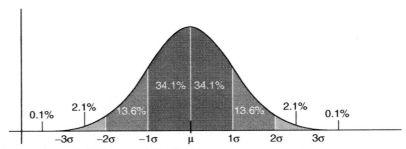

Fig. 2.1 The statistically normal distribution.

Many biopsychological traits are – at least approximately – of this kind, including such as height, speed, strength, IQ, memory capacity, attentional capacity, anxiety, aggression, and so on. The extremes, either lower or higher, are, by definition, relatively rare in the population, and they may create problems. Functioning is always relative to a task and context, and if we are accustomed to the tasks and contexts suitable for the broad average on the trait, then either lower or higher extremes may create problems relative to those tasks and contexts. For example, very low intelligence relative to the average will make it difficult or impossible for the person to carry out tasks that the average person can, and the same goes for low memory capacity, or attentional capacity; or high aggression or impulsiveness. We will then have cases of dysfunction – inability to carry out a task that the average person can – but one that does not involve anything other than principles and processes as in the normal case.

Consider how this applies in clinical examples.

John, age 9, was brought to the clinic because he was disruptive in class, tending to wander around and interfere with other children, instead of getting on with his work, and in the playground he was involved in disputes and fights because, it transpired, when he wanted something he tended to take it, rather than stop and think about consequences, and negotiate sharing. Following detailed clinical interview including information from parents and teachers, eliciting a range of behaviours of particular kinds, John's condition satisfied the diagnostic criteria for ADHD (quoted in the Appendix to the previous chapter). According to the current state of the science, attentional capacity and levels of activity and impulsiveness may well be normally distributed in the child population, and at least some of the children who would receive a diagnosis of ADHD are just high on the extremes; it remains controversial whether there is a severe group that is discontinuous.

Alice, age 8, was brought to the clinic because she had become so frightened of wasps one summer that she refused to leave the house, and before this she had run out several times into busy roads without looking in a panic because of a wasp near her. There was no evidence in the history of Alice having been stung, though there was evidence of other tendencies to high anxiety, for example on separation from parents, and tendency to worry a lot. Alice's state in relation to wasps satisfied the diagnostic criteria for specific phobia (animal type). According to the current state of the science, anxiety is probably normally distributed in the child population, and it is quite likely that at least some of the high anxiety cases presenting at the clinic and receiving a diagnosis are just at the high end of the normal distribution.

Phobic anxiety may be a relatively uncontroversial example of a mental disorder being the extreme end of a normally distributed trait, ADHD is more controversial in this respect, and there are many more conditions that are more or less controversial, including depression, autism, even schizophrenia at least in respect of some of the symptoms. Also the personality disorders may represent the extreme ends of various normally distributed traits; for example, antisocial personality disorder, characterized such as lying, stealing and remorseless aggression, or obsessive compulsive personality disorder, characterized by preoccupation with orderliness, perfectionism and control at the expense of flexibility, openness and task-completion.

Psychology may regard abnormal behaviours as in fact normal by regarding them as extremes of normal variation. A more radical option of the same kind is to suppose that abnormal behaviours characterized as symptoms or syndromes in the psychiatric manuals may not be extremes in the range of normal variation, but in fact more in the middle of it, common in the population. For example, given that up to 25 per cent of the population may at one time or another in their lives experience a major depressive episode, in the sense of the DSM or ICD, it is not plausible to regard this condition as the extreme end of a normal distribution. As another example, there is much current interest in the apparent fact that hearing voices, one of the classical first-rank symptoms of schizophrenia, is in fact a fairly common phenomenon, in people that no one would wish to say were mentally ill, because, for example, they get on with their lives in an (otherwise) normal way, without it causing them any harm. There is also evidence that intrusive, distressing unrealistic thoughts of the kind that characterize obsessive compulsive disorder are fairly common in the population, though not interpreted in the same way as by people suffering from OCD.

This psychological approach to normality has important implications for understanding shifts in the understanding of mental disorder. Mental disorder is mental abnormality, and abnormality has many connotations. First, abnormality carries normative or evaluative weight, so that mental abnormality/disorder implies that the mind is not working as it should. This normative/evaluative sense of abnormality is probably the one closest in meaning to dysfunction and disorder. Second, abnormality commonly connotes rarity. Deviation from the normal in the statistical sense – that is to say, being rare in the population – is a plausible candidate as a marker of disorder or illness, to the extent that, all being well, and pandemics aside, illnesses are usually relatively rare. Third, normality/abnormality is commonly a dichotomous division. With illnesses in mind, it is easy to assume that the difference between normal and abnormal, between being well or ill, is just a twofold one, either/or. Fourth, people making mental disorder attributions typically presuppose that they are themselves mentally normal (reasonable, under-standable, etc.); so 'normal' carries the further connotation of belonging inside the community of mentally normal people, while the abnormal are out-side. These several meanings of normality – normative/evaluative, statistical, binary–categorical, social inclusion – are systematically muddled up in our discourse. The medical model in psychiatry, to the extent that it viewed psy-chiatric conditions as resulting from lesions or disease processes, would have them as failures of function, as usually relatively rare, and as consistent with binary classification – and the social exclusion would be hard to exclude.

This complex of connotations of normality and hence disorder is disturbed by the introduction of a different paradigm, which has psychological traits as typically normally distributed in the population, and some typical mental dis-orders as being extremes of normally distributed population traits, or as even quite common in the population. In this context statistical rarity is now a more or less arbitrary characteristic, depending where you want to draw the line on a continuum. Normality and abnormality are no longer distinguished in a binary–categorical way. The social implications are also undermined: on the normally distributed curve there is no clear 'us' and 'them' – where should we position the other as opposed to ourselves? It is also more clear that the normative/evaluative connotation of mental abnormality – that the mind is failing to function as it should – cannot be captured in terms of statistical abnormality; rather it requires elucidation in terms other than mere differ-ence. The position of the normative/evaluative meaning of normality in this new paradigm is complex: it leads towards the idea that psychological processes may be maladaptive (rather than disordered in some other sense), and will be taken up under this heading later.

Psychology can normalize so-called abnormal conditions in a statistical sense by regarding them as extremes of normal variation, or as being after all, fairly common in the population. A second method of normalizing familiar in clinical psychology has to do with the emotions. Several of the common con-ditions in the psychiatric manuals are a matter of intense, abnormal emotional states, such as anxiety or depression. The abnormality consists in there being apparently no appropriate object for the emotion, or disproportionate inten-sity in relation to the current situation. Normal anxiety is a proportionate response to threat; normal low mood, sadness, a proportionate response to loss. These emotional states in intense form are distressing enough in the normal case, but their persistence in the apparent absence of an appropriate cause or reason multiplies misery and complicates it with confusion. Psychological models typically seek to go beneath the appearances and to detect unrecognized meaning in the emotional responses, either in terms of previous experience, such as childhood trauma or loss, or specific conditioning episodes, or some other aspect of the person's current interpretation of events.

Thus phobic anxiety may signify the extreme end of a normally distributed trait, but it may also result from specific conditioning episodes, such as being bitten in the case of an animal phobia. Major depression following loss of employment may seem to be a disproportionate emotional response, but it may appear more proportionate if the person's job turned out to be critical to their positive view of themselves and/or their sole source of positive reinforcement. Issues like these are entirely typical and familiar in psychological models of mental health problems and in associated therapies. They seek meaning in apparently meaningless emotional responses, making the abnormal appear as more normal after all.

A third way in which psychology normalizes the abnormal is by emphasizing that even in the abnormal case, when something is going badly wrong, the person is still trying to solve problems, consciously or otherwise. The functionality of mental life and behaviour that characterizes the normal case is found also in the abnormal. Typically the person is confronted with a problem, such as a serious threat, or inability to carry out a task. Insofar as the task is unmanageable for the person, for whatever reason, they have to do something, to avoid it in some way, or to do something else that they can manage that is somewhat like it. The resulting behaviours may appear as 'symptoms' of a disorder, but in the psychological view they are rather more or less reasonable attempts at problem-solving. Psychological theory of mental health problems, more or less supported by evidence, abounds in examples of these strategies.

The psychological formulation of John's case, cited above, includes reference to the hypothesis that he is unable to attend for long on class work, gets bored, seeks stimulation, something engaging to do, so talks to, wants to play with, and pesters other children in the class. In the absence of much planning or thoughts about consequences, when John wants the ball very much he takes it, pushing the other child to the ground. He has learnt long ago that he is told off for much of his behaviour, and has become adept at trying to shift the blame to others. The problem for him, from his point of view, is how is he going to negotiate all the situations given his resources, and the solution is what presents as the problem.

In Alice's case the formulation is more straightforward. She sees a wasp, thinks it's going to sting her, or fly in her face, so she runs away fast, or, later, stays in doors to avoid any such risk. Again, the problem that brings the child to the clinic includes her solution to the situation she finds herself in.

Typically in these kinds of formulation the solution involves costs, and has itself become a problem, often the presenting one. In John's case the cost is not only that he makes little use of educational opportunity but also that he becomes unpopular and is socially excluded. In Alice's case her tendency to escape without delay puts her at risk, e.g. from traffic, and her best solution of staying at home has the drawbacks that she misses out on family outings and maybe school as well.

A fourth way in which psychology sees normal functioning in the apparently abnormal is in terms of learnt patterns of behaviour being transferred from the original to an inappropriate environment. Families of children with severe and persistent behaviour problems are often characterized by rapid, frequent, inconsistent commands and punishments, in the context of little attention to and reward for compliant or neutral behaviour. In this regime, the child learns – according to principles of reinforcement modulated by the need to maintain some self-esteem – to ignore commands, to act regardless of threatened sanctions, to get what he wants by taking, and to gain emotional contact by provocation. This pattern of behaviour is at least one kind of reasonable response to the home environment, but it brings with it a host of troubles when taken to school.

Psychology construes behaviour as being as a rule functional: it achieves something for the agent, a satisfaction of some need, or achievement of some goal. The social sciences too tend to construe behaviour as functional, serving for example to enhance group cohesion and facilitate group tasks. Consider for example the following situation.

Jasmine lived in a British African-Caribbean community and was referred to the clinic with a bereavement reaction complicated by post-traumatic stress following the sudden death of her father. In the course of family treatment it emerged that she and her mother heard and felt the father's ghost making threats, and in the mother's case he assaulted her at night. The mother talked every day to her mother in law in Jamaica about the state of mind and activities of the ghost – he also visited his mother – and they compared experiences and formulations. The local faith group understood well what was happening and visited the house daily, carrying out various rites that had the effect of protecting mother and placating the ghost.

This illustrates the way in which behaviour, even if distressing and certainly in distressing circumstances, may activate the social group and its protective and supportive functions. The social ritual around ghosts with malign intent enhances communication and social involvement in grief. It is generally a methodological rule in both psychology and social science to assume and investigate personal and social meanings and functions of behaviour.

This brief case example also illustrates the fact that 'hearing voices' and communicating with them may be normal in a culture that has ghosts and other spirits. Social science and specifically anthropology shows the cultural variation in belief systems which has to be taken into account when defining the rationality of belief. Beliefs are generally acquired by processes of socialization and education, interweaving with personal experiences, and a person's beliefs can be said to be rational if they are so acquired. Stronger requirements of rationality would be that the beliefs are true, or based on scientific methodology, but this debate is best conducted at the cultural not the individual level. Thus, a belief that may appear irrational to us because it is ruled out by our cultural view may nevertheless be rational when the person's cultural context is taken into account. In this way the perspective of the social sciences works in an analogous way at the social level to psychology at the individual level: the apparently meaningless/irrational appears as not so after all, when context – individual learning history or culture – is taken into account. The psychiatric manuals in some contexts follow the methodology recommended by the social sciences, taking culture into account. The general definitions of mental disorder in the DSM-IV and the ICD-10, discussed in the previous chapter, both exclude patterns of behaviour that are sanctioned by the culture. And on delusions and hallucinations the DSM-IV says:

> Clinicians assessing the symptoms of schizophrenia in socioeconomic or cultural situations that are different from their own must take cultural differences into account. Ideas that may appear to be delusional in one culture (e.g., sorcery or witchcraft) may be commonly held in another. In some cultures, visual or auditory hallucinations with a religious content may be a normal part of religious experience (e.g. seeing the Virgin Mary or hearing God's voice).

American Psychiatric Association (1994, p. 281)

In general then psychological models of psychopathology – whether the models are behavioural, psychoanalytic, cognitive or systemic – emphasize normal functioning or continuity with normal functioning, that inappropriate emotions may be more understandable than seems at first sight, and that what typically appear as symptoms are rather strategies for coping with adverse conditions, either constitutional or in the external environment, in the past or in the present.

To all this of course the objection can be made that psychological approaches normalize the psychiatric conditions away – leaving only normality, meaning

and function. It is true that the psychological approaches tend to be antithetical to a particular view of mental disorder, typically identified, with more or
less justification, as the medical model, one that would have mental disorder
as senseless, strategy-less, categorically different from – mere absence of –
normal functioning. However, this rejection of a particular conceptualization
of the phenomena of course does not result in simply the opposite view using
the same concepts. Rather, the medical concept of mental disorder is re-thought
in the clinical psychological paradigm, and new terms of art are needed, of
which 'maladaptive' is among the most common.

Broadly speaking, maladaptive as used in clinical psychological models and
formulations seeks to capture the idea that responses and strategies may
involve more costs for the person than benefits – more harm than good.
Maladaptive is essentially a normative/evaluative concept, not a statistical one,
and it has no particular implications for prevalence rates – groups and whole
societies can and do get involved in maladaptive behaviour. The term invokes
the consequences of a mental state or behaviour, that they are – roughly –
harmful to the agent, running counter to the agent's needs; it is an essentially
evaluative notion, because it involves judgement of what are and are not
harmful consequences. Further, the issue is not just that harmful consequences accrue, but that they outweigh any benefits. This leads to the next
point, that in addition to implying harmful consequences, there is also the
connotation that the mental states or behaviour are in themselves dysfunctional, in the kinds of ways explicit in the diagnostic criteria in the psychiatric
manuals. The normative terms used are distinctively psychological, including
such as unrealistic, irrational, excessive, etc. In effect the underlying idea here
is that we judge the rationality of mental states and behaviour in terms of
whether they accrue more benefits than losses, and to the extent that they do
not, 'irrationality' or some similar term applies, a general one favoured in
psychology being maladaptive.

The importance of this psychological approach to mental health problems –
characterized by terms like maladaptive – will recur through this essay, particularly in Chapter 4 when we reconsider the DSM-IV definition of mental
disorder, which has important features in common with this approach.
The point to be made here is just that the concept of maladaptiveness does not
exclude meaning or strategy, nor normal mental functioning in this sense –
what it says is that some meanings and strategies get us into trouble,
or better: get us into more trouble than they are worth. Though again, this
is likely to be for good reasons, for example, when we are trying to cope with
what we can barely cope with or really cannot manage, feasible accessible
solutions have to be found, whatever the costs. The various coping mechanisms

sketched above – inappropriate generalization of learnt behaviour, irrational behaviour strategies involving substantial risks and losses – all come under this heading.

We turn now to consider another science basic to psychiatry, genetics, which has two main branches, behavioural and molecular. Behavioural genetics studies the relative contribution of genes, environment, and interactions between them, to individual differences in physical, mental or behavioural traits (phenotypes), such as height, onset of cancer, IQ, anxiety, aggression, and so on. The sense of environmental involved here is very broad and amounts to non-genetic, including not only events in the social environment such as early experiences in the family but also e.g. perinatal viral processes that may affect embryonic development, diet, and so on. The methodology involves study of groups of individuals with various degrees of genetic related-ness (twins, mono- and di-zygotic, non-twin siblings, parents, second-degree relatives, etc.) in similar or different environments (e.g. children raised together or in different families), using mathematical models to test observed data (occurrence or degree of the phenotype) against alternative models of the relative contribution of genes and environment. Extensive work has been done recently and is being done currently in estimating the genetic contribution to psychiatric conditions such as autism, schizophrenia, depression and antiso-cial behaviour. The recent and rapidly growing science of molecular genetics is complementary to behavioural genetics, aiming to identify specific genes, at the molecular level, associated with specific phenotypes.

The main question under consideration in this section is what the sciences basic to psychiatry have to say about the notion of disorder or dysfunction. In the case of behavioural genetics of psychiatric conditions, there is little use for the binary categorical distinction disorder/order (or abnormal/normal). Rather, psychiatric genetics like genetics generally works with phenotypes dis-tributed roughly normally in the population. The mathematical modelling used typically makes the assumption of roughly normal distribution, and the observed data is typically consistent with the assumption (otherwise the modelling would be invalid and alternatives would be required).

At the molecular level of gene activity in which DNA is replicated and trans-mitted to the next generation there is a definite use for terms such as error or mistake. Gene replication may lead to an imperfect copy of the original, to what is a different gene, which may be associated with a different phenotype or different range in an existing phenotype. This is called an 'error' but an interesting kind of error it is, since the process – random mutation – is in fact what makes evolutionary development possible. Random mutation may lead to new (variations of) phenotypes that are more or less adaptive than the original in the relevant environment, and if the latter they are more likely to be promote survival of the organism and their own survival. Genetic abnormality compared with the previous generation or with the rest of the population is neutral to whether the associated behavioural expression (if there is one) is adaptive or maladaptive. Adaptiveness or maladaptiveness is a feature of the behavioural expression and is relative to environment including task demands. Thus molecular genetics is so far neutral to the question of maladaptiveness of the associated behavioural phenotype, and probably has no use for notions of dysfunction or disorder otherwise understood.

Psychology and genetics work with concepts in the general area of psychological disorder, but they are of a particular kind, referring to failure of appropriate reactions and strategies, to behaviour that fails to achieve goals, to satisfy needs. In brief, they have a notion of maladaptive behaviour. Whether a behaviour is adaptive or otherwise is a matter relative to perception of needs and goals, whether from the point of view of the agent or some other party. It is not an absolute state, independent of needs and values. Nor can it be defined in terms of statistical abnormality. Nor is it the mere absence of psychological functioning; on the contrary there is functioning, but it goes wrong in the sense defined. Psychology and genetics, sciences basic to psychiatry, thus define a notion of mental disorder which is not the same as is usually attributed to the medical model, at least in its strong reading which excludes function and meaning. The next point to be made is that neuroscience and specifically neuroimaging, much though it has to offer, does not offer an alternative approach to just this problem of defining the difference between mental order and disorder.

Neuroscience – along with molecular genetics the most rapidly expanding area in the behavioural sciences – has subtle relations to notions of dysfunction and disorder. Neuroimaging is a crucial recently developed technology in neuroscience, increasingly used in psychiatry, usually using positron emission tomography (PET) or magnetic resonance imaging (MRI). Neuroimaging studies have two main kinds of design, structural and functional. Structural imaging provides pictorial representations of the physical topography of the brain, distinguishing more or less discrete brain structures and areas, connections between them, and their physical characteristics such as density. Functional neuroimaging, by contrast, provides pictorial representations of the level of activity in areas of the brain and in connections between them, either when the person is in a 'resting state', given no particular task to do, or when carrying out a specific task, in so-called 'challenge' designs.

Structural neuroimaging studies are able to detect signs of neural abnormality or damage, such as atrophy, though for psychiatric compared with neurological conditions the findings tend to be less dramatic and harder to interpret. However, a fundamental point in the present context is that the brain shows high degrees of both redundancy and individual variation, and whether a brain structural abnormality matters in relation to psychological functioning can only be judged in these terms, in terms of the associated psychological functioning, not in terms of the physical characteristics of the brain as such. Structural abnormality of the brain does not necessarily imply abnormality in psychological functioning, and still less does the former capture what is meant by the latter.

Functional neuroimaging studies of people with some specified psychological condition indicate what neural areas and paths of connectivity are implicated in that condition. This methodology applies in the same way whether the condition in question is normal or abnormal, as much to carrying out mental arithmetic, say, as having symptoms of schizophrenia. Analogous to the point just made about structural neuroimaging, the critical point for the present purpose is that whether a specified kind of psychological functioning is normal or abnormal is a matter to be judged in these terms, in terms of psychological or behavioural functioning, not in terms of the brain activity involved. By all means it is the case that if we are assuming that a specific psychological condition is a disorder then we may say in a derivative sense that the brain activity involved in producing it is disordered, but the inferential logic runs this way round, not the other: we do not see from the functional neuroimages that the brain activity (or the areas involved in the brain activity) are disordered, and then infer that the associated psychological functioning is a disorder. Functional neuroimaging is critical for many purposes, it has many scientific and clinical uses, but diagnosing mental disorder – in the sense of telling whether a psychological condition is a mental disorder or is normal – is not one of them. Uses include mapping psychiatric psychological functioning onto brain areas and connections, and investigating whether people with a specific kind of psychiatric condition perform relevant day-to-day tasks using atypical neural areas and pathways, using findings to test neuropsychological or cognitive models of the condition.

These remarks bear on the relation between mental and brain disorder, and physical disorder generally. DSM-IV begins its section on 'Definition of mental disorder' by casting some doubt on the term to be defined:

> Although this volume is titled the *Diagnostic and Statistical Manual of Mental Disorders*, the term mental disorder unfortunately implies a distinction between 'mental' disorders and 'physical' disorders that is a reductionistic anachronism of mind/body dualism. A compelling literature documents that there is much 'physical' in 'mental' disorders and much 'mental' in 'physical' disorders. The problem raised by the term 'mental' disorders has been much clearer than its solution, and, unfortunately, the term persists in the title of DSM-IV because we have not found an appropriate substitute.
>
> American Psychiatric Association (1994, p. xxi)

Probably the main appeal of the term 'mental' in this context is that usually (though not invariably) it is in the domain of the mental that the disorder is identified. It is also for this reason that the neurosciences cannot tell us what mental states are disordered or otherwise – this judgement has to be made within the domain of the mental using criteria appropriate for that domain, involving norms of psychological or behavioural functioning that are explicit or implicit in the diagnostic criteria, as outlined in the previous chapter. In brief, the critical question is whether the mental state or activity is pointless or maladaptive, harm-generating – and this question essentially involves social–psychological appraisal of the context and outcomes of behaviour, and cannot be answered by looking at images of the brain.

These issues lead readily into medicine, historically the parent of psychiatry. The medical model in psychiatry has a range of meanings, but a major inter-pretation of it (not the only one) has the notion of disease entity as fundamental. Biomedical discoveries formed this paradigm in nineteenth cen-tury medicine, and the discovery at the beginning of the twentieth century that general paralysis of the insane was caused by syphilitic infection was a major confirmation of its applicability to psychiatric illness. According to the disease model in psychiatry, psychological explanations of psychiatric condi-tions are somewhere in the range of redundant, misleading and wrong, insofar as the model implies that there is no psychological functioning, no meaning in the conditions, just pure deficit caused by a disease process.

That said, this is an extreme reading of the medical model in psychiatry, and it represents a gross over-simplification of the medical model in medicine itself. Medicine has quite different models of its conditions of interest, far exceeding mere absence of normal functioning, invoking principles of a kind in fact more akin to those familiar in psychology. A classic case was the relatively recent dis-covery that some kinds of hypertension are extremes of normal variation, not caused by disease processes. Another kind of case was the discovery in nine-teenth century medicine that fever was not a symptom of the disease, but rather part of the body's system of coping with disease. In contemporary medicine it is plain that much of the biological resources of the living being function to restore and repair damage or disruption due to various causes, as in the immune system. In this sense what psychology has wanted to say about mental disorder mirrors what medicine has to say about physical disorder. The psychoanalytic use of the term 'defence', for example, is shared with medicine, and the cognitive behavioural notion of coping is similar. The medical model in medicine has always recognized the meaning or function in some features of the presentation and in the underlying mechanisms. Interestingly, however, these themes in the medical model have not travelled well in the transfer to psychiatry – or at least, in the way that the medical model in psychiatry has often been interpreted.

The reason for this is that there have been major complications with deep historical and philosophical roots in precisely the area that is critical: the scientific status of mind and meaning. In fact there never was a shortage of meaningful accounts in psychiatry; there were plenty, but they were confined to psychoanalytic theory and its derivatives, split off from a medical model which came to represent the opposite, the absence of meaning. These complexities point to schisms in the early development of psychiatry, to major problems in the transfer of the medical model from its original domain to psychiatry, to do with the scientific status of mind and meaning. These problems strongly interact with some of the key themes in this essay and therefore require some explicit attention. They involve issues in the philosophy of science and philosophy of mind concerning mental causation and they will be considered in two contexts in the following two sections.

2.3 Mind and meaning in the new behavioural sciences

While psychiatric conditions typically involve disruptions of meaning of one kind of another, some or all may nevertheless involve meaningful responses to the prevailing circumstances, in the inner or outer environments, past or present, or meaningful attempts to manage the near unmanageable. The question then arises to what extent 'mental disorder' is a misleading and unsatisfactory way of characterizing these conditions, but this question does not arise at all unless and until it is supposed that mental, meaningful processes can play a causal role in bringing about behaviour, and this has long been a problematic idea. One simple line of thought in this area runs as follows: since mental disorder is characterized precisely by disruption of meaningful connections, it cannot be explained in terms of meaningful mental processes, but has to be explained dropping to a lower level of explanation, in terms of lesions or disease processes. In terms of Dennett's work on explanatory stances to be considered in more detail in the next section, breakdown of intentionality seems to demand dropping to a lower level, physical stance explanation. On the other hand this simple idea, consistent with a strong interpretation of the medical model, is open to the reply – typical of psychological approaches – that breakdown of meaning may be caused not by physical level disruptions, but by meaningful mental processes themselves. This was Freud's original point about hysterical paralysis. However, this type of explanation will be problematic to the extent that mind and meanings don't do causal work – and this has long been a supposition, though one that has recently changed. The question whether meaningful mental processes could be part of a causal explanation of psychiatric conditions has a long and vexed history, and insofar as the answer was taken to be negative, the only candidate for causal explanation was a lesion or disease process in the body, consistent with a strong – not to say crude – interpretation of the medical model.

The oldest problem was the dualism between matter and mind created with the mechanisation of the western world-picture in the seventeenth century. Among the many insoluble problems created with dualism – known as Cartesian dualism following its clear statement by Descartes – was the problem of mental causation. It never was clear how an immaterial substance could have any causal effect on material things, which moved according to their own mechanical laws. While Cartesian dualism was surpassed in the Kantian philosophy at the beginning of the nineteenth century, it survived in other contexts, particularly positivist science, and it was crucial in the formation of the new psychological science during the closing decades of the nineteenth century. Dualism implied that psychology should study mental states, known by introspection by the subject and otherwise by verbal report, and psycho-physical correlations. This introspectionism had many problems, main ones including the oddity of private data from the point of view of scientific methodology, its incompatibility with the study of non-linguistic animals or pre-linguistic human beings, as well as the underlying problem of mental causation. These kinds of problems led to the development of the only other alternative defined in the Cartesian thought-space: behaviourism, based on the notion of stimulus–response linkage, a not so distant offspring of the Cartesian quasi-mechanical reflex arc, to which mental states were (causally) irrelevant.

The problem of dualism was further and much complicated by another division which cemented the irrelevance of mind to science, a problematic that affected the development of psychiatry more than psychology. The new problem was identified early in the development of psychiatry in its recognizably contemporary form, by Karl Jaspers in his seminal work, the *Allgemeine Psychopathologie*, (*General Psychopathology*), published in 1913, and in English translation in 1963. Central to the work was the attempt to give the new psychiatry a philosophical foundation, the key element in which was the distinction between meaningful and causal connections, and the related distinction between understanding and explaining.

Here is Jaspers explaining the distinctions:

> 1. We immerse ourselves into the psychological situation and understand genetically by empathy how one psychic event emerges from another. 2. We find by repeated experience that a number of phenomena are regularly linked together, and on this basis we explain causally.

(1963, p. 301)

Roughly speaking meaningful connections are those familiar between psychological states such as experiences, beliefs, emotions, desires, and reasons for action, while causal connections are familiar in the natural sciences, involving associations between – typically material – events. Thus:

> In the natural sciences we find causal connections only but in psychology [we find] a quite different sort of connection. Psychic events 'emerge' out of each other in a way which we understand. Attacked people become angry and spring to the defence, cheated persons grow suspicious . . . Thus we understand psychic reactions to experience . . . the development of passion, the growth of an error, the content of delusion and dream . . . how the patient sees himself and how this mode of self-understanding becomes a factor in his psychic development.

Jaspers (op. cit., pp. 302–3)

Jaspers' elucidation of the distinction between meaning and causality and the related distinction between understanding and explaining had enormous implications for the development of psychiatry, and it provided foundations for the teaching of psychiatry in Germany and the UK for many decades. Jaspers did not invent the distinctions however; he inherited them from elsewhere in German scientific activity, seeing their profound implications for psychiatry. The distinctions in question were worked out in Germany in the closing decades of the nineteenth century in the new *Geisteswissenschaften*, a term difficult to translate into English but which may be rendered unsatisfactorily as cultural sciences and which included history, sociology and anthropology. When these subjects were being established as empirical sciences a large problem was encountered, namely, that the phenomena under study – human activities and the meaning that pervades them – did not readily lend themselves to the methodological assumptions of the natural sciences. The problem may be brought mainly under three related headings. First, natural science deals with repeatable phenomena, but historical events and cultural practices are singular, or even unique. Second, natural science aims to explain in terms of general causal laws, while history and social science seek to understand. Third, while the methods of observation in the natural sciences are objective, and the results are meant to be the same for all, understanding draws on subjective empathic abilities that vary from person to person, or from culture to culture, hence raising the question of objectivity and validity. Jaspers was the first to grasp the relevance of the new problematic to psychiatry, and perhaps the last to be able to hold on, even-handedly, to both epistemologies. Jaspers emphasized the importance of both the science of psychopathology and the indispensable need for understand meaning by empathy. However, he had no coherent account of how these two methodologies could together be coherent and valid.

The two dichotomies, mind/matter, and meaning/causality, were hardly directly related, in fact they belonged to distinct philosophies, but the second was superimposed on the first, and both converged on the conclusion that mind and what was essential to it, meaning, were problematic from the point of view of science and scientific methodology. This was the philosophical background – composed of irreconcilable opposites – to the development of the two new sciences of psychology and psychiatry.

In the following decades the conflicts in psychiatry were dealt with in a primitive though effective way, namely splitting: causality as opposed to meaning, explanation as opposed to understanding, organic psychiatry as opposed to psychoanalysis. These divisions became violent in the 1960s, with attacks on the one side by the other, highly charged and highly symmetrical. Mainstream psychiatry was attacked by Laing, Foucault and Szasz among others for systematically stripping madness of its meaning and hence dehumanizing it. Psychoanalysis, the champion of meaning, was rounded upon for being unscientific. The whole development had an inevitability that Hegel would have admired. At the same time as the opposites were reaching a destructive climax there was emerging a new paradigm that effectively combined elements of the old in a new synthesis that was also quite different from either.

The new science was the so-called cognitive or information-processing paradigm that emerged during the 1960s and which is ongoing. Central to the new approach is the idea that information-carrying, semantic cognitive states and processes regulate activity, and that these states and processes are encoded in the brain. These central proposals apparently collapse the two previous dichotomies sketched above, because, first, semantic states now have a causal role in the regulation of behaviour, and because second, the brain is a system for information processing and cognition, and thus – using the original scholastic terminology – the brain as res extensa, spatial material substance – is also res cogitans, cognitive substance. This new paradigm has major implications for the unity of the sciences and for the science of psychopathology.

The divisions between mind and body and between meaning and causality made for a broken up science of psychopathology, barely attached to experience and meaning. In the underlying basic sciences, it has often been asserted or wished that there should be a unified biopsychosocial science, but the dichotomies as considered above made this hardly possible. The incommensurability between biology, psychology and social science has been more in evidence than their cooperative harmony. The new paradigm however holds out more promise here. First, it provides terms which link biology and psychology. Crucially, information-processing models pervade not only psychology, but also biology, famously right down to the level of genes. This has a major impact on what has come to be known as Brentano's thesis, that intentionality is the defining characteristic of mind. 'Intentionality' is a technical term, deriving originally from scholastic philosophy, which pervades current theorizing. To say that a state is intentional is to say: (1) that it is essentially directed to (is about) an object, and (2) that this 'intentional object' may not exist. Mental states such as believing, or striving, are paradigm intentional states. However, with the application of information-processing models in biology as well as in psychology, it is arguable that intentionality in its standard definition (points 1 and 2 above) is actually the mark not of psyche but of bios. Because biological processes have intentionality, biology is not reducible to physics and chemistry. However, the relation between them is comprehensible within this framework: although biological principles are not reducible to laws of physics and chemistry, they never violate those laws, and they generally exploit physico-chemical properties for the purposes of information-processing. There are many elegant examples of this, starting with the so-called translation of the DNA genetic code into proteins.

If intentionality as standardly defined is the mark of bios generally, not of psyche uniquely, then clarification is needed of what has to be added to biological intentionality to produce mind. Probably crucial here, using the same terms that are now grounded in biology, is second-order intentionality, that is, intentional states that represent intentional states. This metarepresentational capacity typically involves language, is central to what has come to be called the 'theory of mind'; it is involved in giving reasons for actions, and hence to concepts of autonomy and responsibility, and (self-)consciousness. In the new paradigm, however, there is no radical and probably incomprehensible break between biological and psychological processes, as was the case in dualism. Rather, as is familiar in the science, the principles here are fundamentally developmental. The crucial matter of interest is the regulation of activity by information-carrying, intentional processes. Intentionality runs through the whole, from the inherited information in genes, to sensorimotor activity, to the later development of second-order intentional processes, the content of which includes the acquired cultural meanings used to interpret the world, each other, and to plan individual and cooperative action. These considerations point to a practically seamless development that can incorporate biology – grounded in but distinct in specified ways from physics and chemistry – psychology, and cultural meanings. There is a kind of unity of science here, but not one achieved by reduction, not one in which one science – physics – is fundamental, but one achieved by integration set in a developmental framework.

This kind of integration of the sciences of the variety of aspects of being human has a great advantage for psychopathology, the science of mental disorder. Models of psychopathology can now incorporate causes of different kinds, without prejudice that one or another kind must be dominant or exclusive. Models of schizophrenia, for example, can now incorporate many different kinds of risk factor, from genes to cognitive vulnerability to social exclusion, in the one conceptual space, in the one statistical analysis of sources of variance. Models of dementia can now incorporate not only neural degeneration and its immediate impacts on psychological functioning, but also the attempts of the patient to make sense of these effects and to come to terms with them. Models of post-traumatic stress disorder, the paradigm mental disorder that has a meaningful cause, can now explore the effects of atypical neural storage of the trauma memory in maintaining the core re-experiencing, as well as for example the second-order appraisals of the original stress response. Models of psychopathology in the twenty-first century can be truly holistic, without giving up the science; or rather, in following the science they will be increasingly holistic.

A related implication of the new paradigm for models of psychopathology is that there are two general kinds of causal pathway, one involving information processing, the other not – though with complex interactions between them. In the normal functioning case biopsychological processes are regulated by information and meaning – they run according to rules. However there are also abnormal cases in which functions break down. In psychological breakdown it has always been tempting to suppose that explanations or understanding in terms of meaning has come to an end, because meaning has by definition run out. This line of thought has been one foundation of the medical model in psychiatry which would posit biological disease processes or lesions of some kind. It has also been clear, however, at least since the psychoanalytic theories of Freud and the behavioural conditioning theories of Watson, that apparently pointless behaviour can be explained not only in terms of the medical model in this sense, but also in terms of the inappropriate intrusion by meaningful processes – meaning is disrupted not by physical lesion, but by *more meaning*. These are the psychological explanations. However, previously the 'medical' and the 'psychological' have been competing general explanations, and this is entirely not the case in the new paradigm. Both kinds of factor may be playing a part in any particular kind or case of disorder. However, the psychological will probably always be playing a part, whether or not as primary cause, at least in terms of strategy for overcoming some psychological challenge, the primary cause of which may be physical, in the sense of not being mediated by information. Just as systems for defence, compensation and restoration are integral to physical illness, so also there is likely to be much method in what we call mental disorder. This conclusion bears on the issues considered in Introduction and Chapter 1: insofar as there is method in what we call mental disorder, there is psychological functioning, not the mere absence of it, and to this extent more neutral terms, uncommitted to absence of meaning, recommend themselves, terms such as 'psychiatric conditions', or 'mental health problems'.

2.4 Varieties of explanation of disorder

In the first half of the twentieth century there was a forced choice between physical explanations of mental disorder, consistent with the medical model, and meaningful explanations, or modes of understanding, championed by psychoanalysis and its many offsprings. With the appearance of the cognitive or information-processing paradigm through the second half of the century, both forms of explanation can coexist, and we need a general explanatory framework that can accommodate these two forms, the relation between them, and perhaps others also. One such general explanatory framework can be found in Daniel Dennett's work on the variety of explanatory stances that can be adopted for explanation of systems characterized by intentionality in the sense defined in the previous section.

Dennett (1979) distinguished three kinds of stance that may be adopted in the explanation and prediction of the moves of a chess-playing computer. One is the *physical stance*, which draws on physical laws applicable to the material of the machine. The second is the *design stance*, referring to design and programme. Here it is assumed that each part is in working order and fulfils its function. Within the design stance the physical constitution of the system is not considered. Now while in principle, Dennett supposes, the moves of a computer are predictable from the design and even from the physical stance, in practice the best chess-playing computers are most efficiently predicted by moving to a third stance, the *intentional stance*. Here it is assumed that the computer will make the most rational move. The assumption of rationality is that of optimal design relative to goals. From the intentional stance, one assumes the possession of certain information and the direction by certain goals, i.e. of beliefs and desires.

These three stances can all be used in the explanation of breakdown of functioning and are familiar in psychopathology. Within his framework, Dennett makes the plausible suggestion, in passing, that in order to explain breakdown of function, for example in the chess-playing computer, we have to drop to the physical stance, there to appeal to such as short-circuits, over-heating, or blown fuses (Dennett 1979, pp. 4–5). The point behind this suggestion is that when function fails we precisely have to abandon the intentional stance, with its reference to rules, strategies, etc. and look instead for physical defined causes. A priori inference of this kind lends support, in the case of psychological disorder, to the medical model in psychiatry, insofar as it posits organic aetiology, brain diseases and lesions. Mental disorder appears as the breakdown of psycho-logic, that is, of meaning, rationality, and so on, and beyond this limit we apparently have to abandon our normal intentional forms of explanation, as used in folk psychology, and posit instead causal processes at the physical level that disrupt normal mental processing.

However, the assumption that breakdown of function can be explained only from the physical stance is invalid, invalid even in the relatively simple case of the chess-playing computer. There are options in the design stance and in the intentional stance itself. Explanations of breakdown of psychological function from the design stance are those that invoke poor fit between specific environments/task demands and psychological dispositions that are either or both genetically inherited or acquired (learned). Explanations of psychopathology from the intentional stance typically invoke disruption of intentional processes by intentional processes. Dennett's three explanatory stances when applied to the problem of explaining breakdown of functioning thus provide a framework for understanding how options in psychopathology have broadened out from just a (crude) medical model to include also the genetic and the psychological.

Consider first the option of explaining disorder from the design stance. The chess-playing computer may make irrational moves, inappropriate to winning the game, because of suboptimal design. Here we envisage a causal pathway to disruption of function in which there is no physical disruption to information processing, but rather use of inappropriate rules. In the case of biological systems, design – the operating rules – may be understood as being acquired by genetic transfer from the previous generation, innate in the offspring, but for biopsychological beings there is also learning, the acquisition of operating rules within generation. For human beings design is acquired from genes, and from learning, and from interaction between the two. The main point for the present purpose is that problematic, maladaptive behaviour need not be explained by dropping right down to the physical stance; there are also options from within the design stance, referring to maladaptive (for the current purpose) operating rules, acquired either genetically or by learning or by some combination of the two.

As to the possibility of explaining disorder from within the intentional stance, this seems to be ruled out a priori – at least at first sight. Disorder appears precisely as the breakdown of intentionality, and hence it does not admit of explanation in terms of intentional processes. The simplicity and power of this line of thought derive primarily, however, from limiting consideration to systems which have only one function. When we consider complex systems (though not more complex than a game-playing computer, or any living being), with many goals and subgoals, routines and subroutines, there arise several possibilities which avoid the apparent contradiction in explaining breakdown of intentionality in terms of intentional processes. An obvious possibility is that two or more sets of rules come into conflict, leading to disorder in action. Another is that one goal can be abandoned in order to achieve a higher goal, that in this sense one function will be sacrificed, but as part of a strategy appropriately described from the intentional stance. A chess-playing computer, for example, may sacrifice the queen for a pawn in order to secure checkmate in three moves. However, an observer who fails to see the point of the sacrifice (fails to see the loss of the queen *as* a sacrifice) would reasonably conclude that the computer had made a radically mistaken move, and shift to the design or physical stance for an explanation.

It should be emphasized that the diagnoses of breakdown of function from the physical and design stances are quite distinct insofar as they make different predictions about future moves, and point to different remedies. If the intentional stance is used for explanation, again there are different predictions as to future moves. In this sense, at least when it comes to the explanation of disorder, the three explanatory stances are genuine alternatives in any one case, and they are (more or less) right or wrong.

The use of Dennett's framework to elucidate explanations of dysfunction requires some amendment to his understanding of the intentional stance and the intentional systems to which it applies. Dennett defines the intentional stance in terms of the assumption of rationality, and intentional systems (trivially) as those to which the intentional stance can be usefully applied (Dennett 1987, 1988). This approach apparently does not envisage the intentional stance being used for predicting irrational behaviour. But apparently it can be. I may learn for example that the chess-playing computer prefers its black bishop to its queen (systematically moves in such a way as to retain the former rather than the latter given these alternative outcomes), and this rule is as useful for prediction as the more rational opposite. Another example is that the computer may be programmed so as never to make a sacrifice (never exchange a higher for a lower value piece). This is a reasonable enough rule, but in some circumstances (when a queen sacrifice would secure mate) it does not lead to the most rational move. What matters to the use of the intentional stance is that some or other identifiable strategy is being used to achieve some identifiable end state; it is not also necessary that the strategy or the end state is (optimally) reasonable. This relies on another way of approach to intentional systems, unlike Dennett's, in which they are understood as systems showing goal-directedness and flexibility according to circumstances. The intentional stance is then seen to explain and predict the behaviour of systems with these characteristics by positing regulation by states which carry information about goals and the current environment.

Thus breakdown of intentionality, such as is involved in the characterization of mental disorders, can arise through a variety of causal pathways, with interactions between them. Physical damage to the brain structures that serve psychological function may disrupt that function, it being recalled that the damage matters in this context only insofar as it does disrupt psychological functioning. There may be design features, either genetic or acquired or both, leading to failure of functioning in specific environments. Finally, there may be intentional processes at work, by which failure of one function is part of a strategy (conscious or otherwise) for preserving another of higher value for the living being. These various kinds of causal pathway may operate separately or in combination. Implications include the following. First, physical damage to neural structures is not necessary for failure of psychological function. There may for example be design features, genetic or acquired, resulting in the person being unable to carry out specific kinds of tasks in specific environments, in the absence of any physical damage to the underlying neural structures. Second, where there are problems at the physical or the design levels (or both), it is likely that intentional level processes will also be brought into play, to adapt to or compensate for those problems. In other words, it is likely that intentional level processes will always play some role.

The clinical presentation – the clinical syndrome as described in diagnostic criteria set out in the psychiatric manuals – may thus involve effects of a variety of causes, perhaps direct effects of physical damage, perhaps extremes of genetically based traits, perhaps maladaptive learning – both of these being essentially environment-/task-specific – and, likely always, methods of coping with the resulting problems.

The main point being drawn attention to in this section, making use of Dennett's influential philosophical work on the variety of explanatory stances in behavioural science, is that current models of aetiology in psychopathology are essentially multifactorial, involving many kinds of causal pathway, with interactions between them. They include, in no particular order: genetic influences on traits, physical and interpersonal environmental impacts on early neural development, pre-, during and post-birth, subsequent adverse life events and chronic stressors, with effects through time evident in psychic life and the underlying neurochemistry, functional abnormalities of the brain, lesions to the brain, by disease processes or injury, styles of information processing evident in neuropsychological experimental paradigms, the operation of meanings drawn from the surrounding culture and subculture, and personal meanings deriving from individual learning histories and modes of interpretation. This is a long list, no doubt not complete, each item of which covers many different kinds of case. There are more or less strong interactions between the kinds of causal pathway. Probably in no kind of psychopathology is there a single cause, though one or another kind or several kinds may be more or less prominent depending on the condition, the subtype of the condition, and on individual differences. Complexity is the rule, hence also uncertainty.

It is not my purpose here to try to summarize or review current models of psychopathology – there are too many, they are always changing, they are sometimes in conflict, they are more or less well integrated, and the relevant data are extensive, and complex. The emphasis here is not on the details of the current science of psychopathology, but on its form, on its multifactorial nature, its complexity and uncertainty, and the chief contrast being drawn is with earlier, simpler assumptions of causality. The old medical model of mental illness, rounded upon in the 1960s, was supposed to have causation as being a matter just of brain disease or lesion, just reductionist physical stance causation, the outcome of which was mental disorder with no meaningful structure or content. However, this kind of causation is only one among many kinds envisaged in the current science, and along with this, it may be more relevant for some conditions or kinds of case than for others. Structural and functional neural abnormalities – abnormalities in the sense that they lead to problematic psychological functioning – may be critical in schizophrenia, for example, or at least in some types of schizophrenia. Specific functional neurochemical abnormalities are likely critical in bipolar disorder, previously called manic depression, and perhaps in recurrent major depressive episodes. These kinds of serious and enduring mental illnesses, as they are now sometimes called, may be contrasted with other kinds of condition listed as mental disorders in the psychiatric manuals, such as first episode depression, likely to be reactive to some adverse life event or accumulation of stressors, interpreted according to cultural and personal meanings. In brief, the current science is pluralist and discriminative: it envisages many kinds of cause, and it teaches differences between kinds of causal pathway more or less prominent in different kinds of condition.

To put this point another way, there is no knowing a priori what is the cause of a particular mental disorder – it is a matter for research, not ideology. The old medical model, understood as having its single preferred cause – a damaged, malfunctioning brain – ran alongside its diametric opposite, psychoanalytic explanation and interpretation of psychopathology in terms of psychic conflicts and unconscious strategies. The one side envisaged no meaning in mental disorder, the other only meaning, but these competing views actually passed one another by, in separate spaces. This schism between mind and meaning on the one hand, and brute physical causation on the other, was considered in the previous section in terms of two deep philosophical divides: mind/body dualism, on which was later superimposed the dichotomy between physical explanations and meaningful interpretations. Dismantling these two divides, bringing the mental and meaningful into the unified space of an animated body and community, has been one of the key philosophical shifts in the new biobehavioural science paradigm. The implication for psychopathology is that mental, meaningful causation now may be envisaged in mental disorder, along with physical lesions or disease processes, and alongside other kinds of risk or protective factors, such as genetically influenced temperamental traits. One protest against the medical model in psychiatry in the 1960s critiques was that it stripped the meaning out of so-called mental illness, disqualifying mental life and the people whose life it is. This alleged dehumanizing was in the context of the assumptions of the time, which excluded the possibility of having mind and meaning, and body and causation, in one ontological and epistemic space. These assumptions have shifted, and now the current science of psychopathology incorporates the role of mental, meaningful processes.

One of the questions to which this essay addressed is the one highlighted in the 1960s debates: is there meaning in mental disorder? The response in the current science is clear enough in principle, along the following lines: there is no simple all or none answer to this question – there certainly can be meaning, there often is, in original causation or in maintenance of the problem, or in more or less adaptive coping, though there also may be, and often are, physical causes, unmediated by information processing but just disrupting it, and the degrees of each and interactions between them will differ from condition to condition and from case to case, and we don't know the general principles or the specifics until we do the research, whether in the clinic or in psychological science or preferably in both. There is complexity and variety, though in this, in any case, meaning has been ruled in, not ruled out.

The general position sketched in this and the previous section is consistent with the one proposed in a recent article by Kenneth Kendler with the title 'Toward a philosophical structure for psychiatry', published in the *American Journal of Psychiatry*, the journal of the American Psychiatric Association. Kendler – a highly credible spokesperson for the current science – seeks to sketch a coherent conceptual and philosophical framework for psychiatry that consists of eight major propositions. Six of these are on the topic of mental causation and explanatory diversity in current models of psychopathology:

+ Cartesian substance dualism is false.

+ Epiphenomenalism is false.

+ Both brain → mind and mind → brain causality are real.

+ Psychiatric disorders are etiologically complex, and we can expect no more 'spirochete-like' discoveries that will explain their origins in simple terms.

+ Explanatory pluralism is preferable to monistic explanatory approaches, especially biological reductionism.

+ Psychiatry needs to move away from a prescientific 'battle of paradigms' towards a more mature approach that embraces complexity along with empirically rigorous and pluralistic explanatory models (Kendler 2005, p. 433).

2.5 **Disorder in evolutionary context**

The concepts of function and dysfunction appear for the first time in biology, then also in psychology where they underpin diagnosis of mental disorder. They do not apply in the physical sciences. The free-fall of bodies under gravity does not admit of the normative distinction between function and dysfunction: there is no failure of function, not without violation of physical laws. Biological systems such as the cardiovascular, by contrast, can and do fail to function, and without breaking any physical laws. This implies that biological systems operate according to mechanisms and principles that, while they are compatible with physical laws, are not themselves physical laws. This matter has been clarified in the new information-processing paradigm that has been applied pervasively in biology since roughly the middle of the twentieth century. In this paradigm the operation of biological systems such as the cardiovascular are described in terms of specialized information detectors, information processing, the use of information in regulating the outputs of the system, producing changes in the environment which are detected, and so on, until the system reaches its end state/range. While these processes exploit the physical properties of the material involved, they can be disrupted without violating physical laws. Physical damage to a specialized information detector may lead to dysfunction, for example, but this has nothing to do with physical laws being broken.

Physics does not deal with parts of nature that 'work' or 'don't work', which function or dysfunction, which 'should' work in a particular way but do not; or rather, physics does not deal with them – is not interested in them – under these descriptions. Its interest is in the processes that follow just physical laws, which never fail to apply. In this sense it is correct to say that normative concepts appear in biology for the first time. That said, however, there is a distinction between order and disorder in contemporary physics, which is sometimes used in stating the second law of thermodynamics. This thermodynamical law can be expressed by saying that physical systems tend to move from order to disorder, from states of lower to higher entropy. Order here refers to differences in temperature or levels of energy, while disorder refers to sameness in these respects. There is an interesting link between this thermodynamic sense of order and biological systems. Schrödinger (1967) observed that living systems may be characterized as local areas in which entropy is in reverse compared with the overall direction stated in the second law of thermodynamics. Biological systems typically work to increase order, to decrease entropy, by taking in energy from the environment, thereby increasing the difference between themselves and their environment. The implied principle here is that living beings create order – for the time being, while alive, until they ultimately tend back to disorder, to sameness with the environment – our ultimately dysfunctional state. The principle that order is created in the biological realm and subsequently in the psychological characterizes the relevant sciences and will be considered at an abstract level in the fourth chapter (4.6) together with its implications for disorder attributions.

Normative concepts in biology belong with the notion of design: the function of a system is what it was designed to do. Darwin famously showed that it was possible to have design without a designer: random variation coupled with selective pressure would result, in the long run, in systems that are designed to achieve particular ends, adapted to survival in a particular environment. In this sense the evolutionary process designs systems, and their normal as opposed to abnormal function is a matter of their functioning as they were designed to do. Evolutionary theory in this way provides a meaning for normative distinctions in biology that may transfer to psychology and which may hence underpin the notion of mental disorder. Evolutionary theoretic approaches to mental disorder have been the dominant ones since about the 1970s. The most elaborate and influential proposal along these lines – due to Jerome Wakefield – is (roughly) that mental disorder is a harmful failure of a psychological system to function in the way designed by evolution. Wakefield's proposal will be considered in detail in the following chapter, but the purpose here is to consider the general effect of introducing evolutionary theory into the theory of mental disorder.

Given the background of the concept of mental disorder in the medical model, the first point to note is that the evolutionary approach can readily accommodate psychological dysfunction due to lesion or disease. From the evolutionary perspective it is plausible to suppose that there are basic psycho-logical competencies, perhaps modular in form, served by relatively circumscribed brain structures, and that damage to these structures, whether by a genetic fault, or some disease process or lesion, would lead to profound disor-der. Autism has been considered in this way, for example, as involving disruption of the basic competency of mind-reading. This kind of approach is compatible also with some current models of schizophrenia. They comprise postulates of a fundamental cognitive dysfunction – such as failure of regulation of sensory input by stored regularities – in the context of neural structural and functional abnormalities, genetic risk, and a hypothesis of specific neural damage in utero. However, while the old idea of a lesion causing profound psychopathology can be accommodated within an evolutionary theoretic approach, this approach in fact points towards a new framework that opens up a wide variety of explana-tory models of dysfunctional, maladaptive behaviour.

Two critical papers in this paradigm shift are Cosmides and Tooby (1999) and Richters and Hinshaw (1999). Both papers acknowledged that Wakefield may have the right analysis of mental disorder, implicating functional failure of some specific designed psychological competency, but the substantial parts of the papers were taken up with other possible pathways to dysfunc-tional mental states and behaviour. These other possible pathways include the following:

1. defensive/coping strategies
2. strategies that involve disruption of function
3. design/environment mismatches
4. phenotypes that look maladaptive but may be adaptive
5. highly evolved learning capacities leading to maladaptive behaviour.

Evolutionary theory emphasizes adaptation and survival, and much of the biological resources of the living being are designed to survive adversity, whether this be in the external environment or the internal, by various forms of restoration, plasticity, and compensation. In brief, living beings use defen-sive/coping strategies. According to this line of thought, when there is a fundamental psychological dysfunction caused for example by damage to the neural structures serving it, then there will be a tendency for the person to seek to act despite this. In this case what shows up in behaviour will be strate-gies for coping, as well as any direct signs of the dysfunction itself. Current models of autism and schizophrenia both use this line of thought, supposing that behaviours characteristic of these disorders, including some regarded as symptoms, may be adaptive. For example, the repetitive, isolated play of the child with autism may sometimes function to avoid situations that require theory of mind, such as cooperative or pretend play. Schizophrenia is also marked by avoidance, the simplest problem-solving strategy, in this case typically avoidance of sensory and social stimulation. It is possible that some positive symptoms, particularly delusions, sometimes function to reduce uncertainty associated with unpredictable sensory experience. The expectation would be, further, that direct signs of the dysfunction may not be open to view, that they will be disguised in some way by coping strategies, and will need special tasks, circumventing the coping strategies, to elicit them, such as theory of mind tasks of the kind used in studies of autism, or the latent inhibition paradigm used in investigations of schizophrenia. Thus while the evolutionary framework can accommodate lesion or disease processes, it involves a rethinking of this old paradigm case, because from the evolutionary biological point of view it is unlikely that damage to a fundamental function, threatening the possibility of action itself, would be left unattended: rather, there would be mechanisms in place to enable the living being to carry on. Further, the evolutionary approach can envisage quite different sources of trouble.

A special though common form of coping strategy involves loss of some function that matters less to the living being, the second kind of causal pathway on the above list. This kind of sacrifice of function presupposes that functional hierarchies are part of human design, and coping strategies may be designed to secure one function at the expense of other functions lower in the hierarchy. There is genuine loss of function, which may appear as disorder, but the loss of function arises from an underlying order. Examples abound throughout psychiatry. Behavioural avoidance strategies are the plainest kind of case, and there are also more complex forms of cognitive avoidance. Thus the person with a phobia of car travel following a road traffic accident avoids it, but this leads, often let us say, to staying at home rather than social engagement, or going to work. There is loss of function, associated with distress, but the loss is strategic, serving to avoid greater loss. Or again, a severely neglected child may act so as to achieve engagement with carers even though this runs the risk of further punishment. Preservation of safety is sacrificed in the hope of having needs met. Behavioural approach–avoidance conflicts have a mental counterpart, with optimistic states of mind alternating with fear.

Although mechanisms of the kinds sketched above, defensive or coping strategies, including those involving loss of function, are compatible with an evolutionary theoretic approach, they are long familiar in psychological models of disorder, starting with the psychoanalytic theories of Freud and the behavioural conditioning theories of Watson, and leading through all subsequent psychology theories of abnormal functioning. As noted earlier in this chapter, these theories emphasize defences or coping, often involving strategic sacrifices, that the presentation is typically of coping strategy not the underlying illness, and that the symptoms are typically signs of problematic coping strategies, the solution being the presenting problem. The evolutionary theoretic approach comes to similar conclusions as psychological theory because both paradigms have as axiomatic the functional, goal-directed nature of behaviour, which persists even in the 'abnormal' case.

The third kind of explanatory model of dysfunctional, maladaptive behaviour in terms consistent with an evolutionary theoretic approach also has a close analogue in psychological theories. The underlying idea is that behaviour is relative to, is shaped in, or is designed to achieve certain results in, specific environments, and that dysfunctional behaviour may arise in transfer to other environments. In an evolutionary context, dysfunctional behaviour may arise due to mismatch between evolutionary design and current environment, if the current environment is different in key respects from that in which the behaviour was designed to function. It has been estimated that about 99 per cent of the evolutionary history of the brain took place when human ancestors were living on the African plains in hunter-gatherer societies. This environment of evolutionary adaptiveness (EEA) probably was characterized by small closely related nomadic groups, sparse population densities with relatively rare encounters with strangers, stable social ties, simple social hierarchies, cooperative ventures organized around basic physical survival needs, with heavy demands on physical endurance, agility and prowess, and outdoor living. Contemporary urban society is different in all these respects, and consequently behaviour may be maladaptive because of design/environment mismatch. A speculative example is the kind of behaviour characteristic of ADHD, which may have been adaptive in the EEA, but is disruptive in our current educational settings.

Another implication of the evolutionary theoretic approach is that even if behavioural patterns seem to be maladaptive, it is unlikely that they would have persisted, would have been selected, unless they had or at least were associated with some adaptive functions. This leads us to the fourth kind of evolutionary approach to disorder, in some ways the most radical. Disadvantageous behaviour as such is likely – other things being equal – to have been de-selected. Conversely, since the so-called mental disorders have persisted, in relatively high rates, the implication is apparently that they have or are at least associated with advantages in the EEA. This remarkable implication suggests a range of new perspectives of mental disorders. One extreme option is that a trait we are usually inclined to call a disorder may turn out not to be a disorder at all from the evolutionary perspective. There has been interest in the possibility that this might be true of sociopathic personality disorder, connected with the fact that individuals so described are not held back from satisfaction of needs by concern for others, and show no remorse or other distress about the costs to others caused by pursuance of their own goals. Another kind of case would be illustrated by the anxiety disorders, which are clearly related to highly adaptive normal anxiety, and certain aspects of which may be more adaptive than apparent at first sight. Another kind of case would be behaviour which evidently involves loss of function, but the loss may itself, in certain circumstances, be adaptive. Depression has been approached in this way, in hypotheses that it has adaptive social functions. A different kind of option is that a syndrome may involve definite loss of function, but is associated genotypically and possibly phenotypically with significant biological gain. As an illustration of this kind of possibility, it has been hypothesized that schizophrenia in the species may be linked to the cerebral lateralization necessary for the acquisition of language.

It is worthwhile noting here some issues regarding testability of evolutionary theoretic hypotheses. Broadly speaking, in all or most of the examples given above, the hypothesized ancestral environments are not so different from our own, and so the hypothesis of advantage can be tested, more or less definitively, by various observational or experimental methodologies. On the other hand there is the risk that a variety of more or less plausible-sounding speculations can be made about possible ancestral environments, and about the advantages of having this or that psychological trait. The new evolutionary psychology avoids 'just so' speculations of this kind. Rather, it hypothesizes that specific functions and behaviours are designed/selected in the EEA to solve particular kinds of problems, and given specific assumptions about the environment and the tasks, specific predictions about cognitive–affective and neural architecture and computational processes can be made and tested.

We turn now to the fifth explanatory approach to dysfunctional behaviour from an evolutionary perspective, last on the list above, to do with the highly evolved learning capacities of human beings. The general point is that we have an evolutionary design that enables us to learn, but we may apply this capacity in ways that lead to dysfunctional behaviour. The simplest and common kind of case is that learnt patterns of behaviour may be transferred from the original to an inappropriate environment. This was considered above in discussion of psychological models. It is the psychological analogue of design/environment mismatch and it brings out that learning complicates the notion of design in human behaviour – an implication to be taken up later in the next chapter in relation to Wakefield's proposed analysis of mental disorder.

In conclusion from the points made so far, the evolutionary framework opens up a variety of possible causal pathways to dysfunctional, maladaptive behaviour, consistent with both the medical model and psychological

approaches, all of which can now be considered together in models of the presenting condition. So how does the notion of mental disorder fare in this new
environment?

Consider the following two examples from papers on the contribution of
evolutionary theory to psychiatry, drawing implications for what mental
disorder is.

> Mental disorders can be recognized as medical disorders when they are viewed in an
> evolutionary framework. As is the case for the rest of medicine, many psychiatric
> symptoms turn out not to be diseases themselves but defenses akin to fever and
> cough. Furthermore, many of the genes that predispose to mental disorders are likely
> to have fitness benefits, many of the environmental factors that cause mental
> disorders are likely to be novel aspects of modern life, and many of the more unfortu-
> nate aspects of human psychology are not flaws but design compromises.
>
> Nesse and Williams (1997, pp. 2–3)

McGuire *et al.* endorse 'biological disadvantage' as an appropriate criterion
for identifying mental disorders, but add:

> It is difficult to know whether a condition is pathological without considering the
> environment in which it occurs. Depression may be adaptive in a supportive social
> environment, just as schizoid personality may be adaptive in isolated areas.
>
> (1992, p. 93)

Thus from the evolutionary point of view many symptoms are likely to be
defences or coping strategies, and not necessarily against an internal disease
process, but perhaps rather against an alien, stressful environment; and some
of the conditions called mental disorders may actually be adaptive in some
environments.

Two main problem areas were identified at the beginning of this essay. First,
whether the norms involved in mental disorder attributions are matters
of natural fact or are rather social; and second, whether the demarcation
between mental disorder and order is valid, particularly whether disorder after
all involves meaning/functionality. In relation to this second set of issues, it
has been suggested in this section that the evolutionary theoretic framework –
like the psychological – plainly highlights the likelihood that many aspects of
what appears to be disorder in fact include functionality, that is to say, order.
The evolutionary theoretic approach also has important implications for the
contrast between natural and social norms, but before considering these in
detail we first consider sociological approaches to mental illness.

2.6 Social order, deviance, and mental illness

Concepts of function and dysfunction in biology make a promising conceptual basis for the understanding of psychological disorder, and psychiatry's

roots in medicine inevitably draws it to notions of biological dysfunction, and to explanations of disruptions of function in terms of disease processes and other lesions. However, biology is not the only science to use distinctions of order and disorder: they pervade social science also, and while the psychological is grounded in the biological, it is also correct to say that the psychological is grounded in the social, in which case psychological disorder may involve not only biological dysfunction, but also may involve social disorder, usually called social deviance.

It would be reasonable to say that social order – the ways in which societies are organized and regulated – is the subject matter of the social sciences. Grand theories include those of the founders of sociology, Marx, Durkheim, and Weber, and diverse subsequent theories, more or less derivative, such as structural functionalism, applied to western and non-western societies, critical theory, ethnomethodology, and so on. The great variety in social theory reflects partly the diversity in societies under study, the cultural position of the theory itself, and methodological differences. In the variety are common themes relating to social organization and regulation, power, patterns of communication and shared practices, inclusion and exclusion, production and distribution of resources, inequalities, systems of law and other forms of social sanction. Models of basic processes of these kinds define social order and hence deviance, behaviour that is contrary to dominant social values and expectations, of which mental disorder is one, more or less distinct kind. However, because of the complexity and diversity of social theory there are no simple lessons to be learned about social disorder, nor about how this may relate to mental disorder, and the topic of mental disorder itself has received relatively little explicit attention. There are notable exceptions, however, and some of these will be reviewed briefly with the focus on issues closely relevant to the themes of the current essay.

It would be fair to say by way of introduction that from the 1960s onwards sociological approaches to the psychiatric notion of mental illness or disorder and its associated practices have generally been critical to hostile. There have been critiques along the following interconnected lines: that the modern western idea of madness has stripped it of meaning, a tendency consolidated by the medical model in psychiatry, which pathologizes the meaning in madness and in so-called mental illness generally, that with increasing psychiatric hegemony, its medical model pathologizes ordinary problems of living; that psychiatry and mental health services in practice have a political function, serving as a method of control of social deviance.

The most important critique and the best starting place is Michel Foucault's seminal study of the modern western idea of madness in his *Madness and Civilisation* (1965). Foucault's primary focus is on the period variously called the 'classical period', or the Age of Reason, or, by Roy Porter, 'the long eighteenth century' (Porter 1987) the period between roughly 1650 and 1800. Here is Foucault in his Introduction anticipating some of his key themes:

> In the serene world of mental illness, modern man no longer communicates with the madman . . . The man of reason delegates the physician to madness, thereby authorizing a relation only through the abstract universality of disease . . . As for a common language, there is no such thing . . . the constitution of madness as a mental illness, at the end of the eighteenth century, affords the evidence of a broken dialogue, posits the separation as already effected, and thrusts into oblivion all those stammered, imperfect words without fixed syntax in which the exchange between madness and reason was made. The language of psychiatry, which is a monologue of reason about madness, has been established only on the basis of such a silence.
>
> (1965, pp. xii–xiii)

These key themes in Foucault – that in modernity the meaning of madness is lost, and that psychiatry was constructed to manage it – may be briefly expanded on as follows.

In the Age of Reason, the prevailing value of rationality was understood in a way compatible with Christian, capitalist, bourgeois family values. What lay on the darker side of reason was deviant behaviour contrary to those values, the boundaries between them being policed by systems of monitoring and control. Differentiations between deviance due to criminality or other moral laxity and deviance attributed to illness were blurred. The critical point in Foucault is that in this western modernity 'madness' became defined negatively as *unreason*, as mere disorder, mere deficit, and hence madness lost its truth, its voice: it became silenced. In setting up the charge that western modernity's construction of madness excluded meaning, Foucault refers in the first chapter to earlier western ideas by way of contrast. He points to the well-known fact that in the Middle Ages, madness, like everything else, was embedded in the context of Christianity, and the other world of spirits, benign or demonic. This meaning of madness was lost, first to the humanist mind of the Renaissance, though in this brief period towards the end of the Middle Ages other meaningful forms of madness were recognized. Foucault cites with literary references four forms: romantic identification (as in Don Quixote), vain presumption, just punishment (Lady Macbeth), and desperate passion (Ophelia, Lear). These forms of meaning too, however, were lost to the rational mind of the Enlightenment. The Enlightenment view of reason had particular characteristics. Paradigms of reason were logic (the law of identity, mathematical deduction) and science (induction); reason was generally contrasted with passion and valued above it; reason was the mark of civilized man, civilization was valued over nature, and in all this, determination of what was rational or not inevitably used local norms.

The insane became physically segregated from civilization, in the eighteenth century, and, in greater numbers, in the nineteenth century asylums. Following Foucault's line of thought, the excessive rationality of the Enlightenment constructed madness as the negation of reason, essentially other, expelled from consciousness, hence it was expelled physically from civilization, out of the community, into the asylums. Further, and inevitably, Foucault's critique continues, there came into being a group who would alone relate to the mad and madness. These were originally religious reformers and the 'mad doctors', the competition between the two eventually being won by the latter, giving rise eventually to the profession of psychiatry. Foucault identifies two strands in the relationship between the mad and their keepers in the asylums: one social, the other medical. The insane were excluded from society, hence there was a need to recreate a society in the asylums, established at first explicitly as communities, modelled on the prevailing norms of social life and values of religious piety. The early asylums aimed to correct the irrational, mad, uncontrolled, antisocial, unreligious ways of the inmates, and to establish normal, sane habits. In any case, there was no question of understanding whatever truth there may be in madness, which by this time, as Foucault observes, was lost. There was emphasis on silencing mad talk, and on stopping mad behaviour, not by manacles, but by 'psychological' methods of authority, training, and instillation of guilt, suggesting Porter's 'mind-forged manacles' (Porter 1987). The second strand in the relationship between the patient and their keepers in the asylums was the medical. As the asylums multiplied they came increasingly under the control of the medical profession, consolidating the idea of insanity as being illness or disease. Traditional medical treatments continued – bloodletting, purging, vomiting, immersion, blistering – based on principles of purification, consolidation of spirits and fibres, though the rationale of such principles was obscure and untested, and the treatments were not well evidenced based. The consolidation and eventual dominance of the medical model of disease was inevitable, so this line of thought runs, to the extent that there no longer existed a meaningful context in which madness – and other forms of mental disorder – could be understood. Foucault suggests that the connection between these two strands in the patient–psychiatrist relationship – the one moral, social and religious, the other medical – was and continued to be problematic, that the former was dominant and the source of power, including the power to cure, though barely understood, and was mystified by the latter. From this obscure background modern psychiatry was born, hearing no meaning in madness, limited to talking about it only, to description of symptoms, classification and diagnosis – the 'monologue of reason about madness' to which Foucault refers in his Introduction (op. cit. p. xiii).

Foucault goes on, in later parts of his work, to note that Freud reversed just this feature, by having the patient speak and the doctor listen. However, Foucault adds a critical qualification, to the effect that psychoanalysis preserved the power relations of the asylums. On this he says:

> There remains, beyond the empty forms of positivist thought, only a single concrete reality: the doctor-patient couple in which all alienations are summarised, linked, and loosened. And it is to this degree that all nineteenth century psychiatry really converges on Freud, the first man to accept in all its seriousness the reality of the physician-patient couple, the first to consent not to look away nor to investigate elsewhere, the first not to attempt to hide it in a psychiatric theory that more or less harmonised with the rest of medical knowledge; the first to follow its consequences with absolute rigour. Freud demystified all the other asylum structures: he abolished silence and observation, he eliminated madness's recognition of itself in the mirror of its own spectacle, he silenced the instances of condemnation. But on the other hand he exploited the structure that enveloped the medical personage; he amplified its thaumaturgical virtues, preparing for its omnipotence a quasi-divine status. He focused upon the single presence – concealed behind the patient and above him, in an absence that is also a total presence – all the powers that had been distributed in the collective existence of the asylum . . . He did deliver the patient from the existence of the asylum within which his 'liberators' had alienated him; but he did not deliver him from what was essential in this existence; he regrouped its powers, extended them to the maximum by uniting them in the doctor's hands; he created the psychoanalytical situation where, by an inspired short-circuit, alienation becomes disalienating because, in the doctor, it becomes a subject.

> (op. cit., pp. 277–8)

This reading of Freud would illustrate how difficult it is to deliver two massive changes at once – the first change involved recognizing meaning in disorder, the second, which had to wait until later, has involved addressing the power imbalance.

The charge that the medical model in psychiatry serves to disqualify the meaning in madness, a process linked to social exclusion of the people so diagnosed, was given a profound sociohistorical interpretation by Foucault. But the same idea ran through other so-called anti-psychiatry critiques of the 1960s. Szasz (1961) questioned the legitimacy of the very idea of mental illness as used in psychiatry, and attacked the associated medicalization of what he described rather as comprehensible 'personal problems of living'. Laing (1960) reframed madness as being an understandable, indeed the only sane response to a confused and contradictory family life.

Sociological field studies in the same period seemed to reinforce the point. In the famous study by Rosenhan (1973) postgraduate students were trained to act somewhat mad with a view to getting themselves admitted to a psychiatric ward. They succeeded, though this was not such a surprise and not the point of the study, which was more to do with what happened next. The second part of the study protocol required the stooges, after being admitted, to cease acting mad, to behave normally instead, and they were eventually discharged as 'in remission'; the diagnostic label was used in assigning significance to what was effectively normal behaviour and talk, and they left with the label still attached. Rosenhan's study was highly influential, though heavily criticized. Its general findings seemed to be consistent with so-called labelling theory, also influential at the time, according to which a critical determinant of social deviance including mental illness is the effects of the labelling process itself: once deviant behaviour had been labelled as mental illness, this label modifies the actions of others towards the labelled person, creating further deviant behaviour.

An extension of these sociological critiques is that psychiatry with its medical model and diagnoses disqualifies and controls not only madness, but also common problems of living. This idea was already prominent in Szasz's early work, and has been elaborated by subsequent commentators, reacting to and increasingly directed towards the increasing size and hegemony of successive editions of the DSM. Kutchins and Kirk for example in their *Making us crazy* (1997) observe that the DSM has grown at such a rapid pace that it includes now over 300 disorders, amounting to the pathologizing of much of what we all do, and stretching the notion of mental disorder beyond breaking point. It has been observed that much of this expansion is driven by healthcare-related considerations, because, for example, access depends on diagnosis, so any condition that is deemed to require treatment gets included. In this case the driving concept is precisely 'what is deemed to require treatment' rather than mental disorder. A related complication often cited is that the pharmaceutical industry has a commercial interest in expanding the range of mental disorders to include more conditions that may be treated by its products, including conditions that may lie within the unhappy part of the normal range, rather than being true disorders. These points will be considered further in later chapters, Chapter 5 particularly.

In this context the theme of social control by psychiatry, evident in the critiques of Foucault, Laing and Szasz, continues to be emphasized. Kutchins and Kirk (1997), for example, consider examples of social control from the past that now appear as barely credible in their outrageousness, for instance the diagnosis of 'drapetomania' applied to enslaved people trying to escape (op. cit., p. 210). They point out, however, that similar charges may be made about more recent diagnostic practice. Feminist critiques of the DSM in the 1970s, for example, highlighted the fact that the commonest mental health problems, anxiety and depression, are much more common in women than in men, arguing that these diagnoses amount to a pathologizing of female stereotypes by male-dominated professional groups. Similar arguments can be used in the case of other groups that are over-represented among those labelled as having mental disorders, the poor, and ethnic minority communities, with these characteristics often confounded (Kutchins and Kirk, op. cit., Chapter 7).

These lines of sociological criticism are diverse and controversial – more or less fair – but in any case they converge on the charge, echoing Foucault, that psychiatry defines its 'conditions of interest' fundamentally according to social values, using categories of pathology and associated practices to disqualify and control what threatens prevailing social power structures, or to enhance its own interests. They are often known as anti-psychiatry critiques, but in their most interesting form they are, as in Foucault, charges against the society that uses psychiatry in this way.

While some of the critiques of psychiatry focused more on the processes involved within psychiatry itself, diagnosis and management, others focused more on the processes within society, including those that lead to involvement of services. With this latter focus, many of the sociological approaches acknowledged or emphasized that critical in the folk attribution of mental disorder (by whatever name) was presumed absence of meaning, some notion that ordinary forms of (meaningful) behaviour and reasoning have run out. Second, however, it was supposed that this meaninglessness was a socially moderated domain, generated and maintained by processes including silencing, disqualifying, social exclusion, and so on – the contrast being with causation by lesions and diseases. These social processes were located in society generally, more proximally in the family, and (eventually) in psychiatric institutions, where they were cemented by the expert's diagnosis. Third, the question arises to what extent this constructed meaninglessness was in fact meaningful. For Foucault there was bound to be silence from the domain of the meaningless. Other approaches obviously allowed for meaning in this domain, as in Rosenhan's study whether the obviously sane apparently could not escape the effects of diagnosis nor therefore the asylum itself. Laing occupied an extreme dialectical position, with the mad sane and the sane mad. Psychoanalytic views of projection were applied at a social level to bolster the view that the meaningless and associated characteristics were projected onto some individual by the social group, in a process sometimes called 'scapegoating' at the time. In brief, sociological critiques of psychiatry did tend to suppose that folk psychiatry like expert psychiatry equated mental illness (at least in severe forms) with meaninglessness, but supposed that this domain was produced by social power processes and structures, not by medical lesions and disease processes – this being exactly the error of pathologizing the social.

Other methodologies in the social sciences were studying problems of order- or meaning-making and communication at the micro level. Garfinkel's ethnomethodological studies in the 1960s illustrated the production of social action in everyday situations including the search for and production of meaning in social interactions, failure of which brought attributions such as 'crazy' into play. Communication between individuals in concrete day to day social situations, the finding of meaning in the other, is the essential basis for our social being, for cooperation and contact, and it is interesting to note that Garfinkel's work in this fundamental domain was influenced by his reading of later work by Wittgenstein. It may be inferred, further, that the methodological rule to find meaning in social interaction, and the disastrous consequences that can follow failure, would apply in all kinds of groups, regardless of social organization and belief, though by all means the culture would help determine where the limits of the meaningful are experienced at any one time. That is to say, there is probably a universally valid problematic here, albeit one that is sensitive to cultural variations. Several sociological books and papers on mental illness in the 1970s and 1980s, drawing on the insights of ethnomethodology made the point that the concept is tied not just to social deviance, but essentially to problems of disruption of meaning and intelligibility.

The anti-psychiatry critiques charge psychiatry with stripping the meaning out of madness, and out of ordinary problems of living, but the broader sociological commentaries have the people involved too. The attitude may then be outrage and blame, or sympathy. Why do people take their family members, or themselves, to mental health services? The simple answer is just that the people, before psychiatry gets involved, find themselves or their kin in highly distressing situations and have typically been unable to understand what is going in normal terms, and unable to find a way of making things better. There are ruptures in the narratives of normality and meaning, in the understanding of a person in terms of their beliefs and desires, or in terms of reasonable beliefs and desires, or in terms of their previous characters, or in a child's development or behaviour compared with others; and so on. These ruptures are typically associated with profound distress or impairment of functioning, relative to the person's own norms or to the norms of the social group. Illness or disorder make their appearance as a particular explanation of failure to meet norms of personal or social functioning. In fact what people recognize is close to the phenomena that are well described in the psychiatric manuals as illustrated and discussed in the previous chapter. That is to say, the people fail to perceive meaningful connections, rationality, appropriate intentionality, normality compared with the peer group, and these are precisely what the psychiatric manuals capture in their characterizations of 'clinically significant' symptoms and syndromes. This line of thought would defend psychiatry against the charge of finding no meaning in madness (or generally in conditions warranting diagnosis), by remarking that psychiatry is just reflecting in this respect what is happening in society at large. The suggestion is just that the psychiatric manuals refine what is already evident to the people; that expert, medical psychiatry simply reflects, and refines, folk psychiatry.

Sociological critiques of psychiatry achieve what one would expect of them: they uncover the social contexts and social dynamics of psychiatry, bringing out that psychiatry like any other form of discourse and practice is embedded in social power structures and subject to their influence, and that it is itself a power structure, interacting with other forms of control of social deviance. These sociological insights are essential for understanding psychiatry's discourse and practice, and since the 1960s and 1970s they have been increasingly incorporated into thinking within and around the mental health professions.

However, while sociological critiques cast much valuable light on the social processes around mental illness, they have a fundamental methodological limitation. What is visible from the perspective of the social sciences are social systems, their structures and functions. At a macro level, the systems are large institutions involved with problems of health, poverty and education, for example. At a micro level they include subcultural organizations, families and couple relationships. The inevitable consequence of the social systemic approach, whether at macro or micro levels, is that dysfunction in the individual, individual distress or disability, is bound to be framed as a characteristic of, created by, group processes. In this sense at least there is a fundamental tension between social science and medicine, including psychiatry. It shows up in many ways, including in clinical practice, for example in the reluctance of systemic family therapists to assign a diagnosis to an individual in the family – a reluctance more or less warranted depending on the kind of case.

The absence of a notion of individual dysfunction – the invisibility of the phenomena which the notion seeks to capture – underlies the charge that the social-systemic critiques of mental illness fail to its reality; fail to see, for example, unbearable psychotic anxiety, hallucinatory and delusional persecution that lead people to kill themselves; or the despair and depression of an individual worn down by trauma or chronic stressors; or the unmanageable distress of the child with autism trying to cope with change that is – for him – too much. The non-individualistic, social-systemic gaze – to be contrasted with the medical – cannot see this individual suffering, or if it does, re-focuses on the group processes involved.

Reconciling social group processes on the one hand and individual agency on the other – or, in the present context, disruption of agency – is a familiar problematic in the social sciences and generally. But it is further complicated by specific assumptions about the construction of meaning, and hence of meaninglessness. The social sciences have tended to dominate the domain of meaning-production, while the natural sciences dominated the domain of causality, this being an aspect of the meaning/causality dichotomy, considered earlier in this chapter. All meaningful content, all interpretation, was taken to be constructed by social processes, hence also its contrasts: the meaningless, the irrational, abnormality of mind. From this point of view, to the extent that concepts of mental illness and disorder turned on perceived absence of meaning, they were bound to be matters determined in social domains: on that particular pitch – elucidating the construction or the deconstruction of meaning – social science was the only player. For this to change, it was necessary first, for psychological science to include content in its domain, and second, to extend the horizons of psychology to envisage mental content caused by nature as well as culture. These changes have happened in the new information processing, cognitive psychology paradigm, subsequently embedded in an evolutionary context, linked to the science of genetics.

2.7 **Evolutionary psychology and social norms**

Here is a passage from Durkheim, quoted by the evolutionary psychologists John Tooby and Leda Cosmides in a chapter entitled 'The psychological foundations of culture', to illustrate what they call the Standard Social Science Model:

> It is clear . . . that the general characteristics of human nature participate in the work of elaboration from which social life results. But they are not the cause of it, nor do they give it its special form; they only make it possible. Collective representations, emotions, and tendencies are caused not by certain states of the consciousness of individuals but by the conditions in which the social group, in its totality, is placed. Such actions can, of course, materialise only if the individual natures are not resistant to them; *but these individual natures are merely the indeterminate material that the social factor moulds and transforms. Their contribution consists exclusively in very general attitudes, in vague and consequently plastic predispositions* which, by themselves, if other agents did not intervene could not take on the definite and complex forms which characterise social phenomena.

> Durkheim (1895/1962, pp. 105–6) quoted, with emphasis added, in Tooby and Cosmides (1992, pp. 24–5)

Key themes in this quotation include the framing of mental life (representations, emotions, and tendencies) as 'collective', not individual – the individual is not the focus in social science, as remarked at the end of the previous section. Further, mental life (as collective) is determined not by human nature, but by social factors; human nature in general and in individuals is vague, indeterminate, plastic material, made specific in and by the social group.

Tooby and Cosmides go on to characterize the Standard Social Science Model and its justification in detail, and they then contrast it with a new proposal, belonging to evolutionary psychology, which they call the Integrated Causal Model. According to this

> Culture is the manufactured product of evolved psychological mechanisms situated in individuals living in groups. Culture and human social behaviour is complexly variable, but not because the human mind is a social product, a blank slate, or an externally programmed general-purpose computer, lacking a richly defined evolved structure. Instead, human culture and social behaviour is richly variable because it is generated by an incredibly intricate, contingent set of functional programmes that use and process information from the world, including information that is provided both intentionally and unintentionally by other human beings.
>
> Tooby and Cosmides (op. cit. p. 24)

An intention behind this statement is to soften the contrast between generality and specificity which has tended to fix the terms in the nature/culture debate. Social science approaches, most obviously in anthropology, delight in variation, in diversity among cultures and cultural practices. The more variation, the more diversity, the more are illustrated the formative roles of local influences, cultural rather than a universal human nature. Conversely, evolutionary approaches – when freed from racism – tend to emphasize the universality of human behaviour. This debate is probably best regarded as a dialectical matter, with what we have in common constantly qualified by differences, and our differences constantly qualified by what we have in common.

The dialectical play has a complex topology, however. There may be examples of mental functioning and behaviour that are entirely evolved, natural, to be contrasted with examples that are wholly attributable to socialization processes. This would illustrate the simplest kind of relation between the natural and the social, amounting to none. In practice however it is more likely that the two are interwoven, in two main kinds of ways, which may themselves interact, as follows.

First, because human evolution has been in social groups, some evolved functions are presumably social. Here the contrast between the natural and the social breaks down. Second, evolved factors may contribute a degree of specific content, but social factors elaborate this in diverse ways. In this kind of case the relative contributions of the two kinds of influence are variable, and the evolved content is typically identified at a more abstract level than the concrete social expression. These possibilities can be illustrated by kinds of mental functioning and practice, with particular reference in the present context to contents that are sometimes implicated in mental disorder.

Evolutionary psychology supposes that the brain–mind has evolved in a modular way, comprising many distinct though interconnected information processing systems which are purpose-/domain-specific. The methodological assumption, consistent with roots in Darwinian evolutionary biology, is that mental modules are adaptations, that is, they have been selected because they serve adaptive functions in the species' environment. However, and this is the main point for the present purpose, some of these modules are essentially involved with social domains and purposes, possible candidates being such as suckling, joint attention, attachment, mind-reading, group cohesion, altruism, concern for others, aggression, and so on – it is a long list. In brief, some forms of social activity are evolved, and genetically inherited, or at least there are strong genetic influences on them. However, in an evolutionary theoretic framework, what is evolved – what is passed on by genetic transmission from one generation to the next – is a clear kind of natural trait. One connotation of 'natural' is: what is with us at birth (innate). The general direction here is to blur the traditional distinction between what is natural and what is social, or again, between nature (what is innate) and culture (what is cultivated).

The interplay between human nature and culture is interestingly at its most vigorous in just those domains where we confront our biological nature and have to manage it with all available resources. In domains such as mating behaviour, birth, child-rearing, illness, eating, competition over resources; and so on, we are in our most biological states, and we are most culturally active. The universality exists at some level of abstraction, while the specifics are real. All societies engage in eating and in mating behaviours, and so on, but how they do it in practice, all the various rules and regulations, show wide variation. On the other hand, it can also be said that eating and mating behaviour are realities common to all. Salman Rushdie, in a novel that plays with cultural diversity, appearances and fantasy also has the narrator remark on just one fact: 'Death, the great fact' (Rushdie 1989, p. 527).

One source of variation in cultural practices is understandable directly from within the evolutionary psychology approach itself, namely, that evolved patterns of behaviour are often in conflict with one another and have to be prioritized. Take for example the complex anxiety response, comprising evaluation of a situation as threatening, physiological arousal in preparation for an appropriate response, such as fleeing or fighting, and the behavioural outcome itself. The anxiety response is a clear enough instance of an evolved information-processing mechanism and response pattern, but it also clearly shows variation at a cultural level. The behavioural outcome is not a fixed pattern invariably triggered by specific stimuli, but is mediated at least in human beings by other considerations, such as the need to protect dependents from threat, to win esteem in the social group, and so on. The pros and cons of behavioural routines have to be balanced, and how these issues are weighed in particular circumstances typically depends on values of the social group. Or again, the tendency to be aggressive when there is something to be gained, for example, may lead to violent and destructive attack, but it has to be weighed against other aims, other values, such as respect for life and property in the social group. While the environment of evolutionary adaptiveness is referred to in the singular it is obvious enough that the aims of and tasks undertaken by our ancestors in it were many and various. So it was then, presumably, and so it is now: and ends and means are sometimes mutually exclusive, so that responding in one way in a particular situation would preclude another; some goals are achieved at the expense of others. Life is full of choices, limitations, and compromises: between aggression and negotiation, selfishness and concern, between aggression and fear of punishment, between rest or play or work, between fearful avoidance and courage; and so on and on. Perseverance in extreme fear against formidable odds, as opposed to flight, may appear to be a definite failure of an evolved mechanism, but it seems so only while we consider the 'anxiety system' in isolation, but for complex social beings it never is in isolation – the anxious fleeing response may be over-ruled by loyalty to the group under threat. There are many possibilities even in those cases, and not less in those cases, where the range of behavioural outcomes is evolved.

The anxiety response can also be used to illustrate variation in relative strengths of influence of the natural and the social in the case of the emotions. At a general, abstract level the anxiety response still has a specific content, to do with detection of threat and fleeing, fighting, or more sophisticated coping. However there is variation in content even at this level: fear of the dark, heights, and animals may be considered among the most primitive, the most natural, independent of culture – but other content, such as social anxiety, characterized by fear of embarrassment of the self in the social group, is clearly socialized, and subject to wide cultural variation. Emotions such as guilt, remorse, pride, associated with blame and praise – the so-called 'moral emotions' – likewise presumably have a natural, evolved basis, but the extent of cultural overlay, cultural meanings and interpretations, is substantial.

There is another major source of variation which criss-crosses an already complex picture, namely, individual differences, this being an expression of the way that the psychological level spans the biological and the social.

Explanations restricted to general human nature (for example the general nature of the anxiety response) emphasize what we all have in common, with no attention to individual variation. Explanations at a social level tend exactly to focus on similarities at a cultural or subcultural level, and individual differences – psychological differences – are again unattended to. The gap in both approaches is addressed by psychology, emphasizing individual variation. For example, prioritizing of incompatible behaviours, whether for example to fight to protect one's comrades or flee from harm's way takes place not only at a cultural contextual level, but also at an individual level; different individuals – with the same general human nature, in the same cultural group, in the same context – do different things.

These and related issues are played out in the new science of genetics, the current expression of our evolutionary history. Behavioural genetic studies have shown that all or practically all psychological phenotypes including many relevant to psychiatry, have some genetic contribution to individual differences, though the extent varies widely, in a range something like between 20–80 per cent. The remaining variance is attributable to environmental factors, in a broad sense, amounting to non-genetic, including such as biological pre-natal environment, postnatal diet, and interpersonal processes involved in infant care and child-rearing. There is no a priori answer to the question of the extent of genetic influence, or to the question of the extent and nature of the relevant environmental (non-genetic) factors – it is all a matter for the science.

Genetics elaborates the methodologies of psychology and social science. As noted above, explanations restricted to general human nature emphasize what we all have in common, explanations at a social level focus on similarities at a cultural or subcultural level, while psychology has attended to individual variation. Genetics methodology introduces more complexity, subtlety and interactions. It is sensitive to differences between groups, between families, and between individuals. Psychology, specifically in its emphasis on learning, on acquired behaviours, is sensitive most straightforwardly to individual differences arising from distinct learning histories. Combined with genetics, however, psychology can recognize both learning histories and genetic/temperamental differences as sources of individual variation. These various kinds of explanations are combined in the new biopsychosocial science paradigm, which can envisage similarities and differences at the social, subcultural, family and individual levels, the relative role of each and their interactions being in principle determinable by research programmes employing appropriately designed studies.

The extent to which the genetic and the social are intertwined is underlined in various recent research programmes in behavioural and molecular genetics.

For example findings are emerging on gene–environment interactions. The term 'interaction' here refers to statistical interaction, whereby the effect of a variable, whether genetic or environmental, is modified by another. So for example, genetic influences on risk for depression may be evident only in the presence of childhood adversities (Caspi *et al.* 2003). There can be various interpretations of such interactions: individuals with one genetic variant may be more susceptible than those with another variant to the effects of adverse experiences such as childhood trauma; alternatively genetic influences may be evident only in the presence of particular types of environmental condition; a third possibility is that there may simply be variation in responsiveness to social environments, whether supportive or adverse, that is to some degree accounted for by genetic variations. Also work in molecular genetics with animals has indicated that generally the replication, translation and expression of genes are typically affected by environmental factors in a broad sense, present not only at birth and not just in the early months or first few years, but in developmental maturation over many years. These environmental factors may include such as physical features in the environment (such as toxins of various kinds), biological factors (such as diet), and also social processes including infant-rearing practices and subsequent social experience. It is generally assumed that these environmental factors affect the influence of genes on brain development and maturation.

In brief, variations in behaviour from birth forwards are affected not just by genetic influences, but by interplay between genes and environment including the social environment and socialization processes within it. The genetics paradigm, like the associated paradigms of evolutionary biology and psychology, breaks up the idea that psychological phenotypes are determined by natural/evolved factors alone, and the natural–social divide itself.

2.8 **Annotated bibliography**

Following an Introduction and overview of the chapter, section 2.2 considered the sciences 'basic to psychiatry' – psychology, genetics, neuroscience, medicine – focusing on what they say or imply about the notion of disorder. Regarding psychology the general points made may be found in any clinical psychology textbook such as Powell and Lindsey (2005) and the extensive Hersen and Bellack (1998). Figure 2.1 – the statistical normal distribution – is copied from the entry under that heading in the web-based Wilkipedia (2006). Basic theory of genetics and application to psychiatry can be found in introductory texts such as Plomin *et al.* (2001), and recent papers include e.g. Bolton *et al.* (2007). Papers on neuroimaging including consideration of what these techniques reveal about causation and pathology include

Carpenter (1987), Fodor (1999), Bechtel and Stufflebeam (2001), and Honey *et al.* (2002). It is noted in the text that the medical model in psychiatry has a range of meanings, but a major interpretation of it (not the only one) has the notion of a disease entity as fundamental. Critiques of the medical model generally include Engel (1977), and commentaries on its application in psychiatry include Guze (1992). A major focus of the essay, the naturalist approaches to mental and physical dysfunctions taken by Boorse and Wakefield definitions, touch on the medical model, for example in the debate between Wakefield and Follette and Houts, cited in the Annotated bibliography at the end of Chapter 1.

The third section of the chapter – on problems of mind, meaning and causation – is intended to explicate the way that current biobehavioural sciences has resolved them in the last 50 years or so in the information-processing/cognitive paradigm. The approach is historical and expository, not primarily conceptual or philosophical. The philosophical literature in the US/UK analytic tradition in roughly the same period (the last 30 years or so), is full of work in and around the problem of mental and semantic causation. Key players include Davidson, Dennett, Putnam and Fodor, each of whom has proposed one or more models of mental causation/explanation, with some strengths and some difficulties. In my view there are two main features that distinguish these philosophical approaches from what I take to be the position of the behavioural sciences. One is that the philosophical approaches retain allegiance to physicalism, the idea that fundamentally all causation is physical, running according to physical laws. The biobehavioural sciences, however, as noted in the text, use causal (regulatory) principles that depend on information carrying, principles that are consistent with physical laws but which are not themselves so – they can fail to apply without any physical laws being broken. The second contrast between current models of mental causation in the US/UK analytic philosophy tradition and what I take to be the position of the behavioural sciences has to do with what concepts of mind are supposed to be for. In the scientific tradition, cognitive (mental) states enter theory because of their role is explaining/predicting behaviour, while there are strong philosophical traditions that link mind essentially to principles of rationality. There is of course much to be said on all these matters – the point here is mainly to say that there is a large philosophical literature on the topics of mind, meaning, and causation, apart from and somewhat at odds with the intended gloss given here of their treatment in the sciences. The material in this essay is covered in more detail in previous material by the present author, and co-author, including Bolton and Hill (2004) and Bolton (2003), where extensive references to related literature may be found.

The fourth section of the chapter explicates the varieties of explanation of disorder by drawing on the hugely influential work of Daniel Dennett on explanatory stances (Dennett 1987, 1988). Again the treatment in the text is based on material from Bolton and Hill (2004), and also in Bolton (2001), where references to related material may be found. Reference is made to the diversity of current models of psychopathology, emphasising that they implicate a diverse range of interacting causal pathways. In Dennett's terms, these causal pathways include physical stance explanations, referring to lower-level disruption of intentionality, such as by neural lesions or disease processes; also design stance explanations, including genetic influences on brain development and behaviour, and temperamental differences typically as a function of the normal statistical distribution of traits in the population, with these design characteristics complicated by differences in individual learning history; lastly, there are components of causal models which refer to cognitive processing and content (for example depressive or depressogenic appraisals and beliefs), invoked from the intentional stance. There are many models/partial models of many conditions that attempt to track these three broad kinds of causal pathway, each comprising distinctive types within it, and the various combinations of interactions between them. Illustrative papers (selecting more or less randomly from many hundreds) include Blair *et al.* (2005) on psychopathy; Hill (2002) on conduct disorder; Murray (1994), Garety *et al.* (2001) and Read *et al.* (2005) on schizophrenia; Hill and Frith (2003), and Happé *et al.* (2006) on autism; Van der Kolk (1996), and Ehlers and Clark (2000) on PTSD; Bolton (1996), Hollander *et al.* (2007) and Westenberg *et al.* (2007) on OCD; O'Keane (2000) and Kendler *et al.* (2002) on depression; Sagvolden *et al.* (2005) and Timimi and Taylor (2004) on ADHD; Antony and Stein (2005) and Chen *et al.* (2006) on anxiety disorders. Textbooks with review chapters on many conditions include Rutter and Taylor (2005); Gelder, Lopez-Ibor and Andreasen (2003), and Andreasen and Black (2006). Increasingly models of psychopathology include a developmental perspective and developmental psychopathology has become a discipline – a multidiscipline – in its own right; theory, method and application to many conditions can be found in Cicchetti and Cohen (2006).

The fifth section – on implications of evolutionary theory for disorder – focuses particularly on the large variety of pathways to current dysfunction that may be envisaged from the evolutionary theoretic framework, and is heavily indebted as stated in the text to papers by Richters and Hinshaw (1999) and Cosmides and Tooby (1999). The radical option opened up in the evolutionary theoretic approach is that mental disorders may be more adaptive than apparent at first sight, given that they have not been de-selected.

The recommended methodology from the evolutionary theoretic perspective is generally to search for the functional, adaptive nature of biological and biopsychological processes, even where they appear – at first glance – to have run out. In this context it may be that the idea of biological disadvantage plays a role, but arguably it is unlikely that action as a whole, including action in much of what we call mental disorder, will carry biological disadvantage: for biological systems in general are geared towards adaptiveness, and biologically disadvantageous behaviour as such is likely – other things being equal – to have been de-selected. Wilson (1993) presents the case for saying that insofar as traits show prevalence rates beyond what is expected as rates of mutation (shown in Hardy–Weinberg calculations), or an unusual range of phenotypic reaction, the implication is that they have or are at least associated with advantages in the environment of evolutionary adaptiveness. Some papers and books on evolutionary approaches to psychiatry are referred to in the text. References for evolutionary theoretic approaches to particular psychiatric conditions mentioned in the text are, for sociopathic personality disorder, Blair (1995), Blair *et al.* (2005), and Mealey (1995); for anxiety disorders, Nesse (1987) and Marks and Nesse (1994); for hypothesized evolved social functions of depression, Price *et al.* (1994) and Watson and Andrews (2002); and for schizophrenia, cerebral lateralization and the acquisition of language, Crow (1997). A useful collection of papers including many of the above is in Baron-Cohen (1997). General principles involved in applying evolutionary approaches to psychopathology are excellently discussed by Leckman and Mayes (1998). The focus of the discussion in the section is on implications of evolutionary theory for disorder, and key reading on theoretical issues and speculative application to psychiatry includes works cited in the text and above. The essay does not attempt a review of evolutionary psychology, key statements and critical discussions of which of which may found for example in Barkow, Cosmides and Tooby (1992), Gould (1991, 1997); Plotkin (1998), Buss (1999) and Buller (2005); see also references relevant to section 2.7 below.

The sixth section of the chapter on sociological approaches to mental disorder cites some key references in the text. Quotations from Foucault are from Foucault (1965). A full English translation of the original French work has recently been published (Foucault 2006). Apart from Foucault's work, key contributions to the 1960s/ early 1970s debates on psychiatry included Laing (1960), Goffman (1961), Szsaz (1961), Rosenhan (1973), with critique from Spitzer (1976), and Scheff's labelling theory (Scheff 1966), recently qualified (Scheff 2005). Hacking's sophisticated work on 'looping effects' in the constructions of kinds, including mental disorders (Hacking 1999), may be regarded as a balanced formulation of some key insights of labelling theory (Charland 2004; Sadler 2004b). Reactive defences of psychiatry following the 1960s critiques included Clare (1976), Roth and Kroll (1986), and Resnek (1991). Reference is made in the text to Garfinkel's ethnomethodological studies in the 1960s see e.g. (Garfinkel 1967) – and to subsequent work on mental illness in the 1970s and 1980s, e.g. Morgan (1975), Coulter (1973), and Ingleby (1982). Recent books on the sociology of psychiatry include Kutchins and Kirk (1997), Bowers (1998), and Horwitz (2002).

Section 2.7 deals with implications of evolutionary psychology for the linkages between the biological, the psychological and the social. This is a much broader set of issues than the specific question of implications for disorder (considered in 2.5), involving core claims of evolutionary psychology which have generated much debate and controversy. Controversial issues include the question of 'universal human nature', the validity of strong adaptationism especially in the psychological realm, and the validity of brain/mind modularity (of the extensive kind envisaged by classic statements of evolutionary psychology). Access to the extensive literature on these and related topics may be gained via the works on evolutionary psychology cited above (in the paragraph on section 2.5), and other works specifically on the relation between biology, psychology and culture include Weingart *et al.* (1997). The points made in Section 2.7 are intended not to rely too heavily on particular positions in these debates, but rather to address specifically the validity of the distinction between what is 'natural' (evolved) and what is 'social' – this taken to be relevant to 1960s and subsequent debates about the norms involved in defining mental disorder. Two main claims are made about the implications of the general evolutionary approach in psychology. First, that because human evolution has been in social groups, some evolved functions are social, in which case the contrast between the natural and the social breaks down. Second, evolved factors may contribute a degree of specific content, but social factors elaborate this in diverse ways, with the evolved content typically identifiable at a more abstract level than the concrete social expression. My intention and hope is that these general claims are plausible in the general evolutionary approach in psychology independently of specific controversial positions. The approach taken in the second claim above is similar to the one proposed by Ronald Mallon and Stephen Stich (2000) in reconciling Tooby and Cosmides' criticism of the Standard Social Science Model with 'social constructionism'. I think it is the right way to go, working well for example in understanding emotions such as anxiety, discussed in the text. Arguments for and against the universal nature of emotional expression are traditionally conducted in terms of whether there are basic emotions (e.g. Stein and Oatley 1992). Variation in cultural expression is most evident in the non-basic ones, including the moral emotions (e.g. Fisher *et al.* 1999). Discussion of the emotions form various angles including the evolutionary psychological is in Griffiths (1997).

Section 2.7 also includes discussion of psychological/psychiatric genetics, general reading for which is given above (in the paragraph on section 2.2). The main topic of the section is interactions of various kinds between evolved and social determinants of behaviour, and there are various research programmes in genetics on this general theme. They include work on gene–environment interactions, including in the development of psychopathology. Kinds of interactions and methodologies required to detect them are elucidated in Rutter, Moffit and Caspi (2005), which includes review of some related work on gene expression; scientific papers on specific psychiatric conditions include Caspi *et al.* (2003), Jaffee *et al.* (2005) and Kim-Cohen *et al.* (2006).

Chapter 3

Mental disorder
and human nature

3.1 The legacy of the 1960s crisis: natural and social norms

The anti-psychiatry critiques of the 1960s attacked the medical model in psychiatry for stripping the meaning out of so-called mental illness, disqualifying and dehumanizing the people labelled in this way. They attacked the concept of mental illness itself, the self-serving pressures in medical practice, and the injustice of the massive social exclusion project in the asylums. These attacks coincided with other major developments that in effect signified changes to correct some of identified excesses. These included, in no particular order:

◆ The closing down of the asylums and the beginnings of care in the community

◆ The beginnings of the movements in which patients regained a voice: the survivor movement, service-user groups, consumer groups.

◆ Increased attention to reliability of diagnoses, this requiring use of agreed behavioural criteria rather that esoteric speculations as to aetiology. This had the effect of demystifying the diagnostic process, opening it in principle and gradually in practice to non-medical researchers and clinicians, even to the public

◆ The split between medical and psychological models was beginning to break down with the emergence of the new cognitive paradigm

◆ Growing influence of evolutionary theoretic ideas in psychiatry, including but not only in psychiatric genetics, emphasizing constructs such as normal variation and adaptiveness.

All of these developments and others in various ways contributed to breaking down the excesses of the medical model in psychiatry, to the recognition that what was called mental illness was or may be in some respects normal, meaningful and valid, not just senseless deficit caused by medical disease or lesion.

Breaking down excesses of the medical model was one matter, however – there never was a question of its retiring from the scene: there were and there remain many reasons why the medical model in psychiatry could not retire. Mental health services remain organized around the training and practice of psychiatrists as medically qualified practitioners, as are related institutions like health insurance, medico-legal pleas, etc. These are the kinds of facts on the ground emphasized in sociological commentaries of psychiatry. In brief, the medical model could not disappear, because it was in practice psychiatry, and psychiatry is there to deal with real, important problems, of all the kinds codified in the psychiatry manuals, people suffering from everything from chronic schizophrenia to an episode of work stress-related depression, breaking down in their lives, needing help of many kinds. While some psychiatric practices could be construed as social control, such as detention of people suffering from a mental illness acting dangerously on the streets, so many other kinds of case could not easily, but are rather healthcare responses to people taking themselves or their children or other dependents to mental health services in unmanageable distress and having tried everything they know to sort things out without enough or without any success. The protection that society occasionally needs, and all the psychological distress, never was going to go away, and help was sought from services entirely formed and run in terms of the medical model.

At around the same time – the 1950s into the 1960s – the pharmaceutical industry developed drugs for the management of psychoses, a critical factor in the closure of the asylums. Subsequently, medications were developed that seemed to alleviate common mental health problems such as anxiety and depression. Effects of these medications were tested in randomized controlled trials, signalling the emergence of psychiatry from the netherworld of untested treatments, placebo effects and frank quackery into the light of evidence-based medicine. In brief, psychiatry began to have tested medical treatments to offer, all the more reason that psychiatry embedded in the medical model was not going to fade away but on the contrary went from strength to strength.

Thus a tense dynamic emerged after the 1960s. On the one hand there were various developments that were working to dismantle core features of the medical model in psychiatry, as sketched above, but on the other the medical model was entirely embedded in social institutions and the problems it was designed to solve were ever-pressing, and it had more to offer, and more promised. These stresses and strains showed up in many ways, but one of particular relevance here is the fate of the notion of 'mental illness'. Under the pressure of the anti-psychiatry movement, and the criticism of Thomas Szasz in particular, the term mental illness gave way to the term 'mental disorder', including in the DSM and ICD, though it never was clear how far this was more than just a terminological shift. Whichever term is used – mental illness or mental disorder – underlying issues remained unresolved. While to a large extent mainstream psychiatry and its medical model found compatibility with psychological models of the conditions of interest, and increasingly absorbed those with scientific credentials, there has been something of a stand-off between the medical model and that theme in the 1960s anti-psychiatry critiques that attacked the medicalization of what were regarded as fundamentally social phenomena. The unresolved question was whether the terms mental illness or mental disorder signify conditions that are indeed matters of medical fact, or whether they are misleadingly applied to conditions that are defined rather by social norms and values.

The problem resurfaced in the 1970s in protests about the inclusion of homosexuality as a mental disorder in the DSM, giving rise to the first attempts to define mental disorder for the purposes of the diagnostic manuals. For some time the issue of medical vs social norms went relatively quiet, at least compared to the furores of the 1960s and 1970s, but it has been played out in a literature concerned with the definition of *mental disorder*. This problem of definition is familiar in the introductions to the DSM and the ICD – considered above in Chapter 1, and to be considered further in the next chapter (4.1) – but there has also been a small but significant cross-disciplinary literature exploring the problem in detail. The underlying issues have been those bequeathed by the controversies in the 1960s, and the subsequent debate has focused on the question of whether the terms mental illness or mental disorder are based in some natural fact, as opposed to being – entirely – a matter of social norms and values.

On this, for example Kendell wrote:

> The most fundamental issue, and also the most contentious one, is whether disease and illness are normative concepts based on value judgements, or whether they are value-free scientific terms; in other words, whether they are biomedical terms or socio-political ones.

> Kendell (1986, p. 25)

The superficial problem facing the view that mental illness or mental disorder is only deviance from social norms is that it fails to discriminate between kinds of explanation of social deviance, specifically the difference between attribution to the agent's free choice, and attribution to some psychological dysfunction which the person cannot help. Social deviance can be regarded as laziness, criminality, eccentricity, or selfishness, but these are distinguished from the person being unable to keep to normal social expectations because of some mental dysfunction. A social theorist may deny that this distinction is very robust, and there is much to be said for that, but nevertheless a distinction it is, and it counts against just collapsing the difference between mental disorder and social deviance. A secondary manoeuvre by the social theorist who wished to pursue this point would then be to say that norms of mental function, including the distinction between attribution of agency and attribution to incapacity through illness, are in any case just another expression of social norms – so the point holds. To evaluate this move consider what social norms are.

Social norms define what is valued in society, especially what is valued by the dominant social grouping. What is valued means what is expected of a person, what is frowned upon or otherwise sanctioned if violated; what is considered appropriate, rational, proportionate, and so on. They apply not only to codes of conduct, but also to individual psychological matters such as displays of emotion, giving reasons for action, holding beliefs. Of course these norms are frequently implicit, and, to complicate matters, when they are made explicit, they are not always thought of as social norms. In some kinds of critical case, such as concentration of wealth and power, there is pressure not to think of social norms as being such, insofar as this may imply the possibility of change, but to think of them rather as built into the nature of things – into human nature, the nature of society, economic processes, etc. So it is at least possible that what we take for granted as being a natural fact, especially when it comes to 'the nature of the human condition' may after all be a feature of social organization.

A grand illustration of this is the wishful irony of Plato's 'noble lie' that would persuade citizens of the Republic that their various positions in society were due to their natural – metallic – qualities and thereby fixed, inhibiting unregulated social change.

> And yet I hardly know how to find the audacity or the words to speak and undertake to persuade first the rulers themselves and the soldiers and then the rest of the city that in good sooth all our training and educating of them were things that they imagined and that happened to them as it were in a dream, but that in reality at that time they were down within the earth being moulded and fostered . . . We will say in our tale that . . . God in fashioning those of you who are fitted to rule mingled gold in their generation, for which reason they are the most precious – but in the helpers silver, and iron and brass in the farmers and other craftsmen.

> Plato, Republic III (1930, 414d–415a; trans. Paul Shorey)

Could the people be got to believe this? Plato replies: 'Not in the first generation, but you might succeed with the second and later generations.' It takes a while for these things to bed down.

A less grand illustration of the interplay between facts of nature and social values is one often cited in the literature on the concept of disease: the changing representation of masturbation. Nineteenth century physicians regarded the behaviour as unnatural, as a disorder or disease, while some time later other representations came into play. This is one of a number of examples which seem to illustrate social values masquerading as medical facts. However, a defender of the distinction, Christopher Boorse – whose 'naturalist' approach to disease is the topic of the next section – writes on masturbation and other examples as follows:

> These examples' influence is as wide as it is, to me, incomprehensible. On their face they look pronaturalist, not pronormativist. One would think they were clear cases of the danger of confusing social values with disease. Yet many authors use them against naturalism to show that even in scientific medicine, the concept of disease depends on values.

(Boorse 1997, p. 72)

Boorse seeks to preserve the claim that the concept of disease is tied to matters of natural fact, not values, and accordingly interprets the shift of representation of masturbation from disease to non-disease as being not primarily a change of values, but simply a change in the science. He goes on to say, citing Engelhardt's essay (1974) on the history of medical views on masturbation:

> 19th-century masturbation science consists of spectacularly false statements. Masturbation does not damage the nerve-tone, much less the spinal chord. It does not cause rickets, blindness, insanity, acne, or even moist palms. Theorists were wrong in their theories, wrong in their data, wrong about virtually everything; almost no statement in the essay contains even a grain of truth.

(Boorse op. cit., p. 74)

However the critical point here is not just that the Victorian doctors had false theories about masturbation, but is rather, how they came by them. Was it by research? By controlled studies? By selective attention to the sexual history of blind patients? From sermon-guided meditation on human nature? What drove what? Did the physicians conduct open-minded clinical research and come to mistaken beliefs about the woes attendant on masturbation, and hence to the view that it was an unnatural act and a medical disorder? An alternative pathway is that the dominant social representation of masturbation was as an unnatural act, according to then current socially embedded religious norms, and the unnatural signified for physicians medical disorder or disease, from which it would have to follow that it has various physical and mental consequences, the direness of which would be with some justice in proportion to the unnaturalness of the act. To resist this interpretation it has to be shown not just that the Victorian doctors had false factual beliefs, but that they did not acquire these false beliefs because of prejudice driven by social norms and values.

The general problem here is how we are to know whether our views as to what is natural and unnatural in the human condition is based on objective grounds – an account of which is owed, but which presumably should rely on current science – or is rather driven by social norms of which we are hardly aware. This problematic pervades the psychiatric manuals and their development. In 1964 the American Psychiatric Association voted, famously, to exclude homosexuality from the list of mental disorders. The issues were complex, including those of the kind involved in the Victorian representation of masturbation considered above – questions of what is natural and unnatural, of what harm accrues, questions of social values. The question whether homosexuality was or was not a mental disorder inspired attempts to define the concept, as will be considered in Chapter 4. More recently, there has been much research on whether 'hearing voices' – one of the first-rank symptoms of schizophrenia – is in fact not uncommon in the general population in European countries, including in people that are not at all mad. Where did the view that this experience was uncommon, found only in mental illness, come from? Not – to be sure – from general population research. In the modern western absolute-world view, radical failure to perceive the world as it is, seeing and hearing things that were not there, was the fundamental epistemological problem, identified by Descartes, who raised the spectre of madness in just this place. Our postmodern or late modern epistemological problems are quite different, to do with relativity and diversity and the like, and in this context there is no longer reason to be aghast at the prospect that citizens can see and hear things that aren't there; this is no longer inconceivable – we can have a look and research this interesting phenomenon, along with many other things.

On the other hand there is an established way of getting purchase on the distinction between what is naturally given in the human condition as opposed to what is socially made, by considering constancies across societies as opposed to what varies. As discussed in the previous chapter, social science methodology mainly illuminates differences, while the biological natural sciences, recently joined by evolutionary psychology, seeks constants and universals. This dialectic plays out in the case of concepts of mental disorder. While different cultures have differing concepts of mind and body, person, agency, and differing views as to the causes of human behaviour and misbehaviour, they all – apparently – work with some notion that some social deviance is caused by illness, though by all means with more or less differentiation between physical and mental. Regarding content, while societies may differ in what counts as reasonable belief, may calibrate the proportionate expressions of emotions in different ways, and may differ in the emotions themselves, still – amidst all the differences – there are common strands to do with behaviour and emotions without appropriate reasons and causes, with a person acting out of character for no apparent reason; and so on.

Take as one example obsessive compulsive disorder (OCD). Research on cultural factors affecting OCD has shown that generally the disorder presents in similar ways in various cultures, including in Judaism, Islam, Hinduism and Catholicism, though the content of obsessions and the nature of compulsions are sensitive to cultural norms and preoccupations. Most attention has focused on the sometimes very striking apparent similarities between OCD and religious beliefs and rituals, but this alongside the fact that within religions it is explicitly acknowledged that observance of the law can go, as it were, over the top, being no longer piety, but eccentricity or sickness. It is here that we get purchase on the idea that concepts of mental disorder are trying to latch on to the idea that the mind is not working as it should because of illness; this is not a moral should, nor a social one, but has to do with the nature of the mind. Further, a crucial point is that in mental illness or disorder there is some harm that results. To continue with the example of OCD, the cross-cultural research shows that in each of the religion-cultures there is authoritative advice as to how to distinguish high degrees of piety from illness. This distinction may be made in terms of neglect of family, for example, antic-ipating the criterion of disorder in the DSM that refers to disruption of social role functioning.

This general idea that the concept of mental disorder is seeking to track fail-ure of the natural functioning of the mind, as opposed to simple social deviance, is obviously of crucial importance and requires careful consideration.

Several writers – most influentially Christopher Boorse and Jerome Wakefield – have tried to elucidate what is the 'natural fact' underlying dis-course on mental disorder, and their proposals have been characterized accordingly as forms of naturalism. Boorse was primarily concerned with physical illness, not mental, and Wakefield vice versa, but both intend that their analysis applies to both. Boorse's approach has the natural fact underly-ing disorder attribution as being a matter of statistical abnormality; Wakefield's approach invokes the evolutionary design of mental and behav-ioural functioning. A fundamental feature of both proposals is that they would resolve the 1960s debate whether mental illness/disorder involves med-ical/scientific norms or social norms by a straightforward compromise in which both kinds of factors are explicitly incorporated into the proposed defin-itions, both necessary, and jointly sufficient. Thus the proposed definitions are of the form, roughly: health (physical or mental) involves conformity to both social norms and natural norms, while illness (or disorder) involves deviance from both. Or again, the general proposal is that mental or physical disorder (or illness) is a condition in which there is divergence from some natural mental (or physical) function, and one which is negatively socially valued. This approach obviously has the virtues of compromise and reconciliation, and has also been taken to fit well with the working definitions of mental disorder in the DSM – though more on this later.

Broadly speaking in the commentaries on Boorse and Wakefield the involvement of social values has been accepted, while the controversies have centred much more on the question of natural norms and how these are to be understood. A core presupposition, more or less explicit, in the primary and secondary literature is the thought that unless some notion of natural dysfunction can be made out, then medicine will be dealing in social norms only, matters of relativity – opening up the possibility that anything can be called illness or disorder, according to fashion, and according to power – subject to sociopolitical uses and abuses. This kind of presumed consequence may be welcomed as recognition of the political nature of medicine and especially psychiatry, or it may be regarded as a reduction of the argument to absurdity or even immorality, but either way the matter is recognized as of fundamental importance. It is meant to be naturalism in the philosophy of illness and disorder that counterbalances social constructionism, and the proposals of Boorse and of Wakefield are recognized as the best worked out theories of this kind. That said, it is also widely recognized that it is hard to make naturalism work in this area (as in many others) – many problems confront attempts to work out the specifics. Insofar as the problems are insurmountable, naturalism fails, and this failure would inevitably open up an array of social issues interacting with psychiatric diagnosis and practice.

In this chapter I shall sketch the theories of Boorse and of Wakefield, focusing on the problems that arise in trying to pin down a notion of natural mental functioning that could underpin the concept of mental order. The conclusion will be that no concept of this kind is viable, either at all, or at least not for the purposes of the psychiatric diagnostic manuals. Most of the chapter is devoted to Wakefield's evolutionary theoretic analysis, which is the most plausible and the most influential version of naturalism. A further issue, explicit in section 3.7, is whether and in what sense this analysis is committed to the idea, attributed to the medical model in the 1960s critiques, that mental disorder lacks meaning. Notwithstanding the plausibility and influence of Wakefield's analysis, the problems it encounters are substantial, so much so that a key assumption and rationale of naturalism receives relatively little

explicit attention – the assumption that in the domain of psychological functioning the natural can be demarcated from the social. This assumption has
already been considered in the previous chapter and seen to be questionable in
the context of evolutionary psychology and genetics.

3.2 Statistical normality and the idealization of the normal

Christopher Boorse proposed in several important papers in the 1970s that
there was a distinction to be drawn between illness and disease: 'disease'
belonged to the science of pathology, where it referred to objectively definable
conditions involving disruption of the natural functioning of bodily organs –
nothing to do with social values; 'illness', by contrast, was a concept embedded
in social values about harm and undesirability, and in social practices relating
to help-seeking and treatment. The critical problem of how to define natural
functioning Boorse proposed to solve in terms of functioning as normal for
the species, in the statistical sense. Thus, Boorse, in a recent résumé and
re-statement of his position:

> Twenty years ago, in four papers, I offered a unified descriptive analysis of health, dis-
> ease, and function. In recent philosophy of medicine, these papers are often treated as
> a standard defense of one pole on the spectrum of views about health: the extreme
> view that, at least at the theoretical foundation of modern Western medicine, health
> and disease are value-free scientific concepts. Theoretical health, I argued, is the
> absence of disease; disease is only statistically species-subnormal biological part-function;
> therefore, the classification of human states as healthy or diseased is an objective
> matter, to be read off the biological facts of nature without need for value judgements.
> Let us refer to this position as 'naturalism' – the opposite of normativism, the view
> that health judgements are or include value judgements. . . Let me call my specific nat-
> uralist theory the 'biostatistical theory (BST)', a name emphasising that the analysis
> rests on the concepts of biological function and statistical normality.

> (1997, p. 4)

In his original papers Boorse contrasted disease in this sense with illness. In
his recent re-statement he has:

> Originally . . . I invoked a contrast between disease and illness to distinguish value-free
> theoretical health from a value-laden practical counterpart, freedom from illness.
> I said that illness was only a subclass of disease, including diseases serious enough to
> have certain normative features. [As follows:]
> A disease is an illness only if it is serious enough to be incapacitating, and therefore is

> 1. undesirable for its bearer;

> 2. a title to special treatment; and

> 3. a valid excuse for normally criticisable behaviour

I then applied this distinction between disease and illness to mental health. Unfortunately, though the idea of value-free theoretical vs. value-laden practical concepts of health still seems to me sound, I now believe that I chose the wrong concept (illness) to illustrate this distinction.

(op. cit., p. 11)

Boorse goes on to explain the reasons for his change of mind on this terminological point but they are not critical for the present purpose, which is to examine Boorse's biostatistical naturalism, and to note that his full account also envisages value-laden practical concepts of health. Biostatistical naturalism wants to say that statistical deviation from a norm can underpin what is meant by disease, mental or physical, or similar concepts, such as dysfunction.

The main objection to this approach is that mere difference will not do for capturing concepts like disease or dysfunction: these concepts already have the connotation that problems are caused, typically to the bearer, while mere difference from average/usual functioning have no such connotation. Further, it is the problems which are most relevant to the attribution of disease or dysfunction; difference from statistical norms as such does little and perhaps no work. While we have the quotes from Boorse to hand, above, it can be remarked that the second passage has: 'A disease is an illness only if it is serious enough to be incapacitating' – but why does the notion of more or less seriousness apply at all to disease in Boorse's definition? Does this mean more or less deviation from the norm? Or – more likely – it is being assumed that 'deviation from the norm' already implies problematic functioning, not just different functioning. In my view this is the main problem with Boorse's analysis and any other attempt to equate dysfunction in health contexts with mere statistical difference.

By all means it may be that different from average functioning may indicate problematic functioning. In some cases below-average functioning may coincide with a more or less catastrophic failure of functioning, as for example in cardiac arrest, or aphasia; in other cases below-average functioning may raise risk for adverse outcomes. Otherwise below-average functioning is just difference from the average, and why should just a difference be described as a disease, or dysfunction?

Difference from average is not sufficient for disease or dysfunction, as above, and it is not necessary either. It is often pointed out in this connection that some diseases such as gum disease are common in the population. Mental disorders are not all uncommon either. Lifetime rates of major depressive disorder may be as high as 25 per cent, for example. The critical point in disease or disorder attribution is that functioning is problematic, not that it just deviates from statistical normality.

So the main problem with the statistical approach to dysfunction and related concepts like disease and disorder is that statistically abnormality – relative rarity – just does not capture what is meant. However, there are also technical problems in making this approach precise, not trivial ones, and they may unravel the whole approach.

One of these technical problems is that defining what is below average for psychological and behavioural traits involves arbitrariness because of the typical kind of distribution of these traits in the population. As was noted in the previous chapter (especially in section 2.2), psychological and behavioural traits are typically 'normally' distributed in the statistical sense, roughly in the shape of a bell. The question then arises: at what point in such a continuous distribution does deviance from the mean become subnormal function, or dysfunction – at one standard deviation below the mean, or two, or three? There is apparently no way of answering this question using statistical principles alone. Of course other factors come into play. In particular, as indicated above, some kinds of below-normal functioning may coincide with a more or less catastrophic failure of functioning, or with risk of adverse outcomes, but then it is the associated harm or risk, not statistical considerations alone, that underlies the cut-off between normal and abnormal functioning.

Another problem with the statistical approach is that statistical normality is always relative to some population – but which one should be used to define dysfunction and disease? For example, depression may indicate subnormal functioning when the comparison is taken to be the group with no genetic vulnerability and with relatively few adverse life events and relatively high social supports; but it may be more typical for a group characterized by presence of those risks and absence of those protective factors. Which group is mean to be the gold standard, as it were, which defines dysfunction and disease?

Boorse casts the net wide, encompassing the whole human species, as in the quote above, allowing elsewhere for age and gender relativity, but it is clear that health-related characteristics, physical and mental, are affected by environmental factors, such as diet and psychological stressors. Given this multiple variability it is unclear that there is any 'species-typical' level of psychological or physical functioning. The same point can be made considering how it would be determined. Epidemiological surveys on the presence or absence or degree of a biobehavioural phenotype do well to collect samples representative of a city or a whole country, but it is unclear what a human species-wide sampling frame would look like, in the present, let alone including the past.

Insofar as there is no determinable, fixed reference group, such as the whole human species, then it is likely that statistical approaches to disease or dysfunction in practice make implicit comparison with some particular group. Perhaps, for example, we would have in mind the dominant social group in a given society, likely to be relatively better resourced. Another possibility, merging into the previous one, is that the gold standard normal group comes to signify an idealized level of optimal functioning – the best possible as we conceive it to be, or would like it to be. The idealization of the normal is an inevitable risk of the statistical approach to disease or dysfunction to the extent that it assigns these qualities to the abnormal, leaving the normal wholly disease and dysfunction free. An idealized, optimal level of functioning would presumably be a function of such as a good diet and good resources and not too much stress, and by this move the disadvantaged have not only poor diet and low resources and high levels of stress, but are also regarded as having subnormal function (and disease and disorder if the outcome is harmful). There are facts of nature involved in all this, but not in the way intended by statistical approaches to disorder. It is a fact of nature that any human being in an environment with poor diet and multiple or chronic psychosocial stressors will be at raised risk for health problems – this is a normal risk profile, typical for the species, but there is no absolute level of normal functioning that can define what is subnormal. Insofar as this is so, the misplaced assumption that there is an objective, statistical notion of dysfunction runs the risk of ending up in practice with an idealized notion of normality, likely to coincide with the functioning of the well-resourced, reflecting after all features of social organization rather than a fact of nature.

In summary, then, Boorse's proposal to construe norms of mental functioning as a fact of nature, in terms of statistical normality, does not work for many reasons. First, because deviance from statistical normality in itself – independent of any problems that may result – does not warrant attribution of pathology, physical or mental. Statistical deviance is indeed a matter of fact, and it may be used as a marker of dysfunction, but in itself it does not constitute dysfunction. Second, statistical rarity is not necessary for disease or dysfunction, so it is neither necessary nor sufficient. Third, in normally distributed traits including the majority of the psychological and behavioural there is no non-arbitrary cut-off in statistical terms alone between what is normal and what is abnormal. Fourth, statistical abnormality is relative to specific reference groups, and these can be selected in various ways, delivering different classifications into what is normal or abnormal. Fifth, Boorse relies on human species typical functioning to define an absolute gold standard group, which would avoid this relativity, but it is unclear whether such a standard exists. Further, in the absence of a fixed fact of nature – human normal functioning – it is likely that understanding of abnormality in statistical terms in practice assumes some fairly well-resourced, well-functioning group, more or less idealized.

The key point is probably the first of these, the mistaken equation of difference with dysfunction. Whatever may have been the attraction of Boorse's analysis several decades ago, as a response to the 1960s controversies, it is particularly problematic now in its proposal that mere statistical difference from some population norm constitutes disease or some mental equivalent. It invites the protest from individuals with such conditions – now that they have a voice – that difference is being pathologized and hence disqualified. Also, invoking the fact that the difference of itself may create problems is open to the rejoinder that such problems are commonly the outcome of imposition of environments and task demands by the majority that are suited for just them. The current moral climate embraces diversity, and in this context pathologizing and social exclusion on the grounds of mere difference are not to be recommended. Characterization of difference as unnatural, contrasted with the conformity to nature of the majority group, only makes matters worse.

Trying to understand the notion of abnormality at work in health contexts in terms of statistical deviance has a long history, presumably because statistical deviance is often linked with problematic functioning, and because it seems to offer a very simple solution to a very complex problem. Wakefield (1992a) has argued that the DSM-III-R definition of disorder, in its stipulation that a disorder must not be merely an 'expectable response' to a particular event (subsequently carried forward to the DSM-IV) relies on a statistical notion of normal and opposed to abnormal functioning, and hence mistakenly confuses normal variation with disorder. Wakefield thinks we can do better – on which more below. To the extent that the DSM and ICD have incorporated this confusion the question arises whether they have been over-inclusive, including in them conditions that are merely relatively uncommon – or as it turns out not so uncommon – population traits, but which are not disorders after all; or at least, are not disorders for this reason. Increasingly research in epidemiology and genetics has shown that many psychiatric conditions are common variations in population traits, perhaps in interaction with environments which are adverse (relative to the trait). For example as noted above the lifetime rate of major depressive disorder is up to about 25 per cent in general populations, and higher in stressful environments. Some current models of autism or autistic spectrum disorder suppose that they represent extremes of general population traits, to take another kind of case. These findings on normal variation in effect broaden our view as to human nature, chipping away at the idealization of normal functioning and the attribution of abnormality and disorder. To the extent that an idealization of normal functioning has driven attribution of disorder, there is now disquiet about the attribution. Or to put the point another way, the more we learn about the diversity of human nature and the human condition(s), the more problematic the notion of disorder becomes.

Boorse presented his view as relying on statistical deviation to underpin the concept of physical disease and its mental equivalent. However, in both the original formulations and in this more recent, Boorse also supposes that statistically normal functioning in a species is a marker of the design of biological or psychological systems, the notion of design being understood in an evolutionary theoretic framework. In this reading of Boorse's position, the critical notion of abnormal function is not tied essentially to statistical deviance, but rather to the notion of functioning as designed in evolution. On the whole, however, Boorse defends his biostatistical theory on the grounds defined by this title, where it encounters the objections above, and for a worked out statement and defence of the proposal linked to design and evolution, we need to turn to Wakefield.

3.3 Wakefield's evolutionary theoretic naturalism: statement and outline of problems

The major alternative to statistical or quasi-statistical versions of naturalism involves evolutionary development. Most major approaches to the definition of physical or mental illness since the late 1960s/1970s have been with reference to evolutionary theory. One of the earlier papers was by the psychiatrist Robert Kendell (1975). Kendell noted that in physical medicine the assumption that medical conditions were caused by lesions or disease processes had recently been undermined by the finding that essential hypertension was rather an extreme of normal variation, as follows:

> The concept of an abnormality or a lesion is quite straightforward so long as one is concerned with deviation from a standard pattern. But as soon as we begin to recognise that there is no single set pattern of either structure or function, that even in health human beings and their constituent tissues and organs vary considerably in size, shape, chemical composition and functional efficiency, it becomes much less obvious what constitutes a lesion; where normal variation ends and abnormality begins. Is, for instance, hypertension a disease, and if so what is the level beyond which the blood pressure is abnormal? And at what point does a raised blood sugar level, or a prolonged response to a carbohydrate load, become the disease diabetes?

> It was in fact the example of hypertension that finally discredited the nineteenth century assumption that there was always a qualitative distinction between sickness and health . . . The demonstration by Pickering and his colleagues twenty years ago that such a major cause of death and disability as this was a graded characteristic, like

height and intelligence, on polygenetic inheritance and shading insensibly into normality, was greeted by shock and disbelief by most of their contemporaries, and the
prolonged resistance to their findings showed how deeply rooted the assumptions of
Koch and Virchow had become.

Kendell (1975, p. 308)

The lesion/disease feature of the medical model, identified as problematic in
psychiatry in the 1960s, was already shifting in general medicine itself. Kendell
in this paper went on to identify the need to consider a new kind of definition
of physical or mental illness, and turns to a proposal made at around the same
time by Scadding (1967), in terms of conferring biological disadvantage.
Kendell proposed that 'biological disadvantage' presumably must embrace
increased mortality and reduced fertility, remarking that 'whether it should
embrace other impairments as well is less obvious' (op. cit., p. 310). Kendell
went on to consider whether mental illnesses do in fact, by reducing either fertility or life expectancy, produce a significant biological disadvantage.
Considering schizophrenia, Kendell reviewed research on the extent to which
low fertility rates resulted from confinement in the asylums, noting the role of
social as well as biological disadvantage. On the other hand, Kendell noted,
quoting other authorities, there is one 'condition' with an apparently clear
detrimental effect on marriage opportunities and fertility, namely homosexuality. In brief, this criterion of biological disadvantage is not as clear-cut as
might have been hoped, nor does it provide anything like a plausible demarcation criterion between mental health and illness, order and disorder.

For these kinds of reason, and probably also because of the persistence of
mental disorders in the population, not much more was heard of the straightforward idea that physical/mental illness/disorder can be defined in terms of
conferring biological disadvantage. Instead the evolutionary theoretic
approach took a sophisticated turn, away from the criterion of biological disadvantage, invoking instead the notion of evolutionary design. Wakefield's
proposed analysis has been the most worked out and discussed theory of
this kind.

Wakefield's proposed his analysis of disorder in a series of papers beginning in
the early 1990s, explicitly focused more on mental disorder than on physical, and,
explicitly tied natural function to evolutionary design rather than, as Boorse had
done, statistical average functioning. Like Boorse before him, Wakefield was primarily concerned with the question of whether there was a distinctive medical,
scientific, objective sense of dysfunction, separable from social norms and values.
Wakefield's analysis has come to be called the 'harmful dysfunction' analysis and
it can be stated briefly along the following lines: A 'mental disorder' is a harmful

failure of a natural function, where 'natural function' is to be understood in terms of functioning in the way designed in evolution.

Wakefield's analysis of disorder is well-argued, plausible, and has a whole range of strengths. Not only is it very well-argued and plausible, it is also has the major advantage, often noted, of being clear and succinct. Spitzer, developer of the DSM-III definition of disorder which survives pretty well intact in the DSM-IV has described Wakefield's harmful dysfunction concept as 'an elegant improvement over my own efforts at this difficult task' (2001, p. 357).

Here is Wakefield introducing his position in an early paper:

> I argue that disorder lies on the boundary between the given natural world and the constructed social world; a disorder exists when the failure of a person's internal mechanisms to perform their functions as designed by nature impinges harmfully on the person's well-being as defined by social values and meanings. The order that is disturbed when one has a disorder is thus simultaneously biological and social; neither alone is sufficient to justify the label disorder.

> (1992b, p. 373)

Wakefield emphasizes that disorder and dysfunction are closely related terms and that if the latter is to be used to explicate the former in a useful way it has to be explained in more basic terms, linking function to design, and design of natural functions to evolution. The function of an object or mechanism, Wakefield suggests, is not just a matter of what it currently does or achieves, but is essentially a matter of its design, part of an explanation of why it is made like it is. In the case of natural functions, the concept of design, the explanation of why things are as they are, involves evolution. The suggestion is that we have first an analysis of a folk concept of disorder in terms of the converse of what is natural – of our human nature. This issue is intimately tied to what made (or designed) nature, and human nature particularly, and what for, and about these questions there are only grand theories, or world views. One kind is the theological, in which 'natural' means roughly as designed or intended by the Creator, and unnaturalness is disorder or wilful perversity, likely to be regarded as sin. Darwin, in our secular age, provided in biology an explanation of creation, natural function and design, which precisely managed without reference to predetermination by a designer. According to the line of thought indicated by Wakefield, contemporary evolutionary theory just is our contemporary view of (biological) nature and natural function, and hence will be the basis of our views and theories of order and disorder.

Here is Wakefield on this line of thought in his early paper:

> In the case of artefacts, it is a prior mental representation of the effect that explains the existence of the artefact. Coming up with a similar demystifying causal explanation in

the case of natural functions has posed an age-old mystery: Why, indeed, should our internal mechanisms be so beneficially designed? Until recently, the mystery could be dealt with only by assuming that there exists a God who purposely created our internal mechanisms with benevolent intentions. According to this theory, our internal mechanisms are artefacts created by a divine entity, so natural functions are reduced to a special case of artefact functions.

Today evolutionary theory provides a better explanation of how a mechanism's effects can explain the mechanism's presence and structure. In brief, those mechanisms that happened to have effects on past organisms that contributed to the organisms' reproductive success over enough generations increased in frequency and hence were 'naturally selected' and exist in today's organisms . . . Because natural selection is the only known means by which an effect can explain a naturally occurring mechanism that provides it, evolutionary explanations presumably underlie all correct ascriptions of natural functions. Consequently, an evolutionary approach to personality and mental functioning . . . is central to an understanding of psychopathology.

(1992b, p. 383)

The conclusion is that 'all disorders must involve failures of naturally selected mechanisms' (op.cit., p. 383). But, Wakefield emphasizes, negative evaluation is also necessary for a condition to be a disorder. This has the consequence that conditions can change from being (considered as) disorders to being (considered as) normal, and vice versa, depending on the prevailing social norms, and in this sense its inclusion in the definition is consistent with the social critiques of the 1960s and subsequent social constructionist views of mental disorders. On the other hand, Wakefield emphasizes as one of his fundamental points, the harmful dysfunction analysis puts a definite limitation on what legitimately counts as a mental disorder, namely, that it has to involve, as a necessary condition, a failure of a natural function, a failure of some psychological mechanism to function as designed in evolution. Problematic or undesirable behaviours as such, in the absence of dysfunction, would not, according to Wakefield's definition, count as disorders, and the labelling of them as such would be, according to the definition, illegitimate and an abuse. In this way Wakefield aims to provide a clear and defensible response to sociological critiques that are radically sceptical about the concept of mental disorder, citing historical examples of frankly absurd and abusive diagnoses. These critiques, which flourished in the 1960s and have continued, were considered in the previous chapter (section 2.6).

Nor of course does this kind of targeted scepticism have historical relevance only. Wakefield has argued from the beginnings of his work that the DSM is over-inclusive according to the harmful dysfunction analysis, and that the analysis can be used to eliminate false positives. For example in his early critique of the DSM (1992a) Wakefield argues that the diagnostic criteria for conduct disorder do not capture that the problematic behaviours described are due to a dysfunction, rather than being appropriate for a problematic environment:

> The three criteria that are the most discriminative of conduct disorder according to the DSM-III-R field trials . . . are stealing (without confrontation of the victim), running away from home, and lying (other than to avoid physical or sexual abuse) . . . Yet these criteria do not enable one to discriminate instances in which such behaviour is caused by internal dysfunctions of, for example, socialization mechanisms, moral development, or impulse control from instances in which such behaviour is the result of social pressure, adaptation to problematic environmental conditions, or other nondisordered causes. An adolescent who behaves in such ways may be rebellious, foolish, coerced, or desperate rather than disordered.
>
> (1992a, p. 242)

In his recent book co-authored with Allan Horwitz (2007), Wakefield has pressed the point strongly that the DSM criteria are over-inclusive, specifically the criteria for depressive disorder, which, the authors argue, can apply to intense sadness which is not disordered but normal. The application of Wakefield's evolutionary theoretic analysis for the purpose of demarcating genuine disorders from non-disorders will be considered later (especially in section 3.7), but the first task is to evaluate its strengths and difficulties.

Wakefield has developed, elaborated and defended his version of the harmful dysfunction analysis – the version that ties dysfunction to evolutionary design – for over a decade and it is undoubtedly the most thorough and sophisticated analysis of mental disorder that has been in play. There is a large critical literature on Wakefield's analysis of mental disorder, testifying both to its importance and to its being problematic. Themes in the commentary on Wakefield's harmful dysfunction analysis can be brought under several headings: first, concerning the way that the analysis seeks to split off the social evaluative from the factual components of the concept of mental disorder; second, those concerning the first component, the 'harmful' part; and third, those concerning the second component, the evolutionary theoretic approach to dysfunction and hence disorder. I consider each in turn, the first two briefly, as they are not the main focus of the critical literature or the present essay, and the third in more detail, because it involves the core of Wakefield's naturalist analysis.

There has been controversy over whether the evaluative component of the concept of mental disorder can be separated out from a factual component, specifically on the question whether dysfunction, including in the evolutionary theoretic sense, is already evaluative. However, I will take it here that the notions of *functioning as designed*, and *failing to function as designed* are plausibly taken to refer to matters of fact, rather than essentially involving social evaluations, and that this is so whether the instrument or mechanism in question is an artefact or is naturally designed. It may be that we value the function positively or negatively, but the question whether the instrument or mechanism is carrying it out, or failing to do so, it itself just a matter of fact. On the other hand there is a subtlety in cases where the design and the mechanism is made by us, for this is presumably going to imply that other things being equal we value functioning as designed positively, and failure to do so negatively. In the case of behaviour that deviates from highly valued social norms, to which we have signed up and seek to maintain, then it seems to be so that we are bound to praise or at least be content with conformity, and to criticise and seek to correct deviance. So we can ask – from the sociological point of view – are judgements about mental disorder like this? This is where Wakefield's naturalism comes into play, to block this move. Wakefield's explicit restriction of mental or behavioural functions to natural functions in his analysis of mental disorder serves in effect to stipulate that the functions in question are not designed by us, are not a matter of social construction, but are designed by independent nature. The point of Wakefield's analysis is to limit the notions of mental and behavioural function and dysfunction which are in play in disorder attributions to what is natural, independent of social design, and hence free of any social norms and values.

Social norms and values are acknowledged to play a critical role in disorder attributions, but not in the crucial dysfunction part of the analysis; rather, they are partitioned off in the harmful part of the analysis. There they have remained, it should be said, largely unattended to in the primary and secondary literature on Wakefield's harmful dysfunction analysis. Broadly speaking, commentators have accepted or acquiesced in the harmful part of Wakefield's analysis, and most attention in the critical literature has been paid to the dysfunction part. Correspondingly, Wakefield's statements, elaborations and defences of this position have focussed mainly on the question of dysfunction, and specifically on the claim that dysfunction in the evolutionary theoretic sense is a necessary condition of disorder.

A direct hit on this critical aspect of Wakefield's analysis would consist of a counter-example, a mental disorder that involves no failure of an evolutionarily designed function. Many kinds of alleged counter-example have been proposed in the critical literature, and Wakefield's responses are typically of one or other of the following kinds, or some combination of both: either the condition really does involve failure of a designed mechanism, notwithstanding appearances, in which case it is, after all – surely all would agree – a disorder;

or, the alleged counter-example really does involve no failure of a designed mechanism, but some other causal pathway, in which case – surely we would all agree – it is really not a disorder. Either way, the alleged counter-example fails, and Wakefield's analysis wins.

One kind of case that has been thought to pose problems for Wakefield's draws on Gould's work in evolutionary theory on 'exaptations' (1991), specifically the proposal that there are current cultural uses of existing biological mechanisms that are distinct from the original function for which they were selected. The relevance to Wakefield's analysis of disorder is that there may be dysfunction in an exaptated function, which if harmful would count as a disorder, but the dysfunction is not of the kind specified in the analysis. Alleged anomalies for Wakefield's analysis along these lines citing dysfunctions in such as reading, writing and arithmetical ability have been constructed by various commentators such as Lillienfield and Marino (1995). In brief, the argument is that according to Wakefield's analysis dysfunctions in such abilities cannot count as disorders, even if they are harmful, because they are cultural inventions, not evolved functions – but this conclusion runs contrary to current diagnostic practice. Wakefield argues as against this that disorder is invoked only when other causes of dysfunction have been excluded, and it is supposed that there is a failure in some internal mechanism that underpins the capacity question. Thus Wakefield on problems with arithmetic:

> Inability to calculate can indicate 'the failure of a system to function as it was designed to function', even if the system was not specifically designed to enable one to calculate. The attribution of the disorder of acalculia is based on a line of reasoning roughly as follows: (a) inability to learn to calculate is a significant harm; (b) the brain was not designed specifically to enable people to learn to calculate; (c) however, when all of a person's brain systems are functioning as they were designed to function, a side-effect is that the person can learn to calculate; (d) therefore, inability to learn to calculate (despite conducive environmental and motivational circumstances) is caused by some (currently unknown) underlying brain function failing to function as it was designed to function, and is a disorder.
>
> Wakefield (1999c, p.383)

And on reading disorder:

> Learning disabilities specialists commonly distinguish sheer failure to learn to read from a reading disorder. Failures to learn occur for all sorts of reasons, such as emotional distractions, lack of motivation, lack of adequate educational opportunity, lack of facility with the language of instruction, and so on. Failure to learn is not considered a learning disorder if it is due to any of these kinds of causes . . . The HD [harmful dysfunction] analysis explains this distinction between similar conditions; none of the mentioned causes imply a failure of internal mechanisms to perform

designed functions, and only by eliminating such causes can one infer the existence of a design failure.

(Wakefield, loc. cit.)

Another kind of alledged counter-example is conduct disorder. Conduct disorder is more controversial because it is one of those conditions which seem to best fit the criticism that psychiatry pathologises social deviance. The potential problem for Wakefield's analysis is that if conduct disorder is just a matter of social deviance, in the absence of a medical dysfunction, then Wakefield's analysis of disorder is apparently wrong. However, his response is simply this: if there is no medical dysfunction, then there is no disorder. This tack can be seen in the quotation from Wakefield above on conduct disorder, illustrating the claim that his analysis can help identify over-inclusiveness in the psychiatric manuals, the inclusion of conditions that are not, at least in some kinds of case, disorders. In effect, Wakefield's response is that such cases are anomalous for the DSM, not for his analysis. The justification for the claim that normal or understandable responses or coping strategies are not taken to warrant disorder attributions is backed up by appeal to clinical judgement.

> Research on disorder attribution to antisocially behaving youths (Kirk, Wakefield, Hseih and Pottick 1999) reveals that clinicians overwhelmingly judge youths whose symptoms satisfy the DSM's criteria for conduct disorder to be non-disordered if the problematic behaviours are explained by learned normal reactions to environmental factors.

Wakefield (2000, p. 261)

My reading of the critical literature that tries to find counter-examples to Wakefield's analysis, and Wakefield's responses to the alleged anomalies, is that the responses are probably successful. Wakefield's analysis is very well designed and crafted, and basically, I think, it sees off all-comers – at least the ones that make a full frontal attack. The critical strength of the analysis, I believe, lies in the fact that it tracks the fundamental idea that in mental disorder something in the person is not functioning as it should. This idea is valid, not to say somewhat tautological. So the problem for counter-examples is that they have to count both as disorders, but also as cases in which nothing in the person is going wrong. The tautological – true by definition – aspect lies in the abbreviated form of Wakefield's analysis: that mental disorder is harmful dysfunction. This is fairly trivial, substituting dysfunction for disorder and emphasizing harm. The substantial part of the analysis derives from the fact that dysfunction is being restricted to natural as opposed to social functioning, and to evolutionary development.

Notwithstanding the strengths of Wakefield's analysis, it has, I shall argue, fundamental flaws. While we have a statement of Wakefield's position and quotes to hand (Wakefield 1992b, pp. 373 and 383, both quoted above), it may be remarked that several of its features are especially relevant to themes in the current essay and signal what I will take to be its key weaknesses.

First, the whole analysis rests on the now doubtful assumption that there is a clear (enough) division between psychological functioning that is natural (evolved and innate), as opposed to social (cultivated). The analysis rests on the assumption, using it to resolve the 1960s debates as to whether psychiatry was diagnosing real medical disorders or simply pathologizing social deviance. The resolution in Wakefield's analysis, as in the other form of naturalism, Boorse's, is to define a domain of natural dysfunction which is the proper domain of medicine and hence psychiatry, while acknowledging that what interests us, the people, and medicine and psychiatry, are only those natural dysfunctions that are negatively socially valued. This resolution was a key strength 20 years ago, but now it has become itself problematic. Both the original problem identified in the 1960s and naturalist resolutions both assume the idea of a radical division between natural, biological norms, and social norms. Since then the sciences have moved on, however, and as evolutionary ideas have influenced not only biology but also psychology and sociology, such a radical division becomes at least questionable, or perhaps useful in some domains but not in others.

A way of putting this point especially relevant to Wakefield's construction of his argument is in terms of the design of human behaviour. Wakefield focuses on evolutionary design because of commitment to distinguishing what is natural from what is social. But human behaviour is also socially 'designed', and the relative contributions of biology and social rules are complex and interwoven, not easy to tease apart. Further, human behaviour shows manifest individual differences, traditionally the subject matter of psychology, so that – in these terms – there is also individual design of human behaviour. Again, these individual design features interact with biological and social conditions. The outcome of these considerations is that the notions of dysfunction and disorder have social and individual meanings, as well as biological, without sharp distinctions, though in some kinds of case one or other will more applicable than others. These issues will be taken up towards the end of the chapter, especially in sections 3.8 and 3.9).

A second kind of difficulty for Wakefield's analysis is the well-recognized problem of determining whether or not a particular problematic mental or behavioural condition does involve failure of a specific evolutionarily designed 'mechanism', as opposed to, say, a reasonable enough response to a problematic environment. If only the former is going legitimately to warrant disorder attributions – as Wakefield would have – then the status of many conditions in the DSM and the ICD as being disorders becomes problematic. Perhaps some of these conditions, or some kinds of presentation of many, may be not disorders after all. In any case, for many conditions or kinds of presentation we do not know whether they are disorders or not in the specified sense – not until the science has been done. In brief, if Wakefield's analysis is correct, then disorder attributions involve a massive hypothesis about the evolutionary design of psychological mechanisms and its relevance to psychiatric conditions, and this would be problematic from the point of view of the psychiatric manuals, which have strived to make diagnostic criteria as observational as possible, as reliable as possible, to ensure basic agreement for clinical and especially for research purposes. This problem and its implications will be the main focus for the remainder of this chapter.

Third, and connected, the idea that if a particular problematic mental or behavioural condition is an appropriate response to a problematic environment, then it is not a disorder – implies that 'true disorders' are basically meaningless, mere failure of function. The role of this line of thought in Wakefield's analysis will be illustrated in later in this chapter (section 3.7). This implication – that 'true disorders' are basically meaningless, mere failure of function – is familiar from the 1960s, in the charge against the medical model that it strips the meaning out of madness, interprets it is as mere deficit. The problem here again is that the science has moved on since the 1960s, again in terms of both paradigm and findings, so that now it is recognized that meaningful processes typically play some role in the development or maintenance of some or all of the conditions and presentations described in the psychiatric manuals. In other words, it no longer works to limit disorders to the meaningless; at least not if we are to catch the conditions in the psychiatric manuals.

Let us turn, then, to the problem of how we distinguish among problematic conditions of the kinds described in the psychiatric manuals between those in which there is a failure of a psychological mechanism to function as designed in evolution, and those which arise from some other causal pathway. Here the critical arguments have come primarily from within the behavioural sciences and evolutionary theoretic frameworks, to the effect that some disorders, or conditions found in the psychiatric diagnostic manuals, do not or may not involve dysfunction in the evolutionary theoretic sense proposed in Wakefield's analysis.

3.4 **Variety of causal pathways to psychopathology**

In a special section on the concept of mental disorder in the *Journal of Abnormal Psychology* published in 1999, there were two papers by behavioural scientists on the implications of evolutionary psychology and psychological theory for the concept of mental disorder, one by Leda Cosmides and John Tooby, the other by John Richters and Stephen Hinshaw. Both papers acknowledged that Wakefield's approach to mental disorder is plausible, implicating functional failure of some specific designed psychological competency, but the substantial parts of the papers were taken up with other possible pathways to mental states and behaviour being problematic in the current environment.

Richters and Hinshaw summarize their approach as follows:

> There are numerous ways in which evolutionarily intact mental and psychological processes, combined with striking discontinuities within and between evolutionary and contemporary social/cultural environments, may cause nondysfunction variants of many widely accepted major mental disorders. These examples undermine many of Wakefield's arguments for adopting a harmful dysfunction concept of mental disorder.

Richters and Hinshaw (1999, p. 438)

And Cosmides and Tooby write on conditions that generate distress:

> The condition may be an evolved defense, normal variation within a universal design, a properly functioning adaptive system in an evolutionarily novel environment, an accommodation to the needs of a different organism (such as a fetus), a dysfunction in an adaptation, or many other things.

Cosmides and Tooby (1999, p. 454)

In brief, there are – from the point of view of psychology set within an evolutionary theoretic framework – various pathways to conditions that generate problems in the current environment, of which Wakefield's analysis captures only one kind. Among other possible pathways are the following five:

1. defensive/coping strategies
2. strategies that involve disruption of function
3. design/environment mismatches
4. phenotypes that look maladaptive but may be adaptive
5. highly evolved learning capacities leading to maladaptive behaviour.

These various pathways leading to dysfunctional, maladaptive behaviour were considered in the previous chapter in section 2.5 under the heading 'Disorder in evolutionary context'. The main point being made then was that introducing an evolutionary perspective into psychology and psychiatry opens up a wide variety of explanatory models of dysfunctional, maladaptive behaviour, beyond the one credited to a traditional medical model, in terms of lesions and disease processes. For the present purpose the point is that this prospect of variety of explanatory models raises a problem for Wakefield's analysis because many of them apparently need involve no disruption of an evolutionary designed function and therefore need not constitute disorder in the sense required by the analysis.

To what extent to do these kinds of case really contradict Wakefield's analysis? Here is Wakefield dealing with the problem of design/environment mismatch:

> There is an active controversy about whether the condition labelled ADHD is in fact a dysfunction of attentional or other mechanisms or just a normal, designed level of child exploratory activity that is problematic in our overly constrained school or home environments. Those who believe the former generally assume that ADHD is a disorder, whereas those who believe the latter generally argue that ADHD is not a disorder. (It seems likely that some conditions labelled as ADHD satisfy one account, and some the other, implying that current criteria are overly inclusive, but that's another story.)

(2000, p. 260)

Thus the argument is that design/environment mismatch is so far not dysfunction, nor therefore disorder. Rather, it is only if these circumstances give rise to dysfunction in the individual (and if it is harmful) that there is reason to attribute disorder (Wakefield, e.g. 1999c, 2000). This move of invoking dysfunction in the individual, together with resulting harm, is crucial and consistent with the definitions of disorder in the DSM and ICD as well as with Wakefield's analysis. Wakefield makes a connected point, though specific to his analysis, in saying that what he wants to capture is not design/environment mismatch, but 'design failure', the former but not the latter being context (environment) relative (1999c, d).

So in what ways might a design/mismatch leading to ADHD lead to harm, to dysfunction in the individual, or to design failure? Here is a simple sketch of a possible adverse developmental pathway leading to a lot of problems:

Suppose (for the sake of argument) that ADHD or a subtype of the condition represents the upper end of normal exploratory behaviour particularly in young males, which was adaptive in the EEA, but is problematic in the current environment, where the children are expected to sit and attend to a (possibly evolutionary irrelevant) task for hours at a time. The child's 'normal exploratory behaviour' in this (evolutionarily) new environment is restless and off-task. The child is also bored and finds out how to get some stimulation, entertainment and attention by irritating the other children and the teacher, so he learns to be naughty as well as restless. Getting told off all the time makes him unhappy, angry and resentful, so he makes up excuses and blames others to avoid as much trouble as he can, and sometimes he is extra naughty and rude. He learns all this at school, and not what he is supposed to be learning, leaves without educational qualifications, applies what he has learnt on the streets as an adolescent, so that he can do it all bigger and better, and he gets arrested for breaking the law.

This is a hypothetical pathway associated with problematic behaviour that can present at any stage to mental health services, satisfying diagnostic criteria for ADHD, complicated by oppositional defiant disorder, possibly also by major depression or dysthymia (minor depression), and developing into conduct disorder, and hence to criminal delinquency which is a matter for the Court.

There would be a general consensus among subscribers to the DSM and ICD that not far along these tracks there is a dysfunction in the individual – persistence of dysfunctional behaviour through time and across contexts – indicating that diagnosis of one or more of the disorders listed above may be warranted. But is there a design failure in Wakefield's sense? There is some uncertainty here due to imprecision in the meaning of this expression and as to what would count as evidence for and against. In any case, what we find is that many or all of the critical stages in this sketched pathway can be interpreted as reasonable or understandable responses to the problems posed for a young person with the characteristics envisaged, though some of the responses undoubtedly lead to major losses of various kinds, and for this reason may be called maladaptive. Thus, the shift to alleviating boredom by irritating those around him leads to loss of (opportunity for) productive and enjoyable relations with peers and adults, but it is a strategy for avoiding something experienced as worse (boredom), illustrating the mechanism by which some strategies can preserve one function by sacrificing another of lesser value. Is this design failure? Presumably not, because the behaviour is operating according to normal learning principles.

Another illustration of a pathway leading to a problematic condition involving the operation of normal learning principles would be the one starting not with ADHD but with a disorganized home environment including insufficient limit-setting which raises risk for oppositional defiance at home and at school and subsequent development of antisocial problems as above. However, Wakefield is quite clear that if a condition results from the operation of normal learning principles then it is not disorder. He writes, as previously quoted:

> Research on disorder attribution to anti-socially behaving youths (Kirk, Wakefield, Hseih and Pottick, 1999) reveals that clinicians overwhelmingly judge youths whose symptoms satisfy the DSM's criteria for conduct disorder to be non-disordered if the problematic behaviours are explained by learned normal reactions to environmental factors.

(2000, p. 261)

In other words, apparently, as a general rule disorder attributions are ruled out if the explanation runs in terms of normal learning. This remains the case, presumably, even if what is learnt is maladaptive, accumulating functional losses along the way, such as loss of educational opportunity, unemployment, imprisonment, etc.

There is another, extreme, possibility of a route to ICD/DSM conditions that apparently involves no failure of evolutionary design, namely, the possibility that some of the conditions may turn out after all to be evolution-arily normal. This option was also considered in section 2.5. Wakefield considers speculative theories about the possible adaptive significance of some conditions currently considered disorders, such as depression, histrionic and antisocial personality disorders, and ADHD, in various contexts, and proposes:

> The evidence is that, if we came to believe that conditions we now consider disorders are in fact naturally selected, we would gradually adjust our judgement about the condition from 'disorder' to 'non-disorder'.

> (2000, p. 259)

In summary, then, it may be that in some of the conditions in the psychi-atric manuals, or in some presentations of them, there is no failure of a mental or behavioural to function as designed by evolution – the only sense of dys-function that Wakefield's analysis envisages – and hence, according to that analysis, no mental disorder.

Wakefield's general strategy here for dealing with alleged counter-examples to his analysis of disorder is the one anticipated in the previous section, along the following lines: either the condition really does involve failure of a designed mechanism, notwithstanding appearances, in which case it is, after all a disorder; or, the alleged counter-example really does involve no failure of a designed mechanism, but some other causal pathway in which everything is working normally, in which case it is really not a disorder. Either way, the alleged counter-examples fail. This is the way that Wakefield deals with prob-lems arising from design/environment mismatch in the above quote. He interprets the situation as meaning that we diagnose disorder only if we sup-pose that there is a dysfunction of an evolutionarily designed mechanism, and if we suppose that there is not, but design/environment mismatch only, then we are inclined not to call the condition a disorder. Hence disorder and failure of function are kept together.

There are two ways of constructing counter-examples to Wakefield's analy-sis, one direct and one indirect. It may well be that the direct approach can be headed off using the strategy outlined above, but the indirect approach is much more interesting conceptually and in its implications. Consider this form of argument in two versions:

> (A) There are causal pathways that do not involve failure of an evolutionarily designed mechanism but which lead (A_1) to mental disorders, or (A_2) to conditions described in the psychiatric manuals, associated with distress and disability.

The stronger version of the argument, (A_1), seeks to score a direct hit on Wakefield's analysis, and may fail – suggesting that the analysis captures mental disorder correctly, especially because it draws heavily on the notion of dysfunction. The weaker version (A_2) leaves open whether the conditions as described in the psychiatric manuals are (really) disorders or not – notwithstanding the fact that the manuals call them so. If the weaker reading of the argument is valid, the implications and options for the term mental disorder and for the manuals are complex and various. Wakefield's analysis of disorder may be correct, in which case the psychiatric manuals are over-inclusive and need shortening. Or, still assuming Wakefield's analysis of disorder is correct, maybe the psychiatric manuals are trying to capture mental disorders plus other kinds of conditions that are not mental disorders but which are best called something else – though what? Or maybe the manuals are right to call all the conditions described disorders, even though some do not involve a failure of evolutionarily designed mechanism – in which case Wakefield's analysis of mental disorder would be considered wrong, and we would need another. Of course there are various other options. Whichever way we turn – if the above weaker form of the argument (A_2) is valid – we enter relatively uncharted territory.

Suppose, then, that there are causal pathways that lead to conditions described in the psychiatric manuals, with associated distress and disability, which do not involve failure of an evolutionarily designed mental or behavioural mechanism. These would be conditions that are called disorders in the manuals, but which are not disorders in the sense of Wakefield's analysis. Where would this leave the analysis? This state of affairs seems fine from Wakefield's point of view: it is just what allows the analysis potentially to be used in prescriptive mode, to adjudicate between what should be in the psychiatric manuals and what should be excluded. It is true, on the other hand, that some of the conditions that would be excluded on the grounds that they fail to meet the conditions specified in the evolutionary theoretic analysis, nevertheless may involve much trouble – distress, disability and risk of adverse outcomes – as in the hypothetical causal pathways and case vignettes above.

A response open to Wakefield to handle this kind of issue is to cite the fact that non-disorders may still be problematic, and that there is a place in the

DSM-IV for them, using the V-code (e.g. Wakefield 1992b, 2000; Wakefield, Pottick and Kirk 2002). Code V in the DSM-IV is for conditions that 'may be a focus of clinical attention' but which are not mental disorders (which do not satisfy any of the diagnostic criteria sets) and which may nevertheless warrant clinical attention, and perhaps, in some kinds of case, treatment. Diverse kinds of case are coded under V, including relationship problems, non-compliance with treatment (for a general medical condition or a mental disorder), malingering, and plain criminality.

So, the suggestion is that if we find that some conditions hitherto thought to be disorders are not disorders after all, then we take them out of the DSM altogether, or reassign them to Code V. These, in brief, are Wakefield's proposals for dealing with the possibility or the likelihood that many conditions or presentations in the DSM and ICD may arise from pathways that do not involve failure of evolutionary design and which are therefore not disorders in the sense of his analysis. This response however wholly underestimates the extent of the problems that arise.

3.5 Evolutionary theory and the reliability of clinical diagnosis

The problems that arise for Wakefield's analysis once it is acknowledged that many conditions or presentations in the psychiatric manuals may not involve failure of evolutionary design are far more radical than can be resolved by the removal of some conditions from the manuals and the reassignment of others within them. The point is rather that for the vast majority of syndromes in the manuals we *just do not know* whether they involve failure of a natural designed function or whether they are designed or acquired strategic responses to environmental conditions, or indeed whether they are designed adaptive responses. There is controversy about ADHD in this respect, as noted by Wakefield in the quote above, and there are more speculative evolutionary theoretic hypotheses about adaptive features of depression, histrionic and antisocial personality disorders. There are also many psychological models of many clinical syndromes which appeal in whole or part to strategic cognitive processing, in response to trauma and other adversities in the immediate environment, or perhaps to problems arising from poor design/environment mismatch, including depression, phobias, PTSD, OCD, autism, borderline personality, and some aspects of schizophrenia. In brief, these considerations problems affect just about every condition in the book, because all the etiological theories are unsettled and controversial. The problem is therefore that amongst all or most of the main conditions of interest we will not know which of them is or is not a disorder, or perhaps which subtypes are or are not disorders, in Wakefield's sense, until a lot more science has been done, and already in the present state of play there is ample reason to anticipate a negative answer in many kinds of case.

What has happened here? Wakefield's analysis has the effect of turning mental disorder into an explanation of the conditions in the psychiatric manuals, not into a simple characterization of them. Moreover, it is an explanation that has competitors, of the kind considered above, and – making matters ever worse – all the various competing explanations are complex, unsettled and to some extent speculative. In brief, the outcome is that diagnosis of mental disorder becomes a highly theoretical matter.

The paper on these issues by Richters and Hinshaw (1999) referred to in the previous section has the title 'The abduction of disorder in psychiatry'. Abduction refers to the mode of inference identified by Pierce (1903) as inference to the best explanation, and is typically used for understanding and explaining phenomena on the basis of incomplete information or imperfect knowledge. Richters and Hinshaw remark that the original abduction of mental disease during the Middle Ages was an improvement over previous prevailing supernatural explanations, but continue:

> Over time, however, the concept of mental disease gradually gave way to the broader concept of mental disorder, and during the closing decades of the 20th century its classification boundaries have been extended far beyond the extreme conditions for which it was originally invoked. Mental disorder now serves as a generic label for the wide array of syndromes of mental and psychological suffering for which individuals and their caretakers seek professional help. Ironically, advances in the scientific study of psychological functioning and behavior during the same period have led to increasingly penetrating questions about whether the mental disorder abduction can be justified any longer as an inference to the best explanation for such a wide variety of conditions.

> (op. cit., p. 438)

Doubtless Wakefield would say that his concept of natural dysfunction is not the same as mental disease, but whatever be the merits of that point, he too is obliged to draw the conclusion that mental disorder is now – in the current state of the science – an hypothesis.

Thus Wakefield, for example:

> My contention is that, when we decide that a condition is likely a disorder, we decide that the best theory of the condition is that it involves a dysfunction.

> (2000, p. 264)

Of course the point is that not only that we are committed to the view that there is a dysfunction – this being a trivial commitment because dysfunction is marginally close to disorder – but specifically we are committed according to Wakefield's analysis to saying that the condition involves failure of some psychological mechanism to function as designed in evolution. That is to say, the theory that such and such condition is a disorder in the sense of Wakefield's analysis is not at all a trivial one, but is highly speculative.

This outcome of Wakefield's analysis – that it has diagnosis of disorder as highly speculative theory – has various interesting consequences to be pursued in later sections of this chapter but which may be anticipated here. First, the implication is that – if the analysis is adopted – we need some way of characterizing the conditions in the psychiatric manuals other than as disorders, while we wait for the science to inform decisions as to which are or are not disorders. In other words, a terminological abyss opens up. A second and connected implication is that the familiar use of the term 'mental disorder' in the psychiatric manuals is problematic. With a background in clinical diagnosis, once a clinician has established that such and such a presentation satisfies the diagnostic criteria for, say, ADHD, that the requisite range of clinically significant symptoms is present, and is associated with distress or impairment, it is apparently not meant to be much of a step to attributing mental disorder – after all the 'D' at the end of ADHD stands for 'disorder' – and certainly not one meant to generate a lot of attention and fuss. Now it seems that, if we follow through on Wakefield's analysis – allegedly the best chance of explicating the notion of disorder at work in the psychiatric manuals in a naturalistic way – there is a big step from symptom syndromes (even when associated with distress or impairment) to the diagnosis of disorder, one that requires confidence in an hypothesis about failure of a system to function as designed in evolution. The expression: 'such and such a presentation satisfies the diagnostic criteria for such and such a disorder' would have no clear use. In this respect Wakefield's attempt to capture the concept of mental disorder in the psychiatric manuals and specifically to bring out its objective, scientific basis turns out to invalidate the way the term is used in the manuals. Science generally deals with hypotheses as much as facts, and the attribution of disorder turns out not to rest on established facts after all but to be one hypothesis among others as to what is implicated in the clinical syndromes, and it cannot be favoured until the science is done or at least reaches some consensus, and in the meantime we need other ways of characterizing the conditions of interest, other than as mental disorders.

Wakefield's analysis of mental disorder has the effect of making disorder a speculative hypothesis, and therefore not obviously available either for clinical use or as a descriptive characterisation of the conditions of interest for the purposes of basic science or outcome research. It was noted in the first chapter that a requirement for clinical and research purposes is at least that we can identify the conditions of interest reliably – so that we know what conditions we are talking about. The DSM and the ICD have been constructed with this aim in mind and have called the conditions mental disorders. Now that Wakefield's analysis of mental disorder turns out to be a theoretical hypothesis which is not known to be correct for all of the conditions, something has to give: either Wakefield's analysis is right about mental disorder and the psychiatric manuals are wrong – or vice versa. Or again, if Wakefield's evolutionary theoretic analysis of mental disorder is correct, we have to choose between reliability and validity of diagnosis. These options are considered further in the next section.

3.6 Options on reliability and validity of diagnosis of disorder

The problem with Wakefield's evolutionary naturalism in relation to the psychiatric manuals, to recap, is this. Consideration of possible pathways to the kinds of conditions described in the manuals show that some but apparently not all of these pathways involve failure of a mental or behavioural mechanism to function as designed in evolution, and that, further, we generally do not know which conditions or which subtypes of conditions arise by which kind of pathway, and therefore which do involve such failure and which do not. One consequence of this line of thought is that diagnosis of mental disorder comes to have the status of an uncertain hypothesis, which is incompatible with the aim of the psychiatric manuals of making diagnosis reliable for clinical and research purposes. A further consequence is that – assuming Wakefield's analysis to be correct – we need some other name for the problematic conditions described in the manuals, some name other than mental disorder, while we wait for the science to sort out which are mental disorders (in the sense of the analysis) and which are not. In short, if one wants to be a naturalist about mental disorder – to have it based in a matter of fact apart from social norms and values – and if one supposes that Wakefield's evolutionary naturalism is the best, if not the only, bet, and if one wants to be able to say that the psychiatric manuals include known mental disorders that can diagnosed in the clinic – then one has a problem, because all these things apparently cannot be had at the same time.

The problematic can be expressed in terms of reliability and validity of diagnosis of mental disorder. The DSM wants reliable diagnosis so makes the criteria observational, but evolutionary naturalism – apparently the only viable kind – wants disorder attribution to be theoretical, to achieve validity.

However there is a tension between these two, which Wakefield has often remarked, beginning in his early papers. For example:

> DSM-III-R attempts to increase reliability by eliminating the inference to internal mechanism failure and relying for diagnostic judgements on the unexpectable nature of the harms alone. However, many of the unexpectable harms that can indicate a dysfunction can also be caused in other ways, such as by normal reactions to stressful environments or by nondysfunctional inner states. Noninferential symptom-based criteria, therefore, fail to discriminate disorders from other causes of symptomatic harms. Consequently, DSM-III-R's strategy for increasing reliability simultaneously decreases validity.

(1992a, p. 242)

If Wakefield's evolutionary naturalism is correct, then the aspiration to achieve reliable diagnosis of disorder in the clinic by basing it in observable data – independent of evolutionary psychological theory speculation – is misconceived. Conversely, if the DSM has the correct methodology, then evolutionary naturalism is incorrect – because there must exist a valid sense of disorder which is not bound up with evolutionary theoretic speculations. In short, we are faced with difficult choices here. Since the tension is between the methodology of the psychiatric manuals and the alleged valid meaning of mental disorder, the two main options involve giving up on one in favour of the other – and both options have serious downsides. Having said that, the issues are complex, so both options are broad and schematic, with room for manoeuvre. On the other hand, again, it is worthwhile to have the two broad options in play, as boundary positions.

Option 1

Naturalism about mental disorder is correct, specifically Wakefield's analysis in terms of harmful failure of natural psychological mechanisms to function as evolutionarily designed. This is the valid definition of (genuine) mental disorder.

Advantages claimed for this option include the familiar aspirations of naturalism:

◆ We retain a factual, objective basis for the medical concept of mental disorder, signifying a principled way of demarcating disorder from normal functioning and responses

◆ Consequently we have a principled, conceptually valid distinction between mental disorder and social deviance, hence e.g. disqualifying social abuses of psychiatry.

Disadvantages are the problems identified above:

◆ Diagnosis of disorder involves risky, speculative, evolutionary theoretic hypotheses about psychological functioning. These hypotheses may well be false for some conditions in the psychiatry manuals, or for some of their presentations. Diagnosis will not be a matter for the clinic. What can be established by standard clinical interviews is just the presence of clinically significant syndromes, with associated distress or impairment.

◆ Reliability of diagnosis of disorder would suffer to the extent that there are divergent schools of thought about evolutionary designed mental functions, and other groups who have not much opinion one way or the other.

◆ In any case we are left with no general category name for the conditions currently in the psychiatric manuals. We would need another name for clinically significant syndromes with associated distress or impairment – some of which may turn out to be mental disorders, some may not be, perhaps depending on the presentation – but in any case while this is being sorted out another, less theoretically committed name would be required. Terminological candidates include, among others, 'treatable conditions', 'psychiatric conditions', and 'mental health problems'. In this scenario 'mental disorder', or 'genuine mental disorder', is envisaged as being used – speculatively but reasonably – for those conditions in which some fundamental, evolutionarily designed psychological mechanism is broken.

In effect this option – retaining Wakefield's evolutionary naturalism as the valid analysis of mental disorder – has the effect of making mental disorders a subset of the conditions in the psychiatric manuals. Wakefield has always acknowledged this to the extent that he envisages it being used in prescription mode to exclude false positives, but behind this point there is divergence from the methodology of the psychiatric manuals. The manuals base diagnosis on information accessible in clinical interview, matched against diagnostic criteria that are reasonably clear, and there is apparently not meant to be much of a gap between establishing satisfaction of diagnostic criteria – the presence of clinically significant syndromes, with associated distress or impairment – and making the diagnosis of disorder. Evolutionary naturalism, by contrast, has disorder attribution as essentially a theoretical move, a matter of evolutionary hypotheses about failure of designed mechanisms, as opposed to involvement of other possible pathways to problematic conditions such as design/environment mismatch, and over-generalized learning, and so on.

Option 2

Retain the concept of mental disorder as a general category name for the conditions defined in the psychiatric manuals in terms of clinically significant symptom syndromes, when associated with marked distress/impairment or risk thereof – in effect jettisoning naturalism in Wakefield's form and probably in general.

Advantages of this option include:

- 'Mental disorder' is retained as a general category heading for the psychiatric conditions (for clinically significant syndromes when associated with distress or impairment or risk)
- Diagnosis is a clinical matter (not a matter of speculation)
- Reliability of diagnosis is preserved and can be worked on (as now).

The disadvantages of this option include:

- We apparently have no scientific, objective basis for the concept of mental disorder. It is quite possible that the norms deviated from in clinically significant syndromes are social and individual, as well as, or as opposed to, being natural.
- Linked to the above, there may be no philosophically or conceptually principled way of excluding social abuses of psychiatry
- Also linked, there will be continuing complaints from within and outside psychiatry that diagnosis of mental disorder pathologizes personal problems and values, disqualifies the meaningful, and socially excludes the so-called disordered.

This option involves a non-naturalist notion of mental disorder and I suggest it is closest to the position currently occupied by the psychiatric manuals. The psychiatric manuals are designed to facilitate diagnosis in the clinic, and have been increasingly refined to improve reliability of clinical diagnosis, and the disadvantages listed above are just those highlighted by sociological and psychological critiques of psychiatry. Non-naturalist approaches will be considered in Chapter 4, and Chapter 5 will take up the issue of whether the medicalization of the problems described in the manuals has been over-extended.

For now we stick with naturalism, the problems it solves and the problems it runs up against. Wakefield's analysis presumably was intended to exclude the main disadvantages of non-naturalist approaches, to distinguish medical/scientific/objective norms from social, but it has ended up being forced into Option 1, which although it succeeds in the original aim, does so at the expense of failing to retain the advantages of the current state of affairs: clinical diagnosis and reliability are lost.

As already indicated, Option 1 implies that while we wait for the science to sort out which conditions or subtypes in the psychiatric manuals are genuine disorders – in the sense of Wakefield's evolutionary naturalism – we would need another general name for the conditions in the manuals, such as mental health problems. We would also need a name for each particular type of syndrome, such as Major Depression, without commitment to whether it constituted a disorder or not. Research would continue into causes and treatments, and would include the programme of primary concern to evolutionary naturalism, namely, establishing which conditions or subtypes or types of presentation do and which do not involve failure of a psychological mechanism to function as designed in evolution. All this research would have to use the fundamental scientific methodology of reliability of observation of basic data, so that we know what is being researched, what conditions the findings are true of, which other samples they are likely to generalize to, how to replicate, etc. Reliability of syndrome ascertainment would be required so that we know what we are talking about in research and in the clinic, and this would best be achieved by using fairly descriptive terminology, or norms of psychological functioning that were generally agreed. In brief, it would all look much like now.

Option 1 is the one which holds on to naturalism, evolutionary theoretic naturalism in particular. However its primary impact, when followed through, is to leave things much as they are, with the exception that evolutionary psychological/psychiatric research goes high up the agenda, and with name changes at two stages. While we are waiting to establish with reasonable confidence which types, subtypes or kinds of presentation of conditions in the psychiatric manuals are genuine disorders in the sense of evolutionary naturalism and which are not, we need another general name for them (such as mental health problems) and other names for specific syndromes which do not include disorder attribution (Major Depressive Disorder would become Major Depression, etc.). Then would come the time eventually, we are supposing, that we would be able to say (most of the time, and albeit with some shades of grey) which types of presentation, or subtypes, are genuine disorders, and which are not. Then what? Suppose we found all this out in time for the ICD-25 and the DSM-11? Should the non-disorder conditions (or subtypes) be removed from the classifications altogether? Here the problem is that they are nevertheless problems – causing much harm, distress and impairment, or risk of adverse outcomes – so why should we in effect classify them by default with happy, well functioning, unproblematic states? Or, should we keep them in the manuals but move them from Axes I/II – the mental disorders – to Code V – the other problems that may come to clinical attention and warrant treatment? Code V would probably then become long and complicated, sufficiently so to require an elaborate classification scheme, probably something like the current one for as Axes I/II – but that is a perhaps just a clerical issue. Or is the clerical point the main point? What is the point? We would have changed the names, moved conditions round in the books, and all else – the conditions, associated harm and risk, clinical need for attention and treatment – stays the same.

The great attraction of naturalism – as applied to mental disorder as elsewhere – is that it identifies facts apart from the uncertainty and relativity of human affairs. The downside is then inherent in it: how do we know these special facts, and what difference do they make (to us)? What difference does it make whether a mental health problem associated with distress, impairment, or risk of adverse outcomes, does or does not involve failure of a psychological mechanism to function as designed in evolution, and therefore is or is not a genuine mental disorder as specified by an evolutionary theoretic analysis? What is the difference? A possible practical implication, over and above the terminological and the clerical, would be that 'non-disorder' mental health problems should not be treated, but if they are associated with distress, impairment, or risk of adverse outcomes, why should they not be treated? They may involve as much harm as genuine mental disorders, for all we know – or more. Who knows, until the evolutionary psychological and psychiatric research has been done?

One problem is what difference naturalist super-facts make, once we get to know them, elevated as they are above the flux. Another problem is how we do get to know. Since naturalist super-facts are by definition independent of human opinions, concerns, values and the like – facts that are just so regardless – we and our words somehow have to access and track them. In so doing we have to use criteria close to hand, and it is probably inevitable that these will after all show the signs of the uncertainty and relativity of human affairs. The question is then whether invoking facts about human nature does any more than give a mythical warrant to our particular opinions and practices.

3.7 Can evolutionary naturalism be used as a demarcation criterion?

As indicated earlier, in section 3.3, Wakefield has always intended that evolutionary naturalism can help to identify false positives in the psychiatric manuals; that is to say, it can be used to identify non-disorder conditions that are by mistake currently included in the manuals as disorders. Wakefield has argued, further, that the psychiatric manuals are at particular risk of mistakenly including non-disorders to the extent that they have used straightforward descriptions of symptoms and syndromes, without paying attention to whether they are normal in context. For example as noted in section 3.3,

Wakefield criticizes the DSM criteria for conduct disorder in this way, citing research suggesting that disorder attributions are ruled out if the explanation of the conduct problems runs in terms of learned normal reactions:

> Research on disorder attribution to anti-socially behaving youths (Kirk, Wakefield, Hseih and Pottick 1999) reveals that clinicians overwhelmingly judge youths whose symptoms satisfy the DSM's criteria for conduct disorder to be non-disordered if the problematic behaviours are explained by learned normal reactions to environmental factors.

> (2000, p. 261)

Wakefield is presumably right that once we have established that a problematic behaviour is learned and normal, we are not inclined to attribute mental disorder. One way of expressing this would be to say that if behaviour makes sense to us, for example has some sensible point, then we consider it normal enough, while conversely, if it makes no sense and has no point, then we think of disorder. Wakefield follows this tack in critical places; for example:

> It would not be particularly surprising if some moderate range of antisocial or histrionic behaviour turned out to be a naturally selected niche strategy, and it is to be expected that some forms of depression represent naturally selected reactions to loss. It does not appear that such behaviours are considered clear cases of disorder. Our intuitions tend to attribute dysfunction and disorder in extreme cases where the behaviour *does not appear to be a useful strategy by any stretch of the imagination* but rather seems to devastate the individual's social functioning and interfere with other designed functions.

> (Wakefield 2000, p. 260: my italics)

Two connected points may be noted about this. First, the use of the italicized expression reinforces the idea that what mental disorder actually tracks is absence of meaning (or functionality, or strategy), an idea mooted at the start of this essay. To the extent that we use a full-strength, no doubts about it, attribution of mental disorder, then we are saying that the condition under scrutiny makes no sense whatsoever, has no conceivable point. The second point to note is that it is the judgement of absence of meaning – in a broad sense encompassing normality, function, strategy – that seems to be driving the intuition that there is a 'failure of a naturally selected psychological mechanism'.

It has been supposed in the Introduction to this essay that attributions of mental dysfunction and disorder typically turn on absence of appropriate meaning, method, and reasons. It was remarked in Chapter 1 that the psychiatric manuals typically though not invariably invoke such notions in the diagnostic criteria. This approach apparently contrasts with Wakefield's claim that it hinges on an hypothesis about failure of an evolutionarily designed mechanism to function as designed. This claim obviously invites the question: how do we tell whether a condition involves such a failure or not? Or again, how does Wakefield's analysis of mental disorder actually work in demarcating what should go in and out of the DSM? Given the nature of the analysis, one would expect elaborations, defences and applications of it to be involved with the latest research on models of psychopathology in relation to current models in evolutionary psychology and their implications for the functional organization of the mind and brain, areas in which one might imagine the issue would be thrashed out, though over a long time. However, Wakefield generally does not go there. Rather, when Wakefield addresses the question how we tell whether such and such a mental state or behaviour involves a dysfunction or not, it turns out that the criteria in play are very close to home, those familiar in the history of the concepts of mental illness and mental disorder, to do with whether the behaviour in question is a reasonable response, or has been acquired by normal learning, or – in brief – makes sense.

So what starts off with the appearance of being a fixed fact of nature – unaffected by our opinions and concerns – turns out to be known in terms of the presence/absence of meaning, a notoriously uncertain, relative fact. How do we know we are not mistaking the one for the other?

In a recent chapter Wakefield (2002) considers what he calls the 'value projection' fallacy, understood as follows:

> [The fallacy] occurs when one inadvertently projects one's values onto the world so that one mistakes what one values for what is naturally designed to happen and thus mistakes what is disvalued for a failure of designed functioning and, consequently, for a disorder.
>
> (2002, p. 154)

This fallacy raises issues of the kind raised by Plato's naturalist myth in the *Republic*, mentioned at the start of this chapter on naturalism. Are we really dealing with facts of human nature – or values embedded in social structures and processes? Wakefield argues that in the case of mental disorder diagnosis we are actually sometimes dealing with values only, but that we should distinguish those kinds of case from genuine mental disorders, which do have a basis in nature, specifically in natural dysfunctions. On the other hand, this distinction will collapse to the extent that identification of 'genuine mental disorders' also turns out to involve socially embedded opinions and values.

Wakefield argues that the value projection fallacy has occurred not only in the past, such as in Victorian views of female orgasm and masturbation, but closer to home, in the DSM. This is Wakefield's analysis of mental disorder in prescriptive mode, helping to distinguish mental disorders from normal psychological functioning – serving as a demarcation criterion. So how does the demarcation work? Wakefield goes on to illustrate the fallacy he has in mind in relation to diagnostic criteria for several disorders characteristic of childhood and adolescence, including separation anxiety disorder, substance abuse, major depressive disorder, selective mutism, oppositional defiant disorder and conduct disorder. In each case, Wakefield claims that some conditions that satisfy the diagnostic criteria are not in fact mental disorders, and the argument runs as follows: there may be presentations that satisfy the diagnostic criteria but in which there are 'normal' reactions or 'reasons'.

For example:

> Separation anxiety disorder is diagnosed in children on the basis of symptoms indicating age-inappropriate, excessive anxiety concerning separation from those to whom the individual is attached, as evidenced in at least three symptoms out of a list of eight symptoms, lasting at least four weeks. The symptoms include, for example, excessive distress when separation occurs, worry that some event will lead to separation, worry that harm will come to attachment figures, refusal to go to school because of fear of separation, a reluctance to be alone or to be without a major attachment figure. These are just the sorts of symptoms children experience when they have a normal, intense separation anxiety response. So, the validity of the criteria in distinguishing disordered responses from normal ones depends entirely on the interpretation of the notions of the age-inappropriateness or excessiveness of the child's anxiety, for which no guidelines are offered; the symptoms themselves are supposed to be the manifestations of the excessiveness. The problem here is that cultural demands placed on children or stressors, such as serious disruption of familial bonds, may arouse what could be construed as an excessive response in normal, non-disordered children. Such contextual factors are not taken into account in DSM criteria.
>
> Wakefield (op. cit., 158)

In this it can be seen that when Wakefield seeks to demarcate disordered from normal reactions the considerations brought to bear seem not to be theory and findings from evolutionary psychological theory after all, but simply clinical judgement about what is a proportionate response to cultural demands and stressors. Further, Wakefield supposes that the diagnostic criteria do not tackle this critical issue of proportionality, and context-dependence generally. Accordingly he construes the DSM criterion for separation anxiety disorder that refers to 'excessiveness' of the distress experienced by the child on separation from major attachment figures, simply in terms of the magnitude/intensity of the distress. Speaking as a clinician I have to say I usually do not interpret excessiveness of anxiety responses in this context-free way, but rather as meaning exactly 'proportionate to context'. What is the point of calling an intense anxiety response excessive/disordered if the child is in a really frightening situation? It is not my aim here to argue about the right way to interpret the DSM, but rather to note that Wakefield is apparently obliged to strip out any genuine dysfunction language in the diagnostic criteria, at least any such concepts that look like they apply to and are judged in the here and now – because the analysis proposes an evolutionary theoretic account of dysfunction. The position adopted in this essay, right from the first chapter, and which I believe is closer to the way the diagnostic manuals work, is that the relevant psychological dysfunction concepts precisely are in the diagnostic criteria, explicitly (for example in the criteria for most of the anxiety disorders) or implicitly, to be applied taking into account the clinical presentation and context as assessed by e.g. multi-informant clinical interview.

Wakefield goes on to illustrate the points made about the diagnostic criteria for separation anxiety disorder:

> For example, a study of the mental health of children of military personnel at three bases (Bickman *et al.* 1995) that happened to take place at the time of Desert Storm, when many parents of the children – including in some cases the mothers – were leaving for the Middle East, where children knew that parents could be killed or injured. The level of separation anxiety was high enough among many of the children that they could clearly qualify as having separation anxiety disorder according to DSM IV criteria; relative to typical separation responses common at their ages, their reactions were 'excessive' and 'developmentally inappropriate'. But in fact they could be considered to be responding with proportional, normal-range separation responses to a highly unusual environment in which an extraordinary kind of separation was taking place and in which they had realistic concerns that the parents would never come back . . . There is no question that there are real disorders of the separation anxiety response, but DSM's criteria for separation anxiety disorder seems inadvertently over-inclusive and reflect our values as much as they do genuine dysfunction in the child's anxiety mechanisms.

(op. cit., pp. 158–9)

We can note here also how use of a statistical criterion of normality – with which Wakefield credits the DSM criteria, rather than genuine dysfunction concepts – is constantly complicated by the question of relativity to groups and environments. And also how this relativity to groups and environments interacts with the problem of meaningfulness of the response (mental normality, appropriateness, etc.): what may look excessive (disproportionate, inappropriate) in relation to one group (children of civilians, or of military personnel in peace time), may be seen to be proportionate (appropriate) in another situation, and statistically normal relative to how 'most children would respond in that situation'. However, the main point here is that Wakefield in practice uses pretty much folk concepts of appropriateness and the like to sort out what is disordered from what is not – not evolutionary psychological models of the separation anxiety response in relation to the latest research from developmental cognitive neuroscience – which probably would not give an answer to just this question anyway. Further, as a corollary, the insistence that psychiatry is trying to capture genuine mental disorders, combined with what may well be the correct take on the folk concept, that it tracks the (perceived) absence of meaning, appropriateness, etc. leads to the problematic conclusion that genuine mental disorders are basically senseless.

Wakefield cites a case in which the proportionality of a high level separation anxiety response is entirely transparent – but in many cases that come to child and family clinics, there is some proportionality to context involving, for example, inconsistent parental care and attention, for various kinds of reason, or reasonable perception of threat, to the child or the parent, for example following accident or assault. Disorder attribution can depend on assessing proportionality – often a fine judgement. The more important questions from the clinical point of view are whether there is a need to treat, turning on the question of significant harm (for example, frequent unmanageable distress, not going to school, not able to go out with friends), and if there is, whether treatment should aim at modifying an inappropriate anxiety response or to help adjustment to what is a reasonably realistic perception of threat. In the first approach the therapeutic aim is change, and the communication could be along the lines: 'Let's try and find out whether mummy really is in as much danger as you fear (for example when she leaves the house, having recently been the victim of an assault) – let's go into it all and find out.' In the second the primary aim is containment of anxiety, and secondarily, better (less interfering) coping, for example along the following lines: 'I can see why you are so worried about your mother (what with her going to war and all), and you (the remaining carers and child) have to spend time thinking about mother and what she is doing, not all dangerous – and while we are about it or at other times we have to try to get on as best we can, trying to go to school, getting on with homework, seeing friends.' All this is just clinical work involving judgements about proportionality, context, harm caused, need to treat, treatment tack – all involving opinions about norms of child and family functioning in particular kinds of environments, and values about harm and need to treat. Nothing I see here fits well with the idea that in some cases we have a real disorder of natural functioning, in others projection of values.

Wakefield goes on to discuss adolescent substance abuse:

> DSM-IV diagnosis of substance abuse requires that any one of the following four criteria be met: poor role performance at work or at home due to recurrent substance use; recurrence substance use in hazardous circumstances, such as driving under the influence of alcohol; recurrent substance-related legal problems; or social or interpersonal

> conflicts due to substance use, such as arguments with family members about it. . .
> Certainly we do not want our adolescents driving under the influence, but given how
> common alcohol is at adolescent parties and the frequent immaturity of adolescent
> judgement in this area, this criterion potentially inappropriately pathologizes a large
> segment of our adolescent population.

(op. cit., p. 159)

The argument here apparently is that if we understand a behaviour pattern in terms of environmental factors (accessibility of alcohol) and adolescent psychology (immaturity) then we should drop our disorder attributions. This again has the effect of keeping disorder attributions tied to responses that make no sense as a psychological response of particular kinds of people, or people in a developmental stage, to particular environments. Apparently, however, the DSM is not approaching the matter in this way: apparently this condition is included in the manual on other grounds, that it causes much harm or risk of harm.

The third example of a DSM-IV diagnosis Wakefield considers is major depressive disorder:

> Depression is one of the most common diagnoses both in adults and in children and
> adolescents. Certainly, sadness is a painful and socially debilitating emotion. However,
> sadness, like other negative emotions, is a natural part of our biologically designed
> repertoire and not in itself a disorder. Unfortunately, the DSM IV's symptomatic
> criteria for diagnosing depression do not adequately distinguish extended periods of
> sadness, which, however painful, can be normal reactions to serious disruptions or
> losses in one's life, from disorders of sadness-generation mechanisms.

(op. cit., p. 160)

Here again, when Wakefield seeks to demarcate genuine disorders from non-disorders he appeals not to evolutionary psychological theory in relation to current cognitive neuroscience, but to an opinion about what is a normal reaction to serious disruption or loss, a matter apparently bound to involve some reference to proportionality, or 'meaningfulness' of the depressive reaction. Again, use of a demarcation criterion of this kind implies precisely that genuine mental disorder is characterized by meaninglessness – mere absence of order – which makes it not only semantically incorrect but also offensive to put the label on understandable, normal responses to adverse life circumstances. Wakefield is being consistent here: he apparently assumes that genuine mental orders have no conceivable point to them, but does not want all the presentations covered in the psychiatric manuals to be labelled in this way, rather he wants the diagnostic criteria tightened up so that – in an ideal world – they would capture all and only the genuine disorders. All the others, the distressing or troublesome mental conditions that are normal (enough) reactions to environmental circumstances, or which have some point to them, would be excluded. However the psychiatric manuals are not obviously headed in that direction, not unambiguously so, apparently acquiescing in the fact that many presentations described in them may indeed be normal enough in the population, or in some groups, and understandable to an extent at least, focusing rather on the harm caused and the need to treat. The ambiguity leaves wide open the problem of whether mental disorder really is a good general name for the conditions in the book. A name for harmful psychological conditions that did not connote meaninglessness, mere absence of order, would be more valid.

If, however, we go down the route of allowing in harmful psychological conditions that are normal enough, understandable to an extent at least, then where and how are we going to be able to draw the line? This problem – which follows on from the failure to find a viable naturalistic definition of mental disorder, or more accurately, from the failure to find a viable naturalistic demarcation criterion for mental disorder – will be considered in Chapter 5, but it can be noted here in the meantime. Wakefield signals the problem following on from the quotation above:

> Unfortunately the DSM IV's symptomatic criteria for diagnosing depression do not adequately distinguish extended periods of sadness, which, however painful, can be normal reactions to serious disruptions or losses in one's life, from disorders of sadness-generation mechanisms. Drug companies appear to be exploiting this failure by encouraging detection of DSM-defined depression in the population at large, for example, through education of physicians to detect formerly undetected depression, and the treatment of such detected depression with psychotropic medication. Thus, a wide range of disvalued conditions are being brought under the umbrella of medical treatment, not all of which may be disorders. Part of this trend is a recent move to give broader FDA approval to the use of psychotropic medication with adolescents for depression and other disorders, which raises serious ethical issues if indeed the DSM criteria tend to encompass normal youth.

(loc. cit.)

This is one of a variety of ethical issues in this area of demarcating mental disorder from order – deciding what gets included in the diagnostic manuals and what is excluded. Boundary problems of various kinds and ethical issues raised will be considered in more detail in Chapter 5. The point for here is that Wakefield intends his naturalistic, evolutionary theoretic definition of mental disorder should hold the line between normality and disorder – though in practice what is invoked are familiar and flexible standards of what judged to be meaningful, or typical in the group (raising the question of which group); etc.

The idea that mental disorder should only be diagnosed when meaning has run out, and criticism of the DSM criteria for not sticking to this rule, are signs of the problematic identified in the 1960s, the charge against mainstream psychiatry that it stripped the meaning out of madness, out of mental illness generally. It may be the case that mainstream psychiatry and its medical model did suppose that there is no meaning in mental illness: presumably no meaning flows from a diseased or otherwise lesioned part of the brain. Wakefield ends up defending this idea – that there is no meaning in mental disorder – but does not suppose that there is no meaning in the conditions described in the psychiatric manuals: we have after all by now enough psychology and social psychiatry to know that there is meaning all over them, so the conclusion has to be that the conditions as described in the psychiatric manuals are not all disorders. The psychiatric manuals, on the other hand, seem content to permit diagnosis of disorder even if there is or may be meaning. There are paradoxes and tensions here, to be taken up in Chapter 4.

In a recent book with Allan Horwitz, Wakefield develops at length the points made about depression in his (2002) chapter discussed above. The book has the self-explanatory title: *The Loss of Sadness: How psychiatry transformed normal sorrow into depressive disorder* (Horwitz and Wakefield 2007). The authors use three criteria to define normal sadness responses, the violation of which, it may be inferred, signifies depressive disorder, as follows:

> They emerge because of specific kinds of environmental triggers, especially loss; they are roughly proportionate in intensity to the provoking loss; and they end about when the loss situation ends or gradually cease as natural coping mechanisms allow an individual to adjust to the new circumstances and return to psychological and social equilibrium.

> (op. cit., p. 16)

It can be seen that these proposed criteria for normal sadness responses invoke relationships of the kind referred to from the beginning of this essay as meaningful connections, terminology deriving from Jaspers. Mental states of emotion, specifically, have to be appropriate in kind to their object (sadness to loss, anxiety to threat, etc.), they have to be proportionate in intensity to their object (much sadness for much loss, much anxiety for much threat, and vice versa), and they have to be appropriate in their duration (anxiety should go down when the threat is removed, more complicated for sadness).

Horwitz and Wakefield accept the official line that the DSM has made descriptive symptomatology the basis for diagnosis, in effect not situating mental states such as low mood in the context of life circumstances and events, and hence not assessing appropriateness in that context. They write:

> In response to criticisms during the 1960s and 1970s that different psychiatrists would not diagnose the same person with the same symptoms in the same way (this problem was known as the 'unreliability' of diagnosis), in 1980 the DSM began to use lists of symptoms to establish clear definitions for each disorder.

(op. cit., p. 7)

Considering the definition of major depressive disorder (MDD) – for this purpose this being the criteria of major depressive episode quoted above in the Appendix to Chapter 1 – the authors conclude:

> The basic flaw ... of the DSM definition of MDD ... is simply that it *fails to take into account the context of the symptoms and thus fails to exclude from the disorder category intense sadness, other than in reaction to the death of a loved one, that arises from the way human beings naturally respond to major losses.*

(op. cit., p. 14: italics in the original)

On this basis Horwitz and Wakefield go on to recommend that diagnostic criteria should be adapted to be context sensitive and hence amenable to the distinguishing what is an appropriate, normal response from what is not.

Whether adopting this recommendation is radical in relation to the psychiatric manuals is a moot point, however. It would be radical if the diagnostic criteria in their present DSM-IV form really were purely descriptive and context-free. However, as argued throughout this essay, there is ample evidence that diagnostic criteria sets often invoke distinctions between normal and abnormal functioning, typically by specifying that the mental states or behaviour involve rupture of one kind or another of meaningful connections. This was signalled in Chapter 1 (section 1.3) as an apparently inevitable limitation to the purely descriptive/observational project recommended by Hempel. In the case of the anxiety disorders, problems with emotions reasonably comparable with depressive disorder, there is frequent reference in the diagnostic criteria to anxiety being excessive or in some other way inappropriate. For example the DSM-IV criteria for separation anxiety disorder refer repeatedly to distress being excessive (American Psychiatric Association 1995, p. 113; see also earlier in this section), the criteria for generalized anxiety disorder refer to excessive and uncontrollable worry (op. cit., pp. 435–6), the criteria for specific phobia refer to excessive or unreasonable fear (op. cit., p. 410), and the criteria for adjustment disorder refer to distress that is in excess of what would be expected from exposure to the stressor (op. cit., p. 626). There is also the fact that the DSM-IV criteria for major depressive episode do in fact exclude (uncomplicated) bereavement, somewhat half-heartedly gesturing to the intent to distinguish normal from abnormal sadness, and, finally, the DSM-IV definition itself (quoted in section 2.2) explicitly excludes from mental disorders expectable responses to stressors. In short, the DSM already does not keep entirely to descriptive symptomatology-based diagnosis. This being so, it would not be such a radical departure from current methodology to include terms like 'excessive' or 'goes on too long' in the criteria for major depression. How much inclusion of such terms would negatively impact on reliability is an empirical question. Any negative impact might be less important in clinical settings, and researchers have methods for dealing with problems of this kind, such as coding manuals illustrated by case vignettes. In any case problems of reliability already exist for other diagnoses for various reasons including use of normative qualifiers of the proposed kind. On the question of agreement over the application of norms of psychological functioning, it was noted when first considered in Chapter 1 (section 1.3), that agreement can be high within a particular group – as high as for what we think of as just descriptions – providing the norms are held in common in the group. This is to say, use of norms (such as excessive emotion for that degree of loss/threat) is not an obstacle in principle to the reliability project.

The issue of principle that is particularly relevant here is whether these kinds of norms invoking the presence/absence of meaningful connections, in a general sense, track the functioning/dysfunctioning of natural evolved mental mechanisms – such as a sadness-generating mechanism. Considerations relevant to the appropriate intensity and duration of sadness are potentially complex, including individual temperamental and previous learning experiences, and the availability and use of protective and recovery mechanisms including social support. These factors show up for example in the implicit or explicit comparison of responses in the individual with those in various reference groups – is appropriateness of intensity and duration to be judged by reference to individuals with protective temperaments, histories and current circumstances, or otherwise? Amongst this complexity and variability, do our judgements of appropriateness or otherwise really track some fact, whether or not the natural, evolved sadness-generating mechanism is functioning as designed?

Horwitz and Wakefield suppose that this is so, consistent with Wakefield's evolutionary naturalist definition of mental disorder as proposed over several decades and reviewed in this chapter. Yet again, there is no construction of a model of normal sadness generating mechanisms that would have testable implications for neural structure and functioning, or from which predictions could be derived about what kinds of losses should appropriately (if the mechanisms were functioning properly) lead to what intensity of sadness, or about the appropriate duration of sadness following particular losses and sadness intensity (if the adjustment /recovery mechanisms were functioning properly).

I am sceptical about whether this would be a sensible aim, given the complexity of moderating variables at an individual level – not to mention at a cultural level, of which more in the next section. In any case, in the absence of specific evolutionary psychological and cognitive neuroscience models with specific predictions, the line of thought that seems to be left is that the three criteria for normal sadness proposed by Horwitz and Wakefield, cited above – appropriateness of the object of sadness (loss), proportionality of the intensity of sadness to the loss, and timeliness of recovery– serve to define the proper functioning of the natural evolved sadness-generating/recovery mechanisms, which has a tautological rather than an empirical air about it. By all means if sadness occurs for no good reason (in the absence of loss), or is too intense for its object (is excessive in intensity), or goes on for too long (is excessive in duration), then there is a dysfunction and possibly a disorder. The point is that these judgements of breakdown of meaningful connections, as they are being called here, are conceptually tied to judgements of dysfunction and disorder – this is a familiar and obvious enough point. So we can analyse mental disorder in terms of mental mechanism dysfunction and this in turn in terms of mental states and processes having no apparent meaning (being inappropriate in some way, or without good reasons, etc.) – but it is not clear that this manoeuvring is homing in on some natural fact of the matter, that a natural mental mechanism is failing to function as designed in evolution, as opposed to expressing our considered view in specific cases or kinds of cases as to what is or is not normal and what does or does not make sense. Nor is it evident that there is a natural fact of the matter here that is independent of social norms and values, a point to be taken up in the next section.

On the other hand, evolutionary naturalism aside, are not Horwitz and Wakefield right to protest if the criteria for major depressive disorder really do allow in – because they make little or no effort to keep out – normal reactions to significant loss? This goes to the heart of the matter as to why conditions are in the psychiatric textbooks. From one natural point of view, disorders are meant to be really different from normal functioning and normal reactions – and this is the intuition that naturalism seeks to justify, though with difficulty. However, there is another way of approaching disorder, which has far more to do with unmanageable distress, disability and risk of adverse outcomes, and in which difference between what is normal and abnormal, and in what sense, is less of an issue. From this point of view, normal troubles and reactions, in the sense of what is common in the population for example, may be just as clinically significant as abnormal troubles and reactions – because they involve just as much unmanageable distress, disability and risk of adverse outcomes.

Bereavement is cited as an exclusion criterion in the DSM-IV diagnostic crite-ria of Major Depressive Episode (quoted in full in the Appendix to Chapter 1), and this may be because it is normal, understandable and common in the population. More critical, I suggest, is that it is understood as a self-limiting condition with no lasting ill-effects on mental state and functioning. This is consistent with the fact that if there are 'complications' of bereavement, such as persistence or marked functional impairment or suicidal ideation, then the DSM-IV does warrant diagnosis of disorder. Many conditions con-sidered as medical illnesses or diseases, or otherwise considered in need of medical attention because they are associated with harm or risk, are common enough in the population and may involve normal responses to more or less damaging or toxic environments. Normality is not the point – harm is. These issues, involving non-naturalist approaches to disorder, will be taken up in Chapter 4.

First, to complete discussion of evolutionary naturalism, we consider the impact of the current paradigm in behavioural science on its presumed fundamental distinction between the natural and the social.

3.8 Evolutionary psychology and social norms: implications for evolutionary theoretic naturalism

Naturalist approaches to mental disorder seek to define a natural fact that underpins the concept. In one version, Boorse's biostatistical naturalism, this fact is claimed to be subspecies-typical functioning; and in the other, Wakefield's evolutionary naturalism, the alleged fact is failure of a mental mechanism to function as designed in evolution. Both versions of naturalism also have social values involved in disorder attribution, recognizing that disor-der is negatively valued. In this way the analyses have the form: mental disorder is harmful failure of natural functioning. The naturalist approaches were responding to problems identified in the critiques of psychiatry in the 1960s and 1970s, with charges that psychiatry was involved in the control of social deviance while masquerading as medical treatment of mental illness. Both sides in the debate accepted the distinction between medical problems and social problems, and the naturalist definitions to mental disorder took up the challenge in just these terms, aiming to resolve the conflicts by including both social values and natural, non-social, medical facts.

However, the science has moved on since the 1970s, and it is likely that the distinctions and dichotomies presupposed in the psychiatry/anti-psychiatry debates, and in the naturalist resolutions of those debates, are no longer viable. The proposal in the previous chapter (section 2.7) is that evolutionary psychology, combined with genetics, serves to break down the underlying contrast between what – in the domain of the psychological – is natural (evolved) and what is determined by social processes. This happens in two main ways. First, because human evolution has been in social groups, some evolved functions are social, in which case the contrast between the natural and the social breaks down. Second, evolved factors may contribute a degree of specific content, but social factors elaborate this in diverse ways, with the evolved content typically identifiable at a more abstract level than the concrete social expression. The implication of this is that natural norms of psychological functioning are typically instantiated by social norms, and breaking one kind may involve breaking the other.

The emphasis in current genetics on gene–environment interactions brings out that psychological phenotypes – including at least some psychiatric conditions – are not simply evolved functions, nor are they produced by environmental conditions alone, including by social processes, but are typically the product of various kinds of interaction between the two.

Insofar as the current science has tended to break down the sharp divide between what is natural, evolved, and what is social, then the rationale for naturalist definitions of mental disorder is also broken down, and behind that, the underlying problematic expressed in the 1960s as to whether psychiatric illness or disorder is essentially defined by medical, scientific facts, or by social norms and values.

Here is a brief indication of the problems for Wakefield's evolutionary theoretic analysis of 'mental disorder' from a recent textbook on developmental psychopathology:

> [Wakefield's] approach appears promising, but it is still problematic to the extent that, for most mental disorders, it has not been possible to identify a biologic dysfunction within individuals, even in those severely impairing conditions where evidence for genetic factors is indisputable (e.g., Autism). In addition, the definition suffers from the tautological definition of dysfunction as a 'biologic system not behaving as it was designed to do' (from an evolutionary perspective); and such definitions invoke anachronistic notions of some hard and fast lines between so-called biologic and sociocultural factors.
>
> Jensen, Hoagwood and Zitner (2006, p. 32)

Here is another commentator elaborating on this last critical point:

> Even if we grant that a specific 'natural' function can sometimes be identified by evolutionary theory, the threshold of dysfunction is undetermined by evolutionary theory because the ecological niche or adaptive context is constantly changing. Consider, for example, psychological systems designed to seek out novelty. When are they functioning well or poorly – that is, what is enough novelty? What about systems

designed for attachment to others? When are these too strong, too weak, or inappropriately directed? Clearly, the normal functioning of these more complex systems cannot be defined without reference to a specific social environment with its attendant cultural values. If this is so for admittedly universal motivations like novelty-seeking, attachment, and aggression, how much more so for socially and culturally acquired systems like the search for prestige, esthetic pleasure, or religious experience. Yet, these more elaborate motivational systems or functions are central to peoples' lives and are the first to be affected by mental disorder.

There are many ways of framing or interpreting the natural functions of our bodies, and the ones we find most convincing reflect our cultural values. For example, we tend to think of adaptation in terms of individuals rather than groups because of the individualistic bias of Euro-American societies, and so we are less likely to recognize and give central place to functions whose main purpose may be intragroup harmony rather than individual fitness. Labelling certain features of human behaviour as natural is one way to ignore their cultural shaping. In fact, there is little consensus on what our psychological systems are for – they are so malleable that they can be for almost anything – and many evolutionary psychologists argue that we have evolved to be able to adapt to situations rather than to have fixed or specific functions. Any change in culture will change the fitness of specific psychological traits, give new meaning and purpose to biological functions, and change their boundaries and interdependence. Beyond a few other relatively simple physiological functions, it is impossible to identify what psychological systems or functions are for in any universal sense.

Kirmayer (1994, pp. 18–19)

This last sentence may make the point too strongly, but this is more matter of dialectical play, since the main point is now probably accepted, that psychological systems or functions are influenced in some degrees by both evolved and cultural factors, and rarely if ever by the one in the absence of the other. It is plausible to say, for example, that the anxiety system or function is for the detection of and dealing with threat, but nevertheless its expressions – its realisations – are sensitive to cultural factors, as well as to individual influences.

The strength of Wakefield's analysis – like evolutionary psychological approaches generally – derives from its focus on what we may assume are the universal, natural, evolved functions, and hence on their failure. The anxiety system or function, understood in the general way above, can be reasonably considered to have broken down if it fails to work in the presence of threat, or does work in the absence of threat. However, determination of presence or absence of threat, of what is a reasonable threshold for anxiety, of when fear should be overcome, not acted upon, because of other priorities – all these matters are not settled by natural, genetic, evolved factors alone, since they are highly sensitive to cultural and personal norms and values. Similar points apply to other principles of appropriate psychological functions and their breakdown, such as: depressed mood and behavioural deactivation are an appropriate response to loss. Or: belief-acquisition systems are designed to use information from experience and education, in a broad sense. Or: learning mechanisms are designed to adjust expectations in exposure to environments that have salient differences compared to the ones in which they were formed. In each case the point is along the lines Kirmayer identifies in the above quote: these general psychological systems and functions are realized in specific cultural contexts, and in specific individuals, and norms of functioning are interpreted accordingly.

Given the terms of the 1960s debates, the challenge was clearly set to define a fundamental non-social, natural matter of fact that would underlie legitimate attribution of mental illness or disorder – as opposed to social deviance. This challenge was taken up by the naturalist definitions proposed by Boorse and in particular by Wakefield, but how does Wakefield manage to define the critical difference required between a natural and a social function? The move is fast – here is Wakefield in one of his early papers:

> What, then, is a dysfunction? An obvious place to begin is the supposition that a dysfunction implies an unfulfilled function, that is, a failure of some mechanism in the organism to perform its function. However, not all kinds of functions are relevant. For example, one's nose functions to hold up one's glasses, and the sound of the heart performs a useful function in medical diagnosis. But a person whose nose is shaped in such a way that it does not properly support glasses does not thereby have a nasal disorder, and a person whose heart does not make the usual sounds is not thereby suffering from a cardiac disorder. A disorder is different from a failure to function in a socially preferred manner precisely because a dysfunction exists only when an organ cannot perform as it is naturally (i.e., independently of human intentions) supposed to perform. Presumably, the functions that are relevant are natural functions.

(1992b, p. 381)

In this example of the function of the nose we have a clear fix on the evolved function (a kind of sense-perception), a clear fix on an additional cultural function that is entirely unrelated (supporting glasses), and 'design' of the nose is pulled only one way. It is all much more complex when we move from glasses and noses to highly evolved social behaviours, such as infant- and childcare, and to socially interpreted evolved behaviours such as fear, whether in response to social or natural stimuli. In these examples the clarity in identification of what is the evolved function and what is the socially designed function, and the sharp demarcation between them, are lost. In these complex cases, which in the realm of the psychological are probably the great majority, the biological evolved mechanism – though it does have content (e.g. anxiety is about threat-perception) – is realized in a concrete social environment, and if the mechanism is failing, so is the concrete social norm. Conversely, if no social norm is being broken, the mechanism is not broken either.

It was the drive to naturalism, the aim of defining a sense of psychological dysfunction and hence mental disorder that rests on an objective, scientific matter of natural fact, not on vagaries of social (let alone personal) norms and values, which led Wakefield to highlight only the evolutionary basis of human behaviour, and to systematically ignore its origins in socialization processes and individual differences; this notwithstanding the fact that all three are clearly, in the current science, all involved and interwoven.

Wakefield's analysis rests on a line of reasoning something like the following:

1. Concepts of systemic function and dysfunction essentially involve the design of the system: normal functioning is functioning as designed; abnormal functioning is not functioning as designed.

2. In the case of psychological functions, we are only interested in those that are naturally designed (as opposed to socially designed).

3. In the case of natural psychological functions, the best scientific account of design that we have is evolutionary selection.

4. Hence, psychological dysfunction (natural dysfunction, the only kind that interests us) must involve failure to function as designed by evolution.

Where is the error? I take it that the first premise is fine, or good enough, and so is the inference to the conclusion from the three premises. The fault lies in the second premise which transfers to the third, and hence to the conclusion. The problem with the second premise is that it assumes an invalid demarcation between natural and social psychological functioning. This invalid assumption affects the third premise, because this now assumes what is also invalid, that evolutionary selection – in isolation from social selection – accounts for the class of psychological functions of interest. These invalidities compound in the conclusion, which postulates failure in a hard to track down natural, evolved psychological function, in which social factors play no role.

Modification of the argument leading to Wakefield's conclusion would replace the second premise – the one that is generally least discussed. We would have to consider the question of the origin and design of psychological functioning. According to the considerations so far, the answers here typically include a complex mixture of genetic, evolved factors, and social factors, with individual differences running though them both. Depending on which is dominant, or which is thought to be dominant, we can attribute the origin – the design – of the behaviour to human nature, to society, to subculture, to family (to family genes or behaviour or both), or to the individual's constitution, character or personal values. In brief, according to current behavioural science in an evolutionary/genetic framework, three kinds of factor are implicated in the design of human behaviour – evolutionary/genetic, environmental, including the cultural, and individual – and, these three kinds of factor interact in complex ways. To each kind of design there corresponds a type of norm: evolutionary/genetic, social, and individual – again with no clear divisions, and interplay between them.

It follows that a mental state or behavioural response can be said to be dysfunctional – to deviate from design norms – in one or more of three ways: first, in that it fails to operate in the way designed by evolution; second in that it fails to operate in the way taught by and sanctioned by the culture; and third, in that it fails to work in the way the person intended, according to his needs and values as he sees them. However, these three kinds of dysfunction are not clearly separated, and they interact. The first kind belongs to an evolutionary theoretic framework and is relative to conditions in the environment of evolutionary adaptiveness. The second kind of dysfunction is the one accessible to social theory; it is immersed in the present, in more or less diverse social realities. There is also a third reading of dysfunctional psychic life, the one at the individual level involving deviation from personal norms and values, evident to the person involved. This meaning has been neglected, to do with the fact that 'madness' was silenced – though it is increasingly apparent in discourse led by service users. These are not, however, three meanings of psychological function and dysfunction – the evolutionary, the social and the individual – they are rather three interwoven themes which run through all kinds of case.

Consider for example what norms are involved in the judgement that, for example, a person's extreme fear of dogs leading to reckless escape behaviour should count as a mental disorder? Well, they are objective, natural norms, because the evolved anxiety response is designed to respond to real threat, and dogs (these ones let us suppose) pose no real threat. On the other hand, how are we to know what counts as a real enough threat, and an appropriate response? That may be an easy case, not causing much disagreement, at least within a given cultural context. Harder cases involve competing views. Is refusal to fight in war because of extreme fear, or fleeing the battle, cowardice, or reasonable, or a mental disorder? Various accounts can be given in terms of what is natural, what is overriding group priority, and what is individual choice. In one account it is natural to try to escape near certain death; in another it is natural, and a social obligation, to want to fight for the group. Views as to what is natural here, or what is the natural way to deal with competing natural responses, are interwoven with complex social purposes, rules and sanctions, and with individual attitudes and values – and all these operate both within the individual in question, and in the person or group making the judgement on him.

Another kind of case, involving the rationality of belief rather than emotion: a person converses with spirits – he says he is, and acts as though he is. In a spirit-free culture, this will be taken to be failure of belief acquisition, cognitive-sensory mechanisms, an hallucination delusion. Unless, that is, it is found that the person lives in a subculture that does converse with spirits, in which case he is only behaving in a normal, socialized way. Unless, again, it turns out that people within the subculture judge that the person is conversing in the wrong way, in a radically wrong way, not following the normal rules and regulations, in which case the person may be ill – disordered – after all. Again judgement of mental disorder apparently involves reference to both natural norms and social norms, which are not clearly separable. Mental disorder attribution may well turn on a view as to what is unnatural as opposed to natural, but since what is natural has been cultivated and shaped by socialization processes, these have to be taken into account.

Another kind of example, involving mainly behaviour: prolonged, repetitive, stylized washing. In a culture that is relatively free of purification rituals, at least of the washing variety, this may well indicate obsessive compulsive disorder. It is not clear what natural function might be failing here – perhaps to do with not wasting large amounts of time doing pointless things while neglecting other things that matter; that is to say, some prioritizing rule. On the other hand, in cultures high on purification rituals, the behaviour may be normal. On the other hand again, typically in these cultures a distinction is drawn between high degrees of piety and going beyond this, as it were, over the top, this being a sign not of piety but of some other process, a disorder, attributable to malign external influence, or illness. How this judgement is made may in turn take into account individual differences: some people are more pious than others, or more conscientious, blending into slow, perseverative perfectionism. A general rule can be broken, a natural norm of behaviour can be violated, but what this amounts to in particular kinds of case depends on social interpretations and individual values.

In general, the same kinds of point apply to all psychological phenotypes, including those of interest in psychiatry. Judgements as to what is normal or abnormal in emotional and cognitive processing such as in anxiety, depression and guilt, in attention, belief acquisition, theory of mind and social understanding, and action itself, such as in ritualistic behaviour, or in antisocial behaviour – in every kind of case these judgements involve, in typically speculative, varying proportions, combinations of grounds invoking what is natural, what is social, and what is individual – in interaction.

In the recent statement of his position in his book with Allan Horwitz (Horwitz and Wakefield 2007) considered in the previous section, Wakefield seems to concede that psychological functioning is not readily teased apart into what is natural/evolved, on the one hand, and what is socialized, on the other. It was noted in the previous section that the authors use three criteria to define normal sadness responses, as opposed to depressive disorder, as follows:

> They emerge because of specific kinds of environmental triggers, especially loss; they are roughly proportionate in intensity to the provoking loss; and they end about when the loss situation ends or gradually cease as natural coping mechanisms allow an individual to adjust to the new circumstances and return to psychological and social equilibrium.

> (op. cit., p. 16)

It was argued in the previous section that these criteria are close to saying, using Jasper's terminology, that normal sadness is meaningful, while disorder is not, and that accordingly they run the risk of being true pretty much by definition, especially in the absence of independent ways of determining what reactions in what circumstances are appropriate and proportionate and which are not. In brief, it is not clear that that these criteria provide an objective way of demarcating between normal sadness and abnormal depressive disorder – they just re-state the difference. However, for the current section the question is this: using criteria of these kinds, what becomes of the difference between natural and social psychological functioning?

Here are Horwitz and Wakefield on the interplay between the natural and the cultural:

> The categories that trigger sadness –losses of attachment, status, and meaning – are common across all societies . . . Nonetheless, culture influences evolutionarily shaped responses in a variety of ways. First, cultural meanings influence which particular events counts as losses. These meanings also influence contextual factors, such as humiliation and entrapment, which determine the severity of loss . . . Cultural values also set the parameters for what are considered proportionate responses to loss. They set the scale of intensity and duration of appropriate responses, shape how emotionally expressive people are, and influence the aspects of the response public expressions of the emotion emphasise . . . Cultural norms also affect what is viewed as the appropriate duration of loss responses.

> (op. cit., pp. 43–4)

Given these points – which are of the sort reviewed earlier in this section, and in more detail previously in Chapter 2 (section 2.7) – it is not clear what remains of the naturalist vision of defining a natural as opposed to a social basis for disorder attribution. The basis seems rather to be natural and social interwoven. The definition of dysfunction of sadness-generating/recovery mechanisms apparently involves deviation from social norms and values as well as from evolutionary design, in which case the social norms and negative evaluation involved in disorder attribution do not after all reside in a distinctive 'harm' component of the concept. In brief, interplay of this kind between natural evolved and social factors in shaping norms of psychological and behavioural functioning undermines the original basis, rationale, and principles of construction of the evolutionary naturalist definition of disorder.

3.9 Summary: problems with naturalism

The 1960s critiques of mainstream psychiatry and its medical model charged it with mistaking social norms for medical, pathologizing what is fundamentally social deviance. Interweaving with this charge was the protest that psychiatry stripped the meaning out of so-called mental illness, disqualifying it and the people so labelled. A major challenge set to psychiatry was to show that that its diagnostic practice was based on some objective, natural matter of fact, not (just) on social norms and values. Two main proposals responded to this challenge, both known as forms of naturalism. In both the resolution was to suppose that the concept of mental illness, increasingly known as mental disorder, involved both kinds of norms: scientific, objective, natural – and social. The factual matter was meant to be that of psychological dysfunction, and social norms and values entered into judgements that dysfunction was harmful and undesirable (causing e.g. high levels of distress, or impairment of desirable social role functioning). The hard work was then to specify with reasonable precision and objectivity, and without the introduction of social norms and values, what psychological dysfunction means. The two main options are as follows. First, correct functioning of some biological or psychological mechanism is just a matter of what it generally does, and dysfunction is a matter of deviation from this statistical norm. Second, correct functioning is a matter of what the mechanism was designed, in evolution, to do, and dysfunction is a matter of deviation from this designed function.

There are several problems with the statistical definition. One is that it has to make mere difference from the usual a dysfunction, and hence, if harmful, into a disorder; but is not clear why mere difference, in the absence of harm, should be thought of as dysfunctional at all. A second and related problem is that difference from the norm is usually a continuous matter not a categorical one, generally and especially for those traits that are (even roughly) normally distributed. The point at which difference becomes dysfunction seems arbitrary from a statistical point of view, and the judgement is most likely to be made by the point at which harm is caused, not distance from the mean as such. Third, all questions of statistical means and deviations are population relative, and populations vary widely in relation to within-individual characteristics (such as age and gender) and environments (physical, biological and social) and interaction between them. This introduces a relativity into judgements of statistical normality and deviance from which it is difficult to find a way out. In practice it is likely that more or less real or idealized population norms do in practice guide judgements as to psychological normality and deviance, but tainted, as it were, by local social experience, and by values, aspirations and hopes.

The alternative to this statistical naturalism is the claim that normal functioning is a matter of design, and hence, in the biopsychological case, of evolution. The most influential and best worked-out theory of this kind is Wakefield's. Wakefield's proposal has much to be said for it, and much against, but one of the major problems focused on here is this: it has the effect of making psychological dysfunction, and hence mental disorder, a hypothesis, and moreover, a complex one pertaining to theories in evolutionary psychology and their implications for mind/brain organization. As such, this interpretation of mental dysfunction and hence mental disorder is not obviously suited for either clinical use or as a descriptive characterization of the conditions of interest for the purposes of basic science or outcome research.

Wakefield's evolutionary naturalism highlights the tension between reliability and validity in the psychiatric diagnostic manuals. The more that they use purely descriptive, observational terminology for defining symptoms and syndromes, the more they may include normal reactions and behaviour. Evolutionary naturalism has a very clear idea as to when disorder attribution is valid, and it entirely antithetical to the suggestion that disorder can be just observed and described. If evolutionary naturalism is adopted, reliability of diagnosis would – presumably – collapse. We would need research programmes in evolutionary psychology and psychiatry to work on distinguishing (genuine) mental disorders, involving failure of a mental mechanism to function as designed in evolution, from the merely apparent: conditions associated with distress, disability or risk that did not, however, involve any mental mechanism failure of the requisite kind. In the meantime we would need another name for the conditions of interest in the manuals – not disorders. What implications the distinction between genuine disorders and apparent disorders has for level of harm, prognosis, need to treat or response to treatment, is unclear. It is possible that evolutionary naturalism's distinction between genuine and only apparent disorders does no practical work – it is a somewhat abstract theory.

Apart from the implications of the difference, how can evolutionary naturalism demarcate between disorders and normality? In practice it seems that the distinction is not drawn by means of complex evolutionary theoretic models related to brain/mind functioning, but on more available phenomena including apparent lack of appropriateness, purpose, rationality or meaning of mental states and associated behaviour. These are the kinds of criteria invoked in the psychiatric manuals, and, like deviance from indeterminate population norms, they are apparently not matters of absolute fact but are flexible.

These criteria are also subject to local norms and assumptions. The validity of the distinction between natural and social functions and norms is not so much an assumption of Wakefield's approach as the explicit terms of the debate in which naturalism is a key participant. The charge against psychiatry in the 1960s was that it disguised social deviance as medical disorder; the conciliatory response from naturalism in the 1970s on was that mental disorder involved both negative social evaluation and medical disorder, this latter being a matter of natural – as opposed to social – fact. Insofar as the presumed contrast what is natural and what is determined by social processes breaks down, then the terms of the debate break down and the naturalist definitions with them. In practice the restriction of the psychological and behavioural functions that we are interested in to natural functions, has to be stipulated. Once this stipulation has been made, evolutionary design can be plausibly introduced as the key to dysfunction/disorder attribution. But this line of thought is invalid to the extent that psychological and behavioural functioning is typically designed not only by evolution, but also socialization processes, and by individual character and choice. These three interweaving origins of design – the genetic, the social and the individual – are all reflected in the complex concept of mental disorder.

3.10 Annotated bibliography

The chapter opens with reference to the 1960s critiques of psychiatry, reviewed more fully in the previous chapter, especially in section 2.6, and references are given there. Various subsequent developments are listed, for which entries to the literature include the following: closure of the asylums and the beginnings of care in the community – UK references include O'Brian (1992) and Rogers and Pilgrim (2001); beginnings of service user groups – UK commentaries include Campbell (1996, 1999); work within psychiatry to improve diagnosis – review and references are in Chapter 1 (especially sections 1.1, 1.2 and 1.6) and in Chapter 4 (especially section 4.1); emergence of a new paradigm in the science – considered with references in Chapter 2, especially sections 2.3 and 2.4; influence of evolutionary ideas in psychology and psychiatry – considered with references in Chapter 2, especially section 2.5; developments in psychopharmacology – see e.g. Lehmann and Ban (1997), Domino (1999), and Ban (2001), with critical commentary by Healy (2002).

The first section of the chapter goes on to introduce some issues around medical and social views of illness. Discussion not referenced in the text includes recent changes of views in psychiatry about hearing voices – see e.g. Romme and Esher (1989), Romme, Honig, Noorthoorn and Esher (1992), and Peters, Joseph and Garety (1999); also remarks on OCD and culture; research includes, in Judaism (Greenberg 1984; Suess and Halpern 1989), Islam (Pfeiffer 1981; Mahgoub and Abdel-Hafeiz 1991), Catholicism (Suess and Halpern 1989), and Hinduism (Chakraborty and Banerji 1975; Sharma 1968).

The second section is on Boorse's biostatistical naturalism. Boorse's main papers include his (1975, 1976a, b, 1977, 1987), with a more recent re-statement, update and response to secondary literature in his (1997). Criticisms have been made of Boorse's proposed distinction between illness and disease, and the broad use of the term disease, but the critical issue for the present purpose is the claim that natural functioning can be defined in statistical terms. Critical commentary includes Hare (1986), Kovacs (1998), Stempsey (2000), DeVito (2000), and Fulford (2001). The issue of pathologizing difference is highlighted in controversies about disability – see e.g. Silvers (1998) for discussion directly related to difference from 'species-typical functioning'; and see also Chapter 5 (section 5.3) for reference to social vs medical models of disability. It is remarked that statistical notions of normal functioning – especially in the absence of a clear reference group – can blur into idealization of the normal. This has been noted by other commentators, for example Davis and Bradley (1996) discuss this usage of 'normal' in medicine.

The third section summarizes some key features of Wakefield's evolutionary theoretic naturalism. The primary and secondary literature on this is extensive, and some key papers are cited in the text.

Key papers for the fourth section on variety of causal pathways to psychopathology from an evolutionary psychological perspective are cited in the text, and there is fuller discussion with references in Chapter 2, section 2.4, and in the accompanying bibliographical section. References to material in sections 3.5–3.8 are in the text.

Chapter 4

Clinical definition
Distress, disability,
and the need to treat

4.1 Definition of mental disorder in the psychiatric manuals – another look

The definitions of mental disorder in the psychiatric manuals were considered in the first chapter by way of introducing the issues under discussion. Some relevant concepts and themes in the current biobehavioural sciences were considered in the second chapter, along with sociological critiques of the medical model of mental illness and disorder, particularly in the 1960s. Subsequent attempts to define an objective, scientifically valid basis of mental disorder, under the heading of naturalism, were considered in the third chapter and found to be problematic in various ways. Against this background this chapter starts by taking another look at the approach to mental disorder in the psychiatric manuals.

Mainstream psychiatry in the second half of the twentieth century was, I suggest, faced with – at least – two kinds of challenge:

1. Respond to the anti-psychiatry charge that the label mental illnes represents the medicalization of what is rather social deviance, and the pathologizing of normal problems of living

2. At the same time, and regardless, to get on with the tasks of clinical and scientific psychiatry – treatment and the understanding of causes – this requiring viable description and classification of its subject matter as a basis for communication between and among clinicians and researchers.

These two tasks were more or less independent. The first task was historically framed, ideological, sociological, about the relationship of psychiatry to society, though with practical resonance, to do for example with management of the problems in healthcare agencies and medicine specifically. The second task was more within psychiatry itself, more a matter for psychiatrists than for any other group, though the DSM in particular became the textual embodiment of the institution of psychiatry, and hence it was up for scrutiny in relation to the first problematic. It was the ideological, sociological problem that primarily gave rise to the need for a definition of mental disorder; left to themselves, occupied with their own tasks, the psychiatric manuals may well have managed without, as was the case through to the DSM-III. This suggests that once the diagnostic criteria have been satisfied, and the presentation is serious enough – causes problems – there is not meant to be a *whole other* question whether the person has a mental disorder or not. However, the 1960s critiques had raised questions that were not going to go away, and it had to happen that they would be raised in relation to the new, highly visible psychiatric diagnostic manuals, with their laudably transparent diagnostic criteria. Are they using medical, scientific norms? Or is mental disorder primarily just another name for what goes against prevailing social norms and values? What is the difference between being normal and having a mental disorder? What is really meant by 'mental disorder'?

In response to the general challenge formulated in the 1960s, reinvigorated by debate in the 1970s, the task was clearly set to define mental disorder, to make clear the basis of why conditions were in the manuals or excluded, and clear that this basis was medical – scientific and objective – not a matter of social rules of normal behaviour. In response to this intellectual and cultural challenge, there were papers in the 1970s through to the early 1990s by very thoughtful psychiatrists tackling the definition of mental disorder, and seminal papers by philosophers applying themselves to the problem, Christopher Boorse, and Jerome Wakefield, also a social worker by training. Boorse and Wakefield produced versions of naturalism already considered in the previous chapter; psychiatrists such as Scadding, Kendell and Klein wrote on related themes, considering the viability of definitions of illness and disorder based on evolutionary theoretic concepts. These writers and others were focusing primarily on the first challenge, listed above, namely, the problem identified in the 1960s: is psychiatry a proper branch of medicine, with a valid notion of illness, or is it a masquerading agency of social control – a psychosocial police force? The emphasis in this task was valid definition of medical-psychiatric as opposed to social disorder, in brief, on conceptual validity.

There was, however, another task, closely connected and interacting, but I suggest distinguishable, the one explicitly tied closely to the development of the psychiatric manuals and their definitions. That is to say, it belonged more to the second challenge mentioned at the start of this section than to the first. This was the task of *trying to define or characterize the conditions in the manuals*, and it was the one taken up primarily by Robert Spitzer, who with colleagues produced the first explicit definition of mental disorder for the

DSM-III, which remains with some amendment in the DSM-IV. While superficially the same as the first task – both come under the heading of attempts to define mental disorder, and though interacting in substantial ways – my suggestion is that the real task undertaken in relation to the psychiatric manuals was not primarily construction of a conceptually valid, intellectually rigorous definition of the concept of mental disorder, preferably one that made clear its scientific basis and specifically its distinction from social deviance. It was rather to try to characterize the psychiatric conditions – why were they psychiatric conditions? What are their common features? Or their essential, defining features? This is a difficult enough task in itself, and leads in directions different to the problem of conceptual validity in the definition of mental disorder. One way of stating the difference is to say that one problem is the meaning of the term mental disorder, while the other is the nature of the phenomena, whatever they may be called. This belongs with the fact, I suggest, that the manuals are somewhat cavalier about the term mental disorder, having it on the front cover (and for good enough reasons) but at the same time expressing discontent with it and just as happy to use others – because, I suggest, the real interest is in the conditions themselves, not in names and conceptual analysis.

The ICD-10 introduces its definition of mental disorder under the heading 'Problems with terminology':

> The term 'disorder' is used throughout the classification, so as to avoid even greater problems inherent in the use of terms such as 'disease' and 'illness'. 'Disorder' is not an exact term, but it is used here to imply the existence of a clinically recognizable set of symptoms or behaviour associated in most cases with distress and with interference with personal functions.

> (World Health Organization 1992, p. 5)

The DSM-IV definition is preceded by extensive caveats and qualifications:

> Although this manual provides a classification of mental disorders, it must be admitted that no definition adequately specifies precise boundaries for the concept of mental disorder ... Mental disorders have ... been defined by a variety of concepts (e.g. distress, dyscontrol, disadvantage, disability, inflexibility, irrationality, syndromal pattern, etiology, and statistical deviation). Each is a useful indicator for a mental disorder, but none is equivalent to the concept, and different situations call for different definitions.

> (American Psychiatric Association 1994, p. xxi)

These passages seem to me to make most sense by supposing that the main problem is not whether the conditions described and classified in the book are mental disorders – they obviously are, but on the other hand this is not the main issue, other words might be used. This is kind of throw-away stuff on terminology, because the real concern is to try to spell out as clearly as possible what characterizes the conditions in the manual.

Having teased apart these two tasks apart – valid definition of mental disorder on the one hand, and characterization of the conditions in the manuals on the other – it has to be said that they interact in complex and confusing ways. First, the task of characterization of the conditions in the manuals of course inherited the preconception that they were mental disorders, until just previously called mental illnesses, because of sound medical science or in any case because of the medicalization of these conditions over some centuries. The problem of characterizing the conditions had to take for granted that they were indeed mental disorders, a variety of medical disorders, so could not comfortably run free of the problem of finding a legitimate definition of these concepts; what was at stake here was the medicalized conception of the phenomena. Second, the characterization problem focuses on the conditions currently in the psychiatric manuals, already there – but there is of course the further major problem as to how and why others should be included or excluded, and behind that, why are conditions in the manuals in there in the first place?

On this point, it was recognized that these were the problems brought by the people to the clinic, and treated as problems by the psychiatrists, but what kind of principles and processes are involved here: social or medical? This question is highlighted as the boundary problem: what is the basis of deciding what is included in and what is excluded from the manuals? The conditions currently in the manuals could be characterized, but this so far does not elucidate the principles involved in inclusion or exclusion – and, given the history, the question arises specifically whether the principles involved are medical, or a matter of social norms and values. All these complications are tangled up, and much simplified under the heading of the problem of definition of mental disorder.

In an historical account of the development of the definition of mental disorder, Spitzer and Williams wrote:

> Physicians rarely concern themselves with defining what a medical disorder is and instead spend their time, as best they can, diagnosing and treating individual patients. Psychiatrists as well, until fairly recently, ignored the issue of what a mental disorder is and left the problem to sociologists, psychologists, philosophers of science and members of the legal profession . . . In the early 1970s, however, gay activists forced American psychiatry to reassess its attitude toward the nosologic status of homosexuality . . . Arguing that homosexuality by itself was not evidence of illness, gay activists insisted that homosexuality be removed from the original classification (then DSM-II).

(1982, p. 16)

Moving to autobiography, Spitzer recalls that as a junior member of the American Psychiatric Association's Task Force on Nomenclature and Statistics at the time, he was given the task of reviewing the controversy and proposing a solution. The authors continue:

> In reviewing the characteristics of the various mental disorders included in the DSM-II, Spitzer concluded that, with the exception of homosexuality, and perhaps some of the other 'sexual deviations', they all regularly caused subjective distress or were associated with generalized impairment in social effectiveness or functioning. It was argued that the *consequences* of a condition, and not its *etiology*, determined whether the condition should be considered a disorder . . . It was proposed that the criterion for a mental disorder was either subjective distress or generalized impairment in social effectiveness.

> (ibid.)

Spitzer and Williams go on in their paper to relate how this criterion provided a solution to the controversy about homosexuality, and how it was received by the Association. They also relate how this piece of work evolved into a complicated definition of medical and mental disorder, though following concerns expressed by psychologists the claim that mental disorders should be conceptualized as a subset of medical disorders was dropped. All this is interesting and important psychiatric–social history. For the present purpose the main point is that when the young Spitzer was given the task of reviewing the controversy about whether homosexuality was or was not a mental disorder, whether it should or should not be included in the DSM, he *reviewed the characteristics of the various mental disorders in the DSM-II* – taking for granted, we may suppose, that this is what they were – and concluded that it was *because of the problems they caused* that they had been included in the diagnostic manuals.

This seems to me to have been the right conclusion. Emphasis on the harm-driven characterization of the mental disorders hangs together with the question of how conditions come to be included in or excluded from the diagnostic manuals: the conditions in the manual are, generally speaking, the ones people have brought to the clinic. A primary concept in the definitions of mental disorder in the psychiatric manuals, both the DSM and the ICD, is that of 'clinically significant', applied to symptoms and syndromes. What does it mean? This is Spitzer's explanation of the key components of the definition:

> The phrase 'clinically significant' acknowledges that there are many behavioural or psychological conditions that can be considered 'pathological' but the clinical manifestations of which are so mild that clinical attention is not indicated.

> Spitzer and Williams (1982, p. 19)

Thus the expression emphasizes the requirement of severity, this being marked, presumably, at least by enough distress and impairment. Further on in the same paragraph, giving examples, the authors remark that caffeine withdrawal syndrome in very heavy coffee drinkers can be very uncomfortable, but 'never leads to seeking professional help' (op. cit., p. 20). Some commentators, for example Wakefield, have emphasized this meaning of clinically significant:

> Sentence 1 [of the DSM-III-R definition of mental disorder] notes that the [manual] will limit itself to 'clinically significant' conditions. This is intended to restrict the manual to conditions that actually come to the attention of clinicians (Spitzer and Williams, 1982).

Wakefield (1992a, p. 234)

So the expression works in the area of severe enough symptoms, association with enough distress and/impairment, enough as judged by the would-be patient, in deciding whether to seek professional help, and enough as judged by the clinician. The expression is appropriately ambiguous between the matters of severity, distress and harm being judged by the doctor on the one hand or by the individual with the problem on the other, and if they ever get to meet to talk about it, the upshot of a successful consultation including an agreement between them. There is much behind this simple first sentence of the DSM definition, and the use of the same phrase – clinically significant – in the ICD. Behind it is the social context, the conditions of the potential consultation and the actual meeting if it takes place, between the patient and doctor; or generally these days, between patient and/or carer, and the mental health professional.

What is signalled here is that the conditions in the psychiatric manuals are those which people in society at large are troubled by and consider taking – if the trouble is enough – to a professional for help, at which point the professional also forms a view about the extent of trouble caused to the person, and the extent of risk of trouble, and the need to treat. This is an excellent pragmatic beginning for an understanding of the conditions in the psychiatric manuals and how they got to be there – albeit put briefly using a technical term of art ('clinically significant'). The pragmatic insight raises important issues about the relation between psychiatric expertise and 'folk psychiatry', and about the social representations and organization that results in these kinds of problems being brought to the psychiatric clinic as opposed to elsewhere – issues to be considered in more detail later.

The characterization of the problems as being originally what people bring to the clinic has not been focused on, however, except for commentary on the point that mental disorder cannot be *defined as* what people bring to the clinic. This would be a desperate definition indeed, and it is often pointed out that what people bring to the clinic depends on many kinds of features of social organization such as availability of resources of both purchaser and provider – as does the clinician's threshold for severity indicating offer to treat. Wakefield (1992a, p. 234) cites Aubrey Lewis on the defect of any criterion of disorder that depends on whether people actually seek treatment for a condition:

> It will fluctuate enormously from place to place and from time to time, it will depend on an attitude by the patient towards his doctor, and it will certainly fail to include many people whom, by any common-sense standard one must call ill.

> (Lewis 1953, p. 119)

Nevertheless, the insight that the folk have *already defined* the conditions described in the manuals as problems, and as problems in need of healthcare, is critical. What are the problems? In general terms it is 'harm': distress or impairment. The detail is in the diagnostic criteria sets, which itemize pretty exhaustively, one supposes, all the many and diverse psychological complaints that have been brought to psychiatry for a century or more, common and rare, classified into syndromes. People coming to the clinic have excessive anxiety, low mood, no enjoyment, poor sleep and concentration. The parents bring children who are withdrawn, too anxious to attend school, whose behaviour is unmanageable; and so on. Carers bring people with bizarre beliefs and breakdown in day-to-day functioning. The police bring people shouting and swearing and intimidating in the streets for no apparent reason except apparently attending to and conversing with voices in the head. The criminal justice system requests psychiatric assessment of criminals convicted for major crimes against the person, about to come to the end of the sentence, or to be eligible for parole, to assess risk of reoffending. Many, many problems come to the clinic – the illustrations above cover some broad kinds only.

The psychiatric manuals do an excellent job in capturing why the problems that people bring to the clinic are problems. The explicit definitions of mental disorder give lengthy explanation, most fully in the DSM. Here is the relevant part of the DSM-IV definition, already quoted in Chapter 1:

> In DSM-IV, each of the mental disorders is conceptualized as a clinically significant behavioral or psychological syndrome or pattern that occurs in an individual and that is associated with present distress (e.g., a painful symptom) or disability (i.e., impairment in one or more important areas of functioning) or with a significantly increased risk of suffering death, pain, disability, or an important loss of freedom.

> American Psychiatric Association (1994, p. xxi)

It may be noted that this definition seems to lose, by neglect, the fact that the harm involved is not always experienced by the person identified as having the problem. It may be that a medical model, when having to be sharply distinguished from a sociological model, tends to be blind to the social and interpersonal aspects of what brings people to the clinic. Be that as it may, the important point is that there are many stakeholders in the perception of harm – parents, carers, neighbours, and the state – as well as the identified patient, a point to be considered further in the next chapter.

This is connected of course with the problem of distinguishing mental disorder from social deviance, identified in the 1960s critiques. It was the elaborate naturalist definitions of mental disorder that responded most directly to this challenge, but the psychiatric manuals do it more simply, bypassing or neglecting the underlying problems, so as to get on with the task of characterizing the conditions in the manuals. In the ICD-10 there is simply:

> The term 'disorder' is used throughout the classification, so as to avoid even greater problems inherent in the use of terms such as 'disease' and 'illness'. 'Disorder' is not an exact term, but it is used here to imply the existence of a clinically recognizable set of symptoms or behaviour associated in most cases with distress and with interference with personal functions. Social deviance or conflict alone, without personal dysfunction, should not be included in mental disorder as defined here.

> World Health Organization (1992, p. 5)

DSM-IV has something similar:

> Whatever its original cause, it [the syndrome or pattern] must currently be considered a manifestation of a behavioral, psychological or biological dysfunction in the individual. Neither deviant behavior (e.g., political, religious, or sexual) nor conflicts that are primarily between the individual and society are mental disorders unless the deviance or conflict is a symptom of a dysfunction in the individual, as described above.

> American Psychiatric Association (1994, p. xxi)

The final qualification – that the syndrome must be due to individual dysfunction, not just a matter of social deviance – is not fully elaborated. Wakefield (1992a) argues that it expresses the correct conceptual point that there must be some inner dysfunction, involving an hypothesis, subsequently captured by his analysis, of failure of an evolutionarily designed mechanism. As against this, however, the judgement whether the presenting problem is a sign of a dysfunction in the individual or simple social deviance is commonly made, and is presumably intended to be made, in the clinic, given sufficient information about the presentation, rather than with reference to textbooks on evolutionary psychology. As noted in the first chapter, the judgement is typically made with reference to the pervasiveness of the dysfunctional behaviour across contexts, using the familiar principle that constancy in behaviours across domains is attributed to the person, while variation is attributed to the context. Thus, an individual who only gets into trouble while in conflict with a particular social group, but who manages his affairs without problem otherwise, will be regarded just as in conflict with that group, not as having an individual dysfunction. Conversely, a person who begins to have problems in one situation, perhaps in work or marriage, but who then, or in any case, develops problems of functioning generally, will be regarded as coming to have an individual dysfunction. This is a clear criterion of practical use, but it bypasses the question whether what we have here is the application of social norms: it may be that the norms being broken pervasively are socially defined.

A fundamental problem is that characterizing the conditions in the manuals in terms of associated harm – distress or impairment – seems to be *too broad* for a definition of mental disorder, which connotes something like 'the mind not working as it should'. There are *many* patterns of behaviour that bring significant harms and risk to the individual (and often to others) including dropping out of school, laziness, criminality (along with benefits), smoking, driving while under the influence, not seeking inoculations against common diseases, taking on too much debt, etc., but these patterns of behaviour apparently do not have anything much to do with mental disorder.

The problem then is: how to tighten up the definition of mental disorder to make it more valid? How do we properly distinguish mental disorder from social deviance, and pathology from normal problems of living? We have to move from the second problem identified at the start of this chapter – characterizing the conditions in the manuals – back to the first, finding a valid definition of mental disorder.

This is the task that leads towards naturalism – and away from the conditions in the manual. Here is Donald Klein, with Spitzer a member of the American Psychiatric Association's Task Force on Nomenclature and Statistics, introducing the problem at the time:

> The recent debate in the American Psychiatric Association whether homosexuality should be included in the *Diagnostic and Statistical Manual of Mental Disorders* is a salutary event. It indicates the growing awareness that labeling some behavioural pattern as a mental disorder has important personal and social consequences.
>
> Klein (1978, p. 41)

This issue was already prominent in the 1960s critiques of psychiatry, but in any case the gay lobby in the US raised it again in the 1970s. The sociological critiques in the 1960s may have focused on mental illness, but terminological change to mental disorder did not resolve the underlying problems. The accusations stayed: some conditions are being illegitimately medicalized and pathologized.

Labelling as pathology and associated social and medical practices matter. So, Klein argues, it is necessary to make diagnosis of mental disorder more rigorous. He continues (loc.cit): 'Psychiatric diagnostic concepts should pass the harsh tests of substantive content, logical consistency, and practical relevance.'

This leads Klein to the matter of definition:

> Strikingly there is no explicit statement within the *Diagnostic and Statistical Manual of Mental Disorders* that defines the sort of condition categorizable within this document. Such a logical lapse is not restricted to psychiatry, however, since the *International Classification of Diseases* also lacks such a statement. It seems plain that these compendia are actually compilations of the sorts of things that physicians treat; a circular classificatory principle but a useful historical clue. Our definitions of illness are derived from medical practice.

> (loc. cit.)

Once the question of definition is raised, it is apparent that the conditions in the manual are just what people bring to the physicians to treat. Klein remarks that this is not much help, however, as a classificatory principle. In particular, it does not help with matters of principle and legitimacy. What has to be clarified are the principles that determine whether a condition *should be* brought to the clinic, should be treated, and should be in the manual of mental disorders.

In the remainder of his 1978 paper Klein elaborates on two themes: first, the suffering and disability that characterize the problems that people to the physician; and second, that what is also necessary for an adequate understanding of disorder or illness is the notion that something has gone wrong, biologically not socially, and this leads to evolutionary theory. For example:

> What justifies considering any particular variation as a disease? Can we arrive at a standard that is not simply an expression of personal preference, but is given to us by the biology of the situation? I propose that evolutionary theory allows us to infer such a standard – suboptimal functioning – and further helps us to objectively specify the optimum. This often allows us to state that something is biologically wrong, not simply that it is rare or objectionable.

> Klein (op. cit., p. 50)

Thus the problem of conceptual validity in relation to mental disorder and medical disorder, to be distinguished from social disorder, was led towards naturalism, to the idea that there must be an underpinning natural fact of the matter: either lowering of function compared with the statistical norm, or compared with some optimal norm, or some disadvantage or dysfunction in evolutionary theoretic terms – either separately or in some combination. These were the options explored rigorously by Boorse and by Wakefield, Wakefield's evolutionary theoretic definition being dominant since the early 1990s.

As previously considered, statistical rarity by itself does not define dysfunction, which probably relies rather on the idea of something having gone wrong, of a system not functioning as it should, perhaps 'not as designed'. However, when this idea in turn is understood in evolutionary theoretic terms, 'mental dysfunction' becomes a problematic, risky hypothesis, lifted out of reach of the diagnosing clinician and research investigator. In brief, we are faced with what was called in Chapter 1 the problem of reliability and validity of diagnosis of disorder in the manuals: that there can appear to be a tension between these two goals, that we cannot have both at the same time.

This problem of reliability and validity has usually been attributed to the drive for reliability following Hempel's advice to the American Psychiatric Association, the outcome of which is seen as stripping out all theory about the conditions being described, even attribution of dysfunction. That may be correct, but consistent with the considerations so far I would put the matter somewhat differently. The reliability in the current diagnostic criteria – to the extent to which they *are* reliable – actually reflects a consensus among clinicians that has existed, or which has developed, over a considerable length of time, concerning the problems of interest, whether they be problems of mood, will, eccentricity of character or belief, and so forth; and indeed a consensus between clinicians and the people who bring the problems to the clinic. In the opening decades of modern psychiatry the presenting problems were more closely observed and characterized, in the work of the psychiatric phenomenologists, and then classified rigorously into syndromes and types of syndrome. What was required to increase reliability between diagnoses was explicit clarification over syndromes and nomenclature, and the removal of speculative hypotheses as to causes emanating from the two main ideological positions current at the time, psychoanalysis and an extreme medical model. I suggest that both the original work by the early nosologists and the later work on increasing reliability were building on the basis of a significant agreement over what the problems were. In brief, the drive to increase reliability of diagnosis from the 1960s onwards was not the origin of consensus. Nor did it give rise to the problem of validity, the **problem** as to whether what the clinicians and the folk had come to regard as medical disorders – suited to take to the psychiatrists – really were mental disorders.

Let us go back to the problem of conceptual validity as it arises in the DSM-IV definition of mental disorder. The definition begins by emphasizing the harmfulness of the conditions in the manuals, the distress and associated impairment, but the question arises how we distinguish among the range of harmful conditions between those that are genuine mental disorders and those which are rather social deviance, or distressing but normal problems of living. We can understand these non-disorder conditions by recognizing that they are, for example, voluntarily entered into, for reasons that we can understand, that have recognizable gains in the short term at least, or as conditions that we can understand as normal, time-limited responses to adverse events; and so on. By contrast, to capture mental disorder we have to find a dysfunction within the process of meaning and rationality, so that, for example, emotions are excessive in degree or duration, beliefs inappropriate, actions not under control of the will; and so on. As noted in the first chapter, these kinds of norms of mental and behavioural functioning pervade the diagnostic criteria, explicitly or implicitly.

In the explicit definition of mental disorder in the DSM-IV, the opening statement that mental disorders in the manual are conceptualized in terms of associated distress or disability is followed by qualifying clause that seems to be intended to demarcate disordered from non-disordered mental functioning (American Psychiatric Association 1994, pp. xxi–xxii): 'In addition, this syndrome or pattern must not be merely an expectable and culturally sanctioned response to a particular event, for example, the death of a loved one.'

This qualification is a vexed one on which much as been written, including in this essay. It is not clear how much weight it can bear, or what exactly it means. The naturalist definitions can be seen as the best attempts to provide a clear meaning, in terms of below species-typical functioning or failure of an evolutionarily designed mental mechanism, but both are problematic in various ways. The latter in particular would blow a massive hole through the reliability of diagnosis of disorder, and if adopted as the definition of disorder would require that the conditions in the manual were called by another name, neutral to whether they were disorders or not in the required sense, until the science sorts out which is which.

In an ideal world the definition of mental disorder – conceptually correct, intellectually rigorous – would coincide with the characterization of the psychiatric conditions as described in the manuals. Actually – things being less than ideal in the real world – they don't coincide. The DSM and the ICD have both wisely steered clear of endorsing a definition of disorder which some think has the best claim to conceptual validity, grounded in the notion of evolutionary design. Reference to failure of mental or behavioural mechanisms to function as designed in evolution does not appear in the psychiatric manuals, presumably in the recognition that while this may be of theoretical interest (along with many other kinds of causal factor), it has no place in a manual designed to characterize and categorize clinically significant syndromes clearly, and to aid reliable diagnosis. Klein's evolutionary theoretic approach to mental disorder, whatever its virtues as a conceptual approach, did not make it into the DSM-III; nor has Wakefield's refined version made it into later editions, at least not the ones developed to date. Nor has the other naturalist criterion of mental disorder – invoking statistical normality – been embraced. While statistical normality figures implicitly or explicitly in some diagnostic criteria in the psychiatric manuals, neither manual defines dysfunction or disorder in those terms. Apparently no one thought that mere statistical deviance will do the job; it is at best simply a marker for what is really critical: significant harm and/or failure of design. Thus the characterization of the conditions in the DSM, its definition of mental disorder, manages without naturalism – as also in the ICD.

What the DSM has instead in its definition are the requirements that mental disorder excludes expectable and culturally sanctioned responses, and excludes social deviance alone. In addition there are in the diagnostic criteria for particular mental disorders many references to what may be called disruption of meaningful connections, using expressions such as inappropriate, disproportionate, excessive, unrealistic, and irrational.

Two connected questions arise here. The first is: what are the features of a non-naturalist approach to mental disorder? and the second: can a satisfactory definition of mental disorder be made out in terms of disruption of meaningful connections? These issues will be considered in the following two sections.

4.2 Harmful dysfunction in the phenomena

Naturalistic definitions of mental disorder have been much criticized in the preceding two chapters, and the main question for this section is how to conceptualize mental disorder without relying on them. The general features of non-naturalist approaches to mental disorder would include the following:

1. The disorder is in the phenomena – in the clinical presentation – in the person's life.

2. Disorder and dysfunction are both closely tied to distress and disability or risk thereof.

3. There is no need – as there is in naturalism – to have a conceptual wedge between disorder and dysfunction.

4. Factors taken into account when attributing disorder or dysfunction typically include distress/disability, deviation from normal functioning in

various, flexible quasi-statistical and idealized senses, and from normal psychological functioning, in the sense that some 'meaningful' linkages in mental life and behaviour are apparently broken.

5. The norms involved in judging disorder/dysfunction are primarily individual and social, not 'natural' in a sense that can be distinguished from these.

6. There is no principled boundary in the nature of psychological phenomena between order and disorder.

The first point is that non-naturalist approaches will recognize *psychological/ behavioural dysfunction in the here and now*, in current experience and social life – as opposed to in a speculative relation with functioning in the environment of evolutionary adaptiveness (EEA), or in relation to some more or less abstract and idealized statistical norm. The second point is that psychological/behavioural dysfunction in the here and now *already causes problems/harm* in the here and now. Here again the contrast is with dysfunction in the evolutionary theoretic sense, which so far, in itself, is neutral to whether there is associated harm; as is dysfunction which deviates from some 'average'. There are certainly issues of *seriousness or severity*: a psychological/behavioural dysfunction may not cause much harm, or hardly any, or even any at all, but the further that we go along this continuum – towards no harm – then the notion of dysfunction gradually loses its grip (though being at the end of the continuum, it may still have retained some). As a corollary to these two points, point 3 on the above list, the sense of mental *dysfunction*, which comes along with harm, is really not much distinguished from mental *disorder*. There is hardly a conceptual wedge between the two, whereas in Wakefield's analysis as in Boorse's biostatistical theory, it is essential to have a real conceptual distinction between the natural fact of the matter (which gets called the dysfunction), typically somewhat elusive, and the harm it may (or may not) cause, which is upfront. If we don't have the naturalist axe to grind, there is no need to distinguish 'disorder here' from 'disorder elsewhere', and we don't need two terms for the purpose; in particular nothing much hangs on the difference between the terms *disorder* and *dysfunction*.

Wakefield's analysis particularly has the effect of deflecting attention away from dysfunction in the present: the required meaning of dysfunction has to be refined and reified, coming to refer speculatively to the evolutionary development of the mind/brain. Rather, the perception of dysfunction by patients, carers and professionals alike is much more open to view – in lived experience, in your face. To put the point another way, in Wakefield's analysis failure of function is understood *relative to the EEA, not necessarily relative to the current environment.* According to this analysis there can be natural dysfunctions all and everywhere and we would never know it because they did not lead to dysfunctions in the current environment. The only way they would come to our attention is because they cause harm. In the alternative, the reason for presentation at the clinic is apparent dysfunctional behaviour in the present.

So what is psychological/behavioural dysfunction in the here and now, and how is it associated with harm? Problems people bring to the clinic typically have two features: first, they involve a level of personal functioning different from some implicit or explicit normal level, and which is negatively valued compared with the norm; the other is that this abnormal function is attributed to some abnormality of mind. Abnormality thus tends to figure twice, though in ways not always clearly separated. The first usage of abnormality, the one that defines a level of functioning different some normal level, is typically a quasi-statistical one, referring either to personal norms or social, either way more or less idealized. This abnormality is negatively valued, but the evaluation can be made by diverse stakeholders, not just or always the identified patient. Complexity pervades both the matter of abnormal functioning and the harm associated with it. The second usage of abnormality – the one that would explain divergence from desired levels of functioning in terms of abnormality of mind – introduces more complexity. It typically turns again on what is considered a normal mental state or way of behaving, but in this context normality has to do with such considerations as whether the mental state is meaningful, appropriate, rational, or whether the behaviour is intentionally chosen as opposed being something the person cannot help. Assumed statistical normality (though relative usually to some undefined group) may be used as a marker of abnormality of mind, but explicit pathologizing of the merely different is generally seen as not a good move: it is likely that 'the mind not working as it should' is more tied to meaning, rationality and intentionality, than it is to statistical normality as such. On the other hand it may be that it works this way round: that we have an idea of what is a meaningful, rational response, and then suppose that it is the typical one for the group (for some idealized group, for the group of rational people, although these will coincide usually with the ones we know). The DSM-IV definition of mental disorder uses the term 'unexpectable' – which wisely allows for various options. In brief, it is hard to imagine a more complex, slippery set of assumptions, values and beliefs than those that underlie attributions of mental disorder. This is not at all to criticize; it is just what comes into view if we give up the simple idea that mental disorder is fundamentally just deficit in some natural state.

Thus, factors taken into account when attributing disorder or dysfunction include distress/disability, deviation from normal functioning in various, flexible quasi-statistical senses, individual and social, and from normal psychological functioning, in the sense that some 'meaningful' linkages in mental life and behaviour are apparently broken. This is point 4 on the above list of features of non-naturalist conceptualizations of mental disorder.

The issues above pervade clinical practice, and in proxy form the psychiatric manuals. Consider for example problems of a negative change in functioning within the individual, more or less sudden or gradual, such as an episode of depression of clinical severity in a person who has not had one before. The extent of low mood, misery, absence of enjoyment, lowered motivation, poor sleep and concentration, inevitably associated with distress, though not always by a significant downturn in social role functioning, is likely to be thought abnormal or dysfunctional – by the person and the clinician – in relation to the individual's own norms, i.e. to what is a normal level of functioning for them. This is a kind of 'statistical' matter, involving within-individual fluctuation through time. The change is obviously a problem, undesirable to the individual: it involves and causes distress. The question whether diagnosis of a depressive disorder requires symptoms to be due to an abnormality of mind as opposed to being a normal reaction to negative life events and chronic stressors, is a complex one, and one over which the psychiatric manuals are ambiguous. The DSM-IV definition of disorder requires disorders to be not expectable, not a normal reaction to events, though it is not clear how this is handled in the diagnostic criteria for major depressive disorder. In any case there is an expectation that the diagnosis requires not just a decline in function but also attribution of abnormality of mind, even if this difference can become difficult to make out in practice. Following assessment the clinician may conclude that the problem is likely to be self-limiting (i.e. a relatively brief episode) and the provision required, if any, is simply monitoring (for worsening or chronicity, or to avoid accumulation of secondary losses and psychological complications). If treatment is recommended and accepted, the aim for both parties is to restore the person to their previous own normal level of functioning. Various episodic problems fall out this way, various anxiety and depressive reactions typically following stressors/losses of many and various kinds. This is probably the simplest kind of case: the values are personal, and common to us all (most of us). After this it gets increasingly complicated.

In recurrent depressive episodes it becomes less clear that there is a stable personal baseline on which there is superimposed a time-limited episode, in which case the standard against which the depressive state is measured ceases to be straightforwardly the individual's own level. Here the dysfunctionality or 'abnormality' is compared with what? Presumably the general level of feeling of well-being and psychosocial functioning in the group? But which group?

The population as a whole, or the relatively stress-free, well-resourced middle classes? Or should we compare with a more limited subgroup, more similar to the person in question. For example, the subgroup of late middle-aged men who are alone possibly following marital break-up? Or the subgroup of low resourced and under-supported young mothers bringing up young children single-handedly? Or adults with childhood histories of abuse and neglect? Choice of reference group determines the extent to which chronically recurrent depression will appear as more or less the norm. This is an aspect of the problem in the mental health field encountered by Boorse's analysis: how to select the reference group that will define dysfunction in factual terms of statistical deviance. Still it can be seen here that, again, the question of abnormality of mind does not figure large, over and above the quasi-statistical, and it is difficult to pin down the idea that the person is not functioning as 'normal'. In any case, what are the values at work in deciding that the condition in question is a dysfunction? Personal, social? The person's wish for a better life and the clinician's wish to help presumably include both of these kinds. Various kinds of recurrent or enduring problems of anxiety and depression fit this kind of description, and some of the so-called personality disorders, especially insofar as they include anxious/depressive features.

Personality features, sometimes though not always apparent in childhood, present other kinds of problems. The child with autism may not mind the condition, provided he is well-supported, not teased or bullied, and there are no serious complications such as highly distressing or impairing anxiety or obsessive behaviours. The parents do mind, and adjust more or less to not having a child who can do and enjoy the things other children can. Or there may be complications of challenging behaviour. Here the values of the parents are personal, but common to all. The attribution of abnormality of mind draws on various considerations, including the hypothesis that individuals with autism lack some basic theory of mind capacity – perhaps failure of an evolutionary designed module, consistent with Wakefield's analysis. On the other hand this is an hypothesis, and more recent theories have the condition as the end of a normally distributed trait of several such traits. This is an example of how 'natural' and 'normal' have been shifted from the colloquial categorical use, also used (with qualification) in the psychiatric manuals, to the idea of the normally distributed curve – much expanding the idea of what is natural and normal. However these various theories of autism pan out – whether the condition turns out to be involve dysfunction of an evolutionary designed mental mechanism, or the extreme end of a trait, or traits – the problems are there anyway: problems of not playing, distress, not mixing with other children, and so on. Consider also the cases of children very high on temperamental features such anxiety, shyness or impulsivity. As they grow up and face increasing task demands and do not meet them very well, interpersonal problems arise such as avoidance or disruption of social situations, typically leading to adjustment problems. Again the norms which these children fall below are not their own personal norms so much as the norms in the social group.

The position is transformed when the would-be patient has no interest in being any such thing. People with conditions characterized by antisocial behaviours are typically unmotivated for treatment. They may be distressed and impaired, but the individual typically regards the problems as other people's fault, not as indicating the need to change. The individuals are not breaking their own norms, probably they and the clinician will agree. The clinician and society regard the individuals as antisocial – for the individual they may still be in the right, but in any case it is not their fault. The terms of this more or less protracted negotiation are social and personal values and norms.

There are other kinds of conditions in which personal, social, and clinical–professional values are typically entangled, such as schizophrenia, and there are within- and between-episode complications. In first-episode schizophrenia, typically in young people, the norms involved are at least personal – the person is falling below their previous normal-for-them level of functioning. If the episode persists or recurs, becoming a chronic illness, the abnormality of social functioning becomes relative to social norms. However, if unusual beliefs are prominent in the presentation, the person is likely to regard themself as right and the clinician and others as wrong; strong personal values may attach to the beliefs and possibly to a way of life that goes with them. Negotiation of treatment in the acute phase, if possible at all, optimally takes account of the beliefs and values of the patient on the one hand and clinicians on the other, and families and carers on still more hands. Between acute episodes other values come into play. The psychiatrist will typically have as at least one main priority that medicine is taken and relapse prevented. This may or may not coincide with the service user or consumer's own aims and values, which may be to avoid the side-effects of medication, to have autonomy and not be treated like a patient, to get a viable life back from the devastation, re-establishing autonomy and respect.

In brief, what presents at the clinic involves various kinds of personal or social problems, distress and other losses, to the patient or to others, with an attribution that 'the mind is not working as it should', involving disruptions of meaning and difference from some standard. All this is accessible, open to view in the clinic – it is upfront: it can be settled in the clinic using the available evidence.

Clinical assessment can ascertain dysfunction at individual and social levels, and psychological dysfunction – in the above senses – as cause. By contrast it cannot determine deviation from the norms defined by naturalism.

Further, as the fifth point concerning the move away from naturalism, the norms involved in judging dysfunction are primarily individual and social, not 'natural' in a sense that can be distinguished from these. In the above examples, what is apparent is deviation from individual and social norms. Dysfunction is judged relative to some norm, and Wakefield may well be right that *normal function* is a matter of what mental functioning is *designed* for. However, as argued in the previous two chapters, there are various sources of design of human mental functioning and behaviour: the evolved genetic, the social and the individual. A person's psychological and behavioural functioning may flout fundamental standards of social conduct, for example involving violence, in ways that indicate a failure of socialization, a failure of social design. This is where the antisocial behavioural traits belong. Second, a person's psychological and behavioural functioning may go against their own perceived needs and wishes. There are many kinds of case that belong here, including those that used to fall under the old heading of neurotic behaviour, in which a person is, for example, persistently anxious and avoidant of situations that they would also like to be able to participate in, and think they should be able to, but – for some reason – they cannot. Or a person finds that they are persistently unhappy, and wants to be otherwise, and does not know why they cannot be. In such kinds of case, there is personal dysfunction, but 'dysfunction' is apparently relative to the person's own perceived needs and values.

'Natural' makes a poor contrast with 'social' in terms of the current science, as argued previously. Natural has to mean evolved, genetically inherited, but evolution and genetic inheritance affect social behaviour too, and there is individual variation, and either way the phenotype typically is the result of interplay between genetic and environmental factors. In other words: what is natural in the sense of evolved is one factor involved in the production of individual and social behaviour, it is not a *third* factor. It would be a third distinguishable factor under the following assumptions: some functions were entirely genetic, others were entirely social, and within those socially acquired functions there were some phenotypes that involved unique learning histories. However this partitioning does not apply to psychological functioning: psychological phenomena are not like this. It is possible that both versions of naturalism were led astray, appeared more plausible than they are, by failing to distinguish psychology from physiology, psychiatry from medicine, and mental disorder from medical disorder. It may be that the natural/social distinction works better in physiology and general medicine.

With naturalism parked, what is left open to view is attribution of psychological dysfunction and disorder that turns on personal and social norms. In these personal and social senses of dysfunction, harm to the person and/or to others is already included – the meaning is precisely that the behaviour in question goes against personal or social norms and values.

The sixth and final general feature of non-naturalist approaches is that there is no principled boundary in the nature of psychological phenomena between order and disorder. Naturalism provides a boundary *if* it can identify a fixed natural fact that is non-negotiable by opinion and values, choice and relativity. Boorse's biostatistical theory is an attempt to identify such a fact, plausible until overwhelmed by relativity to reference groups. Wakefield's evolutionary naturalism is another attempt, but it too is overwhelmed by complexity, in this case complexity of the design of human behaviour. In practice neither kind of naturalism can help to demarcate mental disorder from normal functioning, and the implication is that there are no boundaries from the point of the view of the science, but only boundaries based on personal and social norms, involving primarily perceptions of harm and risk.

The six general features of non-naturalist approaches to mental disorder considered in this section in fact apply, I suggest, to the conditions characterized in the psychiatric manuals, whatever they may be called – mental disorders or some less pathologizing name. Sections 4.4 and 4.5 take up further themes in the conceptualization of mental disorder, or of psychiatric conditions, the conditions in the manuals. First I consider a question that presses on several fronts: is it possible to define mental disorder in terms of breakdown of meaningful connections?

4.3 Mental disorder as breakdown of meaningful connections

Mental disorder may be defined as harmful psychological dysfunction. This definition is by all means not much of an advance; it is innocuous, not to say trivial, but it does highlight that 'disorder' involves harm. Then we have to define 'psychological dysfunction', and we could jump straight to the naturalist positions, but an alternative, at least on the surface, is that we can understand this in terms of disruption of meaning.

The importance of perceived absence of meaning in disorder attributions has shown up in various contexts through this essay so far. 'Meaning' here is a cover expression for various concepts, such as appropriateness of affect and behaviour, rationality of belief and action, functionality of behaviour, strategy, and regulation by information processing. In the Introduction and in the second chapter it was noted that the anti-psychiatry critiques charged the medical model with disqualifying the meaning in so-called mental illness. It was also noted that folk psychiatry may well anticipate or follow professional psychiatry on just this point, attributing disorder at just the point where meaning is perceived to have run out. In the third chapter it was noted that when Wakefield seeks to demarcate mental disorder from normal, understandable reactions to life losses and stresses he does not invoke specific predictions from current evolutionary psychological models but rather the fact that there is – apparently – no understandable cause of the emotion, or no conceivable point in the behaviour. In considering the diagnostic criteria in the psychiatric manuals, in the first chapter, it was remarked that they are pervaded by references to deviation from norms of psychological functioning: affect is excessive, inappropriate, disproportionate; beliefs are unrealistic or irrational, inexplicable in terms of evidence or culture; behaviour is irrational, or compulsive, not based on beliefs and desires, or on reasonable beliefs or desires.

So, can mental disorder just be defined as breakdown of meaningful connections? It should be said that these kinds of breakdown are already likely to be harmful. It is distressing to be persistently anxious and avoidant without due cause; or angry and aggressive, or sad and withdrawn. It is distressing to have intrusive, irrational thoughts or beliefs; or to carry out pointless behaviours for hours on end; and so forth. These problems are also typically disabling – they tend to disrupt daily activities including having difficulty sustaining what is, for the person or for the peer group, normal social role functioning, at school, work and in family life. Failure to meet up to expectations of normal or desirable functioning is intrinsically a cause of distress. In addition, disruptions of meaning bring with them further distress for the person: incomprehension brings with it confusion, feeling overwhelmed, not knowing why they are as they are, or what to do about it. Failure of mutual intelligibility brings with it further distress for families and friends. In brief, these ruptures of meaning are intrinsically distressing and disabling. To strengthen the putative definition, one may want to emphasize that the breakdown of meaning has to carry harm in order for it to count as a disorder, but this is more a matter of severity, serving to exclude mild inappropriate emotions, or conditions that do not interfere much with daily life – but it is not that something quite new is being introduced, in addition to the absence of meaning.

It may work to define mental disorder in terms of breakdown of meaning: this may define a concept of mental disorder in colloquial and professional use. It may be the concept that Foucault identified as the dominant construction of madness in western modernity: madness as fundamentally just deficit of reason and meaning. However, it has serious flaws in the present, because of the psychological approach in psychiatry through the last century.

In considering psychological approaches to mental illness and mental disorder in the second chapter it was noted that psychological models – from those of Freud through to family therapy and cognitive behaviour therapy – are just those that find meaning even where it seems to have run out. Where folk consciousness failed to find meaning, where psychiatry posited lesions, Freud detected functionality and strategy, typically designed to solve problems in the inner environment. Current psychological models are similar, and are now recognized to be causal, alongside models invoking lesions. According to the psychological models, many of the conditions in the psychiatric manuals involve greater or lesser degrees of meaningful processing, whether or not there are also lesions. This being so it will not do to define mental disorder as absence of meaning – it is too strong a condition: it would exclude many or most conditions in the psychiatric manuals.

This shows up, however, the way that scientific and conceptual points in this area interact with terminological problems. Maybe mental disorder does mean absence of meaning, in which case the discovery of meaning in what are called mental disorders just shows they are no such thing – this would be the psychological dissatisfaction with the medical model and its terminology. Or, the conditions in the psychiatric manuals are disorders, notwithstanding the fact that they involve meaning. So what does disorder mean now? Perhaps it means just that ordinary meanings have run out, and much confusion, distress and impairment is generated. Which way do our intuitions run here?

Wakefield rightly claims that disorder attributions are excluded in the context of normal or understandable responses or coping strategies, and that this principle overrides formal diagnostic criteria.

> Research on disorder attribution to anti-socially behaving youths (Kirk, Wakefield, Hseih and Pottick, 1999) reveals that clinicians overwhelmingly judge youths whose symptoms satisfy the DSM's criteria for conduct disorder to be non-disordered if the problematic behaviours are explained by learned normal reactions to environmental factors.
>
> Wakefield (2000, p. 261)

It is true that we begin to think of mental disorder when we fail to find normality and meaning of the kind we are used to, but the point at which this kind of normality and meaning are thought to run out is relative to what we are used to. Sometimes a closer look reveals more meaning, more normality, than we thought. This applies to a whole range of kinds of psychiatric presentation. The quotes from Wakefield given above in Chapter 3, section 3.7, on separation anxiety, depression and substance abuse illustrate some kinds of case in which a broadening of context allows us to see familiar normality and meaning, and – Wakefield is probably right, we would be inclined not to call the behaviours in question disorders – especially if they were not causing too much harm. However, the tension between meaning and disorder can become more difficult to resolve when we move from familiar normality and meaning to less familiar contexts, and when much harm is involved.

As well as risk factors of one or other kinds, psychological aetiological models of psychiatric conditions typically implicate learning processes operating in adverse circumstances, preserving action and the satisfaction of needs so far as possible in at least some restricted domains. These learning processes are abnormal in that they are invoked in relatively unusual situations – extreme challenges to psychological or psychosocial functioning – and in the sense that they typically involve distortions, compromises and losses. It is possible in these terms that maladaptive, dysfunctional behaviour may arise from adverse experiences and subsequent learning to manage them, from processes that are understandable in context. Nevertheless, the behaviour is dysfunctional relative to the person's perceived needs and values – or perhaps our perception of their needs – and hence in this sense does constitute mental disorder.

For example, children that are abused and neglected are at much raised risk for developing depression and suicidal behaviour in adulthood (e.g. Fergusson *et al.* 1996; Hill *et al.* 2001), and people with a diagnosis of borderline personality disorder commonly report seriously abusive childhood experiences (e.g. Zanarini *et al.* 1997). The mechanisms are likely to include maladaptive learning and coping processes. Here is an illustrative case vignette.

Justine was neglected by her mother and raised by her grandmother, who neglected and emotionally abused her; she was taken into care and subsequently had a series of foster home placements. Following a childhood in which Justine appeared to be following a normal enough developmental trajectory, doing reasonably well at school, sometimes described as a perfect child, and with reasonably good peer relations, at age 14 she became extremely abusive to her then current foster mother, truanted from school, and became involved with antisocial behaviour such as stealing. The foster placement broke down, as did the next several; she began to self-injure by cutting her wrists and by overdosing analgesics, requiring emergency medical attention, and she was eventually admitted to an adolescent mental health unit.

Justine's self-injurious behaviour continued there, in the context of strong affective interactions with staff. In the course of psychotherapy on the unit the following interpretations appeared reasonably plausible: that Justine tended to injure herself or to want to injure herself when she perceived that key staff – from her point of view – were neglecting or abusing her, for example by not being on the unit at the weekends, or by spending time with other young people, or, in one circumstance, by becoming pregnant; the perception of neglect and abuse gave rise to extreme anger at the staff concerned, and – insofar as she deserved lack of love, was unlovable, and had such hateful feelings – profound feelings of worthlessness and self-loathing; anger at others gave rise to the impulse to hurt them back, but this was inhibited, out of concern and the wish to preserve the promise of care, and Justine attacked herself instead, which was suited to her self-loathing, and at the same time hurt the staff members exceedingly, because of all the blood and the risk to life, demonstrating their catastrophic failure as care-givers.

The above narrative is a sequence of meaningful enough connections, of problems and solutions, following from early persistent experiences of neglect and abuse by care-givers, but leading to catastrophic mistakes in interpreting others' behaviour and to highly problematic behaviour, associated with persistent breakdowns of care placements, breaking up of important relationships, loss of educational opportunity, loss of sustained peer contact, intense degrees of distress, self-injury and risk of premature death.

Supposing for the sake of argument that Justine's behaviour might be explained in terms of learning processes in response to circumstances that constituted extreme challenge to psychological and psychosocial functioning, would people say that the behaviour is dysfunctional, and that she was suffering from a mental disorder? Presumably few would deny that the behaviour was dysfunctional, and I do not know what people would say about mental disorder in this case because I haven't done the field experiment, but I suppose it is quite possible that some would be inclined to judge that there is mental disorder here. The critical point about the mental disorder attribution here would then be not just whether learning is involved, or meaningfulness for that matter, but the state of mind and associated behaviour that is acquired, and whether that state of mind and behaviour is significantly maladaptive in relation to the hopes and expectations of the individual, or of the clinicians. In any case, whatever this or that person or group may judge about mental disorder in this case as described, the makers of the psychiatric diagnostic manuals, representing the mainstream practice of mental health services, do judge that mental functioning and behaviour of this kind constitutes mental disorder – major depressive disorder, and/or so-called borderline personality disorder.

Clearly this kind of case represents an extreme, but many kinds of psychiatric presentation are extreme, and similar considerations apply. The key point is that if the behaviour is maladaptive enough, if it causes enough harm, then the fact that it can be understood as meaningful, or to evidence effects of learning and coping, is not necessarily enough reason to exclude the attribution of disorder; on the contrary the harmful maladaptive nature of the behaviour may be enough. This brings out what I suggest is an irreconcilable tension at the heart of the notion of mental disorder. It can be applied just on the basis of harmful, maladaptive behaviour – but it also implies that meaning has run out, that there really is absence of (any) psychological order. And the kinds of case that signal the tension are just those in which these two connotations fall apart – where harmful, maladaptive behaviour turns out to be following meaningful principles of learning and coping.

A simpler and less controversial, more empirically validated illustration of the tension here is in panic disorder. Panic disorder is a fairly common, often chronic and highly disabling condition which until recently was very difficult to treat. The person has frequent unexpected panic attacks, characterized by many somatic symptoms, basically the autonomic nervous system in full operation, associated with extreme fear that something catastrophic is happening, such as a heart attack about to result in death. Often the person stays at home because of fear of having such an attack outside, or ventures out only when accompanied by someone who can help if needs be. Absence of meaning is quite clear here: the person has no idea why the panic attacks are occurring – nor until recently did clinicians. The fairly recent cognitive model of panic due to David Clark (Clark 1985, Clark *et al.* 1999) proposed that what is happening is fast, barely conscious mistaken appraisals of somatic activity originally in the normal range, supposition that they are signs of danger, thereby increasing anxiety, leading by positive feedback to full-blown panic and expectation of imminent death. What before appeared meaningless is now meaningful from start to finish. The meanings are by all means mistaken, but meanings they are, and understandable, nonetheless. So is panic disorder a mental disorder in a sense over and above that it is in the books of mental disorders?

As noted previously, a term often used in clinical psychology is 'maladaptive'. In the case of panic disorder, the increasingly catastrophic appraisals of increasing autonomic nervous activity are maladaptive because they are not true, and cause a lot of trouble. 'Not true' is a pragmatic matter open to test. The cognitive therapy treatment of panic brings the appraisals to light, in the context of the model as a whole, and raises the question whether they are true or false, and there are various ways this assessment can be made. The model already provides an alternative construal which is a necessary condition of a belief change. The person may decide to induce some panic symptoms and see whether harm results – having seen the therapist do it.

In some antisocial behaviour problems, the position may be that behaviour styles such as instrumental aggression are acquired in rearing environments that are highly problematic, and become themselves highly problematic when applied to other environments with expectations of more socialized behaviour. Again, the problem is not absence of strategies and meanings, but rather inappropriate, maladaptive ones, generating much distress and impairment.

In summary, then, the idea that mental disorder is breakdown of meaning tends to unravel into several options. It may be interpreted as absence of meaning altogether. This may be valid as a definition of the concept of mental disorder, but it is far too strong as a characterization of the conditions in the psychiatric manuals, given the evidence accumulated in psychological clinical science over the past hundred years; there would be few, if any, mental disorders left – apart from the ones found in the neurological textbooks. The conditions in the psychiatric manuals would need another name, other than mental disorder, which would become all but redundant. Alternatively, the idea may be that mental disorder is absence of meaning on the surface, unperceived by patient, family and clinician. This is probably valid as a construal of day-to-day social practice, but it is evidently flexible and relative, subject to fluctuation according to the perceiver's grasp of psychic life and of the person's life context – it is in any case nothing like a matter of scientific fact. While it may look like meaning has run out, the more we understand about the position, the more we may find meaning after all, albeit maladaptive ones leading to harm.

This idea gives rise to a third possibility: mental disorder involves maladaptive meanings. Maladaptive here would be better applied primarily to mental processes rather than to behaviour directly. There are circumstances in which behaviour may be maladaptive – in the sense that it brings about harm to the person – but which is not indicative of mental disorder: civil campaigning against an unscrupulous social agency would be one kind of example, bravery in battle would be another. Here we understand and have sympathy with the rationale for the behaviour, notwithstanding that it causes or raises risk of harm. It is when the rationale for the behaviour is also thought to be mistaken that the notion of disorder arises. If the underlying beliefs, emotions or values are judged to be in error, and the behaviour leads to persistent problems for the agent – or for others – then we may invoke mental disorder. That said, psychological clinical science has not become entangled in defining and deciding truth and falsity, correctness and error, in mental processes, but has rather settled on the term maladaptive to put the emphasis on the outcome of mental processing – the fact that it brings about harm, and specifically, more harm than good. In this case, the demarcation among behaviours which generate or raise the risk of harm, between those that are maladaptive and those which are thought not to be so, is a matter of implicit understanding and sympathy with the underlying beliefs and values.

4.4 **Diagnosis and the need to treat**

To the extent that mental disorder is defined by a natural dysfunction – as the naturalist definitions would have it – then establishing the presence of a dysfunction would be the primary aim of diagnosis. On the other hand, if mental disorder is not defined by a natural dysfunction, but more by distress and disability associated with various kinds of more or less abnormal psychological functioning, then the primary point of making a diagnosis of disorder as opposed to not making a diagnosis is to say that the level of distress or disability is sufficient to indicate need to treat.

It should be said that 'need to treat' is to be understood in this context in a broad sense. It may include the recommendation of an active treatment intervention such as medication or psychotherapy, but it also includes professional monitoring of the course of presenting problems that do yet require active interventions, either because the problem may well be self-limiting and there is scope for spontaneous recovery in the foreseeable future, or because no harms have yet accrued. The monitoring, sometimes called watchful waiting, may lead to no active intervention if spontaneous recovery does occur, or to active treatment if the problems become chronic and associated with significant harm or risk of harm. This kind of wait and see approach has just as much of a role in mental health services, especially at the primary care level, as in general medicine. Making a diagnosis of a psychiatric condition signifies the need for professional attention but not necessarily the need for active intervention, still less the timing or type of active intervention. For these management and treatment matters we go beyond diagnostic classification manuals to treatment guidelines, to be interpreted by the experienced clinician and taking into account features of the individual case. Treatment guidelines often recommend stepped care, minimal attention for milder cases including watchful waiting, progressing as and when required and indicated to more substantial active interventions.

It has long been apparent that there is a close connection between making a diagnosis of illness or disorder and warranting clinical attention and treatment. Giving a diagnosis presupposes distress, impairment or risk in a degree sufficient to indicate need for clinical care, and diagnosis is commonly required for access to it. Sociologists recognize that giving a warrant for treatment is a major function of diagnostic practice which defines its institutional significance. The psychiatric manuals begin their explicit definitions of mental disorder by reference to distress and disability, or risk thereof, which clearly raise the question of need for treatment. The definitions also invoke the notion of clinically significant symptoms, referring to a blend of the patient's view of the problem as intolerable and in need of help, and the clinician's assessment and consideration of whether attention and possibly active intervention are indicated.

Another theme relevant to the linkage between diagnosis and treatment appears in the work previously considered by behavioural scientists on the nature of mental disorder within an evolutionary theoretic framework. As reviewed earlier in sections 2.5 and 3.4, Cosmides and Tooby (1999) have argued that there are many possible pathways to maladaptive behaviour that do not involve dysfunction in an evolutionary theoretic sense, and which are therefore not disorders according to Wakefield's analysis. Further, insofar as Wakefield's analysis is accepted as valid, the conclusion is that many kinds and instances of maladaptive behaviour, including many of the conditions described in the DSM and ICD, are not disorders. So what are they? This is where the strong connection between diagnostic practice and warrant for treatment can be invoked. Thus, Cosmides and Tooby (1999) agree with Wakefield's definition, noting that it is useful as an analysis of lay and medical usage, and also that it can link up with scientific research programmes. However, they broaden the issue out, noting that there are various options from an evolutionary perspective on conditions generating distress, apart from failure of a system to function as designed, including: evolved defences, extremes of normal variation, proper function in a novel environment, conflict between functions, accommodation to the needs of a different organism, dysfunction in an adaptation, and 'many other things'. They go on to focus on the larger category of interest to health professionals, conditions that may arise by such pathways without involving failure of a system to function as designed, and which are therefore not disorders, and characterize this larger category as *treatable conditions*. So are the psychiatric manuals compilations of treatable conditions?

The viability of this terminological suggestion depends on how it is interpreted. In a straightforward interpretation it is obviously problematic, the problem being that there are conditions in the psychiatric manuals that we cannot treat, or cannot adequately treat, or which in some kinds of presentation we cannot treat, and this cannot sensibly be taken to imply they should on those grounds be omitted. There are untreatable mental health problems, just as there are untreatable physical health problems, and this is a state of affairs that signals the need for further research, on aetiology and treatment, or for rehabilitation, optimizing functioning notwithstanding disability, or for palliative care – not for exclusion from the psychiatric manuals and neglect. On these grounds 'treatable conditions' should mean not conditions that we currently are able to treat, but rather conditions that we wish could be treated/that we would like to be able to treat.

However, this simple and probably inevitable interpretation of the suggestion that the psychiatric manuals comprise treatable conditions plainly has radical implications, which is why the suggestion is instructive. 'Treatable conditions' retains the appearance of being a medical/scientific matter. 'Conditions that we wish could be treated/that we would like to be able to treat' looks anything but a medical/scientific matter, but rather situates the whole problematic back among social structures, choices and values.

This line of thought would have treatable conditions as a cover name for the conditions in the psychiatric manuals on the assumption that Wakefield's analysis of the concept of mental disorder is correct – the consequence being that the term mental disorder is not suitable for all the conditions. Consider another option, sketched in the previous sections and interpreted as being closest to current usage of the psychiatric manuals, according to which mental disorder is retained as a general term, not tied to evolutionary theoretic naturalism, but rather gaining traction in the phenomena described in the diagnostic criteria, in the problematic, maladaptive mental states and behaviours involving disruption of normal, appropriate, typical psychological functioning. In this context – in the psychiatric manuals themselves – what is the linkage between diagnosis and the need to treat?

It was noted in the first chapter that DSM-IV requires for diagnosis of a particular disorder not only presence of the psychological syndrome as specified in the diagnostic criteria for the condition, but also – for many conditions though not all – satisfaction of another criterion requiring the presence of significant distress or impairment in social role functioning. This is consistent with the explicit definition of mental disorder at the beginning of the DSM which states clearly that conditions in the manual are associated with, briefly, distress and/or impairment, or risk thereof. On the other hand, it has often been noted that for many of the psychiatric conditions – most obviously the affective and anxiety disorders – the additional distress or impairment criterion is somewhat redundant, since many of the symptoms already imply distress, if not impairment. So what is the point of the additional criterion?

In clinical practice judgements have to be made about degrees of distress and/or impairment, closely connected to whether treatment should be offered. Sometimes these matters are straightforward one way or the other, but there is also obviously a grey area in between. This is resolved in one way or another in clinical practice, but there is another arena in which assessment, diagnosis and decisions about treatment provision are the primary focus, namely epidemiology and its application to public health services planning. At the community level the boundary problem is magnified: where to draw the line between disorder and normal functioning. To anticipate some of the issues that will be the focus of the next chapter, it can be seen that insofar as mental disorder is tied to distress, disability and the need to treat, the boundary is bound to be somewhat flexible. The problem arises in clinical practice typically on a one-to-one basis, but there is a large-scale problem for epidemiology, in the form of where to define the cut-off for 'caseness' in community samples, in terms of symptom severity, distress and impairment, a decision that significantly impacts on prevalence estimates. One main use of epidemiological studies is public health services planning, so this problem interacts with estimates of need for treatment services. Major epidemiological surveys in the US in the late 1980s/early 1990s found estimates of prevalence of major depressive disorder for example that seemed to be high, giving rise to concerns that the diagnostic criteria were over-inclusive. For example, Regier and colleagues write:

> The high estimates of lifetime disorders that have recently emerged from the NCS and from the two-wave analysis of the ECA raise questions about the clinical significance of all these disorders in such a large proportion of the population ... The high rates in the last studies had led to concerns about the clinical significance of some of these conditions and about the comparability of diagnostic assessments in these different studies. In the current US climate of determining the medical necessity for care in managed healthcare plans, it is doubtful that 28% or 29% of the population would be judged to need mental health treatment in a year. Hence, additional impairment and other criteria should be developed for future epidemiological surveys to identify those most in need of such treatment. If these population defined prevalence rates are useful for determining high risk groups for future prevention purposes, evidence of such clinical course information should also be obtained.
>
> Regier et al. (1998, pp. 113–14)

The explicit distress/impairment criterion had been added to some diagnostic criteria in the DSM-IV in this context, in effect to reduce prevalence estimates,

by serving as a reminder especially in epidemiological surveys to make diagnoses only when the harms indicated in the DSM definition of disorder are
indeed present (Frances 1998). Specifically the criterion helps in epidemiological studies to define a line cutting mild from more severe cases, a cut-off in
what is otherwise probably a normal distribution of e.g. anxiety and depressive
signs in the population.

In clinical practice it is relatively rare to come across people with emotional
problems who do not satisfy the distress or impairment criterion: the diagnostic symptoms are practically by definition distressing, if not impairing. In those
cases where distress or impairment in the patient is not the main presenting
problem, such as antisocial personality disorder, the criterion is (wisely) not
included. In brief, the distress/impairment criterion has limited clinical use;
but it has use in general population studies to exclude mild cases for whom –
given costs and resources relative to harm – decision is made that there is no
need to make treatment resources available.

It may be noted that this use of the distress/impairment criterion to narrow
the class of diagnosable depressive disorder is somewhat suspect from the naturalist point of view: naturalism would just as rather or would prefer to
exclude cases because they do not involve a genuine dysfunction, but are
rather, for example, normal reactions to psychosocial stress. Spitzer and
Wakefield (1999) argued along these lines at the time, as do Horwitz and
Wakefield in their recent book (2007). As argued in earlier in Chapter 3, however, it is not clear that evolutionary naturalism can be used in practice to
demarcate abnormal from normal reactions, and there is the risk that heavy
reliance on this distinction using implicit personal and social norms will jeop-
ardize reliability of diagnosis, especially in the areas of grey that are critical in
epidemiology. In a non-naturalist context, by contrast, reliance on the dis-
tress/impairment criterion simply underscores the fact that psychiatry's
conception of mental disorder is essentially tied to harm, to distress and disability, and there has to be some decision made as to where the threshold is set
for involvement of healthcare, and this is a major issue in epidemiology and
health service planning.

4.5. **The domain of healthcare**

Two main sets of questions central to the problem of mental disorder were
identified in the Introduction.

First, are the norms invoked in psychiatry natural, scientific and medical, or
are they really social? Who or what is the arbiter of the difference between
mental order and disorder, normality and abnormality? Or again: is there a

proper domain for psychiatry: treatment of medical disorder – or does it really and illegitimately just monitor and manage social deviance?

Second, what is the validity of the distinction between mental disorder and order, between abnormal and normal mental functioning? To what extent, notwithstanding appearances, does mental disorder involve meaningful responses and problem-solving – in relation to normal or not so normal problems of living, including extreme psychosocial challenges? Is there after all order in mental disorder? And to the extent that there is, what implications does this have for the viability of the concept?

Broad conclusions of the essay about these problems will be drawn in the last chapter, but one can be signalled here, concerning the proper domain of the medical – and healthcare generally – in relation to the distinction between mental order and disorder. The suggestion, in brief, is that this domain is defined fundamentally by a distinctive kind of response to problems, rather than by a distinctive kind of problem.

Medicine has always been involved in the care of the individual who – in one way or another – is suffering. In this sense the construal of the primary feature of mental disorder as being the suffering of the individual – as in the definitions in the psychiatric manuals – is quite correct. Medicine has always had to deal with a combination of normal and abnormal suffering; practically however these terms might be defined. Normal suffering would include aches and pains, coughs and colds, skeletal fractures, also distress about children, partners, bereavements and growing old – and so on endlessly. Abnormal might include tuberculosis, illness from poor diet, uncontrollable worry, anguish leading to the wish to die – also an endless list – but is there a factual distinction here in the nature of things between normal and abnormal suffering, or between normal and abnormal causes of it? The main conclusion from discussion of naturalist theories of health and illness in the previous chapter is that there is no natural, principled boundary between normal and abnormal conditions of suffering. Physicians have managed them all – using their training, the available science, their own clinical experience, and advice from colleagues who may know such and such a condition better. They draw distinctions as best they can between those conditions which are normal in the community, or normal in certain conditions (ages, genders, socio-economic class), and those which are abnormal, and between conditions which can be expected to remit in the foreseeable future, all being well, and those which raise significant risk and which require treatment – if there is one – or at least amelioration. Physicians can advise about normality in the population, course, risk and need to treat, and they can manage the problems and provide treatment if there is one, on the basis of their training, knowledge and experience – all this they can do – but the question of demarcating between genuine illness and normal suffering is not something required in the course of clinical practice.

So does this mean that there is no proper domain of medicine – or of healthcare generally? Not one that is or can be drawn in terms of a particular type of problem, abnormal as opposed to normal. The domain is not defined fundamentally within the nature of the problems themselves. Rather, what defines the domain is the *response* to the conditions, the physician–patient, the professional healthcare relationship.

Is this not circular? Defining the medical domain in terms of what physicians do? No, because the purpose here is not to define an exclusive domain of medical problems – that would be circular. Rather, it is to define one kind of response to human complaints of suffering among other possible ones.

To illustrate what is intended here, consider the vexed question whether psychiatry, or mental health services generally, confuse medical or healthcare problems with what are rather social problems, or ordinary problems of living. My suggestion is that what is distinctive about the medical or healthcare domain is not a kind of problem, some kind to be kept distinct from social problems or ordinary problems of living, but is a particular kind of response, characterized by seeking to respond to requests for help, at the individual level, using the available science of body and mind. Here are two hypothetical typical cases in which mental health problems and common social problems are interwoven.

A mother of a 10-year-old boy reluctantly brings her son to the community mental health clinic, having been advised to do so by the school because his behaviour is excessively disruptive and he has been excluded. The mother is angry, and correctly points out that UK African and African-Caribbean boys are more likely to get excluded from school than majority white boys, probably for no more disruptive behaviour, and again correctly sets this discrimination within racism in society as a whole. In brief, her son has been excluded because he is black, and to add insult to injury he has now been sent to see a psychologist as if he was mentally ill.

The psychologist – having listened well – responds along the following lines: 'Well you say this, but how many black boys are there in the class, and how many have been excluded? . . . And then let's think about why it is that your son has been excluded and the other boys not. What might the difference be?' This intervention shifts the level of causation/intervention from the social to the individual, away from social group differences to individual – in this context it can probably only be done by a clinician from the same ethnic group (or at least not from the white majority), so that the social group difference can be set aside in the conversation.

This kind of problem is about as socially embedded as it gets, and there is ample scope for social action, action at the sociopolitical level, but even so, the healthcare professional is there for a different purpose – to help this particular individual avoid loss of educational opportunity and other risks of harm.

Another example would be a young single mother with depression. She has many social problems: she has low income, has several young children to care for in inadequate housing, and she has few social supports. Her depression consists in usually low mood, tearfulness, poor sleep, low levels of energy, little enjoyment in her life, irritability with the children; she says she finds it difficult to carry on, she doesn't know how she can keep looking after her children – she worries about money, housing and the children, and sees no way out of her situation.

Again there is ample scope for social action, for example involving the housing department, which may or may not be able to help, or for community organizers to work in the estate. However the clinician, while she may seek to activate these other interventions, operates primarily at another level, the individual, so that again social group differences are partialled out and individual capacities are the focus. The intervention could include something along the following lines: what other mothers do you know around here that are in a similar position? do you know how they are getting on? can you find out? can we find out what they do to get help for themselves? This kind of focus is on help-seeking, self-help and empowerment, and there are other psychotherapeutic options, such as in cognitive therapy or psychoanalytic psychotherapy, but what they have in common is identification of something within the individual that could change to make things better. Pharmacotherapy – prescribing an anti-depressant in this case – shares this same general, individual-level assumption.

There are many kinds of response to problems of human suffering. For example, separately or in combination, the following: helpless ignorance (not knowing what to do); caring ignorance (looking after but with no expertise) attribution of malingering (blaming); attribution of moral weakness, weakness of will or characterological weakness (blaming); expectation that the person should get on with it (belief in self-reliance) – or, shifting to the sociopolitical level, the response to human suffering can be to try to intervene at a community level, as in public health, for example provision of clean water supplies, or to alleviate socio-economic related factors implicated in ill-health, such as poverty, social exclusion, lack of social supports – or, shifting to other levels, suffering can be regarded in a religious cosmological light, with *many* possibilities within and across religions. This is a long and varied list of possible construals of and responses to human suffering, and healthcare of the individual is just one of them; and moreover, the characterization of the problem as 'suffering' is more suited to healthcare and some of the other approaches, but not to all – some constructions would use different names, or none at all.

One implication here is that there are inevitably border disputes and negotiations between the various approaches – between doctors and priests and community workers and politicians – as to what is the proper domain of each. These negotiations depend partly on the domains in which the presenting problem is situated. The problem can be expressed for example as the suffering of the individual, or as complaint about the way society is organized, or as statement of fate, secular or religious–cosmological, or as a religious problem to be solved; and so forth. Different people will have different views about which of these is correct, as they will about the causes: bodily dysfunction, social discrimination, fall from grace, karma and so forth. These issues can to some extent be resolved pragmatically if there is harmony between the parties: it is a matter of what approach looks plausible in any given case or kind of case – and above all a matter of what helps. There is also ample scope for non-negotiation, depending on prevailing conditions, in which case there is something more like turf wars between particular groups, professional or otherwise. The struggle over the control of the asylums involving religious reformers on the one hand, and physicians on the other, described for example by Foucault, is one such example relevant to the themes of the essay. The same possibilities arise within healthcare itself, in the form of negotiations or power struggles between, for example, traditional healers, medical practitioners in different traditions, pharmacists, medics and the other health professions.

All these things are evident in the history and current position of medicine in society, but they are much magnified in psychiatry. This is because the domain in which the problems present is less clearly somatic, relating to bodily dysfunction, and more clearly mental and behavioural (using our western analysed categories), these blurring inevitably into the moral and spiritual and social domains. So all these other approaches are clearly involved, and the boundary disputes are manifest. At the same time western medicine was handicapped in its extension from physical to mental illnesses because mind and meaning were out of reach of natural science. Another science grew up alongside medical psychiatry (though made in large part by medical psychiatrists): the psychological science of psychopathology, and its associated psychological treatments. These twins have become reconciled at a conceptual and scientific level, though turf wars between the professions and professional trainings still have to be played out to a satisfactory conclusion.

One boundary dispute that arises in psychiatry much more urgently than in general medicine is to do with the issue of social control of danger. Psychiatry has had to deal not only with the suffering of the individual, in the traditional role of medicine, but also with individuals who may or may not be suffering themselves, but who are thought to pose a risk to others by reason of mental illness. This gets psychiatry involved with what is properly the activity of the state, a role which fits more or less well – generally not well – with the duty of care to the individual. Issues related to this fundamental and currently critical professional boundary problem will be considered at greater length in the next chapter.

According to the considerations so far in this section, the proper domain of medicine and of healthcare generally is construal of suffering as being such, and attending to it on the basis of professional ethics, training, clinical experience, and the available science of causes and cures. In my view, this is consistent with the approach to the definitions of mental disorder given in the psychiatric manuals, the ICD and the DSM. Both of them – quoted in Chapter 1, section 1.2 – characterize the mental disorders compiled in the manuals primarily in terms of association with distress or disability, or risk of adverse outcomes, with the additional specifications that this is (considered as being) due to a personal dysfunction, and is not just a matter of deviation from social norms. I think these characterizations and specifications can be regarded as a definition in the sense of a position statement: healthcare attends to distress or disability in the individual, therefore regards it as an individual matter, as a procedural assumption, in relation to causes and in any case in relation to response, as opposed to, in particular, a social problem the appropriate approach to which would be sociopolitical.

In this context, I suggest, the qualification of 'personal dysfunction' can be interpreted as a working procedural assumption: attribution of the cause of the problem to the person hangs together with the working assumption that intervening at the individual level can make a difference for the better – for the individual. This stance is obviously not incompatible with the social action working assumption that intervention at the sociopolitical level can make a difference for the better – at the social level, for many individuals, though not necessarily for any particular one. Note that the working assumption is not or does not have to be as strong as that 'the cause of the problem is in the person'. The working assumption required is much weaker, amounting to: there is something in the individual's functioning (biological, psychological or psychosocial) which, if changed in particular ways, would make a difference for the person for the better (would remove or alleviate the harms and risks). This is compatible with the fact that there are many causes at many levels and in many places, and many points of possible intervention, of which the individual is just one.

In a paper associated with the formulation of the DSM definition, Spitzer and Endicott wrote:

> We believe that there are several fundamental concepts in the notion of a medical disorder: negative consequences of the condition, an inferred or identified organismic dysfunction, and an implicit call for action. There is no assumption that the organismic dysfunction or its negative consequences are of a physical nature . . . The purpose of a classification of medical disorders is to identify those conditions which, because of their negative consequences, implicitly have a *call to action* to the profession, the person with the condition, and society. The call to action on the part of the medical profession (and its allied professions) is to offer treatment for the condition or a means to prevent it development, or, if knowledge is lacking, to conduct appropriate research. The call to the person with the condition is to assume the patient or sick role . . . The call to action on the part of society takes several forms which may include giving various exemptions from certain responsibilities to those in the sick role and to provide a means for the delivery of medical of medical care.

(1978, pp. 17–18: italics in the original)

This approach embeds medical problems in their social context, and is consistent with the view proposed here. It needs updating in various ways 30 years on; for example, in its medical profession orientation – psychotherapists, for example, would not necessarily want the person to assume a sick role, but may seek to encourage active engagement in and contribution to the process of change.

Nowhere in this line of thought, however, is there a need to distinguish between normal and abnormal conditions of suffering and disability, or between normal and abnormal causes. If normal means anything here, it is primarily a matter of there being no need to treat, for example if the problems are self-limiting and carry no significant risk of future harms. In this case the only intervention required is giving psycho-educational advice to this effect. In brief, it is all a matter of the consequences of the conditions, not of their intrinsic properties.

On the other hand, the DSM-IV definition of mental disorder adds a further qualification that looks like it is intended to mark a difference in these terms: it is stipulated that to count as a mental disorder a troublesome condition must not be merely an expectable and culturally sanctioned response to a particular event, such as a major loss. Interestingly the original definition in the DSM-III did not have this qualification (American Psychiatric Association 1980; see also Spitzer and Williams 1982), nor does the definition in the ICD have anything to this effect. This stipulation appears to want to rule out normal or normally caused distress and disability, but the term expectable is vague and uncertain and cannot bear much weight. Many medical and psychiatric conditions are expectable in any readily available sense, such as skeletal fractures following a (long) fall, or, for example, stress reaction following profound psychological shock, depression when adverse life events accumulate; and so on. What matters is not expectability or otherwise, but consequences in terms of distress, disability and risk.

However, if the task or challenge is seen as being to define the proper domain of medical or psychiatric care *in terms of the conditions and their causes*, and in particular to distinguish this domain in these terms from normal problems of living, or from social problems, then there is no choice but to go down some route of the kind gestured to in the DSM-IV definition, and thoroughly worked out in the naturalist definitions of disease and dysfunction. We are led towards definitions of abnormality in statistical terms or in terms of failure of the natural design of the body and mind. However – so far as was argued in the previous chapter – all of these attempts lead to problematic and ultimately unviable conclusions. Insofar as this is so, we are left with an understanding of the domains of medical and healthcare of the kind sketched in this section and illustrated in the quote from Spitzer and Endicott's paper above: the domains are socially defined, characterized by individual suffering and the distinctive healthcare responses.

Here is Kendell writing just after the 1960s upheavals:

> The fact is that any definition of disease which boils down to 'what people complain of', or 'what doctors treat', or some combination of the two, is almost worse than no definition at all. It is free to expand or contract with changes in social attitudes and therapeutic optimism and is at the mercy of idiosyncratic decisions by doctors or patients. If one wished to compare the incidence of disease in two different cultures, or in a single population at two different times, whose criteria of suffering or therapeutic concern would one use? And if the incidence of disease turned out to be different in the two, would this be because one was healthier than the other, or simply because their attitudes to illness were different?

(1975, pp. 307–8)

All this is correct. Kendell in his paper had reviewed some of the 1960s critiques of psychiatry, remarked on the need to define the domain of medicine and psychiatry in response, noted that this was generally not a matter of practical concern to medicine, noted that traditional concepts of disease and lesion were changing (as previously quoted to this effect in section 3.3), and reviewed some attempts by psychiatrists to move in the direction of understanding disease, illness, or the proper domain of medicine in terms of the complaints of patients and the medical response. It is in this context that the quoted passage is set. Since the prospects for such a social definition are so poor – absurd from the point of view that disease is a fixed fact of nature – Kendell goes on to consider new ways in which the boundaries of disease can be fixed, not in terms of lesion and disease (note here the shifting nature of the target), which were shifting even in medicine, but rather in terms from evolutionary theory. The appearance of this new approach to defining the real nature and boundaries of disease/illness/disorder was mentioned in section 3.3 as a preamble to discussion of Wakefield's evolutionary naturalism. It is Wakefield's elaborate and refined definition of disorder that has dominated the field for the last nearly two decades, and to the extent that it does not work in the end, as has been argued in this essay, then we are faced with the conclusions and questions that Kendell puts well in the above quotation. They include flexible boundaries in relation to people's tolerance, management and complaints of distress, optimism by doctors as to what they can treat, to which we can add other group that has always offered help, the manufacturers of treatments, and we also have major cross-cultural issues as Kendell indicated. These topics will be pursued mainly in the fifth chapter, with cross-cultural issues arising in the next section.

Defining the proper domain of healthcare without reliance on naturalist definitions inevitably highlights boundary issues of various kinds. Some of them will be considered in more detail in Chapter 5. This chapter closes with a general philosophical view of the contemporary shifts in the representation of mental disorder that underlie many of the themes and proposals in this essay.

4.6 Late- or post-modern views of mental health problems

Foucault's analysis has the idea of madness in western modernity as Unreason, mere deficit, its associated social features being mainly exclusion. What now?

The two great intellectual expressions of modernity were Rationalism and Empiricism, the one seeing the rational order of the Divine and of Nature, His Creation, the other the basis of human understanding and knowledge in the experience of the senses, common to all, shared and objective. These two epistemologies were opposed, until elements were synthesized in Kant, but they both shared the assumption of one Nature and one (correct) knowledge/ representation of it. These great ideas of modernity affected the view of mental disorder like everything else, for example in the following ways, in no particular order:

- Order is a matter of conformity to Nature in reason and experience. There is an absolute distinction between order and disorder (between what is natural, rational, and valid as experience – and their opposites). The boundary between order and disorder will be in the nature of things, an unconditional matter of fact, not at all a matter of opinion.

- All order is fundamentally the same. All rationality is conformity to Nature; all valid ideas and experience likewise. The norms of reason and experience are self-evident, just facts of nature.

- All disorder is likewise fundamentally the same – just absence of order. *Radical* error in the mind is deficit of reason (in Rationalism), or (in Empiricism), it is either or both of deficit in combining ideas of experience (of reason in this sense), or deficit of experience itself. 'Delusion' and 'hallucination' are the defining marks of mental disorder.

- No sense can be heard from the other side of the boundary; it is silent. Disorder is paradoxical, in one sense having no existence – being just absence; but also, what lies on the dark side of order – the unnatural, the irrational, hallucination – is fundamentally chaotic, formless, incomprehensible, unsuited to knowledge, feared and much to be avoided.

The shift away from the episteme of modernity has taken place (as all such shifts) over an indefinite period, roughly, according to some punctuation marks, over the last century, but in any case still in progress. Its most obvious expression has been deconstruction of absolute ideas, by making explicit their assumptions, now seen as discredited, and highlighting the social power structures that have established and maintained them. Examples of this kind of work include feminist critiques of male domination, critiques of colonialism, and so forth. Foucault is among the foremost writers in this general deconstructionist movement, with works on crime and deviance, on medicine, and on madness, considered briefly in this essay in Chapter 2. Other critiques of the idea of mental illness and psychiatry in the 1960s belong in this same movement: repudiating madness, breaking down boundaries between madness and normality, between them and us, reversing them – demolishing the asylums.

Deconstructionism inevitably contains within it the option of negativism. The deconstruction of absolute order as the basis for knowledge, values and social structures inevitably carries with it the possibility of destruction of order full stop, so that all varieties are as good or as bad as all others, with the sole and unreassuring qualification that the most powerful groups will impose their knowledge, values and social structures on hapless others. This kind of option, sometimes associated with so-called postmodernism, lends itself to the charge of moral nihilism. This charge derives partly from remaining convictions of access to some absolute truth. More interestingly, there is the possibility that postmodernism in its deconstructive mode misses positive values in its own foundations, in the conditions of making order in social practice.

'Order' refers to form, patterns, structures, classes, rules, as opposed to absence of these things: formlessness, chaos, randomness. Hence order and similar terms refer to the basis for cognition, values and practice. At this abstract level there are few possible accounts of what order is, probably just two. In one kind of account, order is already given, unconditional, independent of human beings, fixed timelessly; in brief, it is *absolute*. On the other hand, human beings have long been recognized as somewhat lowly epistemic agents, finite, immersed in the flux and relativity of experience and social belief systems. How can human beings, so understood, access unconditioned true knowledge, corresponding to reality as it really is. How to square this particular circle? The solution has always had to be of one general kind: notwithstanding appearances, some human beings can have special access to a form of knowledge that is divine or in some other way superhuman, quasi-divine. Here belong the diverse epistemologies of divine revelation, rationalism, mysticism and other forms of esoteric knowledge. They are all distinct from each other, with quite different affinities, and themselves of many distinct varieties, but they all have in common explaining how human beings can be party to superhuman, non-relative knowledge. The absolute ideas of modernity come under this general heading, and the contrast, found in late- or postmodernity, goes for the other general option, which is not just absence of absolutes, but which has another kind of account of order.

In the alternative account, order is created through time in practice, is relative to conditions of agency, and essentially involves negotiation between agents and their practices/points of view. The principles of making and preserving order in fact assume a kind of absolute status here, in that they meant to underlie all practices, but their existence is not independent of our making them, and is not guaranteed in the nature of things; further, not everyone will agree they are fundamental, or indeed that they matter at all – in all these respects this is not the same understanding of 'absolute' as in dogmatism. Fundamental, interrelated themes in this new late- or postmodern episteme include activity, involving embodiment of subjectivity as agency, and intersubjectivity, grounded in shared, rule-guided practice. These themes pervade twentieth-century philosophy, for example in pragmatism, existentialism, phenomenology, and in the later period Wittgenstein.

The same underlying themes – activity and intersubjectivity – pervade twentieth-century science, especially when it is concerned with epistemological fundamentals. In physics, for example, the Special Theory of Relativity gave up the idea that there are absolute quantities of space and time, independent of the frames of reference, substituting the idea that space and time as measured by rods and clocks interact with the frame of reference, though with rules – the Lorenz transformations – that link frames of reference with the varying results obtained: measurement of space and time depends on regularities in measurements made from various points of view. In developmental psychology, one of its founders, Piaget, emphasized the basis of cognition in action, and another, Vygotski, recognized its basis in the social. All the life-/human sciences have developed in the shift from the old dogmatic philosophies to the new one characterized by the idea that order is created. Evolutionary biology is the classic statement of how order, in this case the design and functional activity of biological organisms, is made up as it – the evolutionary process operating under selective pressure – goes along. Psychological theory from Freud to behaviourism to cognitive psychology has personal and sub-personal processes in the business of meaning-making, signifying the appearance of the idea of human agency in the construction of order. 'Social constructionism' is the general term for this kind of thinking in the social sciences and it pervades them.

The creation of order essentially involves the possibility of error. It was already noted in the second chapter that molecular genetics has a particular view of error, namely as being random genetic mutation which allows for the possibility of evolution itself. Here is Foucault indicating the depth of the shift in conception of error and of nature brought about in the life sciences, (1966):

> But it proved impossible to make up a science of the living being without having to take into account, as essential to its object, the possibility of disease, death, monstrosity, anomaly, error (even if genetics gave this last word a meaning completely different from that intended by eighteenth-century physicians when they spoke of an error of nature).

(pp. 17–18)

> At the heart of these problems [concerning evolution] is that of error. For at life's most basic level, the play of code and decoding leaves room for chance, which, before being disease, deficit or monstrosity, is something like perturbation in the information system, something like a 'mistake'. In the extreme, life is what is capable of error.

(pp. 21–2)

Foucault goes on to elaborate on this theme – error and contrast with truth throughout human history and thought – all this being in the context of commentary on Canguilhem's (1966) dissertation on 'the normal and the pathological'. Here the point is not of course that there is no pathology, but rather that divergence from normality, from existing order, is continuous and essential, and is not yet pathology. As has been argued through the essay, there is nothing intrinsic in particular biopsychological processes that makes them pathological, it is only their consequences, only if they persistently result in seriously more harm than good. This is the kind of idea of error and illness that belongs with the episteme in which order is created rather than already given as absolutely fixed.

In fact there are various ways of understanding how adverse outcomes arise, not sharply distinguished: there is no order at all, randomness only; there is order, but it is pointless (a waste of time, a dereliction of other obligations); there is order, but it leads to much harm – it is in this sense a wrong order – though this may lead to a greater good – in which case it is right after all; or the activity is mistakenly believed to lead to a greater good, in which case it is misguided; or there may be no right way out – all ways lead to harm. These various possibilities in the thought-space frame discourse on normality, pathology, characterological faults, fate and tragedy: they are not sharply distinguished, and distinctions depend on knowledge base, on appraisals and on values, from one point of view or another.

It is in the realm of explicit values – ethics – that relativity is plainly open to view and stock responses to it include on the one hand emphatic dogmatic reassertion of the absolute truth (whichever one the speaker has in mind), and on the other, collapse into a moral nihilism in which every form of behaviour is regarded as neither better nor worse than any other (a view which wins few friends). However, ethical principles are always fundamentally the same as epistemological and ontological ones. In the present case, the epistemology of late- or postmodernity places the highest value on the flourishing and protection of agency and communication, because threats to them are threats to the generation of order – and the origin of order is always the highest good. Dogmatic philosophies whether religious or secular generally are strong on values, proclaiming them loudly, but their inevitable downside is presumed priority of one group over another, this being an obstacle to embracing the whole humanity, except perhaps as a subject for conversion or rule. The downside of the non-dogmatic approach is that it envisages no way of adjudicating between competing claims but recommends negotiation to find common ground, assigning strongly negative value to the denial of rights of others to express their points of view in speech and practices. Although the new episteme contradicts some dogmatic aspects of modernity, as in empiricism and rationalism, in other ways, particularly in assigning equal epistemic and moral value to all, in seeking common ground in reason (reason defined here by the ability to find common ground), and in the high value assigned to freedom of expression, it is better seen as a continuation of the Enlightenment project.

What implications does this have for disorder? All action involves the creation of order. Explanations of actions that are deemed to have no sensible point – no generation of comprehensible order – may be explained from the standpoint of the various sciences: there may be breakdown of some basic biopsychological function, or, the rationale for the behaviour may be hidden from view, or both. As we have seen in Chapter 2, the methodological rule of evolutionary biology, psychology and social science is to seek for strategies that are not open to view. Nowhere in these biopsychosocial sciences do we get a handle on some static called disorder. Apparently there are occasionally in deep evolutionary time meteoric dust clouds that wipe out half the life on earth, but then, even while the dust is settling, life-forms are adapting, finding new niches, new ways of surviving. As in psychology, catastrophic brain insult, if it doesn't kill the person, or destroy mental functioning altogether, is soon followed by the operation of subpersonal compensatory and restorative processes, and attempts by the person to act. Society too can be reduced to rubble and chaos – by natural or human destruction – but, if community remains at all, not for long: rebuilding begins straightaway. There are problems and catastrophes in plenty, but *bios* and *psyche* – unless they are destroyed altogether, try to carry on. This might be said to be our nature – according to the current episteme expressed for example in the sciences. The further aspect is that the boundary between order and disorder is not fixed from one point of view only but is assessed from many – it is a matter of negotiation.

So what uses are there for the term mental disorder in this new episteme? In the strongest interpretation, mental disorder is always just absence of order. In an activity-based philosophy, this means that there is no real activity, no meaning-making, just chaotic behaviour and mentality caused for example by damage to the neural processes that process information and regulate behaviour. Catastrophic brain damage leading to paralysis and cessation of higher mental activity would be a paradigm case, epileptic fit would be another, and both are conditions for neurology, not psychiatry. These are very different paradigms compared with madness, which had its special status before because it offended absolute standards of reason and experience. The expression mental disorder in this strong sense can, however, be applied in psychiatry to express the view that a mental state and associated behaviour has no purpose, no functionality, no meaning, but is no more that the random outcome of a disrupted brain mechanism. Attribution of mental disorder in this strong sense involves an hypothesis, and one difficult to establish for certain, as it involves a negative, but its intended implications are clear, that the attempt to find psychological explanation is misconceived, and is to be given up in favour of, probably, care and pharmacological intervention, if there is one available. Many kinds of psychiatric presentation are plausible candidates, such as severe ADHD, tics and Tourette's syndrome, bipolar disorder, schizophrenia, though in many of these conditions, or in many of their presentations, psychological activity, meaning-making, is also interwoven. Further, this strong connotation of mental disorder requires discrimination between the conditions described in the psychiatric manuals, many of which, or many presentations of which, are not thought to be of this kind, but which rather involve various kinds of maladaptation, that is to say, behaviours and mental processing that do generate order, that do involve information processing, but which consistently lead to harm. These are conditions that involve generation of order, but of an unhelpful kind, and characterizing them as mental disorders is intrinsically paradoxical and misleading, just because there is not simple deficit of mental order. The characterization is problematic because of connotations from the strong, more valid usage, implying that there is no meaning in the presentation when there is, that the person is behaving randomly when they are in fact struggling to best manage some major adversity, that attempts to understand and communicate are misconceived when in fact this is what is needed most; and so on. Psychiatry is characterized by dialectical play between these two usages of mental disorder and their associated practices, not only between conditions, but within any one patient's journey through time. It may be, for example, that in an acute psychotic state the brain is just misfiring, producing no meaningful order, and communication is not possible; but people do not stay in this condition forever, especially with current medications, but begin to recover, and then attempts to communicate and negotiate should resume. These shifts in stance present major challenges to all involved (nurses, doctors, families, and patients).

These issues of mental disorder – terminological and practical – are familiar to the individuals concerned, their families and friends, and to the clinicians involved in care. They have to do with the way that mental normality and abnormality are conceived, how the boundary lines are drawn at any one time, by whom, and how they shift: in brief, they involve negotiation of one broad kind of difference.

Foucault in his study of the modern western idea of madness identified disqualification and social exclusion, but it is obvious that the mad were not the only group at the receiving end of these processes during the period in question. The absolute standards of reason and experience were bound to be conceived in practice in terms of the home culture, in a Euro-centric way, and specifically in terms of the dominant power groups within it. What was referred to above as continuity between the Enlightenment project and late- or postmodernity has primarily involved emancipation and inclusion of previously disqualified and socially excluded groups, within and beyond western culture. Among the processes involved is exposure to the other, most of all the need to negotiate, generally when power balances allow. Mental health services in contemporary western societies face a double challenge, at the interface between two complex sets of boundaries, the one between mental normality and abnormality, the other between western and non-western cultures, following large-scale economic immigration from previously colonized countries and the need to provide mental health services for communities with wide ethnic diversity. Each kind of boundary is complex enough itself, but the challenges interact and exacerbate one another. Members of communities that are already socially excluded on cultural grounds, typically confounded with and compounded by economic disadvantage, face a further disqualification if they become involved with mental health services and receive a diagnosis. Mental health services (among others) have found it hard to engage and provide adequate services for these communities, unfair for various reasons including the major economic benefits they bring. This is partly a matter of social exclusion associated with socio-economic status and explicit or institutionalized racism, but even when there is engagement other more subtle issues come into play to do with barely understood cultural differences in conceptions of mental disorder.

The practical problems of making services accessible to minority culture groups are well-known, though the details are context-specific. A recent UK report by the Sainsbury Centre for Mental Health (2002) identified ten key themes inhibiting engagement, one of which is described thus: 'Divergence in professional and lay discourse on mental illness/distress: different models and descriptions of "mental illness" are used and other people's philosophies or worldviews are not understood or even acknowledged.'

There are several background assumptions and methodologies of western psychiatry that inhibit its grasp of cross-cultural differences and hence its capacity to provide services for multi-ethnic communities. They include rationalism, empiricism, and some uses of the biomedical model. Cross-cultural differences arise in relation to meaning, systems of belief and categorizing, and in relation to rules and regulations of mental life and behaviour. Cultural meanings and values, when they are shared, are commonly invisible, implicit, taken for granted: it is only in diversity that they become visible and more likely to be formulated. Generally speaking it is diversity that drives attention to implicit meanings and values, and homogeneity that drives acquiescence in self-evident facts of human nature. This is a philosophical or sociological point – both disciplines attending much to the matter of implicit assumptions – but it has direct relevance to psychiatry insofar as it practices in communities with socio-economic and ethnic diversity.

The psychiatric diagnostic manuals tend systematically to neglect the matter of norms of mental functioning. This neglect belongs most obviously with empiricist methodology. As noted in the first chapter, empiricist methodology was explicitly recommended by Hempel for use in the development of the psychiatric diagnostic manuals, and was subsequently taken up, consistent with long-standing methodology in western science. The purpose was to identify the basic phenomena that everyone could agree about – the terms used to describe signs and symptoms were to be as 'observational' as possible. Subsequent classification of signs and symptoms into syndromes likewise was meant not to create scope for interobserver variation, by applying the empiricist principle of combining basic observational statements using the truth–functional calculus ('and', 'or', 'not'). Once the diagnostic manuals had been developed in this way in both the ICD and the DSM, structured or semi-structured interviews were developed comprising questions or prompts that would elicit responses directly related to the diagnostic criteria, so that diagnoses could be generated with little or no interpretation, according to an algorithm, sometimes indeed computerized. In this methodology ascertainment of signs and symptoms are assumed to be just a matter of observation of data, indicated by interrater reliability, and the application of normative evaluation is missed.

Systematic neglect of the norms involved in characterizing signs and symptoms of mental disorder also seems to have been reinforced by the use of medical model in the development of the manuals. Here is Wakefield in one of his early papers, discussing the definition of mental disorder proposed by Spitzer and Endicott, and swiftly passing by the distinctive norms of mental life:

> Like Spitzer and Endicott (1978), I focus on *disorder* rather than *mental* because the most heated issues about mental disorder concern whether certain conditions labelled as mental disorders really are disorders, not whether they are mental. Like Spitzer and Endicott, I assume that mental disorder is best taken as a subspecies of medical disorder, with the proviso that this conceptual point does not imply which professions, techniques, or models of intervention are the most appropriate for dealing with particular conditions.
>
> Wakefield (1993, p. 161)

Thus we pass by the fact that attribution of mental states is systematically and intrinsically subject to normative evaluation, expressed by interrelated terms such as appropriate, proportionate, rational, meaningful, as opposed to their opposites such as: disproportionate, excessive, irrational, pointless. Such terms as these used in the characterization of signs and symptoms of mental disorder may partly connote severity (relative to some standard), but they are also normative. Put briefly, what is being neglected are the *rationality constraints* on the mental – or, the constraints that the mental should be meaningful. And how are the norms involved here to be understood? Empiricism had not much to say about principles of rational judgement – meaning just impressed itself on the mind. In the Rationalist tradition there are fundamental principles of Nature – universal, a priori, known to reason. The principles of reason, so also the distinction between rational mental order and disorder, were the province of Philosophy (deserves a capital P here), rather than medicine, say. It may be that this is a conceptual point not favouring one profession over another, but here is Kant making a pitch for the philosophers:

> The delirious talk (delirium) of a person waking in a feverous state is a physical illness and requires medical attention. Only the delirious person, in whom the physician perceives no signs of such a sickness, is called crazy, for which the word deranged is but a mild term. Therefore, if someone has intentionally caused an accident, the question arises, whether any or how much blame should be attached to such an afflicted person. Above all it has to be determined first whether he was crazy at that moment or not. For the solution of this question the court of justice cannot refer him to the medical faculty but must refer him to the philosophical faculty (because of the incompetence of the court regarding this question).

(1798, pp. 110–11)

The competency to adjudicate the difference between mental normality and abnormality has been passed around the faculties, settling eventually with psychiatry constructed for the purpose, according to Foucault's analysis. After the passing around, it can be handed back where it belongs, within society at large, where it will be a matter or more or less agreement between different groups and individuals. Discourse on mental disorder is permeated by normative judgements, referring to rupture of meaningful connections, dysfunction relative to some optimal group, deviance from fundamental social rules. The norms invoked are of many, interwoven kinds: personal, social, biological and psychological. Societies have their own view on matters biological and psychological, and subcultures within it, as to what, for example, counts as being overweight, sexually normal, excessively anxious, as to what is appropriate use of punishment in child-rearing, or appropriate license for adolescents; and so on.

There is ample scope for individual differences on these matters too; and everyone involved is likely to believe that their views represent a fact about human nature, obvious to reason and observation.

The norms of mental life are obscured altogether by empiricism, and their diversity is unrecognized by the mindset of rationalism, which envisages only one standard, to be adjudicated by the appropriate expertise. The same problem – invisibility and failure to recognize diversity – arises for the meaning attributed to mental life, to its malfunctioning, and to associated cultural practices including help-seeking and remedy.

Empiricist methodologies achieved considerable success in harmonizing diagnostic practices in countries in the developed west and underpinned their accelerating research programmes in psychiatry. At the same time the diagnostic interviews were transported to non-western cultures, to address the question whether the western categories are valid in other cultures, but also to assess the biomedical model in psychiatry. The question was: are the same psychiatric conditions found in the west also found in other cultures, consistent with the biomedical model of them as medical diseases? By and large the results of the studies were taken as supporting a positive answer to these questions. Hence it appeared that the fundamental tasks of psychiatry, the diagnosis and treatment of mental illness (or disease), were valid universally and cross-cultural issues were irrelevant or at most secondary. There remains at the end of the DSM-IV, for example, a section called 'Culture-bound syndromes', which describes conditions which are specific to particular cultures; none belongs to the west (all of whose mental diseases are presumably of the universal, culture-free type in the substantial part of the book), which is short, and which can for most practitioners be ignored for most or all or their working lives.

While the results of this international, empiricist, biomedical research programme were coming in, in the 1970s and 1980s, there were dissenting voices, minority but vocal, recommending instead methodologies used in the social sciences and particularly anthropology. Arthur Kleinman in the US and Roland Littlewood in the UK were among the key advocates of the 'new cross-cultural psychiatry'. Here is Julian Leff explaining the contrast between this new approach and the mainstream biomedical point of view, in a lively exchange in the *British Journal of Psychiatry* in 1990:

> This view of psychiatry [the 'new cross-cultural psychiatry'] strikes at the heart of its claim to be a branch of medicine, which has provided ample evidence of the universality of its disease categories. Let us consider the example of smallpox . . . The dominance of the Third World by Western biomedicine is primarily due to its manifest success in treating diseases like smallpox . . . In the 1970s, the remedy for the

bewildering multiplicity of diagnostic systems appeared to be the use of structured interviews, such as the Present State Examination, to ascertain the basic phenomena of psychiatric pathology. This held out the promise that a less rickety superstructure could be built on this solid foundation. Indeed, the series of international collaborative studies conducted by the World Health Organization was developed on this premise. However, this approach has come under heavy criticism from advocates of the 'new cross-cultural psychiatry' for imposing Western concepts of psychopathology on non-Western peoples. This is seen by the more politically minded critics as psychiatric imperialism, enforced by the power of the economic and technological resources of the West.

Leff (1990, p. 305)

One of the background problems was that the empiricist methodology used in the construction of the psychiatric manuals was bound to be of little use in detecting cultural difference, since it is bound to find what it already and always assumes is the case, namely, that everything is basically the same. It achieves this result by supposing that it is possible to describe the phenomena in a theory-free way, using observational terms, so that everyone who has eyes to see will recognize the same phenomena. The terms usually happen to belong to English, but English observational terms have the same meaning as observational terms in other languages, so it doesn't matter. If it were to happen, on the other hand, that no terms in the other language translate, this would be bad news for the other language, not for the project – all valid languages should at a basic level map onto the one observational language (which we just happen to express in English). In brief, empiricism finds that cultural variation is superficial, not fundamental, or variation is disqualified (seen as simply wrong-headed), or it will be not seen at all. Another assumption that is not designed to be sensitive to cultural differences in conceptions of mental disorder is the biomedical model in psychiatry focusing on the science and treatment of smallpox. It has been shown that smallpox is a disease process to which cultural interpretation makes not much difference, but for psychiatric conditions this remains to be shown – it is not suitable as a methodological starting point. Results of applying empiricist diagnostic methodology of course seem to show this, but since it is the wrong methodology for detecting difference, not much is gained.

That the same syndromes can be detected across cultures is not a trivial finding, but it leaves much unsaid about the method of ascertainment. What it leaves unsaid, and under-researched, is the whole matter of cultural interpretation of mental disorder, that in turn being interwoven with the culture as a whole. Outstanding questions include: Are the signs and symptoms as described in western society described in the same way in the other culture? Are they grouped together, categorized in the same way? Is there another classification system in the other culture alongside or more fundamental than what is familiar at home? Either way, are the behaviours so classified regarded in the other culture as mental disorder, as opposed to physical disorder, or as disorder of something more holistic? Do some conditions thought of as mental disorders in western culture have counterparts in the other that are not thought of as disorders at all? Perhaps rather as social problems? Or as normal or abnormal communication with spirits? In general, what has been lost in translation? And behind that, what are the distinctive practices that belong with the other system of meaning and belief?

The kind of cultural variation that is missed or minimized by the empiricist mindset, the more so when it is engaged in reducing the phenomena to their most basic, has to do with the many layers of meaning that belong with the phenomena under study. Empiricist methodology is useless for this purpose because it systematically ignores these meanings, and the method and result becomes the more unviable when there is need for collaborative engagement between cultures.

The methodologies required are those developed in the social sciences and specifically in anthropology, designed to be sensitive to many layers of meaning and the diverse social structures and practices they belong with, typically involving field-work, participation rather than just observation. Several general points are apparent in anthropological accounts relevant to mental disorder – references are in the Annotated bibliography – as follows:

First, there is much cultural relativity in the notions of 'person', 'mind', 'body', and the relation between them. That is to say, it should not be assumed that these modern western European categories and demarcation lines are valid in other cultures; there is reason to be cautious about the 'mental' component of mental disorder (and about switching it to 'physical'). The second point, and subject to the first, is that there seems to be some concept corresponding to mental disorder – 'the mind not working as it should' – in all or most cultures, alongside physical illness, with more or less clear boundary between the two. Third, there is wide cultural variation in the explanations and contextualization of (mental) disorder, in terms of somatic processes, mental processes, and social and spirit contexts and interventions, all of diverse kinds. Fourth, and notwithstanding this last point, the explanations of (mental) disorder can typically be brought under several main headings. One kind of explanation, for cultures with the requisite cosmology, that is to say all or most cultures except the modern western scientific, invokes intervention by magical or spirit forces. Another invokes social and interpersonal context and difficulties. A third kind of explanatory account, typically linked to the first in those that have the first, runs in terms of unbalance of some kind in the body.

This medical model of mental disorder, in the sense of attribution to bodily dysfunction, seems to be a cultural invariant, though set no doubt within much variation as to specifics. The medical model of mental disorder in terms of bodily dysfunction is not as such specific to the modern west, though the separation of body and mind, and the exclusion of spirit forces and communication, may be.

Application of anthropological methodologies and concepts has illuminated differences and similarities across cultures, including the often problematic relationship to western psychiatry's diagnostic categories. The broad framework and the details of the psychiatric manuals are constructed in accord with modern, western, scientific categories, and the norms and values of the home culture. Such manuals do after all have to be constructed somewhere, with some categories, and the dominant culture's values will be used, at least because it is the one that can afford the construction. The psychiatric idea of mental disorder as a natural, biomedical, culture-free fact reflects conception of order as absolute, as does the assumption of a categorical distinction between order and disorder. Of course the assumption of absolute order here is not psychiatry's – no one group in a culture manufactures such an idea, but it belongs rather to the culture as a whole. As Foucault made clear, both the idea of the conditions that psychiatrists treat and psychiatry itself was fashioned in western modernity, and are bound to show the signs of their origins. Against this background, taking into account other cultural views is a daunting task. Here is Leff sketching some of the problems with taking this approach:

> This approach ascribes equal value to folk beliefs about mental illness and its categorization as to the Western biomedical system of psychiatry. It necessitates the study of people who are considered to be mentally ill by the local population, most of whom would be treated by traditional healers in the first instance. The healers themselves need to be interviewed to ascertain the diagnostic systems they use, which may well vary considerably from one healer to another. Through this means, a native lexicon of disease terms and the patterns of behaviour to which they refer can be constructed. Ideally, this work should not be done by someone with a Western psychiatric training, whose perceptions of abnormality will already have been determined . . . The resource demands of this endeavour are such that it has been attempted in only a handful of cultures . . . Yet again, we are faced the paradox that has bedevilled cross-cultural psychiatry throughout its history. The societies that are culturally most different from the West, and hence of greatest interest, are those with the least resources available to carry out the necessary research themselves. Historically, they have been 'exploited' by the Western research workers, who are often blinkered by their own unconscious cultural assumptions.

(1990, p. 306)

These are major problems, but they are no longer, in a globalized world, matters of academic anthropological interest alone. They have to be solved in some way if mental health services are to be relevant to, accessible and usable by ethnically diverse communities in Western societies. Values and norms of behaviour are hardly visible in the clinic when they are shared between the participants. A majority ethnic group male clinician meeting a man from the same (middle/professional) class with a first depressive episode will likely not have to worry much about values – they are implicit and they work well. The doctor–patient relationship is shared, the medical model, the wish to get better, payment – all are understood and evaluated in a similar way by both parties, but the more the social, economic, ethnic and gender variables are mixed, the more likely social norms and values will become evident in the form of conflicts. The easiest conflict to respond to is open discussion, but that already requires much that is shared. Otherwise conflict shows up in the patient dropping out of, or otherwise not adhering to treatment – or commonly in never coming in the first place, or not willingly. Practical steps include increasing the diversity of the workforce to better reflect the communities they serve, this strategy being well-recognized by many kinds of organizations, not only health, and, in the case specifically of mental health-care, seeking to add value to the ways of working of local communities, rather than just offering an alien alternative.

As we move into the twenty-first century what is apparent is that there is much to learn about cross-cultural variation and how to negotiate it in diverse communities. As an example of acknowledgement of lack of cross-cultural knowledge about fundamental matters in mental health, there was a recent Editorial in the *British Journal of Psychiatry* by psychiatrists (Saravanan *et al.* 2004), practising in a multi-ethnic catchment area in South London on the concept of 'insight' in psychosis. The authors note that transcultural studies carried out under the auspices of World Health Organization in the 1980s found that 'lack of insight' was an almost invariable feature of acute and chronic schizophrenia, regardless of setting, and they consider the charge that the concept fails to take into account cultural idioms and is 'Eurocentric'. By way of conclusions the authors say:

> Insight is not only at the interface of biological and psychosocial explanations in psy-
> chiatry, but also at the interface of globalisation and related cultural transitions.
> Globalisation and colonisation in various guises introduce new social effects and
> spread biomedical systems of thought, including causal explanations. Given these
> changes, how does a person find his or her way through this maze of different opin-
> ions? And how do we know what to recommend when trying to improve the mental
> health of a diverse but increasingly interconnected world? Clearly there is a need for a

multi-disciplinary effort, including sociologists and anthropologists interested in insight research. In addition, future studies on insight should focus on cross-cultural validity, reliability and methodological issues related to insight assessments. This must be complemented by open-ended inquiry to capture the complexity of representations and local political dimensions relevant to mental health and illness.

Saravanan *et al.* (2004, p. 108)

Acknowledging uncertainty and the need for constructive engagement is a characteristic sign of the shift of attitude from the absolutes of modernity to the contemporary view.

This section has covered what are – in my view – key shifts away from the modern western idea of madness as explicated by Foucault. The fundamental change is from absolute ideas of order and disorder to boundaries that are fluid and negotiable, this change being worked out both in relation to disorder in the individual and in cross-cultural similarities and differences. There is a further fundamental change from modernity to late- or postmodernity, the appearance of the biopsychological sciences, which, as noted above, express the view that order is generated through time and through agency. The sciences include of course those basic to psychiatry, but fortunately, given that this is already a long section, they have already been addressed in the second chapter of the essay. Foucault was, I think it is fair to say, dismissive of the science of psychiatry and its alleged treatments, and general philosophical reasons apart, probably with good reason in the 1950s. In the half century since, however, biomedicine and the behavioural sciences have made substantial advances in terms of defining the (complex) causes of mental disorders and developing effective, evidence-based treatments. The concepts and findings of these sciences are having profound influence on our understanding of mental disorders – as previously discussed.

This raises various questions about the relationship between various topics addressed in this essay. As we learn more from the science, are we learning more about mental disorder? If so, how does this square with the claim that there seems to be no scientifically determinable fact that demarcates mental order from disorder? Or with the conclusion that it is social norms and values that determine what conditions people bring to the clinic and what psychiatrists consider to be indications for treatment?

The sciences basic to psychiatry study causes of the conditions of interest – complex causal risks and pathways – and remedies. The scientific methodology they use for determining causes and efficacy of treatments, such as controlled experimentation, is culturally relative, but the main point is that for this purpose it is objectively better than any other (better than reading authorities or magic or reading tea-leaves). However, the sciences basic to psychiatry do not depend on the assumption that they are – in any sense other than a terminological convenience – mental disorders: they would work just the same whether the conditions of interest are called mental disorders or something else. This is because the statement that in such and such a condition 'the mind is not working as it should' is not a scientific statement; there is no controlled experiment, for example, that would settle the matter one way or the other. The norms involved are social, not scientific. It is a matter of division of labour – which field of knowledge and expertise deals with what aspect of the problem. Here is Jaspers:

> What health and illness mean in general are matters which concern the physician least of all. He deals scientifically with life processes and with particular illnesses. What is 'ill' in general depends less on the judgement of the doctor than on the judgement of the patient and on the dominant views in any given circle.
>
> (1913, p. 652)

The physician – now the mental health professional or worker – needs to focus on what problems are being brought to the clinic and whether there is a need to treat. In doing this, bearing in mind the need for collaborative engagement where possible, it is as well to understand how the person consulting them views the problem. The mental health professional, depending on training and level of responsibility, should be aware of the science on aetiology and especially on treatments. The scientists including clinicians focus on causes of and treatments for the conditions. Neither group has to worry much about the real meaning of mental disorder, and neither group possesses knowledge or expertise that demarcates mental disorder from order. This, as Jaspers observes, is more a matter of the patients' appraisal and the prevailing conceptions of the contemporary culture.

4.7 Summary and conclusions

The main problem area of this chapter is how to conceptualize mental disorder without reliance on naturalistic definitions, the general conclusion being that the essential features are harm and the professional healthcare response.

The first section reconsiders the definitions of mental disorder given in the psychiatric manuals. Referring to the literature from around the time that the DSM definition was constructed, it is suggested that the aim was not so much to achieve an intellectually rigorous analysis of the concept of mental disorder – a task most suited perhaps for philosophy – but was rather to characterize as accurately as possible the conditions newly compiled in the manuals – this being a task appropriately for psychiatry. The definitions in the manuals emphasize first and foremost the distress, disability, or risk of adverse outcomes. The surrounding literature makes it clear that the manuals were compilations of the kinds of problem people bring to the clinic. This leaves outstanding, however, whether among the problems brought are normal problems of living, or socially defined problems. These issues are left unresolved in the manuals, to be taken up by naturalist theories of mental disorder of the kind discussed and rejected in the previous chapter.

In the second section some key features of mental disorder are considered which are prominent once naturalist theories are removed. The problem – the disorder – is within the phenomena, in the person's life, up front, not relative, for example, to evolutionary history. The norms of functioning that are broken are characteristically personal and social, not natural in a sense that can be distinguished from these. The presenting problem typically though not invariably includes a failure of comprehensibility, a rupture of meaningful connections in psychic life – using Jaspers' terminology.

The third section, 4.3, considers the possibility that mental disorder can be defined in terms of breakdown of meaningful connections. This possibility – which is suggested by folk as well as psychiatric uses of terms relating to mental disorder – is found to be wanting in many ways, especially in the context of psychological models of psychopathology. The main point is that restricting the term mental disorder to cases in which meaning has run out is far too strong, and it would exclude many or most of the conditions and presentations characterized in the psychiatric manuals.

The fourth section explores the implications of diagnosis of disorder being tied to the need to treat, this being understood in the broad sense of warranting mental healthcare professional attention. Judgement that treatment is necessary because of distress, disability or perceived risk is fundamentally one involving personal and social values and priorities. At an individual level this is negotiated between patient and clinician (though other stakeholders are involved); at the social, public health level it involves decisions about healthcare provision and costs. Epidemiological studies used in planning provision of health services try to use a cut-off for 'caseness' that coincides with need to treat, and it was mainly for this reason that the criterion of 'significant distress or impairment' was introduced into the DSM-IV diagnostic criteria for many disorders.

In the fifth section, 4.5, on the domain of healthcare, the conclusion is drawn that insofar as naturalistic definitions of disease and disorder are unviable, the domain of medicine and of healthcare generally cannot be marked out primarily in terms of a special kind of condition to which they apply. There is no hard and fast demarcation between normal and abnormal suffering, or between normal and abnormal causes. Rather, the domain of healthcare is distinguished by one kind of response to suffering, however caused, namely the healthcare response, with characteristic professional ethics, training, use of science, and expertize in management and treatment.

Finally in this chapter, in section 4.6, there in an overview of some large-scale, cultural ontological and epistemological assumptions that have operated in western modernity and which have become involved in the development of western psychiatry. These include naturalism, empiricism, and rationalism. It is noted that assumptions have changed in post- or late modernity, and that these dynamics show up in psychiatry as elsewhere. Absolute ideas of order and disorder characteristic of modernity are contrasted with more relativistic ideas which have order as created through time, in activity, and in intersubjectivity. In this episteme, the notion of disorder as a boundary condition is evasive and complex. Another shift, at the social level, is globalization, which requires western mental services to adapt to different cultural conceptions of health and illness.

4.8 **Annotated bibliography**

References to literature in sections 4.1 to 4.3 are in the text.

Section 4.4 includes material on the introduction of the distress and impairment criterion into the DSM-IV in response to high rates of mental disorders in epidemiological studies. The most relevant epidemiological studies were the Epidemiological Catchment Area study (Robins and Regier, 1991) and the National Comorbidity Survey (Kessler *et al.* 1994). Subsequent discussion, diagnosis of the problem and suggested responses include Regier *et al.* (1998), Frances (1998), and Spitzer and Wakefield (1999).

Section 4.5 on the domain of healthcare makes some references in the text. Histories of medicine including psychiatry that include coverage of demarcation issues of the kind noted in the text include Porter (1996).

Section 4.6 begins with a brief attempt to locate shifts in the concept of mental disorder with general cultural and epistemological changes from modernity to late- or postmodernity. Elucidations of these general changes include Habermas (1985) and Bauman (1992). The section includes reference to work on cross-cultural psychiatry and related anthropological literature. Reports on research on cross-cultural application of the recently developed rigorous diagnostic criteria in the 1970s includes World Health Organization (1973, 1979, 1983), and Leff (1988). At around the same time there was research on cross-cultural conceptions of mental health using non-empiricist methodologies more characteristic of anthropology literature, described in papers collected in Marsalla and White (1982). The contrast between the two kinds of approach and implications for mainstream western psychiatry were highlighted particularly by Arthur Kleinman (1977, 1987, 1988) in the US and Roland Littlewood in the UK (Littlewood 1980, 1985), with a lively exchange and associated correspondence in the *British Journal of Psychiatry* in 1990 (Littlewood 1990, Leff 1990, Kleinman 1990). There is a substantial literature on cross-cultural validity of diagnostic categories and methodologies, including contributions to a recent debate in the *British Journal of Psychiatry* in 2001 (Rogler 1993; Alarcon 1995; Manson 1995; Cheng 2001; Littlewood 2001; Summerfield 2001).

Chapter 5

Boundaries and terminology in flux

5.1 How to draw the line?

The problem of the definition of mental disorder matters most of all in decisions about what to include under the concept, and what to exclude. Here is Spitzer, the main author of the DSM definition, on this point:

> Decisions had to be made on a variety of issues that seemed to us to relate to the fundamental question of the boundaries of the concept of mental disorder. We believed that without some definition of mental disorder, there could be no explicit guiding principles that would help to determine which conditions should be included in the nomenclature, which excluded, and how conditions included should be defined.
>
> Spitzer and Endicott (1978, p. 16)

Paramount in the variety of issues occupying the American Psychiatric Association at the time (as remarked earlier in section 4.1), was the question of whether homosexuality should be in or out of the manual of mental disorders.

So how to draw the boundaries of the concept of mental disorder? The DSM definition, like the one in ICD, is primarily harm-led. Conditions are included that generate much distress or disability, or risk thereof. Frank social deviance as a cause of the harm has to be excluded, and this in practice is done by considering pervasiveness across contexts: only if the distress or disability occurs in several important contexts is dysfunction attributed to the individual; otherwise it can be attributed to the sole context in which it occurs. This approach does not, however, make it clear how to deal with socially deviant conditions that are pervasive across contexts and which generate much harm and risk. Should they be in or out of the book? Are the antisocial behaviour conditions really mental disorders? Another aspect of this problem is that this principle – distinguishing individual dysfunction from social deviance in terms of pervasiveness across contexts – apparently does not exclude distress and impairment associated with pervasive, institutionalized mechanisms of social exclusion on the basis of ethnicity, creed, sexual orientation, or different ability relative to the majority.

The standard response has been that we have to tighten up the notion of dysfunction. At the same time it is admitted that disorder and dysfunction are closely related terms, so definition of the one in terms of the other so far gets us nowhere. The DSM settles for the idea that to count as a mental disorder a harmful condition must not be an expectable response. This idea leads off in many directions, mainly three: two naturalist definitions, and a definition in terms of the response not being appropriate or meaningful. However, none of these leads to satisfactory definitions of mental disorder, as argued previously, and, especially relevant to the present point, none of them does the job of fixing boundaries. Consider this further.

The boundary problems identified in the 1960s critiques of psychiatry could be expressed mainly as these challenges: define the difference between mental disorder and ordinary problems of living, on the one hand, and between mental disorder and social deviance, on the other. The first of these problems arises most readily for depression and anxiety, plainly matters of distress for the person concerned. The second boundary problem, distinguishing between mental disorder and social deviance, splinters into various kinds, depending on the kind of social deviance. Considering antisocial behaviours, the problem was to distinguish between, in colloquial terms, the mad and the bad. Other kinds of social deviance include minority sexual orientation, the boundary problem here being illustrated in the 1970s controversy over whether homosexuality was a mental disorder, as opposed to, for example, a natural though minority trait, or a lifestyle choice.

Boundary problems remain current and urgent. Many of the dominant concerns about mental disorder since the 1960s and currently are boundary problems, arising, I suggest, as mental disorder is located not in the asylum but in the community. We are preoccupied with how much there is the community, what it really is, with how it is different from familiar normality, and how to best respond to it. We are preoccupied, for example, with the problem whether antisocial personality disorder is a real disorder and with the question of who should manage it, and generally with the problem who should manage risk in the community associated with mental disorder. We are alarmed at the apparent growth of anxiety and depression in society and the associated costs: personal, on families, to the public purse in terms of loss revenues and disability benefits, and the costs of treatment, mainly medications supplied by the pharmaceutical industry. Is there really this much disorder in our midst, or are we pathologizing and medicalizing normal problems of living? Then we are worried about the children: do so many youngsters have a mental disorder such as ADHD, or autistic spectrum disorder? Should we be pathologizing and medicating them? Are these real disorders, or just troublesome traits? If there is a mixture, how do we tell which is which, where the boundary lies? To what extent is the associated distress and impairment a function of environments and task demands which are of society's making? And so forth.

The naturalist approaches sought to solve the boundary problems, or to provide a principled way of solving the problems, by specifying some fixed, objective, natural fact that would set a limit to the legitimate diagnosis of disorder. However, as argued in Chapter 3, they run into major obstacles and they are not fit for this particular purpose. The main problems of Boorse's biostatistical version of naturalism (considered in section 3.2) are that statistical difference from the average does not yet mean dysfunction, though it may sometimes be associated with dysfunction, that there is an arbitrariness over what is abnormal in a statistically normally distributed trait, and that statistical deviation from a norm is not a fixed property but depends on choice of reference group. For all these reasons statistical definitions cannot draw a valid, satisfactory line between what is and what is not disorder.

Wakefield's evolutionary form of naturalism (considered in the third chapter from section 3.3 on), like the 1960s debates it was designed to address, relies on what is probably an outdated dichotomy between the natural and the social. Apart from this axiomatic problem, it has the effect of making diagnosis of disorder a highly theoretical claim – invoking failure of a natural mental mechanism to function as designed in evolution – and one which may well be false of some or many of the distressing and impairing conditions in the psychiatric manuals. From the point of view of biopsychological science in an evolutionary theoretic framework there are many pathways to current distress and disability, such as mismatch between evolved design features and current environment and task demands, or inappropriately generalized learning, which apparently do not involve dysfunction in the sense stipulated in Wakefield's analysis. If we are to rely on consensus on models of evolutionary design of mental mechanisms to sort out those distressing, impairing conditions described in the psychiatric manuals that are genuine mental disorders in the required sense from those that are not, we will probably be waiting a long time. Even if this demarcation could be made out, the result would probably be just to break the customary linkage between diagnosis of disorder and the need to treat. Distressing, impairing conditions of the kind described in the psychiatric manuals that are not genuine mental disorders in the required evolutionary theoretic sense may still be thought to require treatment, for example to relieve intolerable distress, to restore functioning, and to reduce risk of future problems. In this case the boundary problem would just reappear in another guise: what to treat and what not to treat?

Leaving to one side models of evolutionary design of natural mental mechanisms, we need to use criteria of disorder and dysfunction nearer to hand. We typically refer to whether the responses make sense in the context, are appropriate, rational, have a point which is at least roughly understandable, or else to whether responses are normal in the population, the population we have in mind, more or less idealized – and so on. It turns out that Wakefield after all uses criteria of these kinds when demarcating disorder from normal functioning (as reviewed in section 3.7), as do the psychiatric manuals in their diagnostic criteria, for many conditions though not all. Criteria of these kinds, used by experts and the folk, serve their purpose, but they do not fix a line between normal and abnormal functioning, only the terms of a negotiation.

Naturalist attempts to define psychological dysfunction – thereby making clear the boundary line between order and disorder – unravel. The inference is that there are no precise, absolute boundaries here; or again, there is no natural fact of the matter that can be determined by the science – rather, social decisions and values are involved.

It may be well be that it would be good if there were a determinate and determinable fact of the matter that would enable us to sort out mental disorder from order, mental health problems from mental health, what should be treated medically or psychologically from what should not – but things being as they are, there apparently isn't. The problem of boundaries – of what conditions should and should not be in the psychiatric manuals, of where the thresholds for diagnosis and treatment of various kinds should be – is real and cannot be conceptually analysed away. Rather it has to be – is being – thrashed out among the various stakeholders: consumers, advocates, service purchasers and providers, different kinds of providers, treatment manufacturers and the like. The key here is the recognition that primarily what drives diagnosis of mental disorder are the problems that people have and take to the clinic, and the responses of clinicians and services – there are no clear boundaries around all these things, but rather fluid processes of social representation and organization. These issues will be taken up through the chapter, beginning with one of the major problem areas identified in the 1960s, psychiatry and social control.

5.2 Psychiatry and social control

Confinement in the asylums was a clear expression of the problem identified by Foucault and other commentators on psychiatry in the 1960s, the tendency for psychiatry to become or to be used as a form of social control of deviant behaviour. This was consistent with the view that this deviance was essentially socially rather than medically defined. The issue of psychiatry and social control remains alive currently in various forms, some of which will be considered in subsequent sections, but soon after the 1960s critiques there gradually became known an extreme form of political abuse of psychiatry, the incarceration of political dissidents in secure psychiatric institutions in the then Soviet Union. The psychiatric practices, the way they became known, and the responses in the western democracies have been well-documented and a brief bibliography is given at the end of the chapter, along with references to papers on related current problems in other countries.

The question for here is the abstract one, the principles by which mental illness can be disentangled from social deviance and from political dissidence in particular. As noted earlier in the essay there were moves to construct a definition of mental illness, by then changed to mental disorder, in the 1970s and 1980s, by the American Psychiatric Association and in theoretical papers. These moves took place against a complex background, including the 1960s sociological critiques of psychiatry and lobbying by activists to have homosexuality de-classified in the 1970s, but also in the context of widespread concern in governments and in psychiatric associations about the abuse of psychiatry in the Soviet Union. One intellectual response to the problem was the perception of need to draw a clear line between mental illness, appropriately treated by psychiatrists, and politically defined social deviance – dissidence – treatment of which is an abuse of medicine.

Here is Spitzer with his co-author explaining part of the DSM-III definition:

> The last statement, '(When the disturbance is *limited* to a conflict between the individual and society, this may represent social deviance, which may or may not be commendable, but is not by itself a mental disorder)', was added to express indignation at the abuse of psychiatry, as when, in the Soviet Union, political dissidents without signs of mental illness are labelled as having mental disorders and under that guise incarcerated in mental hospitals.
>
> Spitzer and Williams (1982, p. 21)

The naturalist definitions of mental disorder were the most elaborate responses to the intellectual task of distinguishing medical disorder from social deviance, of which political dissidence is one important example. The aim was to identify a matter of fact that settles whether beliefs or behaviour really involve a failure of mental functioning. It always was a difficult challenge, and this essay has tried to track some of the main proposals involved and how they have panned out, the conclusion being, in brief, that they are not viable. However, this conclusion has to be brought face to face with the original problem: how then are we to distinguish mental illness from social deviance and from political dissidence in particular? If we fudge the difference, as this essay has ended up doing, if there is not even supposed to be a principled difference, then apparently we cannot even sensibly argue where to draw the line, there is no line – and then, what is supposed to stop the political abuse of psychiatry to label and detain social deviants including legitimate political protestors?

So far as I can see the move here – the one consistent with the direction taken in this essay – has to be like this: prevention of the social abuse of psychiatry cannot be located in the difference between mental illness and social deviance, but has to be located in law, specifically in human rights legislation. What has to be prevented is not primarily the inappropriate diagnosis of mental illness in a mentally healthy individual – a judgement that turns as much on the presence or absence of sympathy with the person's beliefs as on esoteric psychiatric assessment – but the unwarranted deprivation of liberty, this being warranted only by conviction by crime, or perhaps risk. In brief, the response to this crucial question is to be found in social values and the organization of power, rather than in definitions of medical/mental disorder as opposed to social problems.

What stops abuse in practice are the checks and balances of power, human rights legislation, courageous and persistent lawyers, courts independent of executive control, free intellectual life and universities, investigative journalists in a free press; and so forth – in brief, all the apparatus of political democracy. The cases of beliefs and behaviour are different of course and democracies protect freedom of belief by law, while freedom of behaviour is qualified by laws concerning protection of the rights of others. In democracies there is no – or there is less – danger of incarceration in the mental health system by reason of beliefs; the danger is psychiatry being used as a repressive tool in non-democratic, totalitarian political systems. In abusive systems definitions of mental disorder will not help: whatever they are they will be adapted, stretched, interpreted, taught, reinforced, so as to end up with the desired result. All this is run through here only to say what will be obvious to many, that the underlying issues here are fundamentally sociopolitical ones, not a matter of psychiatry in isolation.

In a recent review of the political abuse of psychiatry in the Soviet Union, Richard Bonnie, a professor of law, noted:

> In retrospect, repressive use of psychiatric power in the former Soviet Union seems to have been nearly inevitable. The practice of involuntary psychiatric treatment presents an unavoidable risk of mistake and abuse, even in a liberal, pluralistic society. This intrinsic risk was greatly magnified in the Soviet Union by the communist regime's intolerance for dissent, including any form of political or religious deviance,

and by the corrosive effects of corruption and intimidation in all spheres of social life. Psychiatrists were not immune from these pressures . . . In this respect, abuse of psychiatry in the Soviet Union had less to do with psychiatry *per se* than with the repressiveness of the political regime of which the psychiatrists were a part.

(2002, 138)

Earlier in the paper the author notes the complexities that arise in disentangling medical disorder from socially defined abnormalities:

Political abuse of psychiatry is more complicated than it first appears. Most important, whether the dissident individuals subjected to psychiatric confinement are (or are not) mentally ill is often contestable, especially when culturally embedded features of psychopathology are taken into account . . . The problem is all the more complicated when psychiatrists in different countries are trained to understand normality and psychopathology in different ways.

(op. cit., p. 136)

In summary, prevention of sociopolitical abuse of psychiatry is not– cannot be – essentially a matter of drawing a clear line between mental and social disorder, but rather involves democratic institutional protection of human rights, specifically the right to liberty in the absence of conviction for crime or – perhaps – risk to public safety.

The question of psychiatry and political dissidence is an extreme form of the general question of psychiatry and social control, which had already been raised in the 1960s critiques of psychiatry. Psychiatry responded at a conceptual level by having it clearly stated in the official definitions that mental disorder is to be distinguished from social deviance. Whether this statement was sound, whether it correctly reflected the content of the psychiatric manuals – particularly in the characterization of the antisocial conditions – was another matter. It was the naturalist definitions of mental disorder that made the most elaborate attempts to define medical disorder, physical or mental, as distinct from social deviance. These definitions have a number of problems as reviewed earlier, but most important in the present context is that they assume a sharp and principled distinction between what in human mental life and behaviour is natural, and what is social. This dichotomy is probably no longer valid in relation to the current science – as argued in sections 2.7 and 3.8. Insofar as this is so, the difference between medical mental disorder and social deviance cannot be made out. Does this mean then that psychiatry – or mental health services generally – are in the business of social control?

Several problems here need to be disentangled. First and foremost it is necessary to distinguish between care and treatment of the individual in distress coming to the clinic for help – a task unambiguously assigned to health professions – and control of individuals thought to pose a risk to public safety – a task that belongs properly to the state and is not at all primarily a matter of healthcare. Once that fundamental distinction is in place, it is possible to be somewhat more relaxed about the blurring of boundaries between mental disorder, or mental health problems, and deviance from cultural expectations. Mental life and behaviour is entirely involved with the social, so there is no choice about this anyway, and providing healthcare professionals keep in mind that the voluntary patient is in charge of problem definition and the choice whether and what available indicated treatment to have – then there is so far no social control, at least nothing like compulsory admission of social dissidents. On the other hand, what might be called a more subtle, institutionalized form of social control, distinguishable from state political control, inevitably exists in some form or another in the social representation and organization of problems, self-reliance, help-seeking and provision. There are at any one time and place particular ways of construing problems, whether they need help, and available resources. Problems of personal, socially embedded distress and impairment are ambiguous, available to representations involving self-reliance and autonomy, or need for healthcare, or deviance from social role expectations. Recognition of the inevitable interplay between mental health problems and deviance from social expectations, implying giving up on naturalist conceptions of disorder, helps in understanding the flexibility of boundaries between conceptualizing problems in one way or another. These various issues are taken up through the chapter, beginning with more on the need to distinguish between problems involving personal distress, and problems involving potential harm to others.

5.3 **Harm**

The definition of mental disorder in the psychiatric manuals starts with the harm involved. Here is the first sentence of the definition in the DSM-IV:

> In DSM-IV, each of the mental disorders is conceptualized as a clinically significant behavioral or psychological syndrome or pattern that occurs in an individual and that is associated with present distress (e.g., a painful symptom) or disability (i.e., impairment in one or more important areas of functioning) or with a significantly increased risk of suffering death, pain, disability or an important loss of freedom.
>
> American Psychiatric Association (1994, pp. xxi–xxii)

The naturalist definitions of mental disorder considered in Chapter 3 are also harm-led, invoking 'harmful disease/dysfunction', but (practically) all of the attention is then focused on the 'disease/dysfunction' part, and in particular the problem of defining a natural, social value- and norm-free meaning for these terms – an absorbing, controversial and unresolved challenge. If we focus instead on the harm involved, different issues are raised. Here are two:

• Harm to whom?
• Where are the boundaries around harm?

Psychiatry as part of medicine focuses most clearly on harm or risk of harm that accrues for the individual patient in terms of distress or impairment of social functioning. Harms and risks that accrue for others, specifically to the public at large from various kinds of antisocial behaviour, are apparently not on the list of those associated with mental disorders in the definition, yet they are often the reason for referral to the clinic, and perhaps subsequent treatment. Focus on the individual best fits the traditional doctor–patient model in physical medicine: a patient in distress presents themself and seeks treatment. The other kind of case, in which an individual is brought by others, the reluctant patient with no complaints of their own, is a more problematic fit with the medical model, apparently suiting more the construal of psychiatry as a form of social control. To some extent these two constructions have run in parallel, the medical–psychiatric model and the sociological critique, each with its favoured kinds of example, best ignoring the anomaly of the other kind of case. However, to the extent that we take seriously a conceptualization of mental disorder that primarily turns on harm, as well as the reality of clinical practice, it seems inevitable that we have to make a distinction between harm that accrues to self and harm that accrues to others. To put the point another way, the general heading mental disorder or dysfunction glosses over the distinction, while emphasis on harm highlights it.

The processes by which the distinction between harm to self and harm to others has been obscured are presumably complex. They presumably include the indeterminate and diverse nature of the reasons that people were admitted to the asylums, including both high levels of distress in the patients and perceived danger to others, brought under the general heading of madness. The medicalization of madness however puts the emphasis only on distress and impairment in the patient, so that harm accruing to others is relatively invisible or unconceptualized. So the confusing state of affairs arises in which medical practitioners find themselves to be responsible not only for patients with distressing conditions but also for public safety. The asylum wall represented a solution, but with its dismantling the problem has become more apparent.

Disentangling harm that accrues to the self from harm to others is an essential consequence of having a harm-led conceptualization of mental disorder, and subsequent sections will consider the different issues that arise in each kind of case: treatment of distress on the one hand and management of risk on the other. The other question posed above at the start of this section has to do with boundaries. The boundaries around harm are fluid indeed, and much subject to personal and social pressures and influences. The problem of boundaries is magnified because, as the DSM definition, cited above, has it, we are concerned not only with actual harm, but with increased risk of harm. The problem arises in different ways for both harm to others and harm to the self.

In the case of harm to others, or risk of harm to others, one main problematic has to do with titrating the extent of harm, and especially the extent of risk of harm, to the public, on the one hand, against the severity of measures to control the person thought to pose the risk. Specifically: how much risk justifies compulsory detention, or compulsory treatment?

There are related kinds of boundary issue involved in this area, alluded to above in the distinction between the medical treatment of disorder that gives rise to distress, and social control of persons thought to pose danger to the public. Whose job is the social control? What does it have to do with doctors, or any other mental healthcare professional? Also in the background here: in what way and in what kinds of case is dangerous behaviour a medical mental disorder? What has mental disorder to do with danger to the public?

Turning now to 'harm experienced by the self', the boundaries are apparently elastic. How much distress and disability do particular individuals think they should put up with before seeking help? How much distress and disability should people generally be expected to tolerate or to manage before having healthcare funded by insurance companies or the state? The answer is unclear, so far as I can see, as is the nature of the 'should' in the question – is it ethical, or economic, or what? Once the idea of a fixed category of mental disorder is abandoned – mainly because it cannot be made to work – there are boundary problems, but also the nature of the boundary lines themselves are unclear.

Other boundary problems arise considering harm as disability, some of the main controversies focussing on social vs medical models. The traditional medical model construes disability as caused by an intrinsic characteristic of the individual, a disorder or dysfunction, resulting in reduction of life quality and opportunity, and deserving social resources and medical care to improve the individual's functioning – to make it more normal. The social model in contrast views disability not as a fixed characteristic of individuals but as relative to environments and expectations typically imposed by majority social groups. Such and such a condition would not give rise to disability, it is argued, if the environments and task demands were not incompatible with the condition. In this case diagnosis of disorder is actually a cover for disempowerment, discrimination and social exclusion. This point of view is typically linked to civil rights issues and legislation. The social model of disability can be applied to both physical and mental disabilities, particularly when the disabilities are enduring rather than temporary. Chronic or recurring mental health problems may be associated with enduring disabilities, appropriate for the social model. Temporary, though possibly severe, interference with or impairment of the individual's normal – for them – level of social functioning, associated with an episode of depression, say, typically characterized by extreme distress, which remits spontaneously or with treatment, raises different issues, and may be a better fit with the medical model as above. The issues are complex and much discussed in literature and websites of academic departments, advocacy groups and local government agencies. The main points in the present context are that debates about models of disability indicate one of the many boundary issues around the concept of disorder and associated harm, and like others it is not settled by naturalism but rather involves problems that are fundamentally personal and sociopolitical.

The DSM characterization of the harms that primarily characterize the mental disorders – quoted at the start of this section – ignores the problem of harm to others that underlies at least some of the diagnoses, and passes by the problems of relativity to personal and social opinions and practices. No doubt there are good reasons for this: definition of mental disorder is not the main point of the manuals. Nevertheless the boundary problems that the definition was designed to help solve are better understood when the ambiguity, relativity and shifting nature of harm are opened up.

Against this it can be argued that the harms listed at the start of the DSM-IV definition are actually universal. In an interesting article Gert and Culver (2003) criticize Wakefield's analysis of mental disorder as harmful dysfunction for attempting to locate all the social values and relativity involved in the concept in the harm part (this of course being essential for the purpose of construing the dysfunction part as an absolute, social value free matter of natural fact). They write:

Wakefield's problem . . . is his acceptance of the common view of social scientists that values are constructed by particular societies. By accepting this account, he opens the door to the kind of relativity that the definitions of mental disorder in the DSM-III-R and DSM-IV were designed to close. He does not seem to realise that if harms are determined primarily by social norms, then this opens the door to the criticism that psychiatry primarily enforces social norms . . . Since Wakefield claims that albinism is a failure of nature's design, if a particular society negatively evaluates albinism, then it is a disorder in that society, but not a disorder in a society that does not negatively evaluate it. A person can cease to have a disorder simply by moving from one society to another.

Gert and Culver (2003, p. 421)

This would be an interesting prospect, but Gert and Culver would rule it out on the grounds that values of the kind invoked in the DSM definition are in fact universal:

> Wakefield's acceptance of the common view of social scientists that values are constructed by particular societies is what leads him to think that harm cannot be defined in universal terms. However, it is universally true that, in the absence of reasons to hold otherwise, every society regards death, pain, disability, and loss of freedom or pleasure as harms. No person who is considered rational wants to suffer any of these harms unless he has some belief that he or someone else will avoid what is considered by a significant number of persons to be either a greater harm or a compensating benefit, such as greater consciousness, ability, freedom, or pleasure. The universality of these harms is shown by the fact that nothing counts as a disorder unless it involves one of these harms or a significantly increased risk of suffering them.

(loc. cit.)

This characterization of universal harms with its inevitable qualifications about ranking of harms and compensatory benefits seems to me to have a particularly secular western or North American feel about it (e.g. utilitarian, majority democratic) and I don't know how well it would inter-translate with versions from other cultures. There may be scope for influence by cultural factors, perhaps in the definition of the universal harms themselves, but in any case over prioritizing among harms and benefits, and also over whose opinion should count in the definition and the prioritizing. Some of the cross-cultural controversies that may arise in this kind of area can be seen at work in the real-life attempt to gain international agreement on closely related matters, namely, concerning human rights – understood (roughly) as universally valid rights to certain goods and to protection from certain harms. The controversies are many, various and complex, involving the various international stakeholders – the UN, national governments, NGOs and transnational commercial corporations. They include for example controversies about which states have the right to a place in the UN Commission on Human Rights, and critical commentary by NGOs on which human rights are prioritized. In practice it is not straightforward to find international consensus on harms, on the balancing of greater versus lesser harms, and of harms against greater goods in general or in particular cases, and about whose opinions should count – the issues are culturally and politically involved.

On the other hand, international politics may be irrelevant to the general ethical question of whether there are universally agreed harms. Let us suppose that there are universal harms, and that some are involved in mental disorder, and that the DSM definition has them about right. Still there is much scope for interpretation at a social level and a personal level. There is scope for interpretation, for example, in the matter of what counts as significant distress or disability and over what kinds of distress or disability are viewed as clinically significant, as medical problems, as opposed to, for example, religious problems, or social and political.

Harm associated with mental disorders – with the conditions described in the psychiatric manuals – accrues to the individuals with the conditions, or to others. Each kind of case has distinctive boundary problems and distinctive problems of appropriate management. The blanket term mental disorder used for both kinds of case obscures the differences, even more so with the historical linkage between mental disorder and medical disorder, implying that it is all is a matter of medical expertise. As these constructions become unstable, many problems arise – or rather the other way round: as problems arise, the constructions destabilize. Some of the problems are considered in the following two sections, first in relation to the management of risk in the community, and second in relation to distress of the individual.

5.4 **Management of risk**

The suffering of individuals with unmanageable depression or anxiety, or with psychotic anxiety and confusion, and the concerns of parents for children with developmental problems are consistent with the model for psychiatry derived from general medicine: people in distress come for help, or are brought in need of help by families and carers. However the picture shifts and is complicated when behaviour brings risks of harm to the family, or when disorderly behaviour spills into the streets, as for example apparently threatening behaviour that may occur sometimes in psychotic conditions, or antisocial behaviour characteristic of conduct disorder or antisocial personality disorder. In these kinds of cases law enforcement agencies may become involved, in the interests of public protection, working with psychiatric services. Mental health legislation is designed to protect the public, as well as the individual concerned, authorizing compulsory admission to psychiatric hospital, or disposal by the Court to secure hospitals. It is in these kinds of case, of course, that psychiatry most looks like an agency of social control.

It is important to recall, on the other hand, that general medicine too can get involved in matters of public protection: legislation on infection control is no less socially controlling than its mental health counterparts. The key feature in both cases is that a health condition can present risk to the public, and legal mechanisms are in place to contain it, involving medical services. The crucial additional feature of mental health legislation is that it authorizes detention on the grounds of risk to the self, raising complex issues in psychiatry and in law. In this context self-harming tendencies associated for example with severe depression or psychosis are understood to be episodic, to remit spontaneously or with medication, and the rationale for compulsory detention can be understood, I think, as protection of the future self, when out of episode, reverting to normal for the person. However, these issues are not the primary focus here, which is the management of risk to others and the need to distinguish it from treatment of distress in the person.

In the management of risk to others, the balance shifts away from medical attention to the suffering of the individual and the need to treat, towards legally authorized control of risk to the public. Mental health legislation puts in place judicial and quasi-judicial procedures designed to balance protection of the public against protection of the rights of the individual concerned. Tensions have arisen, however, in relation to several kinds of case, including severe antisocial personality disorder, and schizophrenia involving risk to others.

Following conviction for a crime, a psychiatric assessment may indicate that the person has antisocial personality disorder. The theoretical choice for the Court is between disposal to a healthcare provider or custody in the criminal justice system. These have familiar pros and cons, the relative importance of which varies from case to case and context to context. Disposal to a health institution for treatment is apparently pointless insofar as the tendency to dangerous behaviour is persistent, at least because the person has no interest in change, only at best in the appearance of change so as to get out of whichever institution is holding them; there are no available pharmacological treatments, and probably no psychological treatments either, as all psychotherapies depend on motivation for change. Insofar as all this is correct, or assumed to be so, a health agency has nothing to offer, and the other form of disposal, to prison, would be indicated. However, unresolved problems for the state and the media arise in two kinds of circumstances involving individuals with a diagnosis of severe antisocial personality disorder. They may have completed their tariff in the criminal justice system for crimes committed but appear just as dangerous as before and the criminal justice system cannot detain them. There may be individuals with the diagnosis in community care or in insecure hospital who have not been convicted of a crime and who therefore cannot be held in the criminal justice system. In these kinds of case psychiatrists, as the experts on mental illness and diagnosis, have to assess risk and where appropriate seek to detain the individuals using mental health legislation. If one of these individuals commits murder in the community there is public outcry and recrimination.

For example in one high profile case in the UK recently a question was put from the floor of the Commons to the Home Secretary at the time, Mr Straw:

> Does the Home Secretary believe that further measures will be needed to deal with offenders who are deemed to be extremely violent because of mental illness or personality disorder, but whom psychiatrists diagnose as not likely to respond to treatment? Is he aware that this concern has arisen not simply following the conviction of Michael Stone for those two brutal and horrible murders, but because there has been a tendency in recent years for psychiatrists to diagnose a number of violent people as not likely to respond to treatment?

> [To which Mr Straw replied:] Yes, I entirely agree with the Right Hon. Gentleman that there must be changes in law and practice in that area. We are urgently considering the matter with my right hon. and hon. friends in the Department of Health. Sir Louis Blom-Cooper, who has a distinguished record in this field, said on the radio on Sunday that one of the problems that has arisen is a change in the practice of the psychiatric profession which, 20 years ago, adopted what I would call a common-sense approach to serious and dangerous persistent offenders, but these days goes for a much narrower interpretation of the law. Quite extraordinarily for a medical profession, the psychiatric profession has said that it will take on only patients whom it regards as treatable. If that philosophy applied anywhere else in medicine, no progress would be made in medicine. It is time that the psychiatric profession seriously examined its own practices and tried to modernise them in a way that it has so far failed to do.

Hansard (26 October 2000, column 9)

Some years later we have had a raft of draft legislation designed to modernize psychiatry to make it more fit for the purpose of – among other things – managing risk. Most of it is contentious in the opinions of most groups concerned, professional and otherwise, and the government is pressing on.

Related issues arise in connection with people with a diagnosis of schizophrenia whose hallucinations and/or delusions involve the need or the command to attack others. These people are typically in the care of ordinary community psychiatry services, not specialist forensic. The individuals may be detained in health settings, more or less secure, in the acute phase of the illness, but as the episode wanes, or seems to, probably with medication, while it continues to be taken, nursing staff and the psychiatrist with responsibility have to assess risk, making decisions about the appropriate level of observation and restriction of liberty. The same problem arises in the community: when is risk sufficient to warrant detention? Assessment of risk in such circumstances is well-known to be a difficult matter, and mistakes – including those judged to be so with the benefit of hindsight – are sometimes made. When a catastrophe happens there is typically much media and government attention. High-profile tragic murders are often followed by long and expensive enquiries that find failure in complex systems, sometimes resulting in the end of psychiatrists' careers. Government directives in the UK mean that mental health services use substantial resources for the assessment and monitoring of risk. The problem has come to be seen as how to make psychiatrists and other mental health professionals better trained at assessing risk, and how to have the right legislative framework in place, to prevent catastrophe.

The high level of public concern and expenditure is apparently – so far as the statistics are concerned – entirely out of proportion to the frequency of harm caused to others by people with a diagnosis of mental illness. This point will be taken up in a later in section 5.6, which includes a quote from a publication aptly called 'Scare in the community'.

The main point being made here is that this problem area of management of risk to the public is best distinguished clearly from medical and other mental health professional care of distress. Once mental disorder is conceptualized as being primarily about harm – distress and disability – accruing to the person with the problem, then it is possible and desirable to distinguish it from issues of social control of individuals who pose a risk to the public. This is another kind of problem, properly the activity of the state, not primarily of the medical or any other health profession.

It is clearer to conceptualize these matters of assessment and management of risk to the public as exactly being that – as opposed to matters of diagnosing and treating illness in people in distress. The expertise required includes psychiatry, with its training in for example eliciting subtle features of mental state, and knowledge of prognosis with or without treatment, but other relevant expertise would include statistics, contributing to an understanding of the difficulties inherent in predicting very rare events. Above all, boundaries would be clearer if the responsible officers as well as the context were clearly identified as legal and judicial, not – or not only – as healthcare professionals. Control of individuals for the purpose of protecting others from harm is fundamentally a political activity of the state and its officials. This is obscured to the extent that management of risk to the public is seen as a matter for and assigned to the medical profession – or to any other health profession – the proper activity of which is healthcare of the individual presenting with distress or disability.

The issues here have similarities to those considered above in section 5.2 in relation to the political abuse of psychiatry. In that context the main point was that psychiatric detention of people without conviction for crime is prevented by the apparatus of democracy – rather than by having a clear line between mental disorder and social deviance. Here the point is that if we do want in a democracy to detain people without conviction for crime, on grounds of risk to public safety, then the primary responsibility for this lies with political institutions and officials, subject to democratic checks and balances; discourse on mental disorder linked to the medical or other mental health professions, shifting the responsibility to them, obscures this fundamental point. In these complex matters of protecting the public, psychiatry no doubt has a role, but not as lead.

5.5 **Stakeholders in diagnosis and treatment**

How in practice have particular conditions come to be diagnosed as mental disorders and included, as they were developed, in the psychiatric diagnostic manuals? As considered earlier, presumably the main pathway is that people with these distressing conditions have come to psychiatrists for help, or have been brought for treatment by family and friends. For the most part, it may be supposed, they are conditions which have always been problems for people, under one name or another, and which invoke help-seeking from whichever sources are available. The core ingredients are profoundly troubling and puzzling mental states and behaviours of an individual, requiring someone with expert knowledge and access to resources to help sort it out, or at least contain it. In practice diagnosis is given when thresholds of severity, distress or impairment are such as to indicate need for treatment or some other form of management.

This pathway into the manuals of psychiatric conditions was commonly remarked in the context of the development of the manuals and a definition of mental disorder. Klein has already been quoted in previous chapters to this effect:

> It seems plain that these compendia [the DSM and ICD] are actually compilations of the sorts of things that physicians treat; a circular classificatory principle but a useful historical clue. Our definitions of illness are derived from medical practice.

> (1978, p. 41)

This sociological insight appears implicitly in the definitions of mental disorder in the manuals, in the references to clinical significance. Wakefield for example comments on the DSM-III-R definition (1992b, p. 234): 'Sentence 1 notes that DSM-III-R will limit itself to "clinically significant" conditions. This is intended to restrict the manual to conditions that actually come to the attention of clinicians.'

The needs of individuals and families establish the psychiatrist–patient relationship, and social structures to organize and to fund it. In this complex there are pressures to facilitate diagnosis and access to treatment, and others to inhibit them.

Individuals with the problems – if they want help with them – and their families and advocates, have an interest in inclusivity, in regarding more rather than fewer conditions as warranting diagnosis and treatment, or in setting their thresholds lower rather than higher. Generally speaking, and other things being equal, the groups which provide expertise and treatment have this same interest. Manufacturers of treatment technologies, such as the contemporary pharmaceutical industry, have the same interest. Drivers for exclusivity – for keeping conditions out of the manuals or for keeping diagnostic thresholds higher rather than lower – include those that are typically funder led, government and/or independent insurers, who have to manage limited resources and balance income and expenditure, and possibly profit. Another kind of driver to have particular conditions out of the manuals is pressure from minority groups who see them as variations in life's rich tapestry, as opposed to illness in need of treatment, illustrated in the victory of the gay lobby in the 1970s, and ongoing in some disability lobbying.

Many stakeholders become involved in where the boundaries are drawn in relation to diagnosis and the need to treat for conditions primarily involving distress or impairment in the individual: the individuals concerned, but also families and carers, advocacy groups, manufacturers of treatment technologies, and the funding bodies.

As an illustration of the many kinds of pressure involved, pharmaceutical companies have recently begun direct-to-consumer advertising, identifying problems in the advertisement, encouraging people to request the treatment – and a diagnosis if required. Here is a 2001 news report of the *British Medical Journal*:

> Criticism has erupted in the United States against drug companies that, in violation of a 30-year-old international marketing agreement, have begun aiming their advertising of potentially addictive drugs (used to treat children's behavioural and emotional problems) directly at parents, rather than just doctors. Among those companies is a UK firm, Celltech Pharma, whose US subsidiary, Celltech Pharmaceuticals (based in Rochester, New York), markets the company's Metadate CD, a medication for attention deficient hyperactivity disorder (ADHD), in the United States. Metadate CD is advertised in the August issue of the US monthly magazine *Ladies' Home Journal*, with a mother and son under the headline 'One dose covers his ADHD the whole school day.' Over the page is what the advertisement acknowledges as an 'incomplete list' of the product's side effects, from headache to psychosis.

> Kovac (2001)

This practice may spread from the US to the EU.

> Four of the world's biggest pharmaceutical companies are proposing to launch a television station to tell the public about their drugs, amid strenuous lobbying across

Europe by the industry for an end to restrictions aimed at protecting patients. Pharma TV would be a dedicated interactive digital channel funded by the industry with health news and features but, at its heart, would be detailed information from drug companies about their medicines.. . . The [European] commission is consulting on potential changes to the regulations that ban all direct-to-consumer advertising of medicinal drugs . . . The industry has been lobbying in Europe to be allowed direct access to patients. It argues that lifting restrictions would help its competitiveness and has hinted that companies may relocate to the US, where they can advertise to patients who then demand drugs from their doctors. Profits have soared there as a result . . . But consumer organisations are opposed, warning that the companies will play down risk, and that their real interest lies in boosting profits.

Guardian, London (22 May 2007)

That there are issues and controversies of the kind alluded to above is not intended to be itself a controversial statement – they are open to view. The point in the context of the present chapter and the essay as a whole is that diagnosis of mental disorder – as codified in the psychiatric manuals – is closely tied to judgements of distress, disability, and the need to treat, and as such is subject to many kinds of social pressures from various stakeholders, some pressing for inclusion, some for exclusion, which are best recognized and debated for what they are.

5.6 **Mental disorder in the community**

There is concern that prevalence of mental disorders is on the increase: for example, that rates of diagnosable depression and anxiety disorders are rising in the economically developed west, as are sales of medications for these conditions, and similarly for ADHD in children. This is important in terms of individual suffering, and there is also the matter of cost to national economies, from time lost to work, lost educational opportunity, as well as costs of management and treatment. The position is also somewhat paradoxical in relation to the large research effort in psychiatry in the last few decades and rising. In general medicine, research on the causes and cures of some physical illnesses has led to preventive interventions and/or more effective treatments, resulting in a decline of prevalence rates. In psychiatry, on the other hand, the general trend so far is not clearly in this direction, and may be running for some conditions the wrong way.

Increase in prevalence of mental disorders can be understood in broad terms in several different ways including the following:

1. There are more cases of mental disorders in the population now compared with previously. True rates of major depression and ADHD, for example, are rising.

2. The true prevalence rates are not changing much, or are the same, but we are getting better at detecting cases – either or both of hitherto undetected cases of known disorders, and hitherto undetected disorders.

3. The prevalence of troublesome conditions has probably not altered much, but more and more kinds are being diagnosed as mental disorders, and in particular conditions/cases that are really normal, or at least not disordered, are being pathologized. In brief, the application of the term mental disorder is being illegitimately extended.

The first interpretation is the most straightforward; it points to the need for research programmes to explain the increase and hopefully put it into reverse. The second option has the shift as being not in the phenomena but in the epidemiological technology for assessing them. Neither of these interpretations has much to do with the central topics of this essay. The third interpretation is the one that interacts with the essay's themes, because it implicates shifts in the use of the concept of mental disorder. It belongs with the idea that increasing numbers of conditions are being added to the DSM and ICD, and the suggestion that the threshold for diagnosing disorder is coming down, and expanding to include less severe, or normal, problems.

Here for example is Kutchins and Kirk on a list of ordinary enough feelings and behaviours of the sort friends tell you about, but which can figure as symptoms in psychiatric syndromes:

> Where you thought your friends were just having normal troubles, the developers of the American Psychiatric Association's diagnostic bible raise the possibility that you are surrounded by the mentally ill. Equally disconcerting to you, you may be among them. This easy inclusion of so many quirks and experiences is what we refer to as the pathologising of everyday behaviour.

(1997, p. 22)

On one example, anxiety about an upcoming speech, they continue:

> Worry and anxiety have become big business in the United States. DSM-IV says that 5 percent of the population (about 12 million Americans), two-thirds of them women, will have Generalised Anxiety Disorder (officially coded as 300.02) in their lifetime. The pharmaceutical companies – the makers of Prozac, Xanax, and beta blockers for stage fright – love those numbers because they represent a vast and growing market. . . Sure, giving a speech can be worrisome, but how do normal discomforts become possible signs of mental illness?

(op. cit., p. 23)

This passage from Richters and Hinshaw was quoted earlier in another context:

> Over time, however, the concept of mental disease gradually gave way to the broader concept of mental disorder, and during the closing decades of the 20th century its

classification boundaries have been extended far beyond the extreme conditions for which it was originally invoked. Mental disorder now serves as a generic label for the wide array of syndromes of mental and psychological suffering for which individuals and their caretakers seek professional help. Ironically, advances in the scientific study of psychological functioning and behavior during the same period have led to increasingly penetrating questions about whether the mental disorder abduction can be justified any longer as an inference to the best explanation for such a wide variety of conditions.

(1999, p. 438)

Horwitz and Wakefield's recent book, *The Loss of Sadness: How psychiatry transformed normal sorrow into depressive disorder,* has been discussed previously in Chapter 3 (sections 3.7 and 3.8). Here is part of the publicity announcing its publication:

Depression has become the single most commonly treated mental disorder, amid claims that one out of ten Americans suffer from this disorder every year and 25% succumb at some point in their lives. Warnings that depressive disorder is a leading cause of worldwide disability have been accompanied by a massive upsurge in the consumption of antidepressant medication, widespread screening for depression in clinics and schools, and a push to diagnose depression early, on the basis of just a few symptoms, in order to prevent more severe conditions from developing.

Oxford University Press (2007)

In their book the authors argue that, while depressive disorder certainly exists and can be a devastating condition warranting medical attention, the apparent epidemic in fact reflects the way the psychiatric profession has understood and reclassified normal human sadness as largely an abnormal experience.

The suggestion is, then, that the prevalence of troublesome conditions has probably not altered much, but more and more kinds are being diagnosed as mental disorders, and in particular conditions or kinds of case that that really normal are being pathologized. In brief, the application of the term mental disorder is being illegitimately extended.

This idea, of course, does presuppose that there is a legitimate, reasonably well-defined use of the term, which can then be misused, and that is the problem that this essay has been about. Two readily identifiable positions here are naturalism, specifically the kind that would ground the concept of mental disorder in evolutionary psychology, and a dialectically extreme sociological critique that would regard all mental disorder attributions as illegitimate pathologizing (any extension of the concept would be illegitimate, but in any case the original was to start with).

There is another conception to be distinguished from both of those which is more fluid. It is along the lines characterized in the previous chapter and it is also, I suggest, close to the position in fact occupied in the psychiatric manuals. It is less fussed about having a hard and fast line between mental disorder and normality, hence also about the concept of mental disorder itself. The focus is rather on the distress and disability people bring to the mental health clinic. It may be supposed that these problems are due to a medical or mental dysfunction, but this qualification never has been well-defined, or not in a way that is of much use in the clinic. In brief, according to this line of thought, there never was and there is not now a clear concept of mental disorder distinguished from mental normality. The qualification has rather always been a matter of representing the problems as medical or psychiatric, this representation being built into social structures of help-seeking and healthcare provision. So it was and so it is now, only now the structures are in flux. In brief, the extension of the concept of mental disorder is neither legitimate nor otherwise – it is just a matter of ongoing negotiation between the various stakeholders in the process of help-seeking and help provision.

The structures are in flux. Foucault described the construction of the modern western idea of madness, the confinement of the people labelled as mad in the asylums, and the processes of medicalization resulting in psychiatry and its medical model. The closure of the asylums in the second half of the twentieth century and their replacement by care in the community, clearly signifies a dynamic fluidity in social representations and organization. Increase in diagnosis of mental disorder can be interpreted as the extension of psychiatry's gaze into the community, finding pathology there, here among us, in increasing amounts, but this interpretation refers just to psychiatry, which is part of a more complex social context. There are other, related shifts in social representations. Madness never could be among us – not among *us* – because it was behind the asylum walls. Whatever we may have cannot be the old madness, not something isolated, different, pure deficit, meaningless, with nothing to say – but rather it would have to be something new, more familiar, something we come across in friends and family, on TV and in ourselves, something more understandable, having a voice – something better called something like mental health problems, fading into ordinary or extraordinary problems of living. Madness transforms into something else when it is in the community, representations shift, terminology goes into flux, as do services, and, among all these things and bound up with them, there is more of it; 'it' – whatever it is – is more common.

These changes in representations and social organization have coincided with the development of psychological science and application in psychiatry.

Most evident now are the biomedical and behavioural sciences, consistent with each other though still involved in a degree of turf warfare over which kind of model is most appropriate for particular types or subtypes of psychiatric condition. These piecemeal debates and competing research programmes echo the century-old dichotomy between the epistemologies of meaning and causal explanation, but its old glory is lost in the new paradigms of cognitive psychology and neuroscience. The two transformed approaches are no longer claiming the prize of 100 per cent of the explanatory model, but are rather in negotiation, at its best evidence- rather than ideology-led, over relative contributions of causal pathways involving neural dysfunction of many kinds, and information processing-based functionality of many kinds, these in turn influenced by genetic factors and environmental factors of many kinds. In short, the science has mental disorder now as very complicated, highly diverse, and only partially and provisionally understood – not as unreason caused by a failing brain.

Foucault identified a key shift away from the mechanisms of language in the asylum and in the society that constructed it, as being Freud's methodology of the physician listening for the meaning in the patient's speech. There were 50 or more years of psychoanalytic ideas and their many expressions, in psychotherapy and counselling sessions, in psychiatric training and in the media – establishing new social representations – before more recent psychotherapeutic approaches such as cognitive behaviour therapy have been able to converse with the patient's conscious thoughts and feelings about the problems to negotiate a shared model of the problem and what would have to change, and to work collaboratively on methods of change. (Not, by the way, that this approach has been shown to work for all kinds of psychiatric conditions, and it is unlikely to in just that form). The processes of the patient finding a voice, being empowered, having respect as equal, of common ground being established, being included, are complex and take a long time, but they are among the critical themes in the appearance of mental disorder in the community. The old idea that Foucault identified – madness as absence of reason, mere deficit, to be done to – has no place in the community, though like all old ideas it lingers. Meaning will thread through mental disorder, meaning many interwoven things: being understandable, being familiar, like us, having method, trying to deal with adversity and challenges of many kinds, more or less well, like what we may try to imagine. Meaning threads through mental disorder, in some conditions more than others, to some of those involved more than others, at different times and in different contexts. Sometimes of course it is lost or given up as lost, but these times are now a proportion, not the whole, and probably a small proportion.

Insofar as there is meaning in mental disorder there is mental order – this is to say, this shift in perception effectively destabilizes the concept, creating discontent and the need for others. Another response is this: the idea of mental disorder is left as it is, undisturbed, and then we are disturbed to find that what is now being included under this heading are problems for people that we can understand, understandable responses to ordinary or not so ordinary life adversities, with the thought then that we have to roll the encroachment back – so it covers only real mental disorders which, in this context, is going to have to mean something like: the really senseless. This is a move in the wrong direction; the idea, in this form, is no longer viable – it is only an echo, nothing to do with what we know of from routine clinical practice and the science of the conditions that people bring to the clinic and which are described in the psychiatric manuals.

One expression of the problematic identified by the 1960s debates was the problem of differentiating between mental illness and ordinary problems of living. Thinking of some examples, making this distinction is easy: contrast the terrible desperation of a person in a paranoid psychotic episode, with the stresses and strains of middle class life. However, the difference fades, and its terms unravel, when we think in current day terms, in terms of what we now know about the psychosocial risks for mental health problems, including such as overwork or unemployment, lack of social supports, neglectful or abusive family life, poverty, racism and other mechanisms of social exclusion and deprivation. These are severe problems of living, and people's responses to them, ways of coping with them more or less well, sometimes blur into psychiatric problems. Whether they are considered ordinary problems of living or otherwise depends on where one finds oneself – the community is not one place but many, with different life-problem profiles.

As already suggested, the changes in representations and social organization signalled by the closure of the asylums – the discharge of mental disorder into the community – have coincided with changes in the clinical sciences. One theme already mentioned has been the uncovering of meaning in much that is called mental disorder, and the recognition that it has a causal role. Another relevant theme has been development of the statistical notion of the normal distribution, the discovery that all or most psychological phenotypes are normally distributed in the general population, and the more recent discovery that many psychiatric phenotypes are or may be the extreme or not so extreme end of normally distributed psychological phenotypes. Psychological phenotypes related to depression, ADHD, Autism, and OCD, for example, are normally distributed in the community. The problem then arises as to where to draw the line between a normal depressed reaction and depressive disorder;

or again, between the high end of the normal level of impulsivity or activity in boys, and hyperactive disorder; and so on. Depending what counts as significant enough distress, disability or risk for adverse outcomes, the line might be drawn as high as 12 or 25 per cent – where is the upper limit here? How can so many people, so many of us, have a mental disorder? Is it coherent or affordable to have so many adults and children suffering mental disorder requiring treatment? Should the line for line for diagnosis better be drawn somewhere lower, at 1 or 2 per cent? The degree of arbitrariness involved is obvious, and is confusing only if we think we are trying to track some fixed fact of the matter, the line between genuine mental disorder and normal functioning. The problem can be better understood in terms of balancing the need to treat distress, disability or risk for adverse outcomes, against the drawbacks of referral to mental health services and treatment, such as stigma, and costs, and, so far, neglecting other possible solutions.

Ethical issues are also involved. Insofar as the presenting problems are or may be temperamental or personality characteristics, contributing to the kinds of persons we are, there would be reluctance to try to make changes using psychiatric treatments. Opinions here either way involve social and personal values, in misgivings about prescribing as much as in therapeutic liberalism. Scheurich, for examples, notes this, summarizing his paper on these issues as follows:

> The past decade has seen a growing debate about the expanding use of psychotropic medications. Of particular concerns are current anti-depressants, as well as hypothetical 'mood brighteners' that could modify affect and behaviour in people heretofore classified as being within the normal range . . . Objections to such pharmacologic applications are based on appeals to cultural values – authenticity, diversity, inwardness, and stoicism among others – that are viewed as being under increasing threat in contemporary American culture. Critiques of mood brighteners, like critiques of technological, consumer driven culture, repudiate the ideals of shallow satisfaction and of the self as commodity. The decision to prescribe or not to prescribe a psychotropic medication in any given case is based on cultural values as well as clinical judgements.

> (2006, p. 199)

As an alternative to this unruly scenario there is the more coherent approach of wanting to confine the legitimate domain of prescribing to genuine disorders; ethical, scientific, medical and clinical legitimacies would coincide and give mutual support. This wish creates pressure to roll back the boundaries of disorder, to include only those psychological states and behaviours that are really abnormal, that are different from normal human constitution, resulting from causes such as disease or lesions – from malfunctioning brains: but this is not the way that epidemiologically based behavioural science is going. In practice cut-offs are made in psychiatric epidemiology and in the clinic by considering the distress, disability and risk associated with symptoms, with diagnosis then linked to the decision that there is need to treat. This way of drawing the line is a pragmatic one, unfixed , and it is a matter that inevitably brings into play the various competing pressures on diagnosis and access to treatment, involving various stakeholders as considered in the previous section.

Another theme in Foucault's analysis was that the danger of madness was locked in the asylums, the straightforward implication being that opening the asylum doors lets the danger loose. The old idea of madness as danger unfortunately retains its power still, evident also in the many forms of stigma and social exclusion experienced by people with a diagnosis of mental disorder. It was noted above in section 5.4 that there is much media, political and public concern about the danger to others associated with mental illness in the community, giving rise to increasing political control of mental health services, on a large scale and at high cost. However, the high level of public concern and expenditure is apparently – so far as the statistics are concerned – entirely out of proportion to the frequency of harm caused to others by people with a diagnosis of mental illness.

Here are some quotes assembled by Mind in Manchester (2007) at the beginning on its webpage titled 'Community Scare':

> Tthe risk of [being killed by a psychotic stranger] is around the same as that of being killed by lightening . . . about 1 in 10 million.
>
> Dr George Szmukler (Szmukler 2000)

> There is no evidence that [having psychiatric patients] living in the community is a dangerous experiment that should be reversed.
>
> Professor John Gunn (Taylor and Gunn 1999)

> Most psychiatric disorders are only very occasionally associated with criminality.
>
> Professor Herschel Prins (1990)

> Most people who have schizophrenia are never violent at any stage of their illness.
>
> Dr John Cutting (Cutting and Charlish 1995)

> Statistically we are all 400 times more likely to die from flu than to be killed by a mentally ill patient.
>
> Roger Dobson (1998)

> The people we should really worry about are the people who are drunk or intoxicated.
>
> Dr Robert Kendell, past-President, Royal College of Psychiatrists (Hall 1999)

Fewer than 10 homicides a year – less than 2% of all killings – involved patients with schizophrenia . . . you are 20 times more likely to be killed by a sane than an insane person.

Guardian (1999)

It would be helpful in breaking the stereotypical association between dangerousness and madness/schizophrenia/mental illness if the diagnosis of mental disorder and the assessment of risk to the public were more separated than currently – as suggested above in section 5.4. The main point for here is that major public concern about danger and risk is one of the main outcomes of closing the asylums and care in the community, alongside the issues considered earlier in this section concerning apparent increased spread of mental disorders. The disproportionateness of this major public concern about danger from mental illness in the community – in statistical terms – presumably reflects the unreality of the original idea that it had been confined in the asylum.

5.7 **What's in a name?**

A recent major work by Graham Thornicroft on discrimination against people with mental illness has near the begining:

> At present there is an active international debate on the appropriate words to use in the mental health field – in effect a terminological power struggle. This book reflects such diverse and conflicting views and uses a range of terms to refer to mental illnesses and to people who experience these conditions and their consequences.

(2006, p. xv)

This section considers some of the issues involved in this 'terminological power struggle' from the general perspectives adopted in this essay.

Following the 1960s critiques of psychiatry and its medical model, the term mental illness gave way to mental disorder. This term is subject to the same kind of criticisms as the original, however, insofar as it is used in such a way as to imply that the conditions are medical as opposed to social, and that the conditions are basically senseless. To put the point another way: insofar as we wish to say that the problems in question are social, or are as much social or psychosocial as medical, and that some at least represent meaningful responses to adversities, then the term mental disorder has not much to recommend it. It is unlikely in the present circumstances, however, that there is going to be a single right name on which all we can all agree. Given the diversity of conditions, and what we now know of the complex variety of their causes, and the variety of available responses – medical, psychotherapeutic, social – terminological variety can be expected. Current options include, apart from mental disorder: mental illness (now rehabilitated), mental health problems, maladaptive or dysfunctional behaviour, distress, and emotional well-being (absence of) – to be considered below.

The term mental disorder, like mental illness before it, is best suited for the purpose of saying that the condition in question lacks meaning, cannot be understood in terms of rational beliefs and goals in relation to life-circumstances, but rather is due to a non-meaningful cause, not regulated by information processing, some physical or biochemical disruption of neural information processing or arousal or affect regulation, appropriately described as a medical disorder, and as requiring medical and nursing care, as in hospital admission or day hospital, and medical treatment such as pharmacotherapy. Opinions as to the hypothesized causes obviously rely partly on the science. This however in psychiatry is commonly tentative and partial, and opinions are at the same time forward-looking, constituting decisions that have to be made as to how best to proceed, and how not to. The terms mental disorder and mental illness used in the way described here serve to counterindicate other responses, such as encouraging the person to manage better themselves, blame for not managing better, or using self-exploration or having psychotherapy to understand the reasons why the person is feeling as he is, or doing what he is doing. Conversely the use of the terms mental disorder and mental illness indicate need for the patient/sick role and demand for the best medical and nursing care. Since the existence of lesions is typically unknown and a matter for the science, this discourse is regulated by surface markers, typically including severity and chronicity of distress and impairment, such as in the psychoses, perhaps severe OCD, recurrent major depression and so forth. These kinds of condition and presentation best fit the medical model in psychiatry, as traditionally understood, and the terms characteristic of the model, mental disorder, and even more so mental illness, are suitable, often these days further qualified by severe, or severe and enduring, to emphasize the point.

Not all conditions in the psychiatric manuals, not all mental health problems, are like this, however, which takes us to the next name. In practice in mental health services – note the name – and in many other lay usages the current general term is 'mental health problems'. This term is useful because it connotes problems related to mental functioning, of one kind or another, is probably neutral to aetiology, and it avoids the term disorder which is regarded in many quarters, including by some service users, as stigmatizing and disqualifying – for reasons connected with the familiar points made in the paragraph above. The term mental health problems may be neutral to aetiology, but it remains faithful to the medical model in terms of management, since health belongs to institutions involving medically qualified practitioners, nurses, hospitals, clinics, health insurance, treatment, and so on. In some ways the term mental health problems is the natural heir to the previous mental illness, which was abandoned from widespread usage following the anti-psychiatry critiques of some of the excesses of the medical model, though as mentioned above mental illness has been rehabilitated for a limited class of conditions with particular features, signalled by the qualifiers severe and/or enduring. Mental health problems keeps the problematic embedded in healthcare terminology and institutions, but loses the connotations of chronicity and severity, senselessness and medical causes. It can be used with less risk of discontent for conditions that are relatively milder, less disabling, more akin to the usual, something we all may or do suffer from, in some degree, from time to time, which make some sense to us, and in which social or psychosocial circumstances often seem to be involved. 'Mental health problems' manages fairly well in losing the accumulated history of association with madness, asylums, and otherness, and can therefore be applied to a larger range of conditions, while keeping the link with the social institutions and practices of healthcare, and it might be the best replacement currently on offer as a general category name for the conditions in the DSM and ICD.

On the other hand, this term does not seem so satisfactory from other points of view, in contexts away from health, in non-health agency-based counselling provisions, educational settings, and so on, which deal with problems either not severe enough for mental health services, or in any case not taken to or accepted by these services. In some of these kinds of settings the person presents voluntarily with evident distressing life circumstances, and the general term distress recommends itself. This term also avoids what may be regarded as medicalization and pathologizing of problems of living and circumstances. In the case of problems presenting in children also, for example in schools, parents and other stakeholders may well wish to avoid the stigma of pathologizing, and to emphasize instead that they wish the children to thrive as best possible, and this is not a matter of diagnosing and treating illness. Hence expressions such as absence of emotional well-being. From the point view of highly trained practitioners in mental health services, such terms woefully understate some of the problems they are used to refer to, the more severe, chronic and impairing problems, and it is seen as risky to envisage a break from health agencies, where specialist treatment resources, at least for now, tend to be hosted. On the other hand, for the less severe, chronic and impairing problems, these alternative names and approaches make sense.

Psychologists, psychotherapists and behavioural scientists, as noted previously (in section 2.2), generally focus on strategies for dealing with adverse circumstances, of various kinds, and appeal to principles of psychological meaning, information processing, representation, goal-directed behaviour, coping, and so on. Terms relating to medical causes and medical healthcare are not readily available in this thought-space. In particular, when the task is to formulate the problem that the person is – at some level – trying to solve, the attribution of mental disorder is not fit for purpose: one is looking for order in what is otherwise confusion. Terms such as maladaptive or dysfunctional behaviour will have more appeal, used with a view to finding more adaptive problem-solving. That said, clinical psychologists and psychotherapists are a major presence in public mental health services, for example in the UK, which are health agency-based. Working in these settings, these clinicians may use the psychiatric diagnostic manuals for the purposes of clinical assessment, or for reporting purposes, or for conducting or using research, and in these contexts they may be comfortable with or may at least acquiesce in the term mental health problems.

A crucial complication of these issues, critical in clinical practice, is that the relative suitability of the medical model, terminology and approach, on the one hand, and the psychological or psychosocial, on the other, is not simply a matter of one being suited for one kind of condition and the other for another kind. It would be simple if, for example, psychotherapeutic, psychological or psychosocial terminology and approaches were suited to anxiety and depression, while the medical was more suited to the psychoses. Generally matters are not so simple. Management of a first depressive episode reactive to life events may be best psychotherapeutic, but this is not so clear for recurrent episodes, for which the medical model and treatment may be indicated, or some combination of the two. For the severe and enduring mental illnesses such as the psychoses, medical and nursing management including inpatient and day patient facilities and medication are indicated in episode, but between episodes, or when the acute phase is passed, either with time or more likely with medication, other issues and problems, psychological and psychosocial, require attention. The new cognitive therapy methods for the treatment of schizophrenia developed mainly in the UK focus on the individual's attitude to his illness, his more or less adaptive appraisal of acute symptoms, coping with secondary losses, rehabilitation, and so on. The recovery model developed mainly in the US emphasizes that while best quality medical and nursing care is required in acute phases and for longer-term care, in recovery phases other aspirations come into play, including the need for autonomy and respect, empowerment, help in overcoming obstacles to employment and rewarding social activities; and so on. In these conversations and collaborative activities, as in psychotherapy, the term mental disorder is unhelpful: the purpose is the reconstruction of order.

In summary, the present position on terminology for the conditions of interest is in flux, one might say confusion. This terminology problem – what to call the conditions – interacts with the problem of the appropriate name for the people who seek help for the conditions, current options in use including patient, client, service user, and consumer. This variety reflects many issues: the kind of condition, its severity, its presumed causes, and the kind of provider, but also the matters of perceived agency, the demand for respect, a voice, empowerment, economic contract; and so forth.

The problem with terminology is acknowledged already in the diagnostic manuals themselves, as mentioned in the first chapter. The ICD-10 introduces its definition of mental disorder under the heading 'Problems with terminology', and begins (p. 5):

> The term 'disorder' is used throughout the classification, so as to avoid even greater problems inherent in the use of terms such as 'disease' and 'illness'. 'Disorder' is not an exact term.

The DSM-IV makes extensive caveats and qualifications before proffering its definition:

> Although this manual provides a classification of mental disorders, it must be admitted that no definition adequately specifies precise boundaries for the concept of mental disorder . . . Mental disorders have . . . been defined by a variety of concepts (e.g. distress, dyscontrol, disadvantage, disability, inflexibility, irrationality, syndromal pattern, etiology, and statistical deviation). Each is a useful indicator for a mental disorder, but none is equivalent to the concept, and different situations call for different definitions.
>
> American Psychiatric Association (1994, xxi)

So is mental disorder the right concept here to cover all these things? Is there one right word? I suspect not, in view of all of the many kinds of variety that are now evident. The one words – madness, mental illness, probably mental disorder too – come from another age, the one in which they covered what belonged in the asylums, the most defining feature, within which distinctions were of less interest, and which in any case were only known to and managed by the mad-doctors. Foucault has, in a passage quoted previously (1965, p. xii): 'In the serene world of mental illness, modern man no longer communicates with the madman . . . The man of reason delegates the physician to madness.'

Now postmodern or late-modern people do communicate with madness more, and with people with many other kinds of mental health problem, including familiar anxiety and depression, and this signals rescinding the delegation and taking responsibility back where it belongs – and one sign of these changes among many others is: what word should we use? I don't know. Different groups and individuals want to use different words, for different kinds of problem, depending on the setting and the purpose, depending on what they want to say.

The question arises why we need just one word. Compare the position in general medical services, which are more mature (older) and relaxed. There are general medical practitioners and many medical specialties dealing with many different kinds of problem and these apparently do not have one single name. Recall that Boorse has tried to define a single medical term, disease, and is led to include under this heading conditions that are apparently not diseases in any ordinary or medical sense. Internal medicine deals with diseases, among other things; orthopaedic surgeons with skeletal problems such as fractures; obstetrics and gynaecology deal with a range of problems from diseases to pregnancy, which is not a dysfunction let alone a disease, though it is associated with raised risk of harm. General medical practitioners deal with many kinds of problem, including some which are hardly problems, for more than a week or so, others that are not problems at all, but worries. There is no one word for everything that medical practitioners treat. Why should there be in psychiatry? This line of thought suggests taking seriously the diversity of the conditions in the DSM: phobias, autism, depression, schizophrenia, writing disorder; and so on – a list some hundreds long. Why should one word cover them all?

On the other hand, one word may be needed for convenience and for accounting purposes. There may be a need for one word to put on the front cover of the diagnostic manuals, and for general contracts between purchasers and providers. In fact, however, on this last point, the management of different psychiatric conditions involves such different costs, as in general medicine, that general contracts covering all sorts are insufficiently discriminating from an economic point of view; the accountants have little use for one word. So there is a need for one word for the front cover of books. General medicine can use the word disease as a general term, though without, so far as I can see, the intention of being heavily committed to the view that every condition under this heading really is a disease, and without therefore having to make a definition with the required exact fit. Consider the fact that the World Health Organization's *International Classification of Diseases* – abbreviated to ICD – of which the *International Classification of Mental and Behavioural Disorders* is part, actually has the full title: the *International Classification of Diseases and Related Health Problems*. This relaxed attitude could now be adopted in mental health care, it seems to me, provided the various ghosts from the 1960s debates can be laid to rest – the pressure to distinguish mental health problems from social problems, the paradoxes of meaning in disorder. Since the term mental disorder is the current terminological resting place of these ghosts, it is not fit for the purpose, and other terms of convenience would be better, such as mental health problems, or perhaps some combination of the two.

The real problems of interest are those described inside the manuals. Many have the term disorder appended to the name of the condition, but others do not. In those that do not, the word disorder plays no role, except insofar as the conditions are included in a manual of disorders. In many other cases the term disorder is appended to the name of the condition but could be dropped, leaving the name of the syndrome of clinically significant symptoms. Thus, obsessive compulsive disorder could become obsession–compulsion, PTSD post traumatic stress, and also for the so-called personality disorders, leaving borderline personality, dependent personality, antisocial personality etc. In order to keep the connotation that there is a recognizable pattern of symptoms, at one time or across time, the medical term syndrome could be retained.

The issue arises that these conditions come in various degrees of severity, and the idea was that the diagnosis of disorder marks out the more severe cases. If we have post-traumatic stress without disorder, how would we exclude the milder cases? But the problem would be explicitly where to draw the line on a continuum, which is of course the same problem we have now, but less explicitly. Severity can be defined in various ways, including number of symptoms, distress caused by them, and the extent of interference in daily activities. All or some combination of these are in fact now used to withhold or make a diagnosis, and these criteria would just stay in use. Withholding or making a diagnosis would not be the primary clinical focus, if the term mental disorder were to be dropped. There would be the task, as now, of identifying clinically significant symptoms, classifying them into syndromes, and ranking their severity according to various criteria as above, with some cut-off taken as indicating need to treat (including monitoring of risk). This is just what the diagnosis of a mental disorder now does, and the scenario envisaged is that we could just carry on without the imponderable notion of mental disorder. This approach would be consistent with adopting a dimensional approach, currently under consideration for some conditions for the DSM-V (e.g. First 2005), with the clear indication that categorical cut-off was required for the purpose of signifying, and in terms of, the need to treat.

5.8 **Medicalization and other representations**

Here is Jaspers on who does what:

> What health and illness mean in general are matters which concern the physician least of all. He deals scientifically with life processes and with particular illnesses. What is 'ill' in general depends less on the judgement of the doctor than on the judgment of the patient and on the dominant views in any given cultural circle.

(1913, p. 652)

According to a division of labour along these lines, what counts as mental disorder, or as a mental health problem, is determined by the person in distress seeking help, using available social representations. The community at large, the lay public, generally knows mental disorder when it sees it. We – the people – recognize when a person close to us, including oneself, starts to feel, behave and speak abnormally for them, out of character, and without reason or explanation, and we definitely worry about it if the person is highly distressed, or no longer carries out valued social tasks and obligations, such as childcare, work in or outside the home, personal care. We recognize when a person is angry, sad, anxious for no good reason, or when a person is speaking apparent nonsense, unrelated to what is going on. We recognize and worry when our children cannot do or do not do the things that other children do, learn, play, join in, have fun. Folk psychiatry uses norms of mental states and behaviour based in the usual functioning of an individual, or in the usual mentality and behaviour of an available reference group, perhaps framing them as a belief as to how human beings should function or were made to function. In short, folk psychiatry already identifies the kinds of conditions that are codified in the psychiatric manuals, or at least some of their most prominent features. This folk psychiatry is not based on reading the manuals, rather the other way round: the people recognize the problems and have taken them over the years to psychiatrists, and by this route they end up in a psychiatric book. This direction of travel was common remarked in the context of development of the manuals and the definition of disorder, as has been considered in several contexts above (in 4.1 and 5.5.)

If people are pretty good at recognizing the prominent symptoms of mental disorder as being such, then the traditional view that identification of mental disorder, and before it mental illness, is a matter of expert medical diagnosis, seems to be have been economical with the truth. On the other hand, while the people may know a problem when they see it, there is a further question as to what they see the problem *as*, and specifically how they have come to see the problems of the kind eventually compiled in the psychiatric textbooks as medical problems, mental illnesses, or mental disorders. This raises the complex social historical matter of the construction of medicalization as a form of representation and organization, one account of which is Foucault's. In previous times, prior to the period that is the focus of Foucault's history, people presumably took many problems to the priest rather than the doctor, including some extreme problems that would now come to psychiatry, because the problems were conceived in religious terms, such as sin, or vision. Social representations provide the vehicles for thought and the methodologies for action, and the medicalization of the problems guides people to the clinic rather than elsewhere, rather than to, for example, the priest, the local faith group, family and friends. This medicalization assigned to the physician the authority to diagnose mental disorder, and in this sense it never was a matter for the folk.

The question of medicalization of the conditions of interest is difficult to formulate, even to think about. The expression 'conditions of interest' is as neutral and non-committal a description as I can think of, but it is already imbued – certainly in my mind as someone trained in the field – by the concepts and categories of psychiatry and the medical model, culminating in the clarity of the psychiatric manuals. It is hard to represent without using available representations. This is the point made by Foucault in the preface to his sociohistorical enquiry into the modern representation of madness and reason (1961):

> This is undoubtedly an uncomfortable region. To explore it we must renounce the convenience of terminal truths, and never let ourselves be guided by what we may know of madness. None of the concepts of psychopathology, even and especially in the implicit process of retrospections, can play an organising role. What is constitutive is the action that divides madness, and not the science elaborated once this division is made and calm restored.

On the other hand there are other representations, from the past – Foucault later in his work cites Medieval and Renaissance representations of 'madness' – and from free thinkers – he starts the preface with quotes from Pascal and Dostoievski, and concludes the book with Nietzsche. There are other representations closer to hand half a century on from the time Foucault wrote. Much of the present essay has tried to make sketches of some of them, from the sciences, in interaction with changing social views, and associated shifts in patterns of care, treatments and terminology, with these changes in representations complicated by increased movement of cultures and communication between continents. The calm which Foucault identified is perturbed in these many ways, as was about to be signalled in the 1960s critiques of mainstream psychiatry. Critical points of disturbance – the closure of the asylums and care in the community, the familiar issues of medicalizing the social and pathologizing the meaningful – are superficially problems in psychiatry, but a systemic formulation is bound to implicate broader social representations and practices.

As suggested so far in this chapter, what seems to be found with increasing incidence in the community – because of better awareness or assessment technology, or because true rates are rising – is best understood not in terms of the old representation well identified by Foucault, not in terms of something like 'mental illness akin to madness', but rather in terms of changes in that representation, changes which acknowledge the involvement of social values, the role of meaning, and greater diversity within the normal range. These changes in representation require other words to be used, depending on just what we want to say about the problems in terms of aetiology, context, management and treatment. There are choices between agencies, from mainstream psychiatry through psychotherapy and counselling services, to self-help/empowerment groups. There are also choices between treatments: powerful prescribed psychotropic medications, psychotherapy and counselling of many kinds, durations and costs; alternative/complementary medicines which are probably effective for milder conditions, because of specific naturally occurring ingredients and/or because of powerful placebo effects which are known to be effective – almost as much or even as much as prescribed medications – in common conditions such as single-episode depression. As indicated earlier, choices of these many kinds are not simply a function of the condition, because the same condition in different phases may well warrant quite different responses. In brief, the market is already becoming mixed. People have already freed themselves from the single, absolute idea that everything of the kinds complied in the psychiatric manuals and everything that could be included in them as the thresholds go lower, is mental disorder – insofar as that connotes rare abnormality, deficit of meaning and disqualification, and treatment by psychiatry as part of mainstream medicine.

In the community, before the clinic is reached, there are alternatives to medicalization. Before the problems are medicalized, construed as mental disorder or as mental health problems, they may appear as problems of bringing up children, these being of many kinds, boy/girlfriend/parent generated troubles in adolescence, poverty-related or overwork-related worries, problems of laziness, lack of motivation, shyness, male aggression, problems associated with social exclusion of many kinds, antisocial or criminal behaviour. None of these kinds of problems areas has to be construed as medical or to do with mental health, rather than as problems of living arising from natural human tendencies and forms of social organization. The medicalization of these kinds of problems is one particular kind of social representation and set of practices among others. The practices include specific forms of help-seeking and problem-solving, attending a physician or mental health clinic for assessment and treatment. Once medicalization is established, like all such representations, it is perpetuated: this is the only way, or the dominant way, in which help can be sought – the help is in the clinic. This is a form of institutionalized social control that no one group or law is responsible for, it is rather that things have come to be organized so that this is the way things have to be done. The ground is changing, however, alternatives to health care are clearer, as are some of the pros and cons are deciding between them.

Questions that appear in this changing thought-space include the following. Should we be aiming to change problematic high or low degrees of temperament – activity levels in boys, or shyness, or recklessness, or unhappy disposition – by psychiatric treatments? Should we be aiming to change by psychiatric treatments anxiety and depression related to poverty, poor housing, lack of educational opportunity, and unemployment? These questions obviously raise many issues, pragmatic and economic, and questions of social values: what kind of society do we want to live in? For there are options apart from medical/psychiatric treatments, including such as encouraging social structures that can help individuals to manage distress and unhappiness arising from life events; reorganizing social structures to relieve unrealistic task demands on particular groups, or allocation of resources to alleviate identified risks to public mental health, such as poverty, other forms of social exclusion, child abuse and neglect and so on. It is not my intention here to elucidate in detail these issues in themselves or in relation to specific kinds of case, still less to express an opinion about them – rather it is to make explicit the problem areas that open up once we explicitly abandon the idea that medicalization is the only true representation, warranted by some absolute fact in the nature of things. Medicalization of problems that may be otherwise construed as psychological, psychosocial or social has disadvantages insofar as it deflects attention away from other constructions and responses, at an individual level and in social and political domains.

Further complications arise in cross-cultural contexts as considered in section 4.6. Alternatives to modern western biomedical psychiatry include religious representations of different kinds, systems of belief involving spirits and magic, and what is sometimes called complementary medicine, with roots in medical traditions in other non-western cultures and in the pre-modern west. This last point indicates that under the general heading of medicalization there are various cultural constructions. The modern western medical model, strengthened by its successful reductionist disease model, has reinforced in psychiatry the assumption that mental illness or disorder is best understood in terms of biomedical causes, as opposed to psychological or social causes; and treatment is prescribed accordingly. In other cultural constructions other assumptions and responses are in play, ones which may not so clearly distinguish the social from the medical, or the somatic and psychological within the medical. In the cultural diversity of late- or postmodern western communities, medicalization in its modern western form is not the only medical representation of the problems or the solutions.

The question arises: is or was the characteristically modern western medicalization of the problems currently seen as mental health problems – right or wrong, legitimate or wrong-headed? Some themes and writers in the 1960s critiques of psychiatry and subsequently would have a resounding negative answer: psychiatry wrongly medicalized psychological/psychosocial/ social problems. Orthodox psychiatry with its medical model could be credited with just the opposite view. Expressed crudely like this, it sounds as though the dispute were about some matter of fact that we could be right or wrong about. Systemic, critical thinkers such as Foucault could hardly have such a simple view, so while medicalization can be criticized, and other representations such as the religious are contrasted, on what basis might the one be thought to be any worse or better than any other? As indicated through this essay, explicitly in the epistemological section in Chapter 4 (4.6), the position adopted here is that differing views can be evaluated on pragmatic grounds, to do with their effects in practice and their relative advantages and disadvantages – not in terms of correspondence or otherwise with absolute facts of the matter. Even if another view is taken as to the underlying metaphysics of truth, still there remains the pragmatic issues as to what problems this or that view are good at solving, and in which respects they are more limited.

Here are some outlines of pragmatic criteria on which medicalization in the mental health field can be compared with other representations in terms of advantages and disadvantages:

1. Effectiveness of treatment. This divides into various options depending on the outcomes of interest, such as:
    (a) Better at relieving symptoms
    (b) Symptom relief outweighs adverse side-effects
    (c) Better at improving the person's (perceived) quality of life
    (d) Better at reducing risk of relapse – pharmacologically, or by enhancing coping skills

2. Effective use of what has been identified in current biomedicine as the placebo effect

3. Scientific validity of the underlying models of aetiology and maintenance that inform treatment methodologies, including:

   (a) Understanding of meaningful, understandable psychological processes in causation, maintenance and coping, where they are operating, and addressing/enhancing them in treatment, and

   (b) Recognition of social factors in causation and maintenance, if they are operating, and addressing them in treatment

4. Generally, extent to which the models of aetiology, maintenance and treatment capitalize on coping and management generated by

   (a) self, or

   (b) social group, linked to

5. Compatibility between the model and the views of the people who are in need of help – enabling access, adding value.

6. Value for money, balancing economic benefits of treatment, including prevention of costs of poorer outcomes (e.g. in days lost to work, risk to children), against treatment costs.

These are many issues and they are all of course complex and controversial. A few points may be made briefly here, the purpose being the very limited one of indicating the kinds of discussion that open up when medicalization is not regarded as an absolute or obvious truth, or falsehood, and its pros and cons can be considered according to pragmatic criteria.

The first criterion on the list, 1, belongs with current evidence-based biomedicine in application to psychiatry; we look to open and controlled trials to evaluate effectiveness of medicines. Current medical psychiatry can claim significant advances in this respect; alternative medical approaches have been not much tested, and where they have been they do not clearly or consistently out-perform placebo. On the other hand, emphasis in medical psychiatry and in trials has usually been on symptom relief (1a), and there is increasing attention paid to other outcomes (1b–1d) where advantages are not always as clear. Moving to the second criterion 2, western biomedicine appropriately seeks to distinguish between the effects of active pharmacological agents and non-specific placebo effects which result in poorly understood ways from the psychosocial process of treatment. The size of the placebo effect varies with the psychiatric condition (as with general medical conditions), from large to negligible. For some common mental health problems – such as some presentations of depression and anxiety – it is typically large, sometimes claimed to be as large as for the active drug. Assessment of this point involves meta-analyses of trial findings, published and otherwise, and is a controversial matter.

Complementary medicine methods, whatever other virtues they may have, presumably also exploit the placebo effect fully, being naive to controlled experimentation methodology, raising the probability of good outcomes in conditions highly sensitive to this effect, in patients and communities with the requisite beliefs and expectations. On the other hand western biomedicine has the best, most scientifically validated models of normal and abnormal functioning (criterion 3). Then again, it is increasingly recognized that causes of psychiatric conditions are complex and multifactorial, and theoretical knowledge is at present limited. Western biomedicine in application to psychiatry has arguably done relatively poorly specifically in relation to criteria (3a) and (3b) – this was a major point of the large-scale criticism of psychiatry in the 1960s. To a large extent psychological and psychosocial approaches have filled these gaps in medical psychiatry, as indicated previously (2.2–2.4). A similar point may be made about criterion (4a), capitalizing on self-generated coping and management. There is also the matter of capitalizing on social resources to manage the problems of interest (4b), and on this point psychological therapies probably do no better than medical psychiatry, both sharing a primarily individual-based healthcare concept of malaise and remedy – the exception here being family therapy. Then there is the problem of compatibility (5): the service providers can have the best models and treatments possible, but if the intended users have something different then there are obstacles to access and usefulness, and outcomes are not improved. On the bottom line, criterion (6) is the question of value for money, which ideally has to take into account the whole complex.

As stated above all these issues are complex and controversial. My main concern has not been to express my own particular opinions – neither here nor there for the present purpose, which is simply to signal the problem areas that open up for consideration once we get beyond the simplistic question: 'Is medicalization right or wrong?'; and beyond the view that because western science-based psychiatry is the best in terms of validated theory and evidence-based treatments, it is the best, period.

The section opened with this quote from Jaspers:

> What health and illness mean in general are matters which concern the physician least of all. He deals scientifically with life processes and with particular illnesses. What is 'ill' in general depends less on the judgement of the doctor than on the judgment of the patient and on the dominant views in any given cultural circle.
>
> (1913, p. 652)

The patient's appraisal is that he has a problem involving distress and/or impairment in what he wants to be doing – as opposed to thinking he doesn't have a problem. He also appraises the problem as one to take to the physician, as being a being a medical problem – this appraisal uses dominant conceptions of his culture. These conceptions are what have been called here social representations, of which medicalization is one among others; they vary from culture to culture, from time to time, and they have various culturally embedded advantages and disadvantages, which can be assessed on a variety of pragmatic criteria – as sketched above.

At the start of psychiatry in its recognizably contemporary form, at the time Jaspers wrote, and for at least the half century following, medicalization really was medicalization, tied practically exclusively to medicine, the medical model in psychiatry, and the medical–psychiatric profession. Subsequently during the second half of the twentieth century, psychological approaches have been integrated into the science and into mainstream mental health services, with the result that medicalization has transformed into something broader, the representation being that the conditions of interest are now medical/psychological mental health problems. In the preceding section on terminology (5.7), further shifts in available representations were indicated, non-health related, more embedded in broader social processes and contexts.

Another change in the division of labour indicated in Jaspers' quotation has to do with the growth of the biomedical and behavioural science of mental health problems. Jaspers ran together the physician's concern with the phenomena, with the management and treatment of the problems presented at the clinic, with the scientific point of view. Now – a century on from Jaspers – the scientists can be added as a whole other group, in a major research industry, concerned with causes and treatments, informing and being informed by clinicians' direct knowledge of the phenomena. So there is more like a three-way division, rather than Jasper's twofold.

These three – the dominant social ideas, the clinician's expertise, and the science – all are now in open interaction with one another. The business of deciding which are the problems of interest belongs to society, to the people with the problems, their families, to advocacy and other special interest groups, and to the agencies responsible for planning and funding research priorities and clinical services. That said, social representations of the problems are increasingly influenced by clinical expertise, as summarized in the psychiatric manuals for example, and by the science, which has transformed concepts critical in the understanding of the problems: normality in the population, and the role of hidden or not so hidden method in apparent disorder, understanding of causes, course, risks and outcomes. Lay and expert views influence one another. The manuals inform public perceptions, especially in these days of increased interest in the psychological and the psychiatric, and somewhat less stigma, and the Internet. These days it is not unusual to find people

attending the clinic who already suspect what their condition is, because someone they know knew someone that had a similar problem, or they saw a TV
programme on it, or they have searched the web. People may come already sus-
pecting they have, for example post-traumatic stress (disorder), which everyone
calls PTSD for short, or obsessive compulsive disorder, OCD for short, or
Asperger's syndrome, and so on. Sensibly they usually want expert confirmation of this diagnosis, and in any case they want expert advice and help. People
identify the problems and participate in the social representation of them as
mental health problems; the professions refine description and classification,
which in turn, especially currently, are disseminated to the public at large.
Much of the credit for opening up the dialogue between society at large and clinicians, it seems to me, is due to the work in the ICD and DSM over the last few
decades in clarifying and in effect demedicalizing and demystifying psychiatric
diagnosis. The drive to describe the symptoms in observational terms that
anyone (or anyone with some interest, training and experience) can understand, has made it apparent that the bases for diagnosing mental disorders are
just the problems that people experience and report in clinical interview, and
which are familiar to friends and families. The distinctive professional expertise
lies now not so much in diagnosis itself, but in the process of refinement of
description, nomenclature and classification, but most importantly in knowledge of syndromes, in knowledge of course, risks and need to treat, of whether
the problems are self-limiting and not in need of treatment, or if not, what is
likely to be effective management or treatment, and in therapeutic skills.

5.9 Summary

At the opening of the chapter it was noted that a definition of mental disorder
is required to draw boundaries around the concept, to distinguish between
what is and what is not mental disorder. So far as concerns the psychiatric
diagnostic manuals, the purpose would be assess whether conditions included
as mental disorders really were so, to remove non-disordered conditions
included by mistake, and to assess whether there other disorders that should
be included in the next edition. The definitions of mental disorder given in the
manuals are harm led; that is to say, they emphasize first and foremost that the
conditions in the manuals are characterized by harm, by distress and disability, or risk of adverse outcomes. It is evident that there are many conditions
involving distress and impairment of day-to-day functioning that are not disorders, although it is hard to say in a clear and helpful way what the real
difference is. Gestures are made using terms such as personal dysfunction, and
unexpectable responses. The naturalist definitions of mental disorder are the

most elaborate attempts to demarcate mental disorder from social deviance on the one hand and ordinary problems of living on the other. Problems involved in getting these naturalist definitions to work have been considered in previous chapters, the point for here is that they do not effectively draw boundaries around mental disorder, demarcating what is from what is not. Nor do the harm-led definitions in the manuals.

The second section of the chapter considers a major problem current at the time the definitions of mental disorder were being constructed, the political abuse of psychiatry in diagnosing and detaining political dissidents. The naturalist definitions of mental disorder were the most elaborate responses to the intellectual task of distinguishing medical disorder from social deviance, including political dissidence, and the conclusion that they are not viable has to be brought face to face with the original problem: how then are we to distinguish mental illness from social deviance and from political dissidence in particular? The reply made is that prevention of the social abuse of psychiatry cannot be located in the difference between mental illness and social deviance, but has to be located in law, specifically in human rights legislation.

The third section makes the point that the list of harms associated with mental disorder given in the psychiatric manuals, most fully in the DSM, are those that accrue to the individual with the problems. This is consistent with the general medical practice. However, in psychiatry the harms involved are sometimes more to others than to the self, most obviously so in the antisocial behaviour conditions. Each of these two kinds of case – harm to self and harm to others – raises different boundary issues.

The fourth section considers issues that arise in the management of risk to others. The point is made that control of individuals for the purpose of protecting others from harm is fundamentally an activity of the state. This is obscured to the extent that management of risk to the public is seen as a matter for and assigned to the medical profession – or to any other health profession.

The fifth section on stakeholders in diagnosis and treatment notes that in practice conditions have found their way into the psychiatric manuals not so much because of a prior definition of mental disorder, but because they are the kinds of problem people have brought and continue to bring to the clinic. In practice diagnosis is given when thresholds of severity, distress or impairment are such as to indicate need for treatment or some other form of management. In this process of help-seeking and help provision, there are various stakeholders, not just patients and clinicians, some pressuring to facilitate diagnosis and access to treatment, others to inhibit them. They include families and carers, advocacy groups, manufacturers of treatment technologies, and the funding agencies.

The following section, 5.6, considers various issues under the general heading of mental disorder in the community. It starts with the often-made assumption that prevalence rates of some common mental disorders are rising. It should be said that this assumption is not straightforward, because the epidemiological methodologies to assess it are varied and complicated – see the bibliographical section below for selected references. If prevalence estimates are rising, there are various possible explanations, only one of which is relevant to the themes of this essay, namely, that the concept of mental disorder is being stretched to include more kinds of case, including some that are not really disorders at all. This kind of concern and this boundary problem can be seen as a consequence of the closure of the asylums and the discharge of mental illness/disorder into the community. How much of it there is amongst us and our children, what exactly it is and how it differs from normal problems of temperament, personality, and day-to-day living – all concern us. At the same time the social representation of the problems shifts from the old madness to something more familiar and accessible – something more like mental health problems.

Terminological issues are taken up in more detail in the seventh section. The main point is that there is current a great terminological variety, some would say anarchy, with different words for the conditions of interest being used for different purposes in different contexts; with related variety in what is considered an appropriate name to apply to the people who have the conditions and seek help for them.

Medicalization is the topic of section 5.8, that is to say, the construal of problems as being distress and disability and those in turn as medical problems, as opposed to various other kinds of construction. Alternative constructions include social, political, religious, and moral, each of varying kinds. There are also alternative constructions within the general medical model, more or less distinct from the western biomedical approach. The medical model in psychiatry has also been extended, or transformed, by the incorporation of psychological and psychosocial models. There is no single, fixed standard to use for judging whether medicalization is better or worse in absolute terms, once naturalist approaches to mental disorder are given up. There are however various pragmatic criteria by which different approaches can be compared: on how well they solve particular kinds of problem and in what respects. Regardless whether we think that there is an absolute fact of the matter to which these constructions correspond or fail to correspond, these pragmatic criteria are what is available to us in practice for comparative purposes.

5.10 **Annotated bibliography**

References for the first section – introducing the problems of boundaries – are in the text.

There is a substantial literature on the abuse of psychiatry in the former Soviet Union – considered in the second section. Entry points include Smith (1996), and Bonnie (2002), quoted in the text. There were several important declarations by psychiatric associations emphasizing the fundamental importance of independence of medical practice from state control and the protection of human rights, including the one by the World Psychiatric Association (1989). Attention has shifted away from the Soviet Union following the end of that regime, and has more recently turned to China (Munro 2000; Bonnie 2002; Birley 2002).

The main focus in the third section is on harm as understood in psychiatry, and some references are in the text. The importance of the concepts of harm to self and harm to others in ethics and in law is the subject of influential work by the philosopher Joel Feinberg (1984, 1986). There is reference in the text to an extensive literature on social vs medical models of disability; entry points include Self Direction Community Project (2000–2001), and Disability Awareness in Action (2007). A topic at the end of the section is whether the harms involved in mental disorder are universal or a subject to cultural influences. The discussion includes brief reference to controversies about human rights, for which introductory documents include: on background, the UN web page on human rights (UN 2007); on controversies about membership of the United Nations Commission on Human Rights, see e.g. Human Rights Watch (2003); and for critical commentary on priorities by NGOs, e.g. Oxfam (2005).

Reference is made in the fourth section – on management of risk – to a recent case in the UK. The enquiry into the case was published by Kent County Council (2006), and the quote in the text from the proceedings of the House of Commons is included in the report (first part, p. 24). On the assumption that community care had failed, the UK government published a Draft Mental Health Bill 2004 with wide-ranging provisions including for remand and compulsory treatment (Department of Health 2004). Following widespread criticism the Department of Health subsequently withdrew the Bill, but has suggested instead related amendments to existing mental health legislation; see e.g. Thornicroft and Szmukler (2005), Lepping (2007).

References for the fifth section – on stakeholders in diagnosis and treatment – are in the text.

Section 5.6 on mental disorder in the community opens with the often made assumption that prevalence rates of some common mental disorders are rising. This assumption is not straightforward, however, because the epidemiological methodologies to assess it are varied and complicated. Entries into large literatures for three of the conditions mentioned in the text include the following: for major depression, Murphy *et al.* (2000); for ADHD Timimi andTaylor (2004), and for autism spectrum disorders, Medical Research Council (UK) (2001). What is more clear is that prescription and costs of medication for mental health problems are rising, for example in the US (e.g. Zuvekas 2005), as is demand for more talking therapies, for example in the UK (London School of Economics 2006). Ethical issues raised by medical treatment of conditions that may be normal problems of living are illustrated by a quotation in the text, and other entry points into related literature include Ghaemi (1999), Rego (2005) and Stein (2008). The problem noted at the end of the section is the stereotypical association between madness/mental illness and dangerousness. Quotations complied on a Mind website (Mind in Manchester 2007) are given in the text; the works cited in the compilation are given in the References.

In Section 5.7 on current tensions and diversity in terminology, reference is made to various current therapeutic approaches, introductory references for which include: stepped or staged care involving psychotherapeutic and/or pharmacological interventions, see e.g. NICE guidelines on depression (NICE 2007) and on OCD (NICE 2005); on CBT for schizophrenia see e.g. NICE (2001); and for the recovery model see e.g. Anthony (1993), Jacobsen *et al.* (2001).

Key references for section 5.8 on medicalization include Foucault, discussed in the second chapter in section 2.6. Hacking's work on 'looping effects' in the construction of kinds of illness including mental disorders, noted earlier in the bibliography for Chapter 2 (section 2.6) bears on related problems (Hacking 1999, especially Chapter 4). Passages on pragmatic pros and cons of medicalizing in psychiatry include references to placebo effects, on which see e.g. Harrington (1997), and Moncrieff and Kirsch (2005).

Chapter 6

Some conclusions

Two main sets of questions central to the problem of mental disorder were posed in the Introduction:

First: Are the norms invoked in psychiatry really medical, or are they really social? The clarification of medical disorder typically invokes diseases and lesions, or functioning below the level of the normal group, or failing to function as designed. Sociological critiques, by contrast, emphasize the role of psychiatry in regulating deviance from social norms. How can psychiatry define its proper domain as medical as opposed to social?

Second: What is the validity of the distinction between mental disorder and order, between abnormal and normal mental functioning? To what extent, notwithstanding appearances, does mental disorder involve meaningful responses and problem-solving? These responses may be to normal problems of living, or to not so normal problems – to severe psychosocial challenges. Is there after all order in mental disorder?, and to the extent that there is, what implications does this have for the viability of the concept? Or again, taking a different approach to the distinction between mental order and disorder, what is the 'normal' group that provides a standard by which to judge what is normal as opposed to abnormal mental functioning?

The first set of issues has to do with the processes that define the difference between mental disorder and normality, and the second set has to do with the validity of the difference. The two sets of questions are distinguishable, though obviously they tangle up with one another in complex ways. At the end of the essay we can disentangle some of the themes that run through both, specifically ways of understanding 'mental order' and hence 'disorder'. Order and disorder are somewhat technical terms and it is easier to express the options using the more colloquial 'normal' vs 'abnormal'.

Through the essay various ways of understanding mental normality have been apparent, with mental abnormality as the opposite, as follows:

1. The mind is working as it should (not dysfunctioning)

2. There is meaningful connection between mental states, environment and behaviour, and among mental states: among such as needs, desires, beliefs, and reasons for action

3. Others agree the connections are meaningful

4. Normal means 'like us', in the majority community of normally functioning people

5. Normal = average for some suitably normal group

6. Normal = behaving according to social rules and regulations

7. Normal = states of mind and behaviour are natural – according to our nature

8. Normal = regulates adaptive behaviour – behaviour that is on balance beneficial to the agent (as perceived by them, or us, or really), consistent with their needs and intentions

There are linkages among this complex web of meanings. Here are some.

The first definition, (1), is trivial though reassuring (reassuring us that we mean something clear in case we ever begin to doubt); it is compatible with all the remainder, (2) through (8), and derives non-trivial interpretations from them, in effect because they give meaning to the 'should'.

The second approach (2) – in terms of what have been called here for convenience of brevity meaningful connections – explicates (1) in a way characteristic of psychological approaches. Another characteristically psychological approach is (8), more identifiable with behavioural science in its emphasis on mind as involved in the regulation of activity, which can turn out more or less well for the agent.

Approaches (3), (4), (5) and (6) are social interpretations of normality of the sorts appropriately emphasized by sociological approaches.

The seventh interpretation, (7) – in terms of what is natural in the human condition – is exquisitely ambiguous. It is well-known to invoke social representations, subject to cultural variation, and is interpreted as such in sociological approaches. Alternatively, (7) can be interpreted philosophically as a matter of fixed, given fact, as in naturalism of various kinds including as applied to mental order and disorder, the main contrast being here with sociological interpretation. Naturalism about mental order and disorder can go in two main ways: via design to evolutionary theory; and via what is normal in the naturally defined, one fixed group, probably species-wide. This option in effect makes a naturalist reading of interpretation number (5). Philosophical and sociological interpretations compete over which reading of natural is correct – absolute, fixed fact vs varied social representations. Then again, (7) and aspects of (5) can be seen as the proper domain of the sciences – matters for empirical enquiry to determine.

Amidst this complexity is medicine and psychiatry as one of its offspring. For many kinds of reasons psychiatry faces the challenging task of defining the proper domain of its activity. One set of reasons has to do with the fact that it was born into a scientific culture that had (at that time, the turn of the nineteenth to the twentieth century) no idea what to do with mind and meaning – given this context the domain of psychiatry was immediately somewhere between the problematic and the non-existent; more on these points below. Another set of reasons – exacerbated by the one above – had to do exactly with the problems of defining normality/abnormality in the realm of personal functioning, which is mainly interpersonal and social, hence open to a primarily sociological understanding.

What seemed to be required is some kind of abnormality which is specifically medical – as opposed to socially defined. Some of the interpretations of 'normality' in the list (1) to (8) are hopeless for this purpose. Interpretation (6) – understanding normality as social conformity and hence abnormality as social deviance – is the worst because it effectively defines psychiatry out of existence, equating its practices with those of the police or other agents of social monitoring and control. Interpretation (4), in which normal means 'like us normal people', patently marks the route from judgement of mental abnormality to social exclusion – not what medicine nor therefore psychiatry are about. The sure start for defining a medical meaning of mental disorder is (1) – that in mental disorder the mind is not functioning as it should – certain but somewhat trivial, so it has to be spelt out. What is needed is a domain that is distinct from the social – and there is only one candidate for that (once the problem is posed like this): the natural. This fits well the grounding of psychiatry in medicine, which attends to bodily functioning, using the natural sciences of physics and chemistry, and physiology and biology, bringing them in as natural sciences too. So the best bet for defining the domain of the medical and the psychiatric is (7) – the abnormalities of interest to psychiatry are those involving disruption of natural functioning. However, what is this in detail? The way this thought cannot (for this purpose) be allowed to run is this: mental disorder is socially defined, but by all means it has bodily causes (as all mental and behavioural functioning has), and so these bodily causes are medical malfunctions. This simply has medical norms determined by social – and we are no closer to defining the proper kind of abnormality for medicine. What we need rather (in this line of thought) is abnormality which is itself defined by nature not by culture. Here is where the naturalist definitions come in: either a biostatistical version – drawing on (5) – or an evolutionary theoretic version, which has 'according to our nature' as 'according to natural design' and that in terms of evolutionary selection.

Another dynamic criss-crossing here, noted briefly above, has to do with the fact that psychiatry and psychology were born into a scientific culture that had no place for mind and meaning. The mechanized world-picture of western science had no place for mind – as opposed to the body. There was another later split, at the turn of the nineteenth century, between causal and meaningful connections: the domain of (natural) science was causal connections, while meaning belonged to culture, the domain of social science. In these terms, insofar as psychiatry was grounded in medicine and in natural science, it had no access to meaning (not that this mattered because meaning was not causal) – so all it could define was its absence. This was a practically perfect fit with the then contemporary disease/lesion model of illness including psychiatric illness, which could have it is as pure disruption and deficit. On the other hand – in the thought-space in question – meaning was in the domain of culture, so also the definition of its absence, therefore it was open to the sociological critiques to continue to charge psychiatry with merely following society's lead. Either way, via a scientifically based lesion/disease model or a social representation, the medical model in psychiatry has found itself in the position of seeming to endorse the view that in mental disorder meaning has run out, in effect adopting a strong version of the second interpretation of mental abnormality, (2) above. Accordingly attempts to explicate and authenticate a specifically medical concept of mental disorder tend to end up, more or less intentionally, with defining conditions in which meaning or any other form of normal mental functioning is absent.

Psychology was positioned somewhere in between medical psychiatry and sociological approaches. Psychology as a science arose at the same time as psychiatry and applied itself to clinical problems, as abnormal psychology, and straight away found normal principles involved, classical or operant conditioning, or complicated unconscious meanings that led to dysfunctional behaviour or indeed to no behaviour, mimicking lesions and diseases. These psychological approaches were from the start antithetical to the medical model in psychiatry – or at least the one according to which mental disorder is pure absence.

The ruptures and splits between the medical, the psychological and the sociological, reached a climax in the 1960s, after which things could only get better. The dichotomy between meaning and causality, together with the earlier one between mind and body, were broken down in the new information processing and cognitive paradigm in the biobehavioural sciences, framed in an evolutionary theoretic approach, able to accommodate the medical and the psychological and the social. This major shift impacts profoundly on both the problem areas: on the demarcation between mental normality and abnormality, and on the distinction between natural and social norms.

As regards the distinction between mental normality and abnormality, the new paradigm can incorporate the findings of psychological science that normality of many kinds is – after all – involved in what we think of as abnormality. In particular, mental and behavioural phenotypes are typically not distributed in the population in a binary categorical way, with most individuals having one (normal) value, and a minority having a quite different (abnormal) value; rather the population distributions are typically normal in the statistical sense, bell-shaped, in which there is no clear distinction between what is normal and what is abnormal – between majority and minority. Of course binary categorical distinctions can be made in a normally distributed trait, but this is typically for the purpose of binary decisions (such as whether to provide health services for, or special education for), and does not reflect a sharp categorical difference within the population. In effect this shift in the view of population distribution blurs the difference between normal and abnormal mental functioning in the sense of interpretation (4) in the above list, the one that has normal meaning something like 'like us' in the majority community of normal functioning people.

Or take another interpretation of abnormality – (2) in the above list – in terms of breakdown of meaningful connections. It was emphasized in psychological approaches from the start that there was meaning in apparently irrational behaviour, in psychoanalytic theory. The same conclusion came in a different way in conditioning theory models of such as phobias – normal learning principles (the same as in the normal case) were involved. The same principles were involved as in the normal case, and the abnormality was defined rather in terms of the maladaptive nature of the responses. What was new in the cognitive paradigm was not so much the recognition that meaningful, understandable processes were involved in the abnormal case, but was rather the shift to seeing them as causal, as having a causal role in one or more of the origin of the problem, its maintenance, or in coping with it. Construing meaningful mental states as causes comes to the same as including them in the science, in causal models of psychopathology, so the outcome is that the same principles are involved in psychopathology as are involved in the explanation of normal behaviour. In brief, it turns out that what is called mental disorder in fact may involve order, thus breaking down the dichotomy between the two.

The impact of the new behavioural science paradigm on the other set of questions – as to whether the norms involved in demarcating mental disorder from order are social or medical/natural – is equally profound. 'Natural' has many meanings. As noted above the one required for the purpose of distinguishing medical from social norms is 'natural' as opposed to social. This sense of natural had been reinforced in the turn of the nineteenth century distinction between natural and cultural science, which would among other things have causation in the former and meaning in the latter, an idea that profoundly influenced the development of psychiatry as referred to above. An earlier sense of natural has it as innate, what we have with us at birth. The main contrast here, in the domain of cognition, is with what we derive, after birth, from experience. In empiricism all understanding and knowledge is derived from experience (except the law of identity); in rationalism some – the most important – is innate. These two senses of natural – one in contrast to social, the other as meaning innate – coincide under the assumption that the social is not innate. When the social sciences separated out as fields of empirical enquiry this coincidence was fixed. All this changes with the development of genetics in the context of evolutionary theory. In this context natural means that which is genetically inherited from one generation to the next; so that we have an innate inheritance. Insofar as what is inherited is social, then the two senses of natural fall apart. Some structure and content of cognition and other mental/behavioural characteristics turns out to be both social and innate. Given that much of our evolution has been in social groups, this applies to the majority rather than to the minority of psychological traits. Genetics also reinforces individual variation. In this new paradigm, the sense of natural as opposed to social collapses: psychological traits are typically influenced by both innate, inherited factors and socialization processes, education and training. In this case the attempt to demarcate medical norms from social norms by construing them as natural as opposed to social also breaks down. It was the right way to go, but not any more. Medical norms are interwoven with social norms, and with personal – and the domain of the medical as opposed to the social has to be characterized in some other way.

So what has happened to the two problem areas identified in the Introduction and re-stated at the start of this chapter? One concerns the demarcation between order and disorder, the other how this difference is defined.

As regards the demarcation between order and disorder, it is somewhat broken down, or at least destabilized. If disorder has order in it – some at least – then it isn't disorder. So what then? One tendency is to jettison the word, and there is much to be said for that, although we have changed words around before and what is going on is after all of just as much interest. It is not new to recognize meaning in disorder – psychoanalysis and other psychological approaches appeared at the same time and in the same context as the view of mental illness as disease- or lesion-caused deficit; albeit that they had to be separated from each other as ideologies for many decades. Psychiatry in practice has known since the start that meaning is – sometimes, to some extent – involved, yet words like disorder and before it illness have been and continue to be used. The implication is that these words are being used primarily to pick out something else, not pure deficit of order. This leads to the great traditional medical focus on suffering of the individual and its treatment.

As regards how the difference between order and disorder is defined, all of the various ways of defining the difference (1) to (8), on the list at the start of this chapter, end up as socially involved, value-involved. The only one that does not lend itself to this interpretation is the one defined as not doing so, according to which normality – mental order – is a matter of being according to our nature; number (6) on the list. On the other hand some views of human nature are known simply to reflect and endorse social arrangements, and most importantly, according to the current science, as above, nature and culture in the domain of the mental and behavioural are not two separable realms – and both are permeated by individual differences. So interpretation (6) also becomes socially involved. After all, then, it turns out that medical norms, at least in psychiatry, cannot be defined as a domain separate from the social. However, whatever may have been the dialectical attraction 50 years ago, the possibility that psychiatry might disappear by transforming itself into an agency of social control, now has not much to be said for it. Many of the considerations in this essay apply to medicine as much as to psychiatry, including some of the ways of interpreting the difference between normality and abnormality listed above. Insofar as this is so, it would turn out to be that physical health and illness were not sharply distinguished, and that the differ-ence was drawn in social terms. However, to put it briefly, no one (much) thinks that medicine is anything other than permanent. Medicine helps us when we are in trouble, and the same goes for psychiatry.

In this line of thought, psychiatry is extended to mental health services, comprising different though overlapping areas of knowledge and skills. These areas are represented traditionally in different disciplines: medical psychiatry, nursing, clinical psychology and psychiatric social work, these last two required fundamentally because of the extension of the problems of interest from physical to mental health.

So what is the proper domain of psychiatry; or rather, of multidisciplinary mental health services? The starting place is the matter of harm: the patient's distress and disability. Harm is agreed by (practically) all to be involved in our concept of mental disorder.

Harm is a matter of distress or disability for the individual involved, but in mental health problems the harm or risk or harm is sometimes to others. Harm to others is clearly a socially grounded matter. Distress is personal, a matter of subjective experience, but the expression of distress is typically socially involved, and is regulated both by personal norms and by social norms, with these interwoven. Disability is also a personal matter, concerning the individual's capacity to act, but capacity to act is a function of environment and task demands, and insofar as these variables are socially set, disability too is a function of social organization and norms.

Medicine, psychiatry and mental health services are best regarded, I suggest, as a mode of response to distress and disability, one that intervenes at a personal not at a social level. For this level of intervention to be appropriate at all the person has to express distress – and they have to see themselves as having a problem, and it has to be agreed to be a problem of personal functioning. People who do not see themselves as distressed, or who do not attribute their distress to anything to do with themselves, but rather see it as other people's fault, do not make good patients. Nor do people who regard a disability they may have as attributable to society. In these kinds of case the mental healthcare response is so far counterindicated. On the other hand mental health services may becomes involved if there is perceived risk to others, to known others in the family, for example, or to the general public, and by this move healthcare becomes muddled up with social control, fundamentally the domain of the state. It was remarked above that it was not viable to suppose that psychiatry might disappear by transforming itself into an agency of social control, but in just this area – social control of the reluctant patient on the grounds of risk to others – there is this risk. Many forensic and community psychiatrists in the UK are concerned that current draft legislation would pressure them into a role in which their primary professional duty of healthcare is blurred too much with statutory social control obligations, creating conflict with fundamental medical ethical principles such as confidentiality, acting in the best interests of the patient, and doing no harm.

This highly problematic area at the boundary of healthcare and social control is best considered quite separately from the clear case in which the psychiatrist or other mental health professional is responding to the expressed distress or disability of the individual seeking help. There are many kinds of response within the broad range of mainstream mental health services, ranging from medical interventions such as pharmacotherapy, though psychotherapeutic and psychosocial interventions, themselves of many kinds. There are other kinds of healthcare response, in mainstream healthcare provision or outside, including many kinds of alternative or complementary medical approaches, counselling, and so forth. Which kind is indicated depends on many kinds of factors, including evidence base, availability, cost, and patient choice, which coincide more or less well.

There are many ways in which the same kinds of problems may be responded to, including responses at the individual level distinct from healthcare, for example, suggestions of or demands for self-reliance. There are also responses not at the individual level, but at the level of family, local community, society and the political. The response of healthcare for the individual differs from all of these, though of course it is not incompatible with them. There is much to be said for and against these various options, some of it ideological, but more interesting are the pragmatic criteria as to what helps and in what respects. These criteria too are embedded in values, priorities and choices. Biomedicine has delivered the goods in the understanding and treatment of many kinds of individual suffering, those now accordingly thought of unambiguously as physical illnesses and diseases. The mental health sciences and services seek to emulate this, and now have effective treatments for many kinds of problem, or increased understanding of at least some of the causes and risks, with a view to treatment and prevention.

The suggestion is that the domain of mental health care may be characterized in terms of the patient's expressed distress and wish for help, combined with the response of seeking to help at the individual level, on the basis of training, science and professional expertise. On the other hand this may appear to be far too weak. Is there not also the essential assumption that there is something wrong? Yes, primarily signified by expression of distress and disability, or risk thereof. But further, is there not the assumption that there is a dysfunction in the individual? Yes, but I would unpack this as the methodological assumption that difference can be made by intervention at the personal level. But methodological assumptions – working assumptions which work more or less well in particular kinds of case – are surely pale items of knowledge compared with facts. Surely the assumption that there is something wrong at the individual level is the assumption of some fact of the matter, and it is this fact that would demarcate the proper domain of mental healthcare, and do it properly, demarcating medical problems from socially defined problems on the one hand, and from normal problems of living on the other, distinguishing once and for all between psychiatry and social control, and from the charge of pathologising normality. This would probably all be better, clearer, and an end to all doubts and debates.

The eruptions in the 1960s signalled the closure of the asylums with all their meanings, and profound discontent with medical psychiatry as it was conceived to be, in its new form half a century old, or in its development within the asylums. In this context trying to define a fixed natural fact that would show the difference between mental illness or disorder and socially defined problems, or normal problems in the community – was surely the right way to go. These were the naturalist definitions of mental disorder, either in statistical or evolutionary theoretic terms. To the extent that they do not work, as argued in this essay at length, there is no point in hanging on to this thought that there is some domain of psychiatry fixed by the distinctive nature of the problems – distinct in particular from socially defined problems and from normal problems of living. In this case, the domain of psychiatry – now readily understood to include a broad range of mental health professions – has to be understood more in terms of distinctive responses to the problems. The problems are distress and disability which the person is having trouble with managing and who therefore seeks professional help, and the responses are those which seek to understand the problems and to help at the individual level. Whether and how these problems are socially or personally defined, whether and in what sense they are normal or not – are other matters to be discussed and researched.

The naturalist definitions of mental disorder seek to authenticate the notion of medical disorder in mental and behavioural functioning, but, significantly, they come into conflict in critical respects with the aims and methodology of the psychiatric diagnostic manuals. This has been consistently pointed out by Wakefield in relation to his evolutionary theoretic definition. If this were to be adopted as the valid definition of mental disorder then the diagnosis of a genuine or real as opposed to a merely apparent mental disorder would involve complex hypotheses about failure of mental or behavioural mechanisms to function as designed in evolution. This, however, is a more or less hopeless fit with the aim of being able to diagnose mental disorders reliably in the clinic or in research, whether this be in epidemiological surveys, basic research into causes, or treatment trials. Since reliability is the essential requirement for communication and for any kind of validity, it has to stay as the priority. So either evolutionary naturalism is wrong, or we infer that what we can reliably characterize may or may not be mental disorders, and we need another name, such as 'mental health problems'.

In fact the psychiatric diagnostic manuals do not adopt naturalist definitions, or have not so far. What they have are definitions of mental disorder which state personal distress and disability or risk thereof as the primary feature, followed by the assumption that there is a personal dysfunction, for example as opposed to social deviance only. The DSM-IV definition gestures towards distinguishing normal from abnormal responses, using the term 'expectable', but this can bear little weight, and falls far short of commitment to naturalist definitions, which would be problematic in many ways.

The primary characteristic of the conditions of interest – the reason why they are of interest – is their association with distress and disability, or with risk of these things, if the problem is not self-limiting and may lead to complications such as accumulating losses. This is what matters, not primarily whether the problems are socially defined, or are normal, in the sense for example of common in the population, or in certain subgroups. Harm-led understanding of mental disorders thus does not distinguish well between them and socially defined problems or normal problems of living. Only naturalism can carve nature at those particular joints – and if it doesn't work, the areas remain muddled up. This has always been a more or less problematic fact in psychiatry, and in medicine. It is not a problem caused by the quest for reliability: the transparency of the diagnostic manuals only puts the problem in a certain light.

Insofar as the conditions described in the psychiatric manuals include problems that are socially defined, or which are – at least in some presentations – apparently normal responses to problems of living, and others which are understandable responses to extraordinary problems of living, then mental disorder is not the optimal general word for them all. The term has a background of contrast with socially defined values and with normality, it seems to want to exclude these things, to mark out mental disorders as really different. A less committal term would be better, one with less old baggage attached, such as 'mental health problems'. This term is already in widespread use. The term mental disorder retains a more specific use in some contexts, for example legal, as does the term mental illness, typically used to signify conditions that are severe and enduring, and qualified accordingly. There are various terminological options for a general cover term, including the current mental disorder, or mental health problems, or some combination of the two.

References

Alarcon, R. D. (1995). Culture and psychiatric diagnosis: impact on DSM-IV and ICD-10. *Psychiatric Clinics of North America*, 18, 449–465.

American Psychiatric Association (1980). *Diagnostic and Statistical Manual of Mental Disorders*, 3rd edn. Washington DC: American Psychiatric Association.

American Psychiatric Association (1994). *Diagnostic and Statistical Manual of Mental Disorders*, 4th edn, Washington DC: American Psychiatric Association.

Andreasen, N. C. and Black, D. W. (eds) (2006). *Introductory Textbook of Psychiatry*, 4th edn. Arlington, VA: American Psychiatric Publishing Inc.

Anthony, W. (1993). Recovery from mental illness: The guiding vision of the mental health service system in the 1990s. *Psychosocial Rehabilitation Journal*, 16, 11–23.

Antony M. M. and Stein M. B. (eds) (2005). *Handbook of Anxiety and Anxiety Disorders*. New York: Oxford University Press.

Ban, T. (2001). Pharmacotherapy of mental illness – a historical analysis. *Progress in Neuro-Psychopharmacology and Biological Psychiatry*, 25, 709–727.

Barkow, J., Cosmides, L. and Tooby, J. (1992). *The Adapted Mind: Evolutionary psychology and the generation of culture*. NY: Oxford University Press.

Baron-Cohen, S., Tager-Flusberg, H. and Cohen, D. (eds) (1993). *Understanding Other Minds: perspectives from autism*. Oxford and New York: Oxford University Press.

Baron-Cohen, S. (ed.) (1997). *The Maladapted Mind. Classic readings in evolutionary psychopathology*. Hove, East Sussex: Psychology Press.

Bauman, Z. (1992). *Intimations of Postmodernity*. London: Routledge.

Bechtel, W. and Stufflebeam, R.S. (2001). Epistemic issues in procuring evidence about the brain: the importance of research instruments and techniques. In W. Bechtel, P. Mandik, J. Mundale and R. Stufflebeam (eds), *Philosophy and the Neurosciences, a reader*, (pp. 55–81). Oxford: Blackwell.

Birley, J. (2002). Political abuse of psychiatry in the Soviet Union and in China: a rough guide for bystanders. *The Journal of the American Academy of Psychiatry and the Law*, 30, 145–147.

Blair, R. (1995). A cognitive developmental approach to morality: investigating the psychopath. *Cognition*, 57, 1–29. Reprinted in S. Baron-Cohen (ed.), *The Maladapted Mind. Classic readings in Evolutionary Psychopathology*, pp. 85–113. Hove, East Sussex: Psychology Press.

Blair, R., Peschardt, K.S., Budhani, S., Mitchell, D.G.V. and Pine, D.S. (2005). The development of psychopathy. *Journal of Child Psychiatry and Psychology*, 47, 262–275.

Bolton, D. (1996). Annotation: developmental issues in obsessive compulsive disorder. *Journal of Child Psychology and Psychiatry*, 37, 131–37.

Bolton, D. (2001). Problems in the definition of mental disorder. *The Philosophical Quarterly*, 51, 182–199.

Bolton, D. (2003). Meaning and causal explanations in the behavioural sciences. In Bill Fulford, Katherine Morris, John Sadler, Giovanni Stanghellini (eds), *Nature and*

Narrative. International Series in Philosophy and Psychiatry volume I, pp. 113–125. Oxford: Oxford University Press.

Bolton D. and Hill J. (2004). *Mind, Meaning, and Mental Disorder: The nature of causal explanation in psychology and psychiatry*, 2nd edn. Oxford: Oxford University Press.

Bolton, D., Rijsdijk, F., O'Connor, T., Perrin, S. and Eley, T. (2007). Obsessive compulsive disorder, tics and anxiety in 6-year-old twins. *Psychological Medicine*, 37, 39–48.

Bonnie, R.J. (2002). Political abuse of psychiatry in the Soviet Union and in China: complexities and controversies. *The Journal of the American Academy of Psychiatry and the Law*, 30, 136–144.

Boorse, C. (1975). On the distinction between disease and illness. *Philosophy and Public Affairs*, 5:49–68. Also in M. Cohen, T. Nagel and T. Scanlon (eds), *Medicine and Moral Philosophy*, pp. 49–68. Princeton, NJ: Princeton University Press, 1981.

Boorse, C. (1976a). What a theory of mental health should be. *Journal of the Theory of Social Behaviour*, 6, 61–84.

Boorse, C. (1976b). Wright on functions. *The Philosophical Review*, 85, 70–86.

Boorse, C. (1977). Health as a theoretical concept. *Philosophy of Science*, 44, 542–573.

Boorse, C. (1987). Concepts of health. In D. Van De Veer and T. Regan (eds), *Health Care Ethics: An introduction*, pp. 359–393. Philadelphia, PA: Temple University Press.

Boorse, C. (1997). A rebuttal on health. In James F. Humber and Robert F. Almeder (eds), *What is Disease?* Biomedical Ethics Reviews, pp. 1–134. Totowa, NJ: Humana Press.

Bowers, L. (1998). *The Social Nature of Mental Illness*. London: Routledge.

Buller, D. J. (2005). *Adapting Minds: Evolutionary psychology and the persistent quest for human nature*. Cambridge, MA: MIT Press.

Buss, D. M. (1999). *Evolutionary Psychology: The new science of the mind*. Boston, MA: Allyn and Bacon.

Campbell, P. (1996). The history of the user movement in the United Kingdom. In T. Heller (ed.), *Mental Health Matters: A reader*, pp. 218–225. London, Macmillan.

Campbell, P. (1999). The service user/survivor movement. In C. Newnes, G. Holmes and C. Dunn *This is Madness: A critical look at psychiatry and the future of mental health services*, pp. 195–209. Ross on Wye: PCCS Books.

Canguilhem, G. (1966). Le normal et le pathologique. Presses Universitaires de France. In part reproduction of doctoral thesis in medicine, 1943; partly written 1963–66. With an Introduction by Michel Foucault. English translation by Carolyn R. Fawcett in collaboration with Robert S. Cohen, *The normal and the pathological*, Zone Books, New York, 1991.

Carpenter, W. T. Jr (1987). Approaches to knowledge and understanding of schizophrenia. In the National Institute of Mental Health's *Special Report: Schizophrenia 1987*. Reprinted in *Schizophrenia Bulletin*, 13 (1), 1987, 1–22.

Caspi, A., Sugden, K., Moffitt, T.E., Taylor, A., Craig, I.W., Harrington, H., McClay, J., Mill, J., Martin, J., Braithwaite, A. and Poulton, R. (2003). Influence of life stress on depression: Moderation by a polymorphism in the 5-HTT gene. *Science*, 301, 386–389.

Chakraborty, A. and Banerji, G. (1975). Ritual, a culture-specific neurosis, and obsessional states in Bengali culture. *Indian Journal of Psychiatry*, 17, 211–216.

Charland, Louis C. (2004). A madness for identity: Psychiatric labels, consumer autonomy, and the perils of the internet. *Philosophy, Psychiatry, and Psychology*, 11, 335–349.

Chen, Z.Y., Jing, D., Bath, K.G., Ieraci, A., Khan, T., Siao, C.J., Herrera, D.G., Toth, M., Yang, C., McEwen, B.S., Hempstead, B.L. and Lee, F.S. (2006). Genetic variant BDNF (Va166Met) polymorphism alters anxiety-related behavior. *Science*, 314: 140–143.

Cheng, A. (2001). Editorial. Case definition and culture: are people all the same? *British Journal of Psychiatry*, 179, 1–3.

Cicchetti, D. and Cohen, D. J. (eds) (2006). *Developmental Psychopathology*, 2nd edn. Volume 1, Theory and Method; Volume 2, Developmental Neuroscience; Volume 3, Risk, Disorder and Adaptation. Hoboken, NJ: Wiley.

Clare, A. (1976). *Psychiatry in Dissent. Controversial issues in thought and practice.* Tavistock: London

Clark, D. M. (1986). A cognitive approach to panic. *Behaviour Research and Therapy*, 24, 461–470.

Clark, D. M., Salkovskis, P. M., Hackmann, A, Wells, A., Ludgate, J. and Gelder, M. (1999). Brief cognitive therapy for panic disorder: a randomized controlled trial. *Journal of Consulting and Clinical Psychology*, 67, 583–589.

Cosmides, L and Tooby, J. (1999). Toward an evolutionary taxonomy of treatable conditions. *Journal of Abnormal Psychology*, 108, 453–464.

Coulter, J. (1973). Approaches to insanity. A philosophical and sociological study. London: Martin Robinson and Co.

Crow, T. (1997). Is schizophrenia the price that Homo sapiens pays for language? *Schizophrenia Research*, 28, 127–141.

Cutting, J. and Charlish, A. (1995). *Schizophrenia: understanding and coping with the illness.* London: Thorsons.

Davis, P. and Bradley, J. (1996). The meaning of normal. *Perspectives in Biology and Medicine*, 40, 68–77.

Dennett, D. (1979). *Brainstorms: philosophical essays on mind and psychology.* Sussex: Harvester.

Dennett, D. (1987). *The Intentional Stance.* Cambridge, MA: MIT Press.

Dennett, D. (1988). Précis of *The intentional stance*, with peer commentary. *The Behavioral and Brain Sciences*, 11, 495–546.

Department of Health (2004). Draft Mental Health Bill http://www.dh.gov.uk/en/Publicationsandstatistics/Publications/PublicationsLegislation/DH_4088910. Accessed 17 May 2007.

DeVito, S. (2000). On the value-neutrality of the concepts of health and disease: unto the breach again. *Journal of Medicine and Philosophy*, 25, 539–567.

Disability Awareness in Action (2007). Social model or unsociable muddle? http://www.daa.org.uk/social_model.html Accessed 18 June 2007.

Dobson, R. (1998). Are schizophrenics the lepers of our time? *Independent Review*, 21 July, p. 11.

Domino, E.F. (1999). History of modern psychopharmacology: A personal view with an emphasis on antidepressants. *Psychosomatic Medicine*, 61, 591–598.

Durkheim, E. (1895/1962). *The Rules of the Sociological Method.* Glencoe, IL: Free Press.

Ehlers, A. and Clark, D. (2000). A cognitive model of posttraumatic stress disorder. *Behavior research and Therapy*, 38, 319–345.

Engel, G.L. (1977). The need for a new medical model: a challenge for biomedicine. *Science*, 196, 129–136.

Englehart, H. (1974). The disease of masturbation: values and the concept of disease. *Bulletin of the History of Medicine*, 48, 234–248.

Feinberg, J. (1984). *The Moral Limits of the Criminal Law. Vol. 1, Harm to others*. New York and Oxford: Oxford University Press.

Feinberg, J. (1989). *The Moral Limits of the Criminal Law. Vol. 3, Harm to self*. New York and Oxford: Oxford University Press.

Fergusson, D. M., Horwood, L. and Lynskey, M. T. (1996). Childhood sexual abuse and psychiatric disorder in young adulthood: II. Psychiatric outcomes of childhood sexual abuse. *Journal of the American Academy of Child and Adolescent Psychiatry*, 35, 1365–1374.

First, M.B. (2005). *Dimensional Approaches in Diagnostic Classification: A critical appraisal*. http://dsm5.org/conference13.cfm. Accessed 8 June 2007.

Fisher, A. H., Manstead A. R. and Rodriguez Mosquera, P. (1999). The role of honor-related versus individualistic values in conceptualizing pride, shame and anger: Spanish and Dutch cultural prototypes. *Cognition and Emotion*, 13, 149–179.

Fodor, J. (1999). Let your brain alone. *London Review of Books*, 21 (19), 30 September.

Follette, W.C. (1996). Introduction to the special section on the development of theoretically coherent alternatives to the DSM system. *Journal of Consulting and Clinical Psychology*, 64, 1117–1119.

Follette, W. C. and Houts, A. C. (1996). Models of scientific progress and the role of theory in taxonomy development: a case study of the DSM. *Journal of Consulting and Clinical Psychology*, 64, 1120–1132.

Foucault, M. (1965). *Madness and civilisation: a history of insanity in the Age of Reason*. Trans. by R. Howard of abridged version of *Folie et déraison. Histoire de la folie à l'âge classique*. (Paris: Librairie Plon, 1961). London: Tavistock. Reprinted Routledge 1997. Page references are to this volume.

Foucault, M. (1966). Introduction to Canguilhem, G. *Le normal et le pathologique*. Presses Universitaires de France. English translation by Carolyn R. Fawcett in collaboration with Robert S. Cohen, *The Normal and the Pathological*. New York: Zone Books. Page references are to this volume.

Foucault, M. (2006). *History of Madness*. English translation of *Histoire de la folie à l'âge classique*, Paris: Gallimard, 1972. London: Routledge.

Frances, A. (1998). Problems in defining clinical significance in epidemiological studies. *Archives of General Psychiatry*, 58, 119.

Fulford, K. W.M. (2001). 'What is (mental) disease?' an open letter to Christopher Boorse. *Journal of Medical Ethics*, 27, 80–85.

Garety, P., Kuipers, E., Fowler, D., Freeman, D. and Bebbington, P. (2001). A cognitive model of schizophrenia. *Psychological Medicine*, 31, 189–195.

Garfinkel, H. (1967). *Studies in Ethnomethodology*. Englewood Cliffs, NJ: Prentice-Hall.

Gelder, M., Lopez-Ibor, J. and Andreasen, N. (eds) (2003). *New Oxford Textbook of Psychiatry*. Oxford: Oxford University Press.

Gert, B. and Culver, C.M. (2003). Defining mental disorder. *In The Philosophy of Psychiatry: a companion* (ed. J. Radden). New York, Oxford University Press, 415–425.

Ghaemi, S. (1999). Depression: insight, illusion and psychopharmacological Calvinism. *Philosophy, Psychiatry and Psychology*, 6, 287–294.

Goffman, E. (1961). *Asylums. Essays on the social situation of mental patients and other inmates*. Harmondsworth: Penguin

Gould, S. J. (1991). Exaptation: a crucial tool for evolutionary analysis. *Journal of Social Issues*, 47, 43–65.

Gould, S. J. (1997). Evolution: The pleasures of pluralism. *New York Review of Books*, 44 (11), 47–52.

Greenberg, D. (1984). Are religious compulsions religious or compulsive? A phenomenological study. *American Journal of Psychotherapy*, 38, 524–532.

Griffiths, P. E. (1997). *What Emotions Really Are: The problem of psychological categories*. Chicago, IL: University of Chicago Press.

Guardian, The (1999). It is wrong to rush in. 17 November, p. 192.

Guardian, The (2007). Coming soon: the shopping channel run by drug firms. 21 May.

Guze, S.B. (1992). *Why Psychiatry is a Branch of Medicine*. New York: Oxford University Press.

Habermas, J. (1985). *The Philosophical Discourse of Modernity*. Trans. F. Lawrence. Cambridge, MA: MIT Press.

Hacking, I. (1999). *The Social Construction of What?* Cambridge, MA: Harvard University Press.

Hall, C. (1999) Mentally ill pose less threat than addicts. *Daily Telegraph*, Wednesday 6 January, p. 4.

Hansard (2000). Proceedings in the Commons Chamber. http://www.publications.parliament.uk/pa/cm/cmhansrd.htm#volume. Accessed 17 May 2007.

Happé, F., Ronald, A. and Plomin, R. (2006). Time to give up on a single explanation for autism. *Nature Neuroscience*, 9, 1218–1220.

Harrington, A. (1997). *The Placebo Effect. An interdisciplinary exploration*. Cambridge, MA: Harvard University Press.

Hare, R. M. (1986). Health. *Journal of Medical Ethics*, 12, 174–181.

Healy, D. (2002). *The Creation of Psychopharmacology*. Cambridge, MA: Harvard University Press.

Helzer, J. E. and Hudziak, J.J. (eds) (2002). *Defining Psychopathology in the 21st Century: DSM-V and beyond*. Washington, DC: American Psychiatric Publishing.

Hempel C. G. (1965). Fundamentals of taxonomy. In *Aspects of scientific explanation. And other essays in the philosophy of science*, 137–154. New York: Free Press.

Hersen, M. and Bellack, A. (eds) (1998). *Comprehensive Clinical Psychology*, 11 Vols. San Fransisco, CA: Pergamon.

Hill, E. L. and Frith, U. (2003). Understanding autism: insights from mind and brain. *Philosophical Transactions of the Royal Society Series B*, 358, 281–289.

Hill, J. (2002). Biological, psychological and social processes in the conduct disorders. *Journal of Child Psychology and Psychiatry*, 43, 133–164.

Hill, J., Pickles, A., Burnside, E., Byatt, M., Rollinson, L., Davis, R. and Harvey, K. (2001). Child sexual abuse, poor parental care and adult depression: evidence for different mechanisms. *British Journal of Psychiatry*, 179, 104–109.

Hollander, E., Kim, S., Khanna, S. and Pallanti, S. (2007). OCD and OC spectrum disorders: diagnostic and dimensional issues. *CNS Spectrums*, 12, 5–13.

Honey, G.D., Fletcher, P.C. and Bullmore, E.T. (2002). Functional brain mapping of psychopathology. *Journal of Neurology, Neurosurgery and Psychiatry*, 72, 432–439.

Horwitz, A. V. (2002). *Creating Mental Illness*. Chicago, IL and London: University of Chicago Press.

Horwitz, Allan V. and Wakefield, Jerome C. (2007). *The Loss of Sadness: How psychiatry transformed normal sorrow into depressive disorder*. New York: Oxford University Press.

Houts, A. C. (2001a). The DSM's new white coat and circularity of plausible dysfunctions: response to Wakefield, Part 1. *Behaviour Research and Therapy*, 39, 315–345.

Houts, A. C. (2001b). Harmful dysfunction and the search for value neutrality on the definition of mental disorder: response to Wakefield, Part 2. *Behaviour Research and Therapy*, 39, 1099–1132.

Houts, W.C. and Follette, A.C. (1998). Mentalism, mechanisms and medical analogues: reply to Wakefield (1998). *Journal of Consulting and Clinical Psychology*, 66, 853–855.

Human Rights Watch (2003). *UN Rights Body Admits Abusive Members*. http://hrw.org/english/docs/2001/05/03/sudan135.htm. Accessed 17 May 2007.

Ingleby, D. (1982). The social construction of mental illness. In P. Wright and A. Treacher (eds), *The Problem of Medical Knowledge: Examining the social construction of medicine*, pp. 123–142. Edinburgh: Edinburgh University Press.

Jacobson, N. and Greenley, D. (2001). What is recovery? A conceptual model and explication. *Psychiatric Services*, 52, 482–485.

Jaffee, S. R., Caspi, A., Moffitt, T. E., Dodge, K. A., Rutter, M., Taylor, A. and Tully, L. A. (2005). Nature X Nurture: Genetic vulnerabilities interact with physical maltreatment to promote conduct problems. *Development and Psychopathology*, 7, 67–84.

Jaspers, K. (1913). *Allgemeine pychopathologie*, Berlin: Springer Verlag; 3rd enlarged and revised edn, 1923. English translation of the 7th edn by J. Hoenig and Marian W. Hamilton, *General Psychopathology*, Manchester: Manchester University Press, 1963; Chicago, IL: Chicago University Press, 1963. Page reference of motto quotation is to the fifth edition, 1948, with translation from the German by the present author, the quotation is on page 780 of the English edition.

Jensen, P.S., Hoagwood, K. and Zitner L. (2006). What's in a name? Problems versus prospects in current diagnostic approaches. In Cicchetti, D. and Cohen, D. J. (eds) *Developmental Psychopathology*, Volume 1, Theory and Method, 2nd edn, pp. 24–40. Hoboken, NJ: Wiley.

Kant, I. (1798). Do sciences of the normal and the pathological exist? Introduction to the problem. In H. H. Rudnick (ed.), trans. V. L. Dowdell, *Anthropology from a pragmatic point of view*. Carbondale, IL: Southern Illinois University Press, 1996. Page references are to this volume.

Kendell R. E. (1975). The concept of disease and its implications for psychiatry. *British Journal of Psychiatry*, 127, 305–15.

Kendell, R. E. (1986). What are mental disorders? In A. M. Freedman, R. Brotman, I. Silverman and D. Hutson (eds), *Issues in Psychiatric Classification: science, practice, and social policy*, pp. 23–45. New York: Human Sciences Press.

Kendler, K. (2005). Toward a philosophical structure for psychiatry. *American Journal of Psychiatry*, 162, 433–440.

Kendler, K.S., Gardner, C.O. and Prescott, C.A. (2002). Toward a comprehensive developmental model of major depression in women. *American Journal of Psychiatry*, 159, 1133–1145.

Kent County Council (2006). *Report of the independent inquiry into the care and treatment of Michael Stone*. http://www.kent.gov.uk/publications/council-and-democracy/michael-stone.htm. Accessed 17 May 2007.

Kessler, R.C., McGonagle, K.A., Zhao, S., Nelson, C.B., Hughes, M., Eshleman S., Wittchen, H.-U. and Kendler, K.S. (1994). Lifetime and 12-month prevalence of DSM-III-R psychiatric disorders in the United States: results from the National Comorbidity Survey. *Archives of General Psychiatry*, 51, 8–19.

Kim-Cohen, J., Caspi, A., Taylor, A., Williams, B., Newcombe, R., Craig, I. W. and Moffitt, T. E. (2006). MAOA, early adversity, and gene-environment interaction predicting children's mental health: New evidence and a meta-analysis. *Molecular Psychiatry*, 11, 903–913.

Kirk, S. A. and Hseih, D.K. (2004). Diagnostic consistency in assessing conduct disorder: an experiment on the effect of social context. *American Journal of Orthopsychiatry*, 74, 43–55.

Kirk, S. A., Wakefield, J., Hseih, D. and Pottick, K. (1999). Social context and social workers' judgement of mental disorder. *Social Service Review*, 73, 82–104.

Kirmayer, L.J. (1994). Rejoinder to Professor Wakefield. Debate on 'Is the concept of mental disorder culturally relative?', with J. C. Wakefield. In S.A. Kirk and S.D. Einbinder (eds), *Controversial Issues in Mental Health*, pp. 17–20. Boston, MA and London: Allyn and Bacon.

Klein, D.F. (1978). A proposed definition of mental illness. In R.L. Spitzer and D.F. Klein (eds), *Critical Issues in Psychiatric Diagnosis*, pp. 41–71. New York: Raven Press.

Kleinman, A. M. (1977). Depression, somatization and the 'new cross-cultural psychiatry'. *Social Science and Medicine*, 11, 3–10.

Kleinman, A. M. (1987). Anthropology and psychiatry: the role of culture in cross-cultural research on illness. *British Journal of Psychiatry*, 151, 447–454.

Kleinman, A. M. (1988). *Rethinking Psychiatry: From cultural category to personal experience*. New York: Free Press.

Kleinman, A. M. (1990). Letter. [On 'The new cross-cultural psychiatry']. *British Journal of Psychiatry*, 156, 295–296.

Kovac, C. (2001). News. Drug company breaks 30 year agreement on patient advertising. *British Medical Journal*, 323, 470.

Kovacs, J. (1998). The concept of health and disease. *Medicine, Health Care and Philosophy*, 1, 31–39.

Kupfer D. J., First, M. B., Regier D. A. (eds). (2002). *A Research Agenda for DSM-V*, Washington, DC: American Psychiatric Association.

Kutchins, H. and Kirk, S.A. (1997). *Making us Crazy. DSM – the psychiatric bible and the creation of mental disorders*. New York: Free Press.

Laing, R. D. (1960). *The Divided Self*. Harmondsworth: Penguin.

Leckman, J.F. and Mayes, L.C. (1998). Understanding developmental psychopathology: how useful are evolutionary accounts? *Journal of the American Academy of Child and Adolescent Psychiatry*, 37, 1011–1021.

Leff, J. (1988). *Psychiatry Around the Globe*, 2nd edn. London: Gaskell.

Leff, J. (1990). Editorial. The 'new cross-cultural psychiatry': a case of the baby and the bathwater. *British Journal of Psychiatry*, 156, 305–307.

Lehmann, H.E. and Ban, T.A. (1997). The history of the psychopharmacology of schizophrenia. *Canadian Journal Psychiatry*, 42, 152–163.

Lepping, P. (2007). Ethical analysis of the changes proposed to mental health legislation in England and Wales. *Philosophy, Ethics, and Humanities in Medicine*, 2, 5. http://www.peh-med.com/content/2/1/5. Accessed 17 May 2006.

Lewis, A. (1953). Health as a social concept. *British Journal of Sociology*, 2, 109–124.

Lilienfield S. O. and Marino L. (1995). Mental disorder as a Roschian concept: a critique of Wakefield's 'harmful dysfunction' analysis. *Journal of Abnormal Psychology*, 104, 411–420.

Littlewood, R. (1980). Anthropology and psychiatry: an alternative approach. *British Journal of Medical Psychology*, 53, 213–224.

Littlewood, R. (1985). Social anthropology in relation to psychiatry. *British Journal of Psychiatry*, 146, 552–554.

Littlewood, R. (1990). From categories to context: a decade of the new 'cross-cultural psychiatry'. *British Journal of Psychiatry*, 156, 308–327.

Littlewood, R. (2001). Letter [Case definition and culture]. *British Journal of Psychiatry*, 179, 460.

London School of Economics (2006). *The Depression Report. A New Deal for Depression and Anxiety Disorders*. http://cep.lse.ac.uk/textonly/research/mentalhealth/ DEPRESSION_REPORT_LAYARD.pdf. Accessed 17 May 2007.

Mahgoub, O. M. and Abdel-Hafeiz, H. B. (1991). Patterns of obsessive-compulsive disorder in Eastern Saudi-Arabia. *British Journal of Psychiatry*, 158, 840–842.

Maj, M., Gaebel W., Lopez-Ibor J. J. and Sartorius N. (eds) (2002). *Psychiatric Diagnosis and Classification*. Chichester: Wiley.

Mallon, R. and Stich, S. (2000). The odd couple: the compatibility of social construction and evolutionary psychology. *Philosophy of Science*, 67, 133–154.

Manson, S. M. (1995). Culture and major depression: current challenges in the diagnosis of mood disorders. *Psychiatric Clinics of North America*, 18, 487–501.

Marks, I. and Nesse, R. (1994). Fear and fitness: an evolutionary analysis of anxiety disorders. *Ethology and Sociobiology*, 15, 247–261. Reprinted in S. Baron-Cohen (ed.), *The Maladapted Mind. Classic readings in evolutionary psychopathology*, pp. 57–72. Hove, East Sussex: Psychology Press, 1997.

Marsella, A. J. and White, G. M. (eds) (1982). *Cultural Conceptions of Mental Health and Therapy*. Reidel: Dordrecht and Boston.

McGuire, M., Marks, I., Nesse, R. and Troisi, A. (1992). Evolutionary biology: a basic science for psychiatry. *Acta Psychiatrica Scandinavica*, 86, 89–96. Reprinted in S. Baron-Cohen (ed.), *The Maladapted Mind. Classic readings in evolutionary psychopathology*, pp. 23–37. Hove, East Sussex: Psychology Press, 1997.

Medical Research Council (UK) (2001). *MRC Review of Autism Research: epidemiology and causes*. http://www.mrc.ac.uk/Utilities/Documentrecord/index.htm?d=MRC002394. Accessed 7 June 2007.

Mealey, L. (1995). The sociobiology of sociopathy: an integrated evolutionary model. *Behavioral and Brain Sciences*, 18, 523–541. Reprinted in S. Baron-Cohen (ed.), *The Maladapted Mind. Classic readings in evolutionary psychopathology*, pp. 133–188. Hove, East Sussex: Psychology Press, 1997.

Mind in Manchester (2007). *Community Scare.* http://www.mind-in-manchester.org.uk/campaigning/comscare/community_scare_demythologizing_dangerousness.php. Accessed 4 April 2007.

Moncrieff, J. and Kirsch, I. (2005). The efficacy of antidepressants in adults. *BMJ*, 331,155–157.

Morgan, D. (1975). Explaining mental illness. *Archives européennes de Sociologie*, 16, 262–280.

Munro, R. (2000). Judicial psychiatry in China and its political abuses. *Columbia Journal of Asian Law*, 14, 1–128.

Murphy, D. (2006). *Psychiatry in the Scientific Image.* Cambridge, MA: MIT Press.

Murphy, J.M., Laird, N.M., Monson, M.D., Sobol, A.M. and Leighton, A.H. (2000). A 40-year perspective on the prevalence of depression. The Stirling County Study. *Archives of General Psychiatry*, 57, 209–215.

Murray, R. (1994). Neurodevelopmental schizophrenia: the rediscovery of dementia praecox. *British Journal of Psychiatry* 165, 6–12.

Nesse, R. (1987). An evolutionary perspective on panic disorder and agoraphobia. *Ethology and Sociobiology*, 8, 73–83. Reprinted in S. Baron-Cohen (ed.), *The Maladapted Mind. Classic readings in evolutionary psychopathology*, pp. 73–83. Hove, East Sussex: Psychology Press, 1997.

Nesse, R. and Williams, G. (1997). Are mental disorders diseases? In S. Baron-Cohen (ed.), *The Maladapted Mind: Classic readings in evolutionary psychopathology*, pp. 1–22. Hove, East Sussex: Psychology Press.

NICE (2001). *Schizophrenia: Core interventions in the treatment of schizophrenia in primary and secondary care.* National Clinical Practice Guideline Number 1. Developed by National Collaborating Centre for Mental Health, commissioned by the National Institute for Clinical Excellence. http://guidance.nice.org.uk/CG1/guidance/pdf/English. Accessed 8 June 2007.

NICE (2005). *Obsessive-compulsive Disorder: Core interventions in the treatment of obsessive-compulsive disorder and body dysmorphic disorder.* National Clinical Practice Guideline Number 31. Developed by National Collaborating Centre for Mental Health, commissioned by the National Institute for Clinical Excellence. http://guidance.nice.org.uk/CG31/?c=91523. Accessed 8 June 2007.

NICE (2007). *Depression: Management of depression in primary and secondary care. National Clinical Practice Guideline Number 23.* Developed by the National Collaborating Centre for Mental Health, commissioned by the National Institute for Clinical Excellence. http://guidance.nice.org.uk/CG23/guidance/pdf/English. Accessed 8 June 2007.

O'Brian, J. (1992). Closing the asylums: where do all the former long-stay patients go? *Health Trends*, 24, 88–90.

O'Keane, V (2000). Evolving model of depression as an expression of multiple interacting risk factors. *British Journal of Psychiatry*, 177, 482–483.

Oxfam (2005). *Spoiler countries hold UN hostage.* http://oxfam.org.nz/news.asp?aid=518. Accessed 17 May 2007.

Oxford University Press (2007). Advance notice of *The Loss of Sadness: How psychiatry transformed normal sorrow into depressive disorder*, by Allan Horwitz and Jerome C. Wakefield. http://www.oup.com/us/catalog/general/subject/Medicine/PsychiatryPsychology/~~/dmlldz11c2EmY2k9OTc4MDE5NTMxMzA0OA==. Accessed 17 May 2007.

Peters, E., Joseph, S.A. and Garety, P. (1999). Measurement of delusional ideation in the normal population: introducing the PDI. *Schizophrenia Bulletin*, 25, 553–576.

Pfeiffer, W. M. (1981). Culture-bound syndromes. In I. Al-Issa (ed.), *Culture and Psychopathology*, pp. 201–218. Baltimore, MD: University Park Press.

Phillips, K. A., First, M. B. and Pincus H. A. (eds) (2003). *Advancing DSM: Dilemmas in psychiatric diagnosis*. Washington, DC: American Psychiatric Association.

Pierce, C. S. (1903). Abduction and induction. In J. Buchler (ed.), *Philosophical Writings of Pierce*, pp. 150–156. New York: Dover Publications, 1956.

Plato (1930). *The Republic*, two volumes. English translation by Paul Shorey. Cambridge, MA and London: Loeb Classical Library.

Plomin, R., DeFries, J.C., McClearn, G. and McGuffin, P. (2001). *Behavioral Genetics*, 4th edn. New York: Worth Publishers.

Plotkin, H. (1998). *Evolution in Mind: An introduction to evolutionary psychology*. Cambridge, MA: Harvard University Press.

Porter, R. (1987). *Mind Forg'd Manacles: Madness and psychiatry in England from Restoration to Regency*. Athlone Press, London.

Porter, R. (ed.) (1996). *The Cambridge Illustrated History of Medicine*. Cambridge: Cambridge University Press.

Powell, G.E. and Lindsey, S.E. (2005). *The Handbook of Clinical Adult Psychology*, 3rd edn. Routledge, London.

Price, J., Sloman, L., Gardner, R. Gilbert, P. and Rohde, P. (1994). The social competition hypothesis of depression. *British Journal of Psychiatry*, 164, 309–315. Reprinted in S. Baron-Cohen (ed.), *The Maladapted Mind. Classic readings in evolutionary psychopathology*, pp. 241–253. Hove, East Sussex: Psychology Press, 1997.

Prins, H. (1990). Mental abnormality and criminality: an uncertain relationship. *Medicine, Science and Law*, 30, 247–258.

Read, J., Van Os, J., Morrison, A. P. and Ross, C. A. (2005). Childhood trauma, psychosis and schizophrenia: A literature review with theoretical and clinical implications. *Acta Psychiatrica Scandinavica*, 112, 330–350.

Regier, D.A., Kaebler, C.T., Rae, D.S., Farmer, M.E., Knauper, B., Kessler, R.C. and Norquist, G.S. (1998). Limitations of diagnostic criteria and assessment instruments for mental disorders. *Archives of General Psychiatry*, 55, 109–115.

Rego, M. (2005). What are (and what are not) the existential implications of antidepressant use? *Philosophy, Psychiatry and Psychology*, 12, 119–128.

Reznek, L. (1991). *The Philosophical Defence of Psychiatry*. London: Routledge.

Richters, J. E. and Hinshaw, S. P. (1999). The abduction of disorder in psychiatry. *Journal of Abnormal Psychology*, 108, 438–445.

Robins, L. N. and Regier, D. A. (eds) (1991). *Psychiatric Disorders in America: The Epidemiological Catchment Area Study*. New York: Free Press.

Rogers, A. and Pilgrim, D. (2001). *Mental Health Policy in Britain*, 2nd edn. Hampshire: Palgrave.

Rogler, L.H. (1993). Culturally sensitizing psychiatric diagnosis. A framework for research. *Journal of Nervous and Mental Diseases*, 181, 401–408.

Romme, M. A. and Esher, S. (1989). Hearing voices. *Schizophrenia Bulletin*, 15, 209–216.

Romme, M. A., Honig, A., Noorthoorn, E. O. and Escher, A. D. (1992). Coping with hearing voices: An emancipatory approach. *British Journal of Psychiatry,* 161, 99–103.

Rosenhan, R. (1973). On being sane in insane places. *Science,* 179, 251–258.

Roth, M. and Kroll, J. (1986). *The Reality of Mental Illness.* Cambridge: Cambridge University Press.

Rushdie, S. (1989). *The Satanic Verses.* New York: Viking Books. Reprinted Vintage, Random House: London, 1998. Page references are to this volume.

Rutter, M. and Taylor, E. (eds) 2005). *Child and Adolescent Psychiatry,* 4th edn. Oxford: Blackwell.

Rutter, M., Moffit, T.E. and Caspi, A. (2005). Gene-environment interplay and psychopathology: multiple varieties but real effects. *Journal of Child Psychiatry and Psychology,* 47, 226–261.

Sadler, J. (2004a). *Values and Diagnosis.* Oxford: Oxford University Press.

Sadler, J. (2004b). A madness for the philosophy of psychiatry. *Philosophy, Psychiatry, and Psychology,* 11, 357–359.

Sainsbury Centre for Mental Health (2002). Breaking the circles of fear: a review of the relationship between mental health services and African and Caribbean communities. London: Sainsbury Centre for Mental Health. Executive Briefing. http://www.scmh.org.uk/80256FBD004F3555/vWeb/flKHAL6FAFAU/$file/briefing+17.pdf. Accessed 17 May 2007.

Sagvolden, T., Russell, V.A., Aase, H., Johansen, E.B.and Farshbaf, M. (2005). Rodent models of attention-deficit/hyperactivity disorder. *Biological Psychiatry,* 57, 1239–1247.

Saravanan, B., Jacob, K.S., Prince, M., Bhugra, D. and David, A. (2004). Editorial. Culture and insight revisited. *British Journal of Psychiatry,* 184, 107–109.

Sartorius, N. (1976). Classification: an international perspective. *Psychiatric Annals,* 6, 22–35.

Sartorius, N., Üstün, T.B., Korten, A., Cooper, J.E. and van Drimmelen, J. (1995). Progress towards achieving a common language in psychiatry, II. Results from the international field trials of the ICD-10 diagnostic criteria for research for mental and behavioural disorders. *American Journal of Psychiatry,* 152, 1427–1437.

Scadding, J. G. (1967). Diagnosis: the clinician and the computer. *Lancet,* ii, 877–882.

Scheff, T.J. (1966). *Being Mentally Ill: A sociological theory,* 3rd edn. New York: Aldine de Gruyter, 1999.

Scheff, T.J. (2005). New foreword for re-issue of *Being mentally ill,* 2005. Available at http://www.soc.ucsb.edu/faculty/scheff/45.html. Accessed 17 February 2007.

Scheurich, N. (2006). The prescriber as moralist. Values in the antidepressant debate. Perspectives in Biology and Medicine, 49, 199–208.

Schroedinger, E. (1967). *What is life?* and *Mind and Matter.* Cambridge: Cambridge University Press.

Self Direction Community Project (2000–2001). *The Medical and Social Model of Disability.* http://www.selfdirection.org/dat/training/course01/leve12/04.html?cmd=sessionands=0290991721299605__guest__213218228211. Accessed 18 June 2007.

Sharma, B. P. (1968). Obsessive-compulsive neurosis in Nepal. *Transcultural Research Review,* 5, 38–41.

Silvers, A. (1998). A fatal attraction to normalising: treating disabilities as deviations from 'species-typical' functioning. In Erik Parens (ed.), *Enhancing Human Traits: Ethical and social implications*, pp. 95–123. Washington, DC: Georgetown University Press.

Smith, T. (1996). *No Asylum: State psychiatric repression in the former USSR*. New York, New York University Press.

Spitzer, R. (2001). Values and assumptions in the development of DSM-III and DSM-III-R: an insider's persepctive and a belated response to Sadler, Hulgus, and Agich's 'On values in recent American psychiatric classification'. *Journal of Nervous and Mental Disease*, 189, 351–359.

Spitzer, R.L. (1976). On pseudoscience in science, logic in remission, and psychiatric diagnosis: A critique of Rosenhan's 'On being sane in insane places'. *Journal of Abnormal Psychology*, 84, 442–452.

Spitzer, R. L. and Endicott, I. (1978). Medical and mental disorder: proposed deflnition and criteria. In R. L. Spitzer and D. F. Klein (eds), *Critical Issues in Psychiatric Diagnosis*, pp. 15–40. New York: Raven Press.

Spitzer, R.L. and Wakefield, J. (1999). DSM-IV diagnostic criterion for clinical significance: does it help solve the false positives problem? *American Journal of Psychiatry*, 156, 1856–1864.

Spitzer, R.L. and Williams, J. B. (1982). The definition and diagnosis of mental disorder. In W.R. Grove (ed.), *Deviance and Mental Illness*, pp. 15–31. Beverly Hills, CA: Sage.

Spitzer, R. L. and Williams, J. B. (1988). Basic principles in the development of DSM-III. In J. E. Mezzich and M. von Cranach (eds), *International Classification in Psychiatry: Unity and diversity*, pp. 81–86 Cambridge, Cambridge University Press.

Stein, D. (2008). *Smart Pills, Happy Pills, Pepp Pills. The philosophy of psychopharmacology*. Cambridge, Cambridge University Press.

Stein, N.L. and Oatley, K. (eds) (1992). Basic Emotions. A special issue of *Cognition and Emotion*. Hove, UK: Lawrence Erlbaum Associates.

Stempsey, W. E. (2000). A pathological view of disease. *Theoretical Medicine*, 21, 321–330.

Stengel, E. (1959). Classification of mental disorders. *Bulletin of the World Health Organization*, 21, 601–663.

Suess, L. and Halpern, M. S. (1989). Obsessive-compulsive disorder: a religious perspective. In J. L. Rapoport (ed.), *Obsessive-Compulsive Disorder in Children and Adolescents*, pp. 311–325. Washington, DC: American Psychiatric Press Inc.

Summerfield, D. (2001). Letter [Case definition and culture]. *British Journal of Psychiatry*, 179, 460.

Szasz, T. (1961). *The Myth of Mental Illness: Foundations of a theory of personal conduct*. Harper and Row: New York.

Szmukler, G. (2000). Homicide enquiries: what sense do they make? *Psychiatric Bulletin*, 24, 6–10.

Taylor, P. and Gunn, J. (1999). Homicides by people with mental illness: myth and reality. *British Journal of Psychiatry*, 174, 9–14.

Thornicroft, G. (2006). *Shunned: Discrimination against people with mental illness*. Oxford: Oxford University Press.

Thornicroft, G. and Szmukler, G. (2005). The Draft Mental Health Bill in England: without principles. *Psychiatric Bulletin*, 29, 244–247.

Timimi, S. and Taylor, E. (2004). In debate: ADHD is best understood as a cultural construct. *British Journal of Psychiatry*, 18, 8–9.

Tooby, J. and Cosmides, L. (1992). The psychological foundations of culture. In J. Barkow, L. Cosmides and J. Tooby *The Adapted Mind. Evolutionary psychology and the generation of culture*, pp. 19–136. New York: Oxford University Press.

UN (2007). Human Rights website. http://www.un.org/rights/. Accessed 17 May 2007.

Van der Kolk, B. A. (1996). The body keeps score: memory and the evolving psychobiology of posttraumatic stress. *Harvard Review of Psychiatry*, 1, 253–265.

Wakefield, J. C. (1992a). Disorder as a harmful dysfunction: a conceptual critique of *DSM-III-R*'s definition of mental disorder. *Psychological Review*, 99, 232–247.

Wakefield, J. C. (1992b). The concept of mental disorder: on the boundary between biological facts and social values. *American Psychologist*, 47, 373–388.

Wakefield, J. C. (1993). Limits of operationalization: a critique of Spitzer and Endicott's (1978) proposed operational criteria for mental disorder. *Journal of Abnormal Psychology*, 102, 160–172.

Wakefield, J.C. (1998). The DSM's theory-neutral nosology is scientifically progressive: response to Follette and Houts (1996). *Journal of Consulting and Clinical Psychology*, 66, 846–852.

Wakefield, J. C. (1999a). Philosophy of science and the progressiveness of the DSM's theory-neutral nosology: response to Follette and Houts, Part 1. *Behaviour Research and Therapy*, 37, 963–999.

Wakefield, J.C. (1999b). The concept of disorder as a foundation for the DSM's theory-neutral nosology: response to Follette and Houts, Part 2. *Behaviour Research and Therapy*, 37, 1001–1027.

Wakefield, J. C. (1999c). Evolutionary versus prototype analyses of the concept of disorder. *Journal of Abnormal Psychology*, 108: 374–399.

Wakefield, J. C. (1999d). Mental disorder as a black box essentialist concept. *Journal of Abnormal Psychology*, 108, 465–472.

Wakefield, J. C. (2000). Spandrels, vestigial organs, and such: reply to Murphy and Woolfolk's 'The harmful dysfunction analysis of mental disorder.' *Philosophy, Psychiatry, and Psychology*, 7, 253–269.

Wakefield, J. C. (2002). Values and the validity of diagnostic criteria: disvalued versus disordered conditions of childhood and adolescence. In J. Z. Sadler (ed.), *Descriptions and Prescriptions: Values, mental disorders and the DSMs*, pp. 148–164. Baltimore, MD: The Johns Hopkins University Press.

Wakefield, J. C. (2003). Dysfunction as a factual component of disorder: Reply to Houts, Part 2. *Behavior Research and Therapy*, 41 (8), 969–990.

Wakefield, J.C., Pottick, K.J. and Kirk, S. A. (2002). Should the DSM-IV diagnostic criteria for conduct disorder consider social context? *American Journal of Psychiatry*, 159, 380–386.

Watson, P.J. and Andrews, P.W. (2002). Towards a revised evolutionary adaptationist analysis of depression: the social navigation hypothesis. *Journal of Affective Disorders*, 72, 1–14.

Weingart, P., Richerson, P., Mitchell, S. and Maasen, S. (eds) (1997). *Human by Nature: Between biology and the social sciences.* Englewood Cliffs, NJ: Lawrence Erlbaum Associates.

Westenberg, H., Fineberg, N. and Denys, D. (2007). Neurobiology of obsessive compulsive disorder; serotonin and beyond. *CNS Spectrums*, 12, 14–27.

Widiger, T. A. and Clark, L. A. (2000). Toward DSM-V and the classification of psychopathology. *Psychological Bulletin*, 126 (6), 946–963.

Wikipedia (2006). *Normal distribution.* http://en.wikipedia.org/wiki/Normal_distribution. Accessed 22 May 2006.

Wilson, D. (1993). Evolutionary epidemiology: Darwinian theory in the service of medicine and psychiatry. *Acta Biotheoretica*, 41, 205–218. Reprinted in S Baron-Cohen (ed.), *The Maladapted Mind. Classic readings in evolutionary psychopathology,* pp. 39–55. Hove, East Sussex: Psychology Press.

World Health Organization (1973). *International Pilot Study of Schizophrenia.* Geneva: World Health Organization.

World Health Organization (1979). *Schizophrenia: An international follow-up study.* New York: John Wiley.

World Health Organization (1983). *Depressive Disorder in Different Cultures.* Geneva: World Health Organization.

World Health Organization (1992). *The ICD-10 Classification of Mental and Behavioural Disorders: Clinical Descriptions and Diagnostic Guidelines.* Geneva: World Health Organization, Division of Mental Health.

World Psychiatric Association (1989). *WPA Statement and Viewpoints on the Rights and Legal Safeguards of the Mentally Ill.* (adopted by the WPA General Assembly in Athens, 17 October, 1989). Available at http://www.wpanet.org/generalinfo/ethic6.html. Accessed 17 May 2007.

Zanarini M. C., Williams A. A., Lewis R. E., Reich D. B., Vera S. C., Marino M. F., Levin A., Young I. and Frankenburg F. R. (1997). Reported pathological childhood experiences associated with the development of borderline personality disorder. *American Journal of Psychiatry*, 154, 1101–1106.

Zubin, I. (ed.) (1961). *Field studies in the mental disorders.* New York: Grune and Stratton.

Zuvekas, S.H. (2005). Prescription drugs and the changing patterns of treatment for mental disorders, 1996–2001. *Health Affairs*, 24, 195–205.

Index